CORE SOCIO-ECONOMIC RIGHTS AND THE EUROPEAN COURT OF HUMAN RIGHTS

Core Socio-Economic Rights and the European Court of Human Rights deals with socio-economic rights in the context of the jurisprudence of the European Court of Human Rights (ECtHR). The book connects the ECtHR's socio-economic case law to an understanding of the Court's responsibility to recognize the limitations of supranational rights adjudication while protecting the most needy. By exploring the idea of core rights protection in constitutional and international law, a new perspective is developed that offers suggestions for improving the ECtHR's reasoning in socio-economic cases, as well as contributing to the debate on indivisible rights adjudication in an age of rights inflation and proportionality review. *Core Socio-Economic Rights and the European Court of Human Rights* will interest scholars and practitioners dealing with fundamental rights and especially those interested in judicial reasoning, socio-economic and supranational rights protection.

INGRID LEIJTEN is an assistant professor at the Department of Constitutional and Administrative Law at Leiden Law School, Leiden University, the Netherlands.

D1336164

CORE SOCIO-ECONOMIC RIGHTS AND THE EUROPEAN COURT OF HUMAN RIGHTS

INGRID LEIJTEN

Leiden University

CAMBRIDGE
UNIVERSITY PRESS

CAMBRIDGE
UNIVERSITY PRESS

University Printing House, Cambridge CB2 8BS, United Kingdom

One Liberty Plaza, 20th Floor, New York, NY 10006, USA

477 Williamstown Road, Port Melbourne, VIC 3207, Australia

314-321, 3rd Floor, Plot 3, Splendor Forum, Jasola District Centre, New Delhi - 110025, India

79 Anson Road, #06-04/06, Singapore 079906

Cambridge University Press is part of the University of Cambridge.

It furthers the University's mission by disseminating knowledge in the pursuit of education, learning and research at the highest international levels of excellence.

www.cambridge.org
Information on this title: www.cambridge.org/9781316648216
DOI: 10.1017/9781108182539

© Ingrid Leijten 2018

First published 2018
First paperback edition 2019

A catalogue record for this publication is available from the British Library

Library of Congress Cataloging in Publication data
Names: Leijten, Ingrid, 1984- author.
Title: Core socio-economic rights and the European Court of Human Rights / Ingrid Leijten, Universiteit Leiden.
Description: Cambridge [UK]; New York : Cambridge University Press, 2017. |
Series: Cambridge studies in European law and policy |
Includes bibliographical references and index.
Identifiers: LCCN 2017034631 | ISBN 9781107198470 (hardback : alk. paper)
Subjects: LCSH: Human rights–Europe. | European Court of Human Rights. |
Social rights–Europe.
Classification: LCC KJC5132 .L45 2017 | DDC 342.408/5–dc23
LC record available at https://lccn.loc.gov/2017034631

ISBN 978-1-107-19847-0 Hardback
ISBN 978-1-316-64821-6 Paperback

CONTENTS

SERIES EDITORS' PREFACE

Over the years, the European Court of Human Rights (ECtHR) has acknowledged that the socio-economic sphere cannot be totally disconnected from its work as a human rights adjudicator, albeit one distanced from the domestic legislative sphere where most redistributive decisions continue to be made. The aim of this book is to explain the socio-economic dimension of case law arising out of the enforcement of the European Convention on Human Rights and Fundamental Freedoms (ECHR). Filling a gap in the literature, the author presents an innovative approach for improving the European Court of Human Rights' adjudication in socio-economic rights cases by using a so-called core rights approach. The intention is to go beyond the paradox that can present a roadblock to further development of the ECHR, namely that the rights in the ECHR are overwhelmingly focused on civil and political questions while the ECtHR is frequently faced with questions in which it has to adjudicate around the impact of national legislative measures on the socio-economic rights of claimants. In effect, the core rights thesis posits a 'limit on the limitations', offering a clearer guide as to how the ECtHR has proceeded in previous cases and may proceed in the future.

The centrepiece of this book is the sustained treatment of the so-called core rights doctrine, namely that a distinction should be drawn between the most fundamental aspects of a right and the more peripheral aspects. The author argues, on the basis of a comparative approach that includes the review of core rights doctrines as applied in other contexts (e.g., Germany and South Africa), that a version of such a doctrine has the capacity to enrich the ECtHR's approach to the vexing question of how far it should show deference to national choices whilst at the same time recognizing the need for protection, particularly where complainants are vulnerable and/or dependent upon the state. The key point is that while the role of the ECtHR may so far be relatively minimal in relation to social rights, per se, a core rights doctrine focusing on socio-economic interests may offer a more comfortable basis for adjudicating the question of what degree of deference the Court should pay to contracting parties' choices in the fields of social and economic policy. This is especially relevant in relation to welfare and budgetary issues, and identifying the cases where review of those measures should be robust based on the existing ECHR rights. Ultimately, this provides a better understanding of what the ECtHR, as a supranational court, actually does in such sensitive cases.

Jo Shaw
Laurence Gormley

ACKNOWLEDGEMENTS

It has been a great pleasure to write this book. Rights reasoning never fails to fascinate me, and the effort to make sense of the important protection of socio-economic rights on the basis of the European Convention on Human Rights has been a very rewarding one. I could not have done it all by myself. First of all, I am greatly indebted to Janneke Gerards, who stood at the cradle of the PhD project from which this book originated. Her passion for legal research in the field of fundamental rights has been contagious ever since. I can only hope to someday spark the same interest in my students.

I am grateful to all those who either directly or indirectly contributed to this book, who read and commented on versions of it, who provided opportunities that enabled me to grow as a scholar, or whose work and dedication have been an inspiration along the way. Thank you, David Bilchitz, Eva Brems, Tess de Jong, Rick Lawson, Titia Loenen, Jan-Peter Loof, Christoph Möllers, Sofia Ranchordás, Ymre Schuurmans, Alexandra Timmer, Clara van Dam, Wim Voermans, Jochen von Bernstorff, Armin von Bogdandy, Jerfi Uzman and Katie Young. I am thankful to the Netherlands Organisation for Scientific Research (NWO) for the funding that made this book possible.

I would like to thank the anonymous reviewers for their helpful remarks. For their support in the final stages up to publication, many thanks go to Finola O'Sullivan, Rebecca Roberts, Elizabeth Spicer and their team from Cambridge University Press. I am grateful to the series editors, Laurence Gormley and Jo Shaw, for taking up my book in their series. Esmée Nanninga and Wendy Rodger from Leiden University have provided indispensable help in finalizing the manuscript, for which I want to thank them.

I am deeply indebted to my parents, Ton and Ria Leijten, for enabling me to pursue my dreams. I thank my family and friends for not getting tired of someone who has a hard time putting her work aside. Finally, I thank Ulrich Simon for his love and support.

ABBREVIATIONS

BCLR	Butterworths Constitutional Law Reports (South Africa)
BVerfGE	*Entscheidungen des Bundesverfassungsgerichts* (judgments of the Federal Constitutional Court of Germany)
CC	Constitutional Court of South Africa
CDDH	Steering Committee for Human Rights
CESCR	Committee on Economic, Social and Cultural Rights
CFR	Charter of Fundamental Rights of the European Union
CoE	Council of Europe
dec.	admissibility decision
ECHR	European Convention on Human Rights
EComHR	European Commission of Human Rights
ECSR	European Committee of Social Rights
ECtHR	European Court of Human Rights
ESC	European Social Charter
FCC	Federal Constitutional Court of Germany; *Bundesverfassungsgericht*
GC	Grand Chamber (of the ECtHR)
GG	German Basic Law; *Grundgesetz*
ICCPR	International Covenant on Civil and Political Rights
ICESCR	International Covenant on Economic, Social and Cultural Rights
ILO	International Labour Organization
no(s).	(application) number(s)
OP	Optional Protocol (to the ICESCR)
P1	First Protocol (to the ECHR)
P12	Twelfth Protocol (to the ECHR)
(R)ESC	(Revised) European Social Charter
SA	South African Law Reports
UDHR	Universal Declaration of Human Rights
UN	United Nations
US	United States
U.S.	United States Supreme Court Reports
VCLT	Vienna Convention on the Law of Treaties
WHO	World Health Organization

CASES

European Court of Human Rights (European Commission of Human Rights)

Case relating to certain aspects of the laws on the use of languages in education in Belgium, ECtHR 23 July 1968, nos. 1474/62, 1677/62, 1691/62, 1769/63, 1994/63 and 2126/64

X. v. the Netherlands, EComHR 20 July 1971 (dec.), no. 4130/69

Golder v. the UK, EComHR 21 February 1975, no. 4451/70

Kjeldsen, Busk Madsen and Pedersen v. Denmark, ECtHR 7 December 1976, nos. 5095/71, 5920/72 and 5926/72

Ireland v. the UK, ECtHR 18 January 1978, no. 5310/71

Tyrer v. the UK, ECtHR 25 April 1978, no. 5856/72

König v. Germany, ECtHR 28 June 1978, no. 6232/73

Sunday Times v. the UK, ECtHR 26 April 1979, no. 6538/74

Marckx v. Belgium, ECtHR 13 June 1979, no. 6833/74

Airey v. Ireland, ECtHR 9 October 1979, no. 6289/73

X. v. Austria, EComHR 13 December 1979 (dec.), no. 8278/78

Young, James and Webster v. the UK, ECtHR 13 August 1981, nos. 7601/76 and 7806/77

Bramelid and Malmström v. Sweden, EComHR 12 October 1982 (dec.), nos. 8588/79 and 8589/79

W. v. the UK, EComHR 28 February 1983 (dec.), no. 9348/81

Van der Mussele v. Belgium, ECtHR 23 November 1983, no. 8919/80

Stewart v. the UK, EComHR 10 July 1984, no. 10044/82

X and Y v. the Netherlands, ECtHR 26 March 1985, no. 8978/80

Abdulaziz, Cabales and Balkandali v. the UK, ECtHR 28 May 1985, nos. 9214/80, 9473/81 and 9474/81

James a. O. v. the UK, ECtHR 21 February 1986, no. 8793/79

Feldbrugge v. the Netherlands, ECtHR 29 May 1986, no. 8562/79

Deumeland v. Germany, ECtHR 29 May 1986, no. 9348/81

Gillow v. the UK, ECtHR 24 November 1986, no. 9063/80

Germany

South Africa

United Nations Committee on Economic, Social and Cultural Rights

United States

~

Introduction

Reasoning Indivisible Rights

Despite its civil and political rights mandate,[1] the European Court of Human Rights (ECtHR; the Court) increasingly rules on cases concerning socio-economic rights. It decides whether the replacement of a social benefit was proportional[2] or whether the reduction of a pension was justified.[3] Other complaints lead it to reflect on whether the authorities' efforts to provide adequate housing were sufficient[4] or whether a state should have done more to prevent health damage that results from environmental pollution.[5] Dealing with socio-economic issues is a risky endeavour that highlights the complexity of the task the ECtHR faces as the final arbiter of fundamental rights conflicts under the European Convention on Human Rights (ECHR; the Convention).[6] It illuminates the difficulties inherent in striking the right balance between providing effective individual rights protection and deferring to the national authorities whose (democratic) decisions – especially in a field like social policy – need to be respected. Essentially, the puzzle presented by this development is how a supranational Court that proceeds on the basis of civil and political rights norms can protect socio-economic rights without overstepping the boundaries of its legitimate task. The Court is criticized for not providing very transparent socio-economic rulings characterized by consistent reasoning. Because of its vulnerable position and the fact

[1] Council of Europe, European Convention for the Protection of Human Rights and Fundamental Freedoms, 4 November 1950, ETS 5.
[2] See, for example, *Stec a. O. v. the UK*, ECtHR (GC) 6 July 2005 (dec.), 65731/01 and 65900/01.
[3] See, for example, *Valkov a. O. v. Bulgaria*, ECtHR 25 October 2011, 2033/04, 19125/04, 19475/04, 19490/04, 19495/04, 19497/04, 24729/04, 171/05 and 2041/05.
[4] See, for example, *Winterstein a. O. v. France*, ECtHR 17 October 2013, 27013/07.
[5] See, for example, *Dubetska a. O. v. Ukraine*, ECtHR 10 February 2011, 30499/03.
[6] In fact, protecting socio-economic rights is a difficult endeavour for courts in general. See, for example, Jeff King, *Judging Social Rights* (Cambridge University Press, 2012), 8–9, who holds that 'the best argument' against social rights adjudication is that it is a 'risky enterprise'.

that the effectiveness of the Convention system is dependent on the acceptance and implementation of its judgments by the member states, this reasoning, as well as the ECtHR's role in protecting social rights in the first place, is in need of further clarification.

The argument I develop in this book is that the notion of core rights protection can explain, as well as guide, the ECtHR's socio-economic rights protection. It provides a justificatory explanation for its engagement in this field while presenting a structured approach for the ECtHR's reasoning that fits its unique role and task in a multilevel system of fundamental rights protection. The notion of core rights, briefly stated, entails that a distinction can be made between more and less important, or fundamental, aspects falling within the (potential) reach of a fundamental right. This idea allows for expounding the connection between the Court's emerging socio-economic practice and the role of the Strasbourg system of fundamental rights protection. Why exactly it makes sense to explore a core rights perspective in regard to the ECHR's socio-economic dimension will be elaborated on shortly. I will start by giving some broader context to the questions that are central to this book by introducing the ECtHR and its relation to certain features of and developments in judicial fundamental rights protection.

The ECtHR and Developments in Fundamental Rights Protection

The ECtHR is a supranational court tasked with the interpretation and application of the rights enshrined in the European Convention. This treaty was signed under the auspices of the Council of Europe (CoE) in 1950 and designed 'to take the first steps for the collective enforcement of certain of the rights stated in the Universal Declaration'.[7] Being the first of its kind, the ECtHR, together with the former European Commission of Human Rights (EComHR; the Commission), has developed the idea of fundamental rights protection at a level beyond the state, including the power to render binding judgments on the basis of individual complaints.[8] As natural as this may seem today, in the 1950s supranational judicial enforcement of fundamental rights was a novel phenomenon; it is due in great part to the success of the ECtHR that since then the importance of international and supranational rights adjudication has generally increased worldwide.

---

[7] Preamble to the ECHR.   [8] Art. 46 ECHR.

What is this success story about? Starting with ten CoE member states, presently there are forty-seven European states that have signed and ratified the Convention and are therefore subject to the jurisdiction of the Court. Especially after the fall of the Berlin wall at the beginning of the 1990s, the number of states parties increased significantly and many Eastern European states entered the Convention. This has not been without problems as regards the quantitative increase of complaints, as well as the qualitative standard the Convention could set throughout the continent.[9] Nevertheless, the Court has managed to maintain and even consolidate its important role as a safety net for individuals confronted with interferences in their fundamental rights by the state. Since then, it has created an immense and rich body of case law, which has given content to the rights norms laid down in the Convention and in the several protocols that have been added thereto, but has also influenced the understanding and the protection of fundamental rights in national legal orders.[10] The ECtHR's decisions and judgments are broadly accepted in the member states and widely discussed by legal academics around the world.

The ECtHR is not only known for its successful, pioneering role as a supranational fundamental rights adjudicator. In legal debates, the Court and its practice are referred to as being exemplary of several European and global legal and doctrinal trends related to fundamental rights protection. These trends and developments illuminate what are perceived as some of the hallmarks of the ECtHR's practice, which provide an important background to the topic of this book.

First, there is the Court's emphasis on *proportionality review* and *balancing* in cases concerning interferences with fundamental rights. Where Aleinikoff speaks of an 'age of balancing',[11] and Möller of the emerged 'global model of constitutional rights',[12] both underline the current predominance of a 'proportionality paradigm' in dealing with

---

[9] Cf. Steven Greer, *The European Convention on Human Rights: Achievements, Problems and Prospects* (Cambridge University Press, 2006), 105 ff.; Wojciech Sadurski, *Constitutionalism and the Enlargement of Europe* (Oxford University Press, 2012), Ch. 1.

[10] See, for a comparative study on the implementation of the Strasbourg case law, Janneke Gerards and Joseph Fleuren (eds.), *Implementation of the European Convention on Human Rights and of the Case Law of the ECtHR in National Case Law* (Antwerp/Oxford/New York: Intersentia, 2014).

[11] T. Alexander Aleinikoff, 'Constitutional Law in the Age of Balancing', *Yale Law Journal*, 96 (1987), pp. 943–1005.

[12] Kai Möller, *The Global Model of Constitutional Rights* (Oxford University Press, 2012).

clashes between individual and collective freedom. The proportionality test – which has been developed to an important extent by the Federal Constitutional Court of Germany (FCC; *Bundesverfassungsgericht*), and has carefully been expounded by scholars such as Alexy[13] and more recently Barak[14] – consists of multiple subtests. These concern the questions whether an interference with fundamental rights served a legitimate aim and whether it was 'suitable', 'necessary', and finally proportional *stricto sensu*. Of these different tests, the latter is especially seen as illustrative of what proportionality is about. Proportionality in the strict sense boils down to weighing and balancing the rights of the individual against the general interest and/or the rights of others. It finds much expression in the Court's approach, in the sense that the reasoning of the ECtHR discloses a clear preference for proportionality review, and especially balancing. This can partly be explained by the wording of the various provisions of the Convention. Articles 8–11 ECHR require a limitation to be 'necessary in a democratic society', while Article 1 of the First Protocol (P1) speaks of the possibility of 'necessary' controls on the use of property. Starting from this wording, the Court's review of interferences with Convention rights is usually guided by the question of whether a fair balance has been struck between the individual and the general interests at stake. To generate an answer to this question, the Court takes account of the various considerations relevant on both sides of the scale to then reach a conclusion on whether or not a Convention right has been breached.[15]

Second, the ECtHR's case law can be seen as prototypical of another important doctrinal development in the field of fundamental rights, namely the recognition of *positive obligations*. Just like proportionality review, positive obligations are also considered part of the 'global model of constitutional rights'.[16] The link between the two indeed seems

---

[13] Robert Alexy, *Theorie der Grundrechte* (Baden-Baden: Nomos, 1985) (Robert Alexy, *A Theory of Constitutional Rights*, transl. Julian Rivers [Oxford University Press, 2002]).

[14] Aharon Barak, *Proportionality: Constitutional Rights and Their Limitations* (Cambridge University Press, 2012). Also Möller's 'global model of constitutional rights' can be understood as a moral theory of rights in which proportionality plays the leading part (Möller 2012 (n. 12)). See also Matthias Klatt and Moritz Meister, *The Constitutional Structure of Proportionality* (Oxford University Press, 2012).

[15] See, generally, Jonas Christofferson, *Fair Balance: Proportionality, Subsidiarity and Primarity in the European Convention on Human Rights* (Leiden/Boston: Martinus Nijhoff Publishers, 2009). See also Barak 2012 (n. 14), 183–184; Möller 2012 (n. 12), 13–14, Ch. 7.

[16] Möller 2012 (n. 12), 5–10.

obvious: besides in the context of measures taken by the state, the question of whether something was proportional or not can just as well apply to situations in which a state allegedly failed to take action in breach of a fundamental right. In its case law, the ECtHR has expressly created a doctrine of positive obligations. It holds that the rights enshrined in the Convention also give rise to positive duties on the part of the state.[17] Accordingly, if states wish to comply with the rights enumerated in the ECHR, they have to take deliberate action and 'interfere' with the situations of individuals. When the Court started to develop its doctrine of positive obligations, which it already did in the 1960s, this was found remarkable – especially since the ECHR's rights norms are phrased negatively and do not, on the face of it, demand state engagement.[18] However, partly also due to the example set by the ECtHR, the concept of positive obligations has become generally accepted in modern legal debate and practice worldwide.[19]

Third, an apparent trend in constitutional law, and fundamental rights protection in particular, is the increased prominence of *socio-economic fundamental rights*.[20] Although this may seem less obvious, also in this connection the practice of the Strasbourg Court may be considered relevant. Ever since economic and social rights were laid down in international documents, they were considered to have a second-rank status.[21]

---

[17] *Marckx v. Belgium*, ECtHR 13 June 1979, 6833/74, para. 31; *Case relating to certain aspects of the laws on het use of languages in education in Belgium*, ECtHR 23 July 1968, 1474/62, 1677/62, 1691/62, 1769/63, 1994/63 and 2126/64, para. 9. See, on this doctrine generally, Alastair Mowbray, *The Development of Positive Obligations under the European Convention on Human Rights by the European Court of Human Rights* (Oxford: Hart Publishing, 2004); Dimitris Xenos, *The Positive Obligations of the State under the European Convention of Human Rights* (London/Oxford/Edinburgh: Routledge, 2012); Laurens Lavrysen, *Human Rights in a Positive State: Rethinking the Relationship Between Positive and Negative Obligations under the European Convention on Human Rights* (Antwerp/Oxford/New York: Intersentia, 2016).

[18] The ECHR provisions generally start with the words 'No one shall . . .' or 'Everyone has the right to . . .', which mirrors a negative duty of the state to refrain from interfering with the different rights. Cf., J.G. Merrills, *The Development of International Law by the European Court of Human Rights*, 3rd ed. (Manchester University Press, 1993), 102–103.

[19] As a well-known exception, the United States can be mentioned. Cf., *Deshaney v. Winnebago County Department of Social Services*, 489 U.S. 189, 169 (1989).

[20] See, for example, Murray Wesson, 'The Emergence and Enforcement of Socio-Economic Rights' in L. Lazarus, Ch. McCrudden, and N. Bowles (eds.), *Reasoning Rights: Comparative Judicial Engagement* (Oxford: Hart Publishing, 2014), pp. 281–297; Möller 2012 (n. 12), 5.

[21] Sandra Fredman, *Human Rights Transformed: Positive Rights and Positive Duties* (Oxford University Press, 2008), 1–2.

The dominant philosophical account of fundamental rights holds that fundamental rights foremost prescribe areas of freedom related to the civil and political sphere.[22] Yet whereas the debate has long been whether socio-economic guarantees can, properly speaking, be seen as 'rights', it has gradually shifted towards a more constructive approach. This shift is visible in particular in national constitutional developments, where it can be seen that especially younger and non-Western constitutions include a reference to economic and social guarantees. These can be phrased as directive principles,[23] but also as self-standing individual rights that can serve as the basis for individual constitutional complaints.[24] At the international level, socio-economic rights catalogues have been supplemented by additional protocols and (collective) complaints mechanisms, allowing states to be held accountable for shortcomings in the provision of socio-economic rights in a more forthright manner.[25] In line with these developments, the ECtHR's case law has supported and even strengthened the emerging perception that there is or should not be a clear distinction between '"permissible" civil and political rights review and "impermissible" social rights review'.[26] As I will demonstrate in this book, the ECtHR's case law illustrates that it is impossible to strictly distinguish between civil and political and economic and social rights protection.[27] The Convention norms are of a classic, civil and political kind, but the Court has interpreted them broadly, thereby expounding their socio-economic dimension.[28] Its increasing engagement in cases concerning topics like housing, health care and social security underlines that no fatal tension exists between socio-economic rights and judicial

---

[22] Möller 2012 (n. 12), 2.

[23] Cf., Part IV (Directive Principles of State Policy) of the Constitution of India.

[24] Cf., the Constitution of South Africa. See Ch. 5, S. 5.2.

[25] See the Additional Protocol to the European Social Charter (Council of Europe, 5 May 1988, ETS 128 [entry into force 5 September 1992]), creating a collective complaints mechanism, as well as the Optional Protocol to the International Covenant on Economic, Social and Cultural Rights (UN General Assembly, 5 March 2009, A/RES/63/117, entered into force 5 May 2013), with a possibility for individual communications. The Charter of Fundamental Rights of the European Union (OJ 18 December 2000 (2000/C 364/01)), under the header of 'Solidarity', also contains a number of socio-economic rights.

[26] Colm O'Cinneide, 'The Problematic of Social Rights – Uniformity and Diversity in the Development of Social Rights Review' in L. Lazarus, Ch. McCrudden, and N. Bowles (eds.), *Reasoning Rights: Comparative Judicial Engagement* (Oxford: Hart Publishing, 2014), pp. 299–317, 300. See also Ben Saul, David Kinley and Jacqueline Mowbray, *The International Covenant on Economic, Social and Cultural Rights: Commentary, Cases, and Materials* (Oxford University Press, 2014), 1.

[27] *Airey v. Ireland*, ECtHR 9 October 1979, 6289/73, para. 26.   [28] Möller 2012 (n. 12), 9.

review of individual cases in this field. Even in a supranational judicial context, where this appears even more problematic than at the national and constitutional level, the practice of the ECtHR shows that it is possible for a court to decide on socio-economic measures.[29]

The role the ECtHR plays in regard to the different developments in fundamental rights protection emphasizes its prominent position and forerunner role. The ECtHR not only sets an unprecedented example of supranational rights adjudication as such; when it comes to more particular doctrinal and other developments, its practice can be seen as avant-garde as well. It often breaks ground, if not by instigating new trends, then at least by confirming ongoing changes in the perception of fundamental rights and the way these rights should be dealt with. Notwithstanding this, it must not be forgotten that the Court is constantly moving on thin ice. It needs to be mindful of its supranational position and take stock of the prevailing ideas on fundamental rights in the states that are a party to the Convention. In part because it cannot do without the states parties' support, the Court should be careful not to overstep the boundaries of its competences. In this regard, the question arises whether the success story of the Court may in some way also be endangered by the various developments mentioned. The Court's task is a limited one, and especially when joining the different trends, there appears to be a risk that it obtains a greater role than it can legitimately claim. The recognition of positive obligations in combination with Convention requirements related to economic and social rights can lead to all-encompassing rights review in the sense that the Court's jurisdiction – and thereby its involvement in national policy and democratic decisions – is hardly curtailed. Moreover, it can be questioned whether proportionality review and especially balancing exercises are always the appropriate means for a (supranational) judicial body to decide on a broad range of issues while also trying to steer away from political decisions on the distribution of rights and goods throughout society. These approaches have, after all, been criticized for creating room for judicial discretion and thereby activism.[30] At least in theory, it can be

---

[29] For an extensive overview of this case law, see Ida Elisabeth Koch, *Human Rights as Indivisible Rights: The Protection of Socio-Economic Demands under the European Convention on Human Rights* (Leiden: Martinus Nijhoff Publishers, 2009).

[30] See, for example, Francisco J. Urbina, 'A Critique of Proportionality', *American Journal of Jurisprudence*, 57 (2012), pp. 49–80; Ariel L. Bendor and Tal Sela, 'How Proportional Is Proportionality', *International Journal of Constitutional Law*, 13 (2015), pp. 530–544.

argued, the various developments of which the ECtHR's practice is considered a powerful example together may have the result that the ECtHR becomes the final decision-maker in virtually all conflicts concerning individual interests. Especially in a Europe characterized by diversity, this hardly seems desirable.

In addition, there is a practical downside to the success of the Convention system connected with the developments mentioned. A first problem is the recent 'docket crisis'. The immense number of applications that have reached the Strasbourg Court has put pressure on its work almost to the point of collapse. Serious institutional measures had to be taken,[31] and even though the immediate danger has subsided, the question remains whether this issue has been tackled in a lasting manner. The caseload problem cannot be seen apart from the Court's expansive interpretation of the Convention rights, including the socio-economic aspects thereof. That is, its case law might give the impression that it is possible to phrase almost every thinkable interest in terms of the ECHR, thereby qualifying for Convention protection.[32]

A second, related issue is the criticism that is voiced concerning the practice of the ECtHR by both academics and lawyers, but even more prominently by politicians who in some member states even suggest leaving the Convention.[33] Although this criticism may not specifically be related to the positive, socio-economic protection the Court is offering,[34] it does concern the too far-reaching impact of the Convention

---

[31] Protocol No. 14 to the ECHR, for example, has amended the Convention so that it is now possible for single judges to reject manifestly inadmissible applications; committees of three judges may now declare an application inadmissible and decide on the merits of a case where the matter at hand is determined by well-established case law of the Court (see Arts. 27–28 ECHR).

[32] Cf. Janneke Gerards, 'The Prism of Fundamental Rights', *European Constitutional Law Review*, 8 (2012), pp. 173–202, 179–180.

[33] At the time of finishing this book, particularly in the UK, politicians propelled the idea to leave the Convention. Also in the Netherlands and Belgium, the Court is regularly criticized. See, generally, Janneke Gerards, 'The European Court of Human Rights and the National Courts: Giving Shape to the Notion of "Shared Responsibility"' in J.H. Gerards and J. Fleuren (eds.), *Implementation of the European Convention on Human Rights and of the Case Law of the ECtHR in National Case Law* (Antwerp/Oxford/New York: Intersentia, 2014), pp. 13–93, 86–88.

[34] See, however, Marc Bossuyt, 'Should the Strasbourg Court Exercise More Self-Restraint? On the Extension of the Jurisdiction of the European Court of Human Rights to Social Security Regulations', *Human Rights Law Journal*, 28 (2007), pp. 321–332 (cf., also Marc Bossuyt, 'The Court of Strasbourg Acting as an Asylum Court', *European Constitutional Law Review*, 8 [2012], pp. 213–245).

and the allegedly activist role of the Court in this regard.[35] It is considered problematic that the ECtHR assumes the final say on a broad variety of topics that not always concern what were originally thought to be the fundamental rights protected by the Convention. Besides, the way in which the Court reaches its conclusions, i.e., by balancing case-specific interests and hence in an ad hoc manner, does not seem convincing to some critical observers, adding to the doubts about the broad influence of the Convention.[36]

Thus, the Court's engagement in the socio-economic sphere, combined with the increasing role of positive obligations and the idea that the Court – or (supranational) courts in general – is not very well placed for dealing with 'polycentric' issues of this kind, may constitute a risk for the successful functioning of the Convention system. Even without having regard to the current criticisms, moreover, a fundamental question remains why, and how, a court like the ECtHR should deal with cases concerning economic and social rights that cannot literally be found in the Convention.

Socio-Economic Protection and Core Rights Reasoning

Especially in the context of socio-economic rights protection, the tension between judicial protection and the Court's subsidiary task becomes readily apparent. Social rights issues may be of a fundamental nature, but the scope of the Convention prevents the Court from assuming law-making capacities in this regard. Several authors have addressed the socio-economic dimension of the Convention.[37] They highlight

---

[35] See, for example, Lord Hoffmann, 'The Universality of Human Rights', *Judicial Studies Board Annual Lecture* (2009), paras. 27 and 36; Patricia Popelier, Sarah Lambrechts, and Koen Lemmens (eds.), *Criticism of the European Court of Human Rights: Shifting the Convention System: Counter-Dynamics at the National and EU Level* (Cambridge/Antwerp/Portland: Intersentia, 2016).

[36] Cf. Stavros Taskyrakis, 'Proportionality: An Assault on Human Rights?', *International Journal of Constitutional Law*, 7 (2009), pp. 468–493; Jochen von Bernstorff, 'Kerngehaltsschutz durch den UN-Menschenrechtsausschuss und den EGMR: vom Wert Kategorialer Argumentationsformen', *Der Staat*, 50 (2011), pp. 165–190; Jochen von Bernstorff, 'Proportionality without Balancing: Why Judicial Ad Hoc Balancing in Unnecessary and Potentially Detrimental to the Realisation of Individual and Collective Self-Determination' in L. Lazarus, Ch. McCrudden, and N. Bowles (eds.), *Reasoning Rights: Comparative Judicial Engagement* (Oxford: Hart Publishing, 2014), pp. 63–86.

[37] See Ida Elisabeth Koch, 'Social Rights as Components in the Civil Right to Personal Liberty – Another Possible Step Forward in the Integrated Human Rights Approach?', *Netherlands Quarterly of Human Rights*, 20 (2002), pp. 29–51; Ida Elisabeth Koch, 'The

important socio-economic cases and point out welcome developments, whereas some also note the shortcomings in the Court's decisions and judgments.[38] Only few authors have addressed more fundamentally the question of how the Court should 'reason indivisible rights', i.e., deal with conflicts between the general interest and individual socio-economic interests that can be linked to the norms enshrined in the Convention. In her articles on the socio-economic protection by the ECtHR, and especially of work-related rights, Mantouvalou has provided a normative account of how the Court should handle socio-economic complaints based on a positive account of freedom.[39] In addition, Koch has developed a 'hermeneutical' perspective to fundamental rights protection under the Convention that includes civil and political as well as socio-economic rights.[40] In this work, Koch presents an extensive overview of the case law of the Court in different socio-economic fields.[41] The current book aims to add to these important works by providing a more up-to-date impression of the socio-economic protection offered by the Court related to housing, health, and social security. Moreover, it explicitly places the socio-economic dimension of the ECHR in the broader context of questions surrounding the legitimate role of the ECtHR, and

---

Justiciability of Indivisible Rights', *Nordic Law Journal*, 72 (2003), pp. 3–39; Virginia Mantouvalou, 'Work and Private Life: Sidabras and Dziautas v. Lithuania', *European Law Review*, 30 (2005), pp. 573–585; Ida Elisabeth Koch, 'Economic, Social and Cultural Rights as Components in Civil and Political Rights: A Hermeneutic Perspective', *The International Journal of Human Rights*, 10 (2006), pp. 405–430; Eva Brems, 'Indirect Protection of Social Rights by the European Court of Human Rights' in D. Barak-Erez and A.M. Gross (eds.), *Exploring Social Rights: Between Theory and Practice* (Oxford: Hart Publishing, 2007), pp. 135–167; Colin Warbrick, 'Economic and Social Interests and the European Convention on Human Rights' in M.A. Baderin and R. McCorquodale (eds.), *Economic, Social and Cultural Rights in Action* (Oxford University Press, 2007), pp. 241–256; Colm O'Cinneide, 'A Modest Proposal: Destitution, State Responsibility and the European Convention on Human Rights', *European Human Rights Law Review* (2008), pp. 583–605; Ellie Palmer, 'Protecting Socio-Economic Rights through the European Convention on Human Rights: Trends and Developments in the European Court of Human Rights', *Erasmus Law Review*, 2 (2009), pp. 397–425; Ellie Palmer, 'Beyond Arbitrary Interference: The Right to a Home? Developing Socio-Economic Duties in the European Convention on Human Rights', *Northern Ireland Legal Quarterly*, 61 (2010), pp. 225–243; Virginia Mantouvalou, 'Labour Rights in the European Convention on Human Rights: An Intellectual Justification for an Integrated Approach to Interpretation', *Human Rights Law Review*, 13 (2013), pp. 529–555. See also Koch 2009 (n. 29).

[38] See Ch. 2, S. 2.3.2.   [39] Mantouvalou 2013 (n. 39). See also Mantouvalou 2005 (n. 37).

[40] Koch 2006 (n. 27). See also Koch 2002 (n. 27); Koch 2003 (n. 27); Koch 2009 (n. 29).

[41] Koch 2009 (n. 29), Ch. 5–9.

especially of developments in fundamental rights adjudication and legal reasoning. It addresses the gap that exists in the justificatory explanations given for the ECtHR's socio-economic practice and provides a constructive response that is in line with a future-proof understanding of the position and competencies of the Court while allowing effective socio-economic protection.

In doing so, this study contemplates the notion of core rights protection. Why is this seen as a notion worth exploring, and hypothesized as having potential added value in the Strasbourg context? The concept of core rights, i.e., the idea that one can differentiate between the various aspects of a fundamental right in the sense that some of these aspects are more essential and hence deserve more protection than others, is regularly considered redundant. This has to do with the common understanding that balancing rights and interests is the appropriate means for dealing with rights conflicts, and this leaves no room for core rights protection.[42] Moreover, it is considered that determining the core of a right is very difficult, if not impossible. How can we know what belongs to the inherent essence of a right? And in case there is no objective answer to this question, who is to decide on this matter?[43] Nevertheless, regardless of these sceptical outlooks, the notion of core rights fails to fade into oblivion. It is regularly taken up in new constitutions,[44] and the Charter of Fundamental Rights of the European Union (CFR), entered into force in 2009, also contains a reference to this idea where it states, 'Any limitation on the exercise of the rights and freedoms recognised by this Charter must ... respect the essence of those rights and freedoms'.[45]

The protection of core rights is considered relevant in the field of economic and social fundamental rights, which provides an additional reason for researching its potential in relation to the development of the

---

[42] In Germany, for example, it is often considered that proportionality analysis will automatically secure the protection of the essence of a fundamental right, albeit in an implicit manner. See Ch. 4, S. 4.3.3.

[43] Cf. Katherine G. Young, 'The Minimum Core of Economic and Social Rights: A Concept in Search of Content', *Yale Journal of International Law,* 33 (2008), pp. 113–175.

[44] A few examples are the Constitution of Colombia of 1991, Art. 334 ('In no case shall the essential core of a right be affected.'); the Constitution of Kenya of 2010, Art. 24(2)(c) ('[A] provision in legislation limiting a right or fundamental freedom ... shall not limit the right or fundamental freedom so far as to derogate from its core or essential content.'); and the Constitution of Angola of 2011, Art. 236(b) ('Alterations to the Constitution must respect ... [e]ssential core rights, freedoms, and guarantees.').

[45] Art. 52(1) CFR.

ECHR's socio-economic dimension.[46] In the end, the idea that fundamental rights catalogues are there to protect, first and foremost, the 'core' of the rights they enumerate is hard to contradict. When rights are not understood as 'trumps'[47] but instead as requirements that can be limited in the light of the general interest or the rights of others, it is generally agreed that at least their essential aspects should be secured.

This study explores the notion of core rights in relation to fundamental rights adjudication and links it to the Strasbourg context. A choice was made for exploring the idea of core rights protection in German constitutional law, in relation to the International Covenant on Economic, Social and Cultural Rights (ICESCR), and in the debate on socio-economic rights adjudication under the South African Constitution. While not drawing from the complete experience of core rights theory and practice worldwide, this illuminates the most important features thereof and provides the necessary inspiration. I show how the idea of core rights can connect the ECtHR's socio-economic practice to an understanding of this Court's task that recognizes the need for effective rights protection, as well as deference, and provides an answer to the challenges lying ahead in this regard. The Court's task is a complex, multidimensional one. Besides ensuring effective individual protection, it needs to respect the leeway of national decision-makers, but also provide sufficient clarity as to what is demanded for complying with the Convention. The explanations given thus far for the Court's socio-economic case law have primarily focused on the former (effective protection), while the doctrines of proportionality and the margin of appreciation as such fail to sufficiently address in particular the latter two aspects (deference and guidance).[48] Moreover, combined with an expansive interpretation, these doctrines do not always accord sufficient attention to the important interests concerned. A core rights perspective forms the 'missing piece of the puzzle' in that it completes the justificatory explanation given for the ECHR's emerging social dimension. At the same time, it offers a structure for the Court's reasoning in social rights cases that resonates its past achievements and current struggles.

---

[46] See Ch. 5 and Ch. 6, which discuss the notion of core rights, or 'minimum core(s) (obligations)', in the context of the ICESCR and the South African Constitution.

[47] For the idea of rights as trumps, see Ronald Dworkin, 'Rights as Trumps' in J. Waldron (ed.), *Theories of Rights* (Oxford University Press, 1984), pp. 153–167. See however Möller 2012 (n. 12); Jacob Weinrib, *Dimensions of Dignity: The Theory and Practice of Modern Constitutional Law* (Cambridge University Press, 2016), 245–251.

[48] Ch. 2.

It is worth stressing that the overall argument of this book does not concern the protection of socio-economic fundamental rights more broadly speaking. The development of economic and social rights protection and the growing importance of these rights as justiciable norms is reason for a lively, ongoing debate in which scholars and practitioners alike present their different views on these important issues.[49] Although inspiration is definitely drawn from this debate, this book does not directly contribute to the broader discussion on socio-economic rights. The various findings do not necessarily apply to other (judicial) actors and norms outside the Convention that somehow safeguard economic and social rights. The argument I develop concerns the protection of socio-economic rights under civil and political rights norms, and more specifically the ECtHR's unique position and context. Limits to socio-economic rights adjudication that apply in the field of the Convention may be absent where economic and social rights norms are involved. Another point to note is that when it comes to interpreting and reviewing limitations of rights, even if they all share a proportionality paradigm, the ECtHR does not stand on the same footing as national constitutional courts. Of course, lessons may be drawn from the core rights insights this book presents and comparisons may be made with other legal contexts, yet it does not aim at suggesting what core rights and/or socio-economic protection in general should be about. In turn, this means that although the particular role and position of the ECtHR are taken as the point of departure, the findings of this study cannot be transposed one-on-one to the protection of civil and political rights under the Convention. The core rights perspective is specifically tailored to the subject matter of socio-economic rights, and hence cannot automatically be applied to the Strasbourg adjudicative process in general.

---

[49] For some important, recent contributions to this debate, see, David Bilchitz, *Poverty and Fundamental Rights: The Justification and Enforcement of Socio-Economic Rights* (Oxford University Press, 2007); Fredman 2008 (n. 21); Malcolm Langford, 'The Justiciability of Social Rights: From Practice to Theory' in M. Langford (ed.), *Social Rights Jurisprudence: Emerging Trends in International and Comparative Law* (Cambridge University Press, 2008), pp. 3–45; Sandra Liebenberg, *Socio-Economic Rights: Adjudication under a Transformative Constitution* (Cape Town: Juta and Company, 2010); Conor Gearty and Virginia Mantouvalou, *Debating Social Rights* (Oxford: Hart Publishing, 2011); King 2012 (n. 6); Paul O'Connell, *Vindicating Socio-Economic Rights: International Standards and Comparative Experiences* (London: Routledge, 2012); Katherine G. Young, *Constituting Socio-Economic Rights* (Oxford University Press, 2012).

In addition, it must be highlighted that in answering the question of how the Court can strike the right balance between the effective protection of individual rights and deferring to member states' decisions in socio-economic rights cases, the focus lies on the reasoning of the Court. That is, the scope of this study is limited to the interpretation of the Convention and the review of cases that fall within its scope. Consequently, although interesting questions may also arise, for example, as to the remedies provided in socio-economic rights cases, these will not be addressed here.

With regard to the terminology used, it is important to clarify that generally I use the term 'fundamental rights' rather than the also commonly used 'human rights'. Although the latter term certainly is appropriate in the context of the ECtHR, I chose to refrain from using it in most instances. This has to do with the broader meaning that can be given to the notion of 'fundamental rights'. Contrary to the term 'human rights', 'fundamental rights' encompasses both fundamental rights protected at the international or supranational level and 'constitutional rights' that can generally be found in national constitutions. Thus, it enhances the comparability of issues and doctrinal insights from both the supranational and the national level. The term 'human rights', moreover, might wrongly suggest that what is concerned is some kind of meta-notion that is relevant foremost in the political and theoretical spheres, rather than in the legal sphere. This would fail to recognize the fact that the ECtHR is a distinctly legal actor, and that the rights it protects are of concrete relevance at the national level and in the practice of national courts.[50]

A second remark on terminology relates to the use of the term 'socio-economic rights' or 'economic and social rights'. Both terms are used interchangeably and refer to fundamental rights concerning topics like welfare benefits, education, the provision of health care and housing – but also work-related rights, etc.[51] The use of these terms demonstrates, moreover, that I am not dealing with cultural rights. Especially in the context of the International Covenant on Economic, Social and Cultural

---

[50] According to Art. 46 ECHR the judgments of the ECtHR are binding for the parties to the case. Moreover, due to their *res interpretata* effect, the judgments and interpretations of the Court are of general relevance throughout the member states (cf. Gerards 2014 (n. 35), 21–27).

[51] Occacionally, I also use the term 'social rights', because of the primarily social character of the cases on housing, health and health care and social security discussed in Ch. 8.

Rights (ICESCR), cultural rights seem to form a natural extension of the category of economic and social rights. However, cultural rights, and particularly claims for recognition, are of a different nature than issues concerning social measures and redistribution, and for that reason they are expressly not considered.[52]

Last, 'core rights' should not be understood as a label that is attached to rights or rights norms that are more important than others. It does not refer to a hierarchy amongst rights, in the sense that the right to life would, for example, be a core right, whereas the right to property would not. What this term, admittedly somewhat confusingly, instead refers to is that *within* the potential scope of rights (norms), some aspects can be distinguished that are more important or more fundamental than others. The term 'cores of rights' could also have been adopted to express this; however, for reasons of legibility and because it is the term customarily used in the literature, 'core rights' is preferred here.

Towards a Core Rights Perspective

In order to connect the ECtHR's emerging socio-economic rights practice with the legitimate role of this Court by means of a core rights perspective, several issues must be tackled. First of all, we need a clear picture of the position and tasks of the Strasbourg Court, as well as the different possible approaches to rights reasoning and the limits thereto. Besides this, a sufficient impression is needed of the Court's socio-economic case law, including the (normative) explanations that have been given for it. Various core rights doctrines provide the necessary inspiration for grasping the idea and potential of core rights reasoning. Together, the insights on the role and practice of the Strasbourg Court and the idea of core rights protection allow the development of a core rights perspective tailored to the ECtHR.

The outline of this book is as follows: Part I is called 'Setting the Stage'. It provides the background needed for exploring the idea of core rights protection in relation to the ECtHR's practice. Chapter 1 introduces the ECHR, the ECtHR and the Court's socio-economic case law. The European Convention can be characterized as a civil and political human rights document; it was originally meant to include merely negative rights, and economic and social rights norms were expressly left out. In

---

[52] Cf. Young 2008 (n. 45), 119–120.

the CoE, the latter were protected separately in the European Social Charter (ESC).[53] The ECtHR's task is a complex one. Three main dimensions to its role as the interpreter and guarantor of the Convention rights can be distinguished. The first relates to the aim of effective individual rights protection:[54] the ECHR is meant to form a safety net shielding individuals from interferences with their fundamental rights by the state, with the ECtHR holding states accountable and providing individual relief. Besides, the ECtHR is a supranational court *par excellence*, positioned too 'far away' from decisions taken at the national level to always assume the final say in rights matters. Not being part of a national balance of powers amongst the legislature, executive and judiciary, its outsider position requires it to grant the state – the bearer of the ECHR obligations – a degree of deference.[55] Third, the task of the ECtHR has become more 'constitutional', i.e., the Court expounds the meaning and implications of the Convention in a way that transcends the contours of individual cases.[56] Moreover, the constitutional task of the ECtHR is 'built in' in the sense that it is primarily up to the member states to guarantee the Convention rights – and for that they need the guidance of the Strasbourg Court. This is all the more so because the rights and duties stemming from the ECHR have become more encompassing. Its 'living tree' character has resulted in a constant extension of the fields covered by the Convention and a growing number of suggestions for compliance. The Convention protection in the field of socio-economic rights forms an important illustration. The final part of Chapter 1 deals with the Court's emerging socio-economic case law. Besides Article 6 ECHR (the right to fair trial) – in the context of which the Court clarified that there is no 'water-tight division' separating the social sphere from that of the Convention[57] – the prohibition of discrimination of Article 14 (and Article 1 of Protocol No. 12 to the ECHR) does not *a priori* distinguish between civil and socio-economic interests. Yet also the negatively phrased substantive rights found in Articles 2 (the right to life), 3 (the prohibition of torture), and 8 (the right to respect for private and family life) ECHR, as well as in Article 1 of the First Protocol (the protection of property), have proven to be vehicles for the Court's often implicit economic and social

---

[53] Council of Europe, European Social Charter, 18 October 1961, ETS 35.
[54] *Soering v. the UK*, ECtHR 7 July 1989, 14038/88, para. 87.
[55] Cf. Art. 1 Protocol No. 15 ECHR, referring to the 'margin of appreciation'.
[56] Cf. *Loizidou v. Turkey*, ECtHR 23 March 1995, 15318/89, para. 75.
[57] *Airey v. Ireland*, ECtHR 9 October 1979, 6289/73, para. 26.

rights protection. Its socio-economic case law is diverse, yet the gap between prima facie and definite protection is considerable – just like the lack of clarity on precise socio-economic obligations.

Chapter 2 addresses the underlying normative explanations for the Court's engagement in the field of economic and social rights. To grasp this phenomenon, a distinction is made between the rights norms as they form the starting point for the adjudication of a case (the provisions), and the interests (claimed to be) protected on the basis thereof. In the ECHR, the former are civil and political, whereas the latter can be socio-economic as well. This has been explained as resulting from the Court's efforts to effectuate the Convention rights, which requires a broad interpretation unconstrained by distinctions between different categories of rights. The idea of the indivisibility of human rights presents a complementary justificatory explanation: rights are 'indivisible, interdependent and interrelated', including in the legal and, increasingly, in the judicial sphere.[58] This is why the ECtHR takes into account socio-economic rights when interpreting and applying the Convention. Yet the ideas of effectiveness and indivisibility at most provide an incomplete answer to the puzzle of supranational socio-economic rights protection on the basis of classic rights norms. The interpretive room both prescribe is not countervailed by any clear idea on how to render definite the socio-economic rights (potentially) covered by the Convention. Proportionality analysis and the doctrine of the margin of appreciation cannot claim to fill this gap. In fact, both are part of the problem in the sense that their opaque use prevents a clear image of the ECHR's social dimension.

To address these issues, something must be said in more general terms on 'reasoning rights'. Chapter 3 discusses the different stages of fundamental rights reasoning: the first concerns the determination of the scope of a right and the second the review of a limitation thereof. The distinction between the two stages is important, especially for supranational courts, because it demarcates their jurisdiction illuminating what fundamental human rights are about. Determining a right's scope is a matter of interpretation. The preferred interpretative methods are linked to the particular adjudicative context. The ECtHR has preferred teleological or comparative approaches over textual and originalist approaches, which, however, does not mean that the ECtHR is prevented from choosing

---

[58] See, for example, the Limburg Principles on the Implementation of the International Covenant on Economic, Social and Cultural Rights, UN doc. E/CN.4/1987/17, Annex, reprinted in *Human Rights Quarterly*, 9 (1987), 123, para. 3.

between a more or less broad interpretation of the different provisions. At the review stage, the room for limitations corresponds to the inclusiveness of the interpretation: when fundamental rights are broadly applicable, limitations will often be justified and vice versa. I already mentioned that, today, proportionality review is the dominant approach to reviewing conflicts involving rights.[59] It means that courts will (eventually) balance individual rights against the general interests at stake in a given case. An alternative approach would be a more categorical one, in which predetermined rules suggest a particular outcome. At the review stage, and in supranational rights reasoning especially, regard must be paid to the intensity of the review or margin of appreciation. This intensity or the degree of deference granted may also be determined in an ad hoc manner having regard to all the circumstances of a case.[60] An alternative approach relies on categories based, for example, on the right that is at stake. Having an idea of the pros and cons of the different approaches to rights reasoning allows a better insight in the choices the Court makes at the different adjudicatory stages, as well as the place a core rights perspective could play therein.

A comprehensive understanding of supranational protection of socio-economic rights on the basis of civil and political rights norms must deal with the interpretation of rights provisions and the review of limitations or omissions in an integrated fashion. Different to general theories of rights, it starts from written provisions, the elaboration of which is subject to legal, political and cultural constraints. Such an explanation is needed for vindicating the socio-economic dimension of the ECHR and guiding its further refinement. Several authors have brought up the idea of core rights protection in relation to the ECtHR's socio-economic practice.[61] A superficial treatment of this idea, however, underscores the one-dimensional interpretation it is generally given. Core rights are seen as inflexible aspects of rights that must at all times be protected; but this view contrasts with reality and leads to overlooking core rights' potential. Part II explores various core rights doctrines that contrast or at least enrichen this dominant account. Rather than looking at the Strasbourg context, I elaborate on how the idea that some aspects of rights are more important than others has been theorized and applied at both the

---

[59] Cf. Alexy 2002 (n. 13); Möller 2012 (n. 12); Barak 2012 (n. 14).
[60] Cf., for example, *Petrovic v. Austria*, ECtHR 27 March 1998, 20458/92, para. 38.
[61] Koch 2002 (n. 37), 46; Koch 2003 (n. 37), 23; Koch 2009 (n. 29), 181; Palmer 2009 (n. 37), 408; Brems 2007 (n. 37), 167.

constitutional and the international level. Although the focus lies on core socio-economic rights, Chapter 4 starts with a discussion of constitutional core rights protection in a classical rights context. Article 19(2) of the German Basic Law (*Grundgesetz*; GG) holds, 'In no case may the core content of a constitutional right be infringed'. This provision has been discussed in depth by German legal scholars, which has led to a plurality of understandings that are conceptually inspiring, even when not always workable. What they have in common is that the protection of the *Wesen* of a right is understood to translate into a limit to their limitation. Rights should not be hollowed out by the legislature entirely – or in fact by any of the three national branches. The discussions of whether this guarantee secures an objective institution or an individual claim, is circumstantial or more predictable, are still partly unresolved. It is nevertheless clear that in their function as 'limits to limitations', core rights also apply to positive rights, i.e., it is possible that 'too little' is provided.

There are other uses of core rights as well. Social rights often are not expected to be complied with (immediately) entirely. In the ICESCR, this was translated into the requirement of progressive realization. But how can a state be held accountable for such realization 'in the light of available resources', when there is no agreement on what it should do first?[62] In Chapter 5, I discuss the core obligations recognized in response to this dilemma. In the context of monitoring compliance with the ICESCR, the minimum core is used to pinpoint what should be prioritized in aspiring full compliance with socio-economic rights.[63] In turn, in South Africa and by the South African Constitutional Court, the idea of core rights has been contemplated for adjudicational purposes. The Constitutional Court concluded, however, that core rights cannot be determined.[64] Continuing the debate, scholars have overcome the dichotomy between core rights protection and reasonableness review. Just as in the General Comments of the Committee on Economic, Social and Cultural Rights (CESCR), it is emphasized that core rights can be a matter of content, i.e., of the (justiciable) scope of rights without the determination of which state measures – or the lack thereof – cannot be evaluated. This is corroborated by the German right to an *Existenzminimum* (subsistence

---

[62] Art. 2(1) ICESCR.
[63] Cf. CESCR, General Comment No. 3: The Nature of States Parties' Obligations (Art. 2(1) of the Covenant), 14 December 1990, E/1991/23, para. 10.
[64] See, for example, Government of the Republic of South Africa v. Grootboom & Others 2001 (1) SA 46 (CC).

minimum). Recognized under the guarantee of human dignity in conjunction with the social state principle, this right allows for individual
claims whenever minimum, core social guarantees are at stake.[65] The
Existenzminimum does not protect social rights broadly understood.
Important aspects thereof can, however, form the starting point for a
constitutional complaint, even though it remains up to the legislature to
decide what exact minimum must be provided.

Core rights are indeterminable, or at least that is what is held against
them. Still, a look at the minimum core obligations determined by the
CESCR shows that a pragmatic approach is possible. Several categories of
core socio-economic rights can be identified. Chapter 6 focuses on the
core rights and obligations belonging to the rights to access to housing,
the highest attainable standard of health and social security. On closer
inspection, their cores include both negative and positive duties; they
entail not only obligations to respect, but also to protect and fulfil certain
rights. Non-discrimination can be seen as a core requirement, and so
is the protection of disadvantaged and marginalized individuals and
groups. Hence, minimum social protection must be available for all.
Besides, long-term programmes and procedural safeguards are crucial
for progressively realizing the various social rights. Broadly speaking, two
ways of identifying cores exist: The first looks at the right itself and
searches for the inherent nucleus thereof; depending on one's normative
starting point, though, this may point in different directions or at least
leave unclear the exact level of protection required. Second, taking
account of information apart from the right itself, such as consensus or
broad agreement on core aspects or expert determinations thereof, may
add to an understanding that is neither fixed nor court-centred. In fact,
when referring to cores as setting a threshold for adjudication, there need
not be a detailed understanding of what the core entails: recognizing, at
least prima facie, that a minimum level of socio-economic protection is
to be provided already seems helpful in this regard.

Part III turns again to the ECtHR and its protection of socio-economic
rights, but not before drawing together some of the main findings from
the core rights chapters, especially as to how core rights tap into the two-
phased structure of rights adjudication. Core rights can be absolute but
also relative, and this goes for both rights' interpretation (content) and
the review of interferences or omissions in regard thereof (protection). In

---

[65] Art. 1(1) in conjunction with Article 20(1) GG; BVerfGE 125, 175, 1 BvL 1/09 of
9 February 2010 (*Hartz IV*).

Chapter 7, I argue that a core rights perspective departing from absolute content while offering relative protection best fits the Strasbourg Court's role in connection with socio-economic rights. It could provide an answer to the existing gap in the explanation and justification for the Court's engagement in this field that connects the two stages of rights adjudication. While showing that the scope of the rights enshrined in the Convention need not be limitless in order to provide for effective protection, it suggests ways for rendering definitive prima facie core socio-economic rights on the basis of classical rights norms. A core rights approach suggests that once the Convention is held admissible to a complaint about core social rights, the margin of appreciation should be adjusted accordingly. Automatically granting a wide margin in cases involving socio-economic policy fails to do justice to the indivisibility of rights and the importance of minimum guarantees in this field. The different aspects of the proportionality test should be sufficiently strict to see whether core socio-economic rights have been guaranteed. Prima facie social rights may also translate into procedural requirements. Without having to define what desirable social policies would look like, recognizing that core individual needs must be taken into account in national decision-making furthers the aim of protecting minimum social rights that seem indispensable for effectuating the rights of the Convention.[66]

In Chapter 8, the core rights perspective is confronted with the Court's socio-economic case law. What happens when we view the Court's reasoning in these cases through a core-rights lens? I show that the Convention appears to guarantee, at least prima facie, core socio-economic rights protection in the fields of housing, social security and health and health care. Albeit the Court remains hesitant to explicitly recognize this, minimum protection, both positive and negative, must be ensured in the case of evictions or when someone is seriously ill. Protection against disproportional interferences with social benefits is granted so as to ensure that a minimum subsistence level is guaranteed. A core rights perspective, thus, together with the ideas of effectiveness and indivisibility, provides a comprehensive explanation for the Convention's emerging socio-economic dimension. The various cases presented illustrate how the idea of core rights protection 'fits' the Strasbourg practice,

---

[66] On the development of procedural fundamental rights review, see, for example, Janneke Gerards and Eva Brems (eds.), *Procedural Review in European Fundamental Rights Cases* (Cambridge University Press, 2017).

and also illuminate the shortcomings of the Court's reasoning as discussed in Chapter 2. A core rights perspective in this regard provides a structure that allows the Court to address the different issues and improve its case law. That is, it provides suggestions for how to reason indivisible rights where both deference and robust, consistent protection are required. These relate to the stages of fundamental rights adjudication while placing core socio-economic rights first.

PART I

Setting the Stage

1

The ECHR and Socio-Economic Rights Protection

The European Convention on Human Rights is a civil and political rights document. The rights norms it contains are classic ones. They guarantee civil and political liberties, i.e., the existence of a personal sphere in which government is not allowed to interfere. Yet to protect the rights of the Convention, the European Court of Human Rights is also confronted with complaints of a socio-economic kind. These concern, for example, housing, health and health care or social security. Socio-economic complaints give rise to the question, first, whether they deserve prima facie protection under the ECHR. If this is the case, the issue becomes whether protection must be granted in the individual circumstances at hand .[1] Over the past decades it has become clear that the Court does not categorically exclude economic and social interests from protection under the Convention. It has held that issues ranging from pension cuts to environmental pollution and the non-provision of medication can be covered by the ECHR. In a significant number of socio-economic cases, moreover, the ECtHR has found a violation of one or more Convention rights.

As the Court itself has underlined, a clear distinction between the civil and political and the economic and social sphere cannot be made.[2] Regardless of the Convention's classical starting point, thus, the protection of socio-economic interests seems merely inevitable. Yet this does not mean that review of economic or social issues is immune to concerns about the legitimate role of the ECtHR. Judicial socio-economic protection is often thought to sit uneasily with notions such as (democratic) legitimacy, subsidiarity and expertise.[3] Even though it is impossible to

---

[1] See, on the different stages of fundamental rights adjudication, Ch. 3.

[2] *Airey v. Ireland*, ECtHR 9 October 1979, 6289/73, para. 26.

[3] These concerns also feature in the debate on the adjudication of constitutional or treaty-based economic and social rights. See, for example, Gearty, in Conor Gearty and Virginia Mantouvalou, *Debating Social Rights* (Oxford: Hart Publishing, 2011), 57–64; Paul

exclude the socio-economic sphere from the protection of the Convention altogether, the scope and depth of the ECHR's economic and social dimension may thus be a point of debate. This is because of the ECtHR's intricate role in a multilevel system of fundamental rights protection, which amplifies the question of the potential limits to the Court's authority to deal with socio-economic complaints. In line with this, it may be asked whether the ECtHR's socio-economic case law is based on a particular theoretical outlook on economic and social rights protection, or what standard of review the Court should apply in this field.

Before I further elaborate on these questions, this chapter first gives an overview of the socio-economic dimension of the ECHR. Besides the 'civil and political' Convention and the complex task of the ECtHR, it introduces the Convention articles most relevant to the development that is central to this book. Chapter 2 will then 'make sense' of this phenomenon by discussing how the Court's socio-economic case law can be understood, and by addressing the chances and (potential) pitfalls of its current approach.

This chapter is set up as follows. In Section 1.1 I present some background information on the ECHR as a civil and political rights document. This section also addresses the position and the role of the ECtHR as a fundamental rights adjudicator in a multilevel legal system. Section 1.2 introduces the socio-economic case law of the Court by showing how several Convention articles provide for indirect socio-economic protection. Finally, in Section 1.3, I give a brief overview of the substantive Convention norms relevant to the ECHR's socio-economic dimension, as well as of the case law rendered on the basis thereof.

1.1   The Civil and Political ECHR and the ECtHR

1.1.1   The ECHR as a Civil and Political Rights Treaty

The European Convention on Human Rights embodies an agreement between states striving for the protection of human rights and fundamental freedoms. Its inception can be understood against the background

---

O'Connell, *Vindicating Socio-Economic Rights: International Standards and Comparative Experiences* (London: Routledge, 2012), 8–17; Jeff King, *Judging Social Rights* (Cambridge University Press, 2012), 3–8. In relation to the ECHR, see Heike Krieger, 'Positive Verpflichtungen unter der EMRK: Unentbehrliches Element einer gemeineuropäischen Grundrechtsdogmatik, leeres Versprechen oder Grenze der Justitiabilität?', *Zeitschrift für ausländisches öffentliches Recht und Völkerrecht*, 74 (2014), pp. 187–213.

of the human rights movement that evolved in response to the atrocities that had occurred in the first half of the twentieth century. Particularly, the origins of the ECHR can be viewed as beginning with the Universal Declaration of Human Rights (UDHR). In 1948 the UDHR was adopted by the General Assembly of the United Nations.[4] The creation of this international bill of rights formed a major step in the development of fundamental rights protection beyond the state and 'has retained its place of honor in the human rights movement' ever since.[5] It contains an extensive set of fundamental rights that is not limited to what are generally termed classic or civil and political rights. Next to, for example, the right to life, the prohibition of torture and the right to take part in the government of a person's country, the UDHR also enumerates economic and social guarantees. Some examples of this are the rights to work, to education, as well as to an adequate standard of living.

There is no indication in the UDHR of a hierarchy amongst the different rights. This suggests that civil and political, and economic and social rights were considered equally important.[6] In fact, however, against the backdrop of the Cold War and due to the prominent role of the United States in the universal human rights movement, the equal status of these rights had become more contentious over the drafting period.[7] The UDHR did not obtain the character of a legally binding instrument. Rather, it was meant to function as a springboard for treaties that would have more than merely political significance. This made the differences between the two sorts of rights less immediately relevant. When eventually binding legal norms were drafted, the contents of the UDHR were divided over two separate covenants.[8] The first came to include only civil and political rights, while the economic, social and cultural ones obtained a separate covenant.

---

[4] United Nations General Assembly Resolution 217A(III) of 10 December 1948.

[5] Henry J. Steiner, 'Securing Human Rights: The First Half-Century of the Universal Declaration, and Beyond', *Harvard Magazine* (September–October 1998), pp. 45–46, 45.

[6] See, however, Matthew C.R. Craven, *The International Covenant on Economic, Social and Cultural Rights* (Oxford University Press, 1995), 17, n. 87, for the argument that there seems to be some preference for civil and political rights, because these are listed first.

[7] Henry J. Steiner, Philip Alston and Ryan Goodman, *International Human Rights in Context: Law, Politics, Morals*, 3rd ed. (Oxford University Press, 2007), 136.

[8] See the analysis, prepared by the United Nations, of the drafting process: Annotations on the Text of the Draft International Covenants on Human Rights, UN Doc. A/2929, 10th Session (1955), 7.

It is well known that the International Covenant on Civil and Political Rights (ICCPR) and the International Covenant on Economic Social and Cultural Rights (ICESCR) differ in important respects.[9] Whereas ICCPR rights are phrased as individual, subjective rights, ICESCR rights merely require states to take steps towards the fulfilment of socio-economic guarantees, subject to the requirement of progressive realization and in the light of the available resources.[10] In line with this weaker and non-individualized wording, the latter remain to be understood as second rank. Even in the twenty-first century, economic and social rights are famously labelled the 'Cinderella of the human rights corpus'.[11]

In line with the international human rights movement, at the European level, too, efforts were made after the Second World War to create a 'Charter of Fundamental Rights'.[12] In May 1948, a preliminary draft of the ECHR, prepared by the legal committee of the European Movement, was adopted.[13] Article 1 of this draft held that 'every State a party to this Convention shall guarantee to all persons within its territory' a list of no less than eleven fundamental rights. These included several freedoms (of speech, religion, association and from arbitrary arrest, detention and exile and slavery) as well as equality guarantees and freedom from discrimination. Also listed was the 'freedom from arbitrary deprivation of property'.

In 1949 the Consultative Assembly of the Council of Europe set up a legal committee that had to decide on which rights would eventually

---

[9] United Nations General Assembly, International Covenant on Civil and Political Rights (ICCPR), 16 December 1966, 999 U.N.T.S. 171 (entry into force 23 March 1976); United Nations General Assembly, International Covenant on Economic, Social and Cultural Rights (ICESCR), 16 December 1966, 993 U.N.T.S. 3 (entry into force 23 March 1976).

[10] See further Ch. 5, S. 5.1.

[11] Sandra Fredman, *Human Rights Transformed: Positive Rights and Positive Duties* (Oxford University Press, 2008), 2.

[12] Pierre-Henri Teitgen, 'Introduction to the European Convention on Human Rights' in R.S.J. Macdonald, F. Matscher and H. Petzold (eds.), *The European System for the Protection of Human Rights* (Leiden: Martinus Nijhoff Publishers, 1993), pp. 3–14, 5; Ed Bates, 'The Birth of the European Convention on Human Rights – and the European Court of Human Rights' in J. Christofferson and M.R. Madsen (eds.), *The European Court of Human Rights between Law and Politics* (Oxford University Press, 2011), 18 ff.

[13] Teitgen 1993 (n. 12), 5; Ed Bates, *The Evolution of the European Convention on Human Rights: From Its Inception to the Creation of a Permanent Court of Human Rights* (Oxford University Press, 2010), 20–21.

deserve a place in the Convention. According to Pierre-Henri Teitgen, the legal committee's rapporteur at the time:

> [T]he committee agreed without difficulty that the collective enforcement should extend solely to rights and freedoms: (a) which imposed on the States only obligations 'not to do things,' which would thus be susceptible to immediate sanction by a court; and (b) which were so fundamental that human dignity and democracy were inconceivable if they were not respected; it followed that so-called economic and social rights should be excluded, at least to begin with.[14]

It was decided that the 'borderline right' to protection of property from the previous list was to be left out.[15] Together with the right to education this right was only incorporated in Protocol No. 1 to the Convention.

The 1950 European Convention for the Protection of Human Rights and Fundamental Freedoms eventually entered into force on 3 September 1953.[16] According to the Preamble, its aim was to 'to take the first steps for the *collective enforcement* of *certain* of the rights stated in the Universal Declaration'. The eventual document merely enumerates the civil and political guarantees that would later become part of the ICCPR within the UN system.[17] One reason for this was that the rights included were to be collectively enforced, i.e., had to be suitable for adjudication by a court. Important in this regard, moreover, was the rise of communism.[18] That economic and social rights were left out of the eventual Convention did not mean that the inherent value of these rights was put into question.[19] Rather, the time was not yet considered ripe for these rights to be included in a document containing binding human rights norms subject to international judicial enforcement.

The Convention's civil and political rights norms can be placed under different headers. First of all, the ECHR includes classic freedoms: the right

---

[14] Teitgen 1993 (n. 12), 10.

[15] See Janneke Gerards, 'Fundamental Rights and Other Interests: Should It Really Make a Difference?' in E. Brems (ed.), *Conflicts between Fundamental Rights* (Antwerp/Oxford/New York: Intersentia, 2008), pp. 655–690, 659; Bates 2011 (n. 12), 24.

[16] Council of Europe, European Convention for the Protection of Human Rights and Fundamental Freedoms, 4 November 1950, ETS 5.

[17] Some exceptions are the right to equality before the law, freedom of movement and residence and the right to a nationality.

[18] David J. Harris, Michael O'Boyle, Edward P. Bates and Carla M. Buckley, *Harris, O'Boyle and Warbrick: Law of the European Convention on Human Rights*, 3rd ed. (Oxford University Press, 2014), 1, Bates 2011 (n. 12), 18–19.

[19] See, Council of Europe, Consultative Assembly, First Session, Reports, 1949, 1144.

to life (Article 2), the prohibition of torture (Article 3), the prohibition of slavery and forced labour (Article 4), the right to freedom and security (Article 5), no punishment without law (Article 7), the right to respect for private and family life (Article 8), freedom of thought, conscience and religion (Article 9), freedom of expression (Article 10), freedom of assembly and association (Article 11) and the right to marry (Article 12). These freedoms protect an individual sphere that does not allow for interference by the state. In the case of several rights, this prohibition is relative in the sense that limitations can be justified in certain circumstances. Second, there are the procedural safeguards: the right to a fair trial (Article 6) and the right to an effective remedy (Article 13). Rather than protecting substantive rights, these provisions ensure the entitlement 'to a fair and public hearing within a reasonable time by an independent and impartial tribunal established by law' as well as 'an effective remedy before a national authority' in case of a violation of the Convention. Finally, there is the prohibition of discrimination (Article 14), which prohibits unjustified unequal treatment in the enjoyment of Convention rights.

Over the years, the Convention has been supplemented by various protocols, which contain institutional changes[20] as well as additional fundamental rights norms. It was already mentioned that the First Protocol to the ECHR enshrines the right to protection of property (Article 1) as well as the right to education (Article 2). Other examples are the right to free elections (Article 3, Protocol No. 1), the abolishment of the death penalty (Protocol No. 13) and the 'free-standing' non-discrimination clause (Article 1, Protocol No. 12). The latter provision ensures that also in the absence of a direct link with another Convention right, complaints of alleged discrimination can be dealt with under the Convention. The protocols are optional, and not every party to the Convention has ratified every protocol or all provisions thereof. This shows that, regardless of their 'classic' character, some of the rights added are too controversial to be agreed upon by all states partaking in the Strasbourg system of human rights protection.[21]

From the 1970s onwards, some efforts have also been made to create a protocol to the ECHR that would include socio-economic

---

[20] See, in particular, Protocol No. 11 to the ECHR, 'restructuring the control machinery established thereby'.

[21] Charts of signatures and ratifications can be found on the Court's website: www.echr.coe.int.

rights.[22] In 1970 and 1978, recommendations that argued in favour of such a protocol were adopted, but the initiatives were rejected.[23] Also more recently, explicit protection of economic and social rights within the ECHR framework was incentivized.[24] In 2005, however, the Steering Committee for Human Rights (CDDH) concluded that 'it was obvious that such an activity would have no political support at the present time'.[25] Attention for the topic has since faded.

Just like in the UN system, also under the umbrella of the Council of Europe, economic and social rights have ended up in separate document. In 1961 the European Social Charter (ESC) was adopted.[26] The ESC contains an extensive list of economic and social rights norms that are directed at the Member States and phrased as positive rights. Amongst other things, they require states to ensure the effective exercise of the right to work and just conditions of work, of the right to protection of health and of the right to social security. Like in the UN human rights context, the enforcement of the economic and social rights at the CoE level differs from that of the civil and political ones. The ESC has been revised and consolidated, and in addition to a reporting procedure now also has a complaints procedure.[27] This has resulted in an illuminating body of decisions by the European Committee of Social Rights (ECSR). Complaints can however only be made collectively, and the decisions of the ECSR do not have the same legal status as judgments of the ECtHR,

---

[22] Klaus Berchtold, 'Council of Europe Activities in the Field of Economic, Social and Cultural Rights' in F. Matscher (ed.), *The Implementation of Economic and Social Rights, National, International and Comparative Aspects* (Kehl: N.P. Engel Verlag, 1991), pp. 355–370.

[23] Council of Europe, Consultative Assembly, Recommendation 583 (1970), and Council of Europe, Parliamentary Assembly, Recommendation 838 (1978), respectively. See also Pieter van Dijk, Fried van Hoof, Arjen van Rijn and Leo Zwaak (eds.), *Theory and Practice of the European Convention on Human Rights*, 4th ed. (Antwerp/Oxford/New York: Intersentia, 2006), 5.

[24] Council of Europe, Committee of Ministers, Declaration on the Occasion of the 50th Anniversary of the Universal Declaration of Human Rights, 10 December 1998; Council of Europe, Parliamentary Assembly, Recommendation 1415 (1999), Additional Protocol to the European Convention on Human Rights Concerning Fundamental Social Rights.

[25] Council of Europe, Report of 29 June 2005 from the Steering Committee for Human Rights, CDDH(2005)009, S. 5.4, para. 17. See also Council of Europe, Report of 18 May from the Working Group on Social Rights GT-DH-SOC(2005)007.

[26] Council of Europe, European Social Charter, 18 October 1961, ETS 35. A revised version of the Charter ((R)ESC) was adopted in 1996: Council of Europe, European Social Charter (Revised), 3 May 1996, ETS 163.

[27] Additional Protocol to the European Social Charter Providing for a System of Collective Complaints, 9 November 1995, ETS 158.

which makes it harder to ensure concrete follow-up at the national level. Unsurprisingly, thus, it is particularly the protection offered by the civil and political ECHR, rather than (also) that of the ESC's economic and social rights, that is often considered the most effective example worldwide of supranational fundamental rights protection.

1.1.2   The ECtHR as a Supranational Fundamental Rights Adjudicator

According to Teitgen:

> [T]he Convention which was envisaged had firstly to list the *fundamental* human rights and freedoms to be respected and safeguarded in every Member State of the Council of Europe, and secondly to set up a system of collective enforcement of those rights for all those States.[28]

A central reason why the ECHR has come to be perceived as a 'human rights protection system of unparalleled effectiveness',[29] is that it is backed by a supranational court that renders binding judgments on the basis of individual applications. A novel phenomenon at the time, this today ensures that individuals in the 47 member states can resort to the ECtHR if they feel national courts have not dealt with their fundamental interests in an adequate manner.[30]

Originally, the collective enforcement mechanism of the ECHR consisted of the European Commission of Human Rights (EComHR) and the European Court of Human Rights in collaboration with the Council of Ministers of the CoE. In this setup, the EComHR played the major part in dealing with fundamental rights complaints, and only a limited number of cases were referred to the ECtHR. This changed after the entry into force of Protocol No. 11 on 1 November 1998. A single and permanent European Court of Human Rights replaced the combination of the part-time EComHR and ECtHR.[31] In addition to interstate applications,[32] this court 'may receive applications from any person, nongovernmental organisation or group of individuals claiming to be the victim of a violation by one of the High Contracting Parties of the rights set forth in the Convention or the Protocols thereto'.[33] There is still a possibility for

---

[28] Teitgen 1993 (n. 12), 3. Cf. also the ECHR's Preamble.

[29] Rolv Ryssdal, 'The Coming of Age of the European Convention of Human Rights', *European Human Rights Law Review* (1996), pp. 18–29, 18.

[30] According to Art. 35(1) ECHR, '[t]he Court may only deal with the matter after all domestic remedies have been exhausted'.

[31] Art. 19 ECHR.   [32] Art. 33 ECHR.   [33] Art. 34 ECHR.

internal appeal: within three months after a seven-judge Chamber judgment, the parties to the case may in exceptional circumstances request a referral to the Grand Chamber of the Court (GC). When a panel of five judges accepts this request, the Grand Chamber – consisting of seventeen judges – delivers a final judgment.[34]

It is the Court's task to interpret the rights enshrined in the Convention and the protocols thereto and apply them to specific complaints.[35] For several reasons related to the character and position of the ECtHR, this is a particularly complex task.[36] First of all, the ECtHR can be characterized as a supranational court that is part of an international organisation (the CoE). In this respect, it plays a subsidiary role in a complex, multilevel legal order, which implies that it may only step in when national authorities have failed to provide the necessary protection. At the same time, the ECtHR is a human rights court dealing with the adjudication of fundamental rights. In this capacity, it has the important task of protecting individuals' most fundamental interests, which requires particular consideration of their circumstances and needs. Finally, the ECtHR has also been labelled, or at least compared to, a constitutional court.[37] Albeit being unable to strike down laws for their incompatibility

---

[34] Arts. 43 and 44 ECHR.   [35] Art. 32 ECHR.

[36] On the specific 'problematic' of the Court, see, for example, Janneke Gerards, 'Judicial Deliberations in the European Court of Human Rights' in N. Huls, M. Adams and J. Bomhoff (eds.), *The Legitimacy of Highest Courts' Rulings. Judicial Deliberations and Beyond* (The Hague: T.M.C. Asser Press, 2009), pp. 407–436, (with further references).

[37] See, for example, Ryssdal 1996 (n. 29); Evert Alkema, 'The European Convention as a constitution and its Court as a constitutional court' in P. Mahoney et al. (eds.), *Protecting Human Rights: The European Perspective* (Studies in memory of Rolf Ryssdal) (Cologne: Carl Heymanns Verlag, 2000), pp. 41–63, 59–60; Luzius Wildhaber, 'A Constitutional Future for the European Court of Human Rights?', *Human Rights Law Journal*, 23 (2002), pp. 161–166; Steven Greer, *The European Convention on Human Rights: Achievements, Problems and Prospects* (Cambridge University Press, 2006), 173; Luzius Wildhaber, 'The European Court of Human Rights: The Past, The Present, The Future', *American University International Law Review*, 22 (2007), pp. 521–538, 528; Alec Stone-Sweet and Helen Keller, 'The Reception of the ECHR in National Legal Orders' in A. Stone-Sweet and H. Keller (eds.), *A Europe of Rights: The Impact of the ECHR on National Legal Systems* (Oxford University Press, 2008), pp. 11–36, 7; Gerards 2009 (n. 36), 409–412; Wojciech Sadurski, 'Partnering with Strasbourg: Constitutionalisation of the European Court of Human Rights, the Accession of Central and East European States to the Council of Europe, and the Idea of Pilot Judgments', *Human Rights Law Review*, 9 (2009), pp. 397–453; Stéphanie Hennette-Vauchez, 'Constitutional v. International? When Unified Reformatory Rationales Mismatch the Plural Paths of Legitimacy of ECHR Law' in J. Christofferson and M. Rask Madsen (eds.), *The European Court of Human Rights between Law and Politics* (Oxford University Press, 2011), pp. 144–164; Nicolas

with the Convention, the Court and its case law are understood to play a leading, or in any case guiding, role.[38] These three different role perceptions, i.e., the supranational/subsidiary adjudicator, the human rights protector, and the (semi-)constitutional court, can explain what makes the task of the Court so particularly challenging.[39] All three roles impose different, and at times incompatible, expectations on the ECtHR. To illustrate this, the different demands the Court faces can be presented by sketching two dilemmas the Court is confronted with practically on a day-to-day basis.

First, the ECtHR has to ensure *effective fundamental rights protection* while at the same time taking a *deferential stance* towards the member states. The Court was set up to guarantee a certain level of fundamental rights protection throughout the Council of Europe Member States. Its role cannot be merely symbolical: it must ensure that the ECHR guarantees are not 'rights that are theoretical or illusory but rights that are practical and effective'.[40] This means that the Court regularly interprets rights in a manner that was not foreseen at the time the Convention was drafted.[41] It also implies that the Court will sometimes reach a conclusion

---

A.J. Crocquet, 'The European Court of Human Rights' Norm-Creation and Norm-Limiting Processes: Resolving a Normative Tension', *Columbia Journal of European Law*, 17 (2011), pp. 307–373, 308; Wojciech Sadurski, *Constitutionalism and the Enlargement of Europe* (Oxford University Press, 2012), 47; Steven Greer and Luzius Wildhaber, 'Revisiting the Debate about "Constitutionlising" the European Court of Human Rights', *Human Rights Law Review*, 12 (2013), pp. 655–687; Harris et al. 2014 (n. 18), 4.

[38] This is underlined by the *res interpretata* effect of the judgments. Because the ECtHR does not have the power to strike down national laws, it will never become *fully* constitutional (Sadurski 2009 (n. 37), 448). The ECHR nevertheless has many 'constitutional' features: it protects a rather inflexible set of justiciable rights that seem at least *de facto* – though this depends to some extent on the jurisdiction – superior to other laws (cf. Joseph Raz, 'On the Authority and Interpretation of Constitutions' in L. Alexander (ed.), *Constitutionalism: Philosophical Foundations* (Cambridge University Press, 1998), pp. 152–193, 153–154).

[39] Cf. Janneke Gerards, 'The Prism of Fundamental Rights', *European Constitutional Law Review*, 8 (2012), pp. 173–202, 184–186 (speaking of the 'backup' role, the standard-setting role and the agenda-setting function), and on the Court's task and the notion of 'shared responsibility', Janneke Gerards, 'The European Court of Human Rights and the National Courts: Giving Shape to the Notion of "Shared Responsibility"' in J.H. Gerards and J. Fleuren (eds.), *Implementation of the European Convention on Human Rights and of the Case Law of the ECtHR in National Case Law* (Antwerp/Oxford/New York: Intersentia, 2014), pp. 13–93.

[40] *Airey v. Ireland*, ECtHR 9 October 1979, 6289/73, para. 24.

[41] See, for example, *Tyrer v. the UK*, ECtHR 25 April 1978, 5856/72, para. 31 (where corporal punishment was held to fall within the scope of Art. 3 of the Convention).

that goes against strongly held national beliefs or long-standing policies or practices. In its human-rights protector role, thus, the ECtHR sometimes needs to be merciless in order to ensure effective protection. At the same time, the Court remains a supranational court par excellence; it must keep a certain distance from what is decided at the national level.[42] A deferential attitude is not only imperative having regard to the setup of the Convention system,[43] it also has a pragmatic purpose. The ECtHR is dependent on the willingness of the member states for the implementation of its judgments.[44] Deferring to national policies and practices where possible is important in this regard. When the Court renders far-reaching judgments that encroach upon national laws and democratic decision-making to a serious extent, this potentially conflicts with its judicial role as well as its subsidiary position. That is, whereas the role ascribed to courts is limited by definition, the supranational position of the ECtHR exacerbates the need for a cautious approach. If the Court fails to keep this in mind, the inclination of the member states to comply with the Strasbourg case law may decrease.[45]

The aims of ensuring effective protection and showing deference to the national authorities need not always be in conflict. The CoE member states have willingly subjected themselves to the jurisdiction of the Court and have endowed it with the power to interpret and apply the Convention. At the same time, it is not hard to imagine that both demands do in fact regularly collide. Ensuring that fundamental rights are non-illusory may require a strict stance by the Court that has unwelcome consequences for the state involved. A famous example is the case of *Hirst v. the United Kingdom*, in which the Court held that the UK had violated Article 3 of Protocol No. 1 by restricting the right to vote of convicted prisoners.[46] Its judgment has been received with much criticism, and there has been a continuing debate over whether and how to change the legal system accordingly.[47] Situations like these can have a chilling effect

---

[42] See, for example, *Case relating to certain aspects of the laws on the use of languages in education in Belgium*, ECtHR 23 July 1968, 1474/62, 1677/62, 1691/62, 1769/63, 1994/63 and 2126/64, para. I.B.10.

[43] See Arts. 1 and 35(1) ECHR.   [44] Cf. Krieger 2014 (n. 3), 200.

[45] See Gerards 2014 (n. 39), 41–46.

[46] *Hirst v. the UK (No. 2)*, ECtHR (GC) 6 October 2005, 74025/01.

[47] See Steve Foster, 'Reluctancy Restoring Rights: Responding to the Prisoner's Right to Vote', *Human Rights Law Review*, 9 (2009), pp. 489–507; Ed Bates, 'Analysing the Prisoner Voting Saga and the British Challenge to Strasbourg', *Human Rights Law Review*, 14 (2014), pp. 503–540.

on the relation between the Court and the state, which in turn might have a negative impact on the reputation and effectiveness of the supervisory system as a whole.

The second, related dilemma can be sketched as follows: The ECtHR must offer *individual protection* while at the same time providing *general guidance*. As a fundamental rights guarantor, it offers a safety net for individuals who need to be shielded against majority decisions unfavourable to their fundamental interests.[48] In order to guarantee the subjective rights of the ECHR, the Court thus needs to focus on the individual circumstances of a case.[49] When these circumstances call for action, the Court arguably should not be hampered by the text of the Convention or other formalistic concerns. An individual focus moreover fits what is generally understood to be the limited task of the judiciary, seen in relation to the other powers.[50] Although it is generally accepted that they do, to some extent, engage in lawmaking activities, courts are not equipped nor legitimized to make general rules. Rather, it is their task to 'fix' individual cases in which general rules have undesired effects or are applied contrary to higher laws. Concurrently, however, the Strasbourg Court needs to provide some 'objective' guidance. The constitutional role of the Court is more than just a modern label attached to the ECtHR's practice that nicely fits the broader notion of 'constitutionalism beyond the state'. Rather, the constitutional task of the Court is embedded in the system of the Convention. It is first and foremost up to the member states to ensure compliance with the rights and freedoms of the ECHR.[51] Because these rights and freedoms allow for multiple

---

[48] See, for example, Gerards 2012 (n. 39), 184–185.

[49] *Sunday Times v. the UK*, ECtHR 26 April 1979, 6538/74, para. 65; *Young, James and Webster v. the UK*, ECtHR 13 August 1981, 7601/76 and 7806/77; Johan Callewaert, 'The Judgments of the Court, Background and Content' in R.S.J. Macdonald, F. Matscher and H. Petzold (eds.), *The European System for the Protection of Human Rights* (Leiden: Martinus Nijhoff Publishers, 1993), pp. 713–731, 728; Franz Matscher, 'Methods of Interpretation of the Convention' in R.S.J. Macdonald, F. Matscher and H. Petzold (eds.), *The European System for the Protection of Human Rights* (Leiden: Martinus Nijhoff Publishers, 1993), pp. 63–81, 64.

[50] Cf. Ingrid Leijten, 'Separation of Powers and the Limits to the "Constitutionalization" of Fundamental Rights Adjudication by the ECtHR and the CJEU' in H.M.Th.D. ten Napel and W.J.M. Voermans (eds.), *The Powers That Be: Rethinking the Separation of Powers: A Leiden Response to Christoph Möllers* (Leiden University Press, 2015) pp. 275–293.

[51] See also George Letsas, *A Theory of Interpretation of the European Convention on Human Rights* (Oxford University Press, 2007), 9; Françoise Tulkens, *How Can We Ensure Greater Involvement of National Courts in the Convention System?* Dialogue between Judges (European Court of Human Rights, Council of Europe, 2012), pp. 6–10.

interpretations, yet need to guarantee the same level of protection throughout the CoE, there is a need for clarification by the ECtHR. In line with this, although in principle the judgments of the Court are only binding for the parties to the case,[52] it is widely recognized that they *de facto* work *erga omnes*.[53] The effects of the Court's judgments thus reach beyond the contours of a particular case. Once the Court interprets the Convention in a particular manner, the example set will not only trigger individuals in a comparable situation to invoke their Convention rights, but is also likely to be taken as a point of reference by national authorities – including national courts. This implies that clear answers from the supranational ECtHR are very welcome at times, even when it can generally be argued that courts should not always have the final say. Thus, because of the specific position of the Court in a multilevel system, sometimes the Court needs to render principled, comprehensively reasoned judgments that provide states with more than just the outcome of a single case.[54]

The demands of individual justice and of constitutional justice may be seen to be in conflict with one another. As a human-rights protector, the Court is likely to emphasize individual, circumstantial protection, whereas it benefits its guiding role more with general reasoning. The Court's subsidiary function seems to demand both: The judicial interference is circumscribed by 'minimal' judgments that only concern one particular situation. Yet in order to protect rights in a sufficient manner without the Court having to interfere, states also profit from more objective information.

Thus, the Strasbourg Court is entrusted with a complicated, multidimensional task. Against this background it can hardly be blamed for not only receiving praise, but criticism as well. Especially over the past years, this criticism has intensified.[55] In the media, as well as in the political

---

[52] Art. 46(1) ECHR.
[53] See, for example, Gerards 2009 (n. 36), 409–410; Gerards 2014 (n. 39), 21. George Ress, 'The Effects of Decisions and Judgments of the European Court of Human Rights in the Domestic Legal Order', *Texas International Law Journal*, 40 (2005), pp. 359–382, 374 (speaking of an 'orientation effect').
[54] See, for example, Gerards 2014 (n. 39), 69–70.
[55] Cf. the discussions that evolved since the end of the 2000s in the United Kingdom but for example also in the Netherlands. See, generally, Gerards 2014 (n. 39), 86–88; Patricia Popelier, Sarah Lambrechts and Koen Lemmens (eds.), *Criticism of the European Court of Human Rights: Shifting the Convention System: Counter-Dynamics at the National and EU Level* (Cambridge/Antwerp/Portland: Intersentia, 2016).

arena, prominent actors have voiced their doubts about the functioning and future of the Court's fundamental rights protection. The Court has been accused of interfering with member states' laws and policies more than necessary and of overstepping its boundaries as a judicial body. At the time, the most visible effect of this criticism is the United Kingdom's threat to leave the Convention. At the end of 2016, Prime Minister Theresa May announced that this topic will be a central aspect of her 2020 re-election campaign.

Another problem that has come to the fore more recently is the enormous caseload of the Court. Since the 1980s, the number of applications has grown steadily.[56] With the inception of the new ECtHR in 1998 and then the accession of several Eastern European states, the pace of this growth has become more rapid.[57] A few years ago, the caseload became a real threat to the functioning of the system.[58] In order to keep the amount of applications pending before the Court manageable, this has resulted in a number of measures. Of crucial importance has been the entry into force of Protocol No. 14 to the Convention. This protocol includes several institutional amendments to enable the Court to deal with a greater number of cases in a shorter period of time.[59] At the High Level Conferences on the Future of the European Court of Human Rights in 2010 in Interlaken, Switzerland, and in 2011 in Izmir, Turkey, some further concrete actions were agreed upon.[60] At the High Level Conference in Brighton in 2012, moreover, it was decided to devise a new protocol to the Convention.[61] Once all the member states parties to the

---

[56] Cf. Greer 2006 (n. 37), 33–41. Statistical information on the number of applications, judgments by state, etc. can be found via www.echr.coe.int (under Statistics).

[57] The latter development has led to difficult questions regarding the appropriate level of fundamental rights protection as well as structural problems. See Letsas 2007 (n. 51), 2; P. Leuprecht, 'Innovations in the European System of Human Rights Protection: Is Enlargement Compatible with Reinforcement?', *Transnational Law and Contemporary Problems*, 8 (1998), pp. 313–336; Greer 2006 (n. 37), 105 ff.; Sadurski 2012 (n. 37), Ch. 1.

[58] As it has often been said, the Court became a 'victim of its own success'. See Marie-Benedicte Dembour, '"Finishing Off" Cases: The Radical Solution to the Problem of the Expanding ECtHR Caseload', *European Human Rights Law Review*, (2002), pp. 604–623, 604.

[59] Protocol No. 14, amongst other things, has amended the Convention so that single judges can now reject manifestly inadmissible applications; committees of three judges may now declare an application inadmissible and decide on the merits of a case where the matter at hand is determined by well-established case law of the Court (see Arts. 27–28 ECHR).

[60] Interlaken Declaration, 19 February 2010; Izmir Declaration, 27 April 2011 (the different declarations can be found on the website of the Court: www.echr.coe.int).

[61] Brighton Declaration, 20 April 2012.

Convention have ratified this Protocol No. 15, it shall add a new recital to the ECHR, reading:

> Affirming that the High Contracting Parties, in accordance with the principle of subsidiarity, have the primary responsibility to secure the rights and freedoms defined in this Convention and the Protocols thereto, and that in doing so they enjoy a margin of appreciation, subject to the supervisory jurisdiction of the European Court of Human Rights established by this Convention.[62]

The very fact that it was considered necessary to codify the notion of subsidiarity and the margin of appreciation doctrine demonstrates that merely solving the backlog problem does not answer all the Court's concerns.

The criticism of the Court's encroaching upon national prerogatives is more than a problem in the margins. It is also relevant for the purposes of this study, as the Court's task as a protector of socio-economic rights cannot be meaningfully assessed without having regard to the acceptance and effectiveness of its judgments. In this regard, it is important for the Court to not just focus on one of its roles, but instead discharge *all* of its functions. First, its subsidiary role implies that the Court cannot provide for an all-encompassing rights order covering every possible conflict of interests. Second, it needs to strive for as much effective protection as possible in individual cases. Finally, in order to ensure an enduring, well-functioning system of European fundamental rights protection, it is important that its case law provides some clarity on the standards set by the Convention. Only this will allow the member states to confidently and effectively apply ECHR standards in their own legal orders. It is a principal aim of this book to deal with the issue of how the Court can live up to these expectations when socio-economic rights are concerned.

1.2 No Watertight Division

1.2.1 The Airey case

At the beginning of this chapter, I explained that the ECHR is a typical civil and political rights document. Its wording shows that first and foremost it protects negative freedoms.[63] Article 10, for example, stipulates

---

[62] Art. 1 Protocol No. 15 ECHR.
[63] The factsheet on 'welfare rights', that used to be on the Court's homepage, stated: 'The European Convention on Human Rights ... guarantees *civil and political rights* (such as

that '[e]veryone has the right to freedom of expression', and that '[t]his right shall include freedom to hold opinions and to receive and impart information and ideas without interference by public authority and regardless of frontiers'. Taken literally, it is not that obvious that the Convention imposes more than mere duties not to interfere. It has, however, become apparent from the Court's case law that the ECHR also includes positive obligations, and thus requires states to take action.[64] An early example is presented by the *Marckx* judgment, in which the Court held that Belgium had violated the right to respect for family life (Article 8 ECHR) because no maternal affiliation could be established directly after the birth of an illegitimate child.[65] Thus, a possibility to do so had to be created in order for Belgium to comply with the Convention.

Another point is that the ECHR guarantees cannot always meaningfully be characterized as entirely civil or political in nature. Even a brief look at the case law of the Court reveals that economic and social interests are protected therein as well. Under the header of rights to private life, property and non-discrimination, the ECtHR has, for example, reviewed numerous complaints concerning social security payments, housing laws and environmental nuisances. Inasmuch as the ECHR norms may still be characterized as 'civil and political', this no longer holds true for all of the interests they protect.[66]

Although in legal scholarship positive protection and socio-economic rights protection are often seen as being closely related,[67] two different things are concerned here. The positive obligations belonging to the ECHR do not always concern economic or social rights, whereas the socio-economic guarantees the Court recognizes are not always of a

---

the right to life, the right to liberty and security and the right to a fair trial). Meanwhile, other Council of Europe instruments, notably the European Social Charter, concern *economic and social rights* (such as housing, health, education, employment legal protection and social welfare)'.

[64] See, generally, Alastair Mowbray, *The Development of Positive Obligations under the European Convention on Human Rights by the European Court of Human Rights* (Oxford: Hart Publishing, 2004); Dimitris Xenos, *The Positive Obligations of the State under the European Convention of Human Rights* (London/Oxford/Edinburgh: Routledge, 2012); Laurens Lavrysen, *Human Rights in a Positive State: Rethinking the Relationship Between Positive and Negative Obligations under the European Convention on Human Rights* (Antwerp/Oxford/New York: Intersentia, 2016).

[65] *Marckx v. Belgium*, ECtHR 13 June 1979, 6833/74.

[66] See, further on the distinction between norms and interests, Ch. 2.

[67] See, for example, Kai Möller, *The Global Model of Constitutional Rights* (Oxford University Press, 2012), 5.

positive kind. Yet it must be admitted that the two do overlap, and that socio-economic protection in fields like housing or health often requires that at least some active steps be taken.

The adjudication of economic and social matters under the ECHR is not a recent phenomenon. Although the number of socio-economic rulings of the Court has clearly increased over the past years, it was recognized at a relatively early stage that the civil and political character of the ECHR must be nuanced. In a 1979 case under Article 6(1) ECHR (the right to a fair trial), for the first time the Court made explicit that the Convention also safeguards interests one would rather expect to be protected by socio-economic rights treaties.[68] In *Airey v. Ireland*, the question was whether the Article 6(1) guarantee of access to court also gives rise to positive state duties. Mrs Airey wanted to go to court to obtain a separation from her violent, alcoholic husband, but could not afford any legal assistance. The ECtHR held that the right to free legal aid under circumstances can also be invoked in civil law suits. It emphasized the importance of procedural safeguards, even when this has substantial implications for a national legal system bringing along significant costs. More precisely, Article 6 'may compel the state to provide for the assistance of a lawyer when such assistance proves indispensable for an effective access to court'.[69]

The Government had submitted that 'the Convention should not be interpreted so as to achieve social and economic developments in a Contracting state'. Rather than ignoring this sensitive point, the Court responded as follows:

> Whilst the Convention sets forth what are essentially civil and political rights, many of them have implications of a social or economic nature. The Court therefore considers, like the Commission, that the mere fact that an interpretation of the Convention may extend into the sphere of social and economic rights should not be a decisive factor against such an interpretation; there is no water-tight division separating that sphere from the field covered by the Convention.[70]

It thus clarified that a real distinction between the civil and the social sphere cannot be made. The *Airey* case put an end to the idea that the Convention is concerned solely with civil and political interests. It

[68] Martin Scheinin, 'Economic and Social Rights as Legal Rights' in A. Eide et al. (eds.), *Economic, Social and Cultural Rights: A Textbook*, 2nd ed. (Leiden: Martinus Nijhoff Publishers, 2001), pp. 29–54, 34.
[69] *Airey v. Ireland*, ECtHR 9 October 1979, 6289/73, para. 26.   [70] Ibid.

showed the ECtHR's willingness to conclude on costly obligations for the state that can be interpreted as being primarily of a social or economic nature.

The paragraph quoted above is often referred to in the Court's case law, showing that *Airey* is not an anomaly.[71] Quite the contrary, the overlap between the civil and political sphere and the field of economic and social rights is visible in an expanding number of decisions and judgments. These concern Article 6, but also several other provisions of the Convention.

1.2.2   Socialization through Articles 6 and 14 ECHR

The *Airey* case was dealt with under Article 6 ECHR, which contains classic procedural guarantees.[72] Besides this procedural route, there is another route that typically tends to hinder the distinction between civil and political and socio-economic protection. The non-discrimination principle enshrined in Article 14 ECHR also does not allow for a clear dividing line between different kinds of guarantees. It can easily trigger social obligations, perhaps even more obviously than Article 6. After all, once a practice is considered discriminatory, this means privileges or benefits provided to one group need to be distributed to others as well, regardless of whether they are of a social kind.

Both Article 6 and Article 14 thus provide for socio-economic rights protection as a by-product. They do not protect substantive socio-economic interests; rather, the protection of these interests flows from ensuring procedural safeguards or combating discrimination. Let me give some more information on both articles and the corresponding case law in order to illustrate this.

---

[71] See, for example, *N. v. the UK*, ECtHR (GC) 27 May 2008, 26565/05, para. 44. There, however, the reference was used to underline that '[a]lthough many of the rights it contains have implications of a social or economic nature, the Convention is essentially directed at the protection of civil and political rights'. The dissenters in this case (Judges Tulkens, Bonello, and Spielmann) have drawn attention to this 'incomplete and thus misleading quotation', which according to them ignores 'the social dimension of the integrated approach adopted by the Court' (para. 6).

[72] See, for a classical reading of the judgment, Colin Warbrick, 'Economic and Social Interests and the European Convention on Human Rights' in M.A. Baderin and R. McCorquodale, *Economic, Social and Cultural Rights in Action* (Oxford University Press, 2007), pp. 241–256, 245–246.

First, Article 6 ECHR forms one of the cornerstones of the ECHR and covers a broad range of fair trial guarantees.[73] Its procedural focus implies that it is not the Court's function 'to deal with errors of fact or law allegedly committed by a national court unless and in so far as they may have infringed rights and freedoms protected by the Convention'.[74] The rights guaranteed by Article 6 apply in the context of criminal charges as well as in disputes concerning 'civil rights and obligations'. It is the Court's broad interpretation of the latter notion that is crucial for the right to a fair trial's indirect social protection.

The Court has interpreted the notion of 'civil rights and obligations' in an autonomous manner – that is, without considering the defendant state's qualification of what is at stake to be decisive.[75] Thereby, and by 'expanding its scope over time, the position has been reached in which most substantive rights that an individual may arguably claim under national law fall within Article 6 unless they quintessentially concern the exercise of the public power of the State'.[76] Whereas, notably, disputes concerning the entry, conditions of stay and removal of aliens as well as issues concerning public service employment and taxes are not considered to be 'civil' in nature, Article 6 of the Convention covers a wide range of other topics. Most illustrative for the socio-economic dimension of Article 6 is the application of this provision in the field of social security. Whereas the Court in several earlier cases balanced the 'private' and 'public' aspects of disputes concerning this topic in order to determine whether Article 6 applied,[77] later it more generally incorporated disputes concerning social security, including social assistance.[78] In fact, the Court's broad interpretation of 'civil rights and obligations' implies that besides social security disputes, all kinds of other social rights disputes, such as those related to work, are covered as well. The social protection that follows from this is often more indirect compared

---

[73] *Perez v. France*, ECtHR (GC) 12 February 2004, 47287/99, para. 64.

[74] *Garcia Ruiz v. Spain*, ECtHR (GC) 21 January 1999, 30544/96, para 28.

[75] *König v. Germany*, ECtHR 28 June 1978, 6232/73, para. 88.

[76] David J. Harris, Michael O'Boyle, Edward P. Bates and Carla M. Buckley, *Harris, O'Boyle and Warbrick: Law of the European Convention on Human Rights*, 2nd ed. (Oxford University Press, 2009), 212.

[77] *Feldbrugge v. the Netherlands*, ECtHR 29 May 1986, 8562/79, para. 40; *Deumeland v. Germany*, ECtHR 29 May 1986, 9348/81, para. 60.

[78] *Salesi v. Italy*, ECtHR 26 February 1993, 13023/87, para. 19. See also Ida Elisabeth Koch, 'Social Rights as Components in the Civil Right to Personal Liberty – Another Possible Step Forward in the Integrated Human Rights Approach?', *Netherlands Quarterly of Human Rights*, 20 (2002), pp. 29–51, 36.

to what was granted in *Airey*; cost-free assistance of a lawyer is after all a particularly concrete social advantage. In most cases, Article 6 merely ensures an appropriate procedure without thereby guaranteeing a substantive individual interest of an economic or social nature. Nevertheless, at least this means that the various detailed guarantees of Article 6(1) of the Convention must be complied with, as well as that in social rights disputes covered by Article 6 access to court must be provided.[79]

Second, Article 14 ECHR guarantees the enjoyment of other Convention rights without discrimination.[80] It is therefore described as 'parasitic' and as having 'no independent existence'.[81] The application of Article 14, however, 'does not necessarily presuppose the violation of one of the substantive ECHR rights. It is necessary but also sufficient for the facts of the case to fall "within the ambit" of one or more of the Convention Articles'.[82] This 'within the ambit' formulation can be understood as pointing at something that is more inclusive than the strict scope of a particular ECHR provision.[83] The Court has come to recognize that Article 14 extends beyond the enjoyment of the Convention rights that states are required to guarantee. It also attaches to additional rights voluntarily provided by the state, as long as they fall within the 'general scope' of any Convention article.[84] In other words, as soon as measures or decisions taken by the state touch upon a provision

---

[79] *Golder v. the UK*, EComHR 21 February 1975, 4451/70.

[80] It reads: 'The enjoyment of the rights and freedoms set forth in this Convention shall be secured without discrimination on any ground such as sex, race, colour, language, religion, political or other opinion, national or social origin, association with a national minority, property, birth or other status.'

[81] *Chassagnou and Others v. France*, ECtHR (GC) 29 April 1999, 25088/94, 28331/95 and 28443/95, para. 89. See, on the (limited) scope of Article 14, for example, Robert Wintemute, '"Within the Ambit": How Big Is the "Gap" in Article 14 European Convention on Human Rights? Part 1', *European Human Rights Law Review* (2004), pp. 366–382 and Robert Wintemute, 'Filling the Article 14 "Gap": Government Ratification and Judicial Control of Protocol No. 12 ECHR: Part 2', *European Human Rights Law Review* (2004), pp. 484–499. See also Oddný Mjöll Arnardóttir, *Equality and Non-discrimination under the European Convention on Human Rights* (Leiden: Martinus Nijhoff Publishers, 2003), 35–37; Oddný Mjöll Arnardóttir, 'Discrimination as a Magnifying Lens: Scope and Ambit under Art. 14 and Protocol No. 12' in E. Brems and J.H. Gerards (eds.), *Shaping Rights in the ECHR: The Role of the European Court of Human Rights in Determining the Scope of Human Rights* (Cambridge University Press, 2014), pp. 330–349, 331.

[82] See, for example, *Abdulaziz, Cabales and Balkandali v. the UK*, ECtHR 28 May 1985, 9214/80, 9473/81 and 9474/81, para. 71.

[83] Wintemute 2004 (n. 81), 370; Arnardóttir 2014 (n. 81).

[84] *Case relating to certain aspects of the laws on het use of languages in education in Belgium*, ECtHR 23 July 1968, 1474/62, 1677/62, 1691/62, 1769/63, 1994/63 and 2126/64, para. 9.

of the Convention – and irrespective of whether the Convention requires that they be taken – they must comply with the requirement of non-discrimination.[85] That a measure is of a socio-economic nature is not material in this regard.

In relation to Article 1 of Protocol No. 1 (the protection of property), for example, the accessory character of Article 14 implies that when a social security right is created by the state, a complaint about a difference in treatment relating to that right will fall within the ambit of this Article for the purpose of applying Article 14. In the words of the Court: 'Although Protocol No. 1 does not include the right to receive a social security payment of any kind, if a State does decide to create a benefits scheme, it must do so in a manner which is compatible with Article 14'.[86]

Similarly, the Court has held that 'there is no right under Article 8 of the Convention to be provided with housing', but if a state provides benefits in this field, it must nevertheless comply with the requirements of Article 14.[87] The non-discrimination principle has been applied to cases concerning the differential treatment of a former civil servant who was a tenant of the state,[88] the succession of a tenancy after the death of a same-sex partner[89] and the denial of priority treatment under the applicable housing legislation because of the applicant's son's immigration status.[90]

Because of its broad scope of application, thus, 'Article 14 may have a socialising effect on the rights and freedoms laid down in the Convention'.[91] Economic and social rights are not explicitly taken up in the Convention, but because of the non-discrimination principle, they can nevertheless be protected. Violations have, for example, been found in cases concerning the refusal of parental leave allowances to fathers,[92] access to a social security fund that was linked to a nationality requirement[93] or

---

[85] See, for example, *Kafkaris v. Cyprus*, ECtHR (GC) 12 February 2008, 21906/04, para. 159.

[86] *Stec a. O. v. the UK*, ECtHR 6 July 2005 (dec.), 65731/01 and 65900/01, para. 55. Article 14 may thus lead to positive obligations. See, for example, Ida Elisabeth Koch and Jens Vested-Hansen, 'International Human Rights and National Legislatures – Conflict or Balance', *Nordic Journal of International Law*, 75 (2006), pp. 3–28, 20.

[87] *Bah v. the United Kingdom*, ECtHR 27 September 2011, 56329/07, para. 40.

[88] *Larkos v. Greece*, ECtHR (GC) 18 February 1999, 29515/95.

[89] *Karner v. Austria*, ECtHR 24 July 2003, 40016/98.

[90] *Bah v. the United Kingdom*, ECtHR 27 September 2011, 56329/07.

[91] Van Dijk et al. 2006 (n. 23), 1051.

[92] *Petrovic v. Austria*, ECtHR 27 March 1998, 20458/92.

[93] *Luczak v. Poland*, ECtHR 27 March 2007 (dec.), 77782/01.

pension eligibility in post-Soviet constellations.[94] The socializing effect is not as promising as it might seem, though, because 'a right does not arise when the preferential treatment by the authorities is intended precisely to remove an existing inequality or – according to the case law developed by the Commission and the Court – may be justified on other objective and reasonable grounds'.[95] As the Court has established as early as 1968, this will be the case when the distinction does not pursue a 'legitimate aim', or lacks a 'reasonable relationship of proportionality between the means employed and the aim sought to be realised'.[96] Distinctions between groups and individuals in the field of health care policy or social security legislation are omnipresent. Importantly, it cannot always be argued that persons falling in different categories, according to, for example, their place of residence, find themselves in a comparable position.[97] Even if this is the case, moreover, distinctions can serve a legitimate aim and be considered proportional in the light thereof. In a case concerning a refund for life-saving medication, the Court found a justification for the alleged discrimination 'in the present health care system which makes difficult choices as to the extent of public subsidy to ensure a fair distribution of scarce financial resources'.[98] It also accepted that adjustments to pension schemes that distinguished between men and women must be carried out gradually and should not be forced on the state by a supranational court.[99]

Finally, the Court sometimes also refrains from addressing discrimination complaints in the field of social rights. Examples are several Roma housing cases, where differential treatment is either considered absent[100] or not discussed because it did not raise a 'separate issue' in relation to other alleged violations of the Convention.[101] Although relevant for ECHR protection in the socio-economic sphere, thus, Article 14 does not necessarily provide a successful path for obtaining social rights protection.

---

[94] *Andrejeva v. Latvia*, ECtHR (GC) 18 February 2009, 55707/00.

[95] Van Dijk et al. 2006 (n. 23), 1051.

[96] See, for example, *Chassagnou and Others v France*, ECtHR (GC) 29 April 1999, 25088/94, 28331/95 and 28443/95, para. 91.

[97] Cf. *Carson a. O. v. United Kingdom*, ECtHR 4 November 2008, 42184/05; *Ramaer and Van Willigen v. the Netherlands*, 23 October 2012 (dec.), 34880/12.

[98] *Nitecki v. Poland*, ECtHR 21 March 2002 (dec.), 65653/01, para. 3.

[99] *Andrle v. the Czech Republic*, ECtHR 17 February 2011, 6268/08.

[100] *Buckley v. the UK*, ECtHR 29 September 1996, 27238/95, para. 88.

[101] See, for example, *Connors v. the UK*, ECtHR 27 May 2004, 66746/04, *Yordanova a. O. v. Bulgaria*, ECtHR 24 April 2012, 25446/06.

1.3   Socio-Economic Protection through Substantive ECHR Rights

1.3.1   The Right to Life (Article 2 ECHR)

More forthright, yet also characterized as 'collateral',[102] is the protection of socio-economic interests under the (other) substantive rights laid down in the Convention. What is effectively claimed under Articles 6 and 14 is a fair trial or non-discriminatory treatment, while claims based on the other articles relevant here may appear more straightforwardly socio-economic. This has to do with the broad terms of these provisions, as well as with the recognition of positive obligations for states. When it comes to socio-economic claims concerning housing, social security and health and health care, a first example is Article 2 ECHR. The first paragraph of this article reads:

> Everyone's right to life shall be protected by law. No one shall be deprived of his life intentionally save in the execution of a sentence of a court following his conviction of a crime for which this penalty is provided by law.

The right to life is not absolute as paragraph 2 allows several exceptions. Nevertheless, and unsurprisingly, it can be considered amongst the most fundamental rights of the Convention.[103] The prohibition to deprive someone of his or her life is directed at national authorities, agents of the state and individuals for which the state can be held responsible.[104] The exceptions summed up must, moreover, be read narrowly.[105] The use of force resulting in the deprivation of life 'must be shown to have been "absolutely necessary" for one of the purposes in sub-paragraphs (a), (b) or (c) and, therefore, justified in spite of the risks it entailed for human lives'.[106] A successful invocation of one of these exceptions will hence be very rare.

Although Article 2 primarily contains a negative obligation for the state, it 'may, as other Convention articles . . . give rise to positive obligations on

---

[102] Warbrick 2007 (n. 72), 247.

[103] See *McCann a. O. v. the UK*, ECtHR (GC) 27 September 1995, 18984/91, para. 147.

[104] Alistair Mowbray, *Cases, Materials and Commentary on the European Convention on Human Rights*, 3rd ed. (Oxford University Press, 2012), 83; Van Dijk et al. 2006 (n. 23), 352.

[105] Van Dijk et al. 2006 (n. 23), 403. See also Mowbray 2012 (n. 104), 83.

[106] *Stewart v. the UK*, EComHR 10 July 1984, 10044/82, para. 15. Mentioned in Art. 2 are '(a) in defence of any person from unlawful violence; (b) in order to effect a lawful arrest or to prevent the escape of a person lawfully detained; (c) in action lawfully taken for the purpose of quelling a riot or insurrection.'

the part of the State'.[107] 'Protection by law', first of all, implies certain procedural duties. The Court has held that Article 2(1), read in conjunction with Article 1 of the Convention, 'requires by implication that there should be some form of effective official investigation when individuals have been killed as a result of the use of force by, inter alios, agents of the State'.[108] More generally, the first sentence of Article 2 is understood to mean that states are required to take 'appropriate steps to safeguard the lives of those within their jurisdiction'.[109] They have a 'primary duty' to secure this right by creating 'an appropriate legal and administrative framework to deter the commission of offences against the person, backed up by law enforcement machinery for the prevention, suppression and punishment of breaches of such provisions'.[110]

The positive interpretation of the right to life has resulted in the application of Article 2 not only in situations of conflict or violence, but also in more daily contexts. It was considered relevant in cases concerning the lack of information and health monitoring after exposure to radiation which had caused leukaemia and where a life-threatening disease was not diagnosed on time.[111] More generally, the Court has stated that the positive obligations under Article 2 apply in the public health sphere and

> require States to make regulations compelling hospitals, whether public or private, to adopt appropriate measures for the protection of their patients' lives. They also require an effective independent judicial system to be set up so that the cause of death of patients in the care of the medical profession, whether in the public or the private sector, can be determined and those responsible be made accountable.[112]

This has led to a violation in a case where no sound investigation was conducted, and the necessary treatment was refused to a pregnant woman who died after not being able to pay for this treatment on the spot.[113] Additionally, the Court has held that 'an issue may arise under Article 2 of the Convention where it is shown that the authorities of a Contracting

---

[107] *W. v. the UK*, EComHR 28 February 1983 (dec.), 9348/81, para. 12.
[108] *McCann and Others v. the UK*, ECtHR (GC) 27 September 1995, 18984/91, para. 161.
[109] See, for example, *L.C.B. v. the UK*, ECtHR 9 June 1998, no. 14/1997/198/1001, para. 36.
[110] *Makaratzis v. Greece*, ECtHR (GC) 20 December 2004, 50385/99, para. 57. Regulations must be enforced by 'an effective judicial system' (*Öneryildiz v. Turkey*, ECtHR (GC) 30 November 2004, 48939/99, para. 92).
[111] *L.C.B. v. the UK*, ECtHR 9 June 1998, no. 14/1997/198/1001 and *Powell v. the UK*, ECtHR 4 May 2000 (dec.), 45305/99, respectively.
[112] *Calvelli and Ciglio v. Italy*, ECtHR (GC) 17 January 2002, 32967/96, para. 49)
[113] *Mehmet Senturk and Bekir Senturk v. Turkey*, ECtHR 9 April 2013, 23423/09.

State put an individual at risk through the denial of health care which they have undertaken to make available to the population generally'.[114]

Issues concerning (the provision of) medication have also come up, such as a complaint concerning a request for a refund of the cost of life-saving drugs.[115] A violation was found in a case where anti-cancerous medication was not provided even though this had been ordered by the domestic courts.[116] Another issue that has been linked to Article 2 is the treatment – or lack of appropriate treatment – of prisoners. In particular, the Court has dealt with various cases of suicide by prisoners, where it has held that '[i]t is incumbent on the State to account for any injuries suffered in custody, which obligation is particularly stringent where that individual dies'.[117] In other situations in which individuals are dependent on the state, the right to life involves obligations of a particularly socio-economic kind. In a case concerning the death of fifteen children and young adults in a care home that had to cope with a lack of heating, food, medical care and medication during a severe economic crisis, the Court concluded that the state had failed to comply with its obligations and should have provided the necessary care.[118]

Finally, the right to life can be applied in relation to the responsibility of the state for environmental pollution.[119] This was the case in a case concerning a methane explosion on a rubbish tip that caused the death of thirty-nine people.[120] Depending on the danger of the situation concerned, there can be an obligation for the state to provide information and take the necessary measures in order to avoid a violation of the Convention.[121]

1.3.2   The Prohibition of Torture (Article 3 ECHR)

Article 3 ECHR prohibits 'torture or . . . inhuman or degrading treatment or punishment.' The brevity of this provision can be explained by its

---

[114] *Cyprus v. Turkey*, ECtHR (GC) 10 March 2001, 25781/94, para. 219.

[115] *Nitecki v. Poland*, ECtHR 21 March 2002, 65653/01.

[116] *Panaitescu v. Romania*, ECtHR 10 April 2012, 30909/06.

[117] *Keenan v. the UK*, ECtHR 3 April 2001, 27229/95, para. 91.

[118] *Nencheva a. O. v. Bulgaria*, ECtHR 18 June 2013, 48609/06.

[119] See, for example, *L.C.B. v. the UK*, ECtHR 9 June 1998, no. 14/1997/198/1001 (concerning radiation).

[120] *Öneryildiz v. Turkey*, ECtHR (GC) 30 November 2004, 48939/99.

[121] Cf. *Budayeva a. O. v. Russia*, ECtHR 20 March 2008, 15339/02, 21166/02, 20058/02, 11673/02 and 15343/02.

absolute character: no justifications can be provided for what is prohibited under this article. It covers a broad range of issues and plays a supplementary role; whereas Article 2 provides 'protection against deprivation of life only',[122] '[o]ther injuries to the physical – and mental – integrity may in many cases be brought under Article 3'.[123]

Next to ensuring that state officials do not actively expose individuals to torture or other forms of ill treatment, the ECtHR has held:

> [T]he obligation of the High Contracting Parties under Article 1 of the Convention to secure to everyone within their jurisdiction the rights and freedoms defined in the Convention, taken together with Article 3, requires States to take measures designed to ensure that individuals within their jurisdiction are not subjected to ill-treatment, including ill-treatment administered by private individuals.[124]

Primarily, these positive measures must constitute effective deterrence as well as ensure an effective investigation. For complying with these obligations, it is important to know what exactly the terms 'torture' or 'inhuman and degrading treatment' mean. In this regard, the Court has made clear that a limited overview of the situations covered by Article 3 cannot be given. Instead, it has held that in order for this provision to apply, the situation an individual is confronted with must 'attain a minimum level of severity'.[125] It has further explained that '[t]he assessment of this minimum is, in the nature of things, relative; it depends on all the circumstances of the case, such as the duration of the treatment, its physical or mental effects and, in some cases, the sex, age and state of health of the victim, etc.'.[126] This means that there is no single, clear criterion that is decisive for judging whether something counts as ill treatment. Thus, the question of whether particular circumstances demand individual protection has to be decided on a case-by-case basis.

This relative way of approaching Article 3 does not *a priori* exclude socio-economic protection. For example, Article 3 has been applied in cases where houses were destroyed,[127] but also where applicants – as a consequence of such destruction – had to live for years in deplorable circumstances without heating, in cellars and while sleeping on the

---

[122] *X. v. Austria*, EComHR 13 December 1979 (dec.), 8278/78, para. 1.

[123] Van Dijk et al. 2006 (n. 23), 353.

[124] *Moldovan a. O. v. Romania*, ECtHR 12 July 2005, 41138/98 and 64320/01, para. 98.

[125] *Ireland v. the UK*, ECtHR 18 January 1978, 5310/71, para. 162.   [126] Ibid.

[127] See, for example, *Selçuk and Asker v. Turkey*, ECtHR 24 April 1998, 23184/94 and 23185/94.

floor.[128] In the latter case, it was not merely the lack of an appropriate place to live that was the reason for holding Article 3 applicable. Rather, it was the combination of (aggravating) factors at stake that made the Court decide that in the circumstances at hand, the prohibition of ill treatment was violated. A similar conclusion can be distilled from cases concerning prison circumstances, which sometimes also attain the minimum level of severity required – for example, when the health of prisoners requires special treatment or other accommodations in order to prevent serious humiliation.[129]

Most prominent in terms of the social dimension of Article 3 are perhaps the cases concerning health and medical treatment apart from those involving prison situations. The Court has, for example, dealt with complaints concerning the refusal of requests for experimental cancer medication. Although Article 3 may apply when 'suffering which follows from a naturally occurring illness … is, or risks being exacerbated by treatment stemming from measures for which the authorities can be held responsible', in this case there was no obligation to alleviate the disparities between the levels of health care available in different countries and thus provide the medication.[130] Another important subset of the Court's health-related case law under this article concerns complaints of persons suffering from serious illness who are about to be deported to their country of origin. According to the Court, this can amount to a violation of Article 3 ECHR,[131] but only in very exceptional circumstances.[132] It has clarified that 'exceptional circumstances'

> should be understood to refer to situations involving the removal of a seriously ill person in which substantial grounds have been shown for believing that he or she, although not at imminent risk of dying, would face a real risk, on account of the absence of appropriate treatment in the receiving country or the lack of access to such treatment, of being exposed to a serious, rapid and irreversible decline in his or her state of health resulting in intense suffering or to a significant reduction in life expectancy.[133]

---

[128] *Moldovan a. O. v. Romania*, ECtHR 12 July 2005, 41138/98 and 64320/01.

[129] See, for example, *Farbtuhs v. Latvia*, ECtHR 2 December 2004, 4672/02, para. 56; *Khudobin v. Russia*, ECtHR 26 October 2006, 59696/00, para. 93.

[130] *Hristozov a. O. v. Bulgaria*, ECtHR 13 November 2012, 47039/11 and 358/12, para. 111.

[131] *D. v. the UK*, ECtHR 2 May 1997, 30240/96.

[132] *N. v. the UK*, ECtHR (GC) 27 May 2008, 26565/05.

[133] *Paposhvili v. Belgium*, ECtHR (GC) 13 December 2016, 41738/10, para. 183.

In a similar vein, in a case concerning an individual asylum seeker who was living in extreme poverty, the Court has underlined that

> it has not excluded 'the possibility that the responsibility of the State may be engaged [under Article 3] in respect of treatment where an applicant, who was wholly dependent on State support, found herself faced with official indifference in a situation of serious deprivation or want incompatible with human dignity'.[134]

In this case the Court held the state responsible and thus inferred a positive socio-economic obligation from Article 3 ECHR.[135] Another violation focused on the lack of guarantees concerning appropriate accommodation for an Afghan family that was to be returned to Italy.[136] Finally, cases in which someone obtains a wholly insufficient amount of pension or is left bereft of essential medical treatment, may, in principle, also lead to protection under Article 3 of the Convention.[137]

1.3.3   The Right to Respect for Private and Family Life (Article 8 ECHR)

Article 8 ECHR contains the right to respect for private and family life. More precisely, '[e]veryone has the right to respect for his private and family life, his home and his correspondence'. An interference can be justified when it is 'in accordance with the law and is necessary in a democratic society in the interests of national security, public safety or the economic wellbeing of the country, for the prevention of disorder or crime, for the protection of health or morals, or for the protection of the rights and freedoms of others'. The Court interprets Article 8(1) in an autonomous manner – that is, independent from how the different rights are understood at the national level.[138] Notably, however, instead of providing for clear definitions, the Court has interpreted Article 8 in a case-by-case manner. This makes it generally difficult to know exactly what guarantees can be distilled from this provision of the Convention. With regard to 'private life', however, the Court has held:

---

[134] *M.S.S. v. Belgium and Greece*, ECtHR (GC) 21 January 2011, 30696/09, para. 253.
[135] See Ida Elisabeth Koch, 'The Justiciability of Indivisible Rights', *Nordic Law Journal*, 72 (2003), pp. 3–39, 23.
[136] *Tarakhel v. Switzerland*, ECtHR (GC) 4 November 2014, 29271/12.
[137] *Laroshina v. Russia*, ECtHR 23 April 2002, 56869/00; *Budina v. Russia*, ECtHR 18 June 2009, 45603/05.
[138] Harris et al. 2014 (n. 18), 522.

> [I]t would be too restrictive to limit the notion [of private life] to an 'inner circle' in which the individual may live his own personal life as he chooses and to exclude therefrom entirely the outside world not encompassed within that circle. Respect for private life must also comprise to a certain degree the right to establish and develop relationships with other human beings.[139]

It has become clear that interference with physical or moral integrity is covered by 'private life', and so is sexual orientation and activity. Besides, the right to respect for private life can also be triggered in cases concerning the employment sphere.[140]

Especially relevant for Article 8's social dimension is the Court's broad interpretation of 'home'. Whether something constitutes a home for purposes of the Convention depends on 'the existence of sufficient and continuous links with a specific place'.[141] In this regard,

> the length of temporary or permanent stays ..., frequent absence ... or ... use on a temporary basis, for the purposes of short-term stays or even keeping belongings in it, do not preclude retention of sufficient continuing links with a particular residential place, which can still be considered 'home' for the purposes of Article 8 of the Convention.[142]

A 'home' need not be owned or established legally, which means that also individuals who – due to a lack of alternatives – have established a place to live without having the permission to do so can expect protection under the Convention. This has been important especially in cases concerning Roma housing, which often concern situations in which the requisite planning permissions have not been granted.[143] The Court has emphasized, though, that '[t]he interests protected by the notion of a "home" within the meaning of Article 8 include the peaceful enjoyment of one's existing residence', thereby seemingly excluding the right to obtain a home.[144]

Yet although Article 8 speaks of 'respect', especially the private and family life limb of this provision has given rise to positive obligations as well. In the words of the Court, it

---

[139] *Niemietz v. Germany*, ECtHR 16 December 1992, 13710/88, para. 29.
[140] *Sidabras and Džiautas v. Lithuania*, ECtHR 27 July 2004, 55480/00 and 59330/00, para. 47.
[141] *Lazarenko a. O. v. Ukraine*, ECtHR 11 December 2012 (dec.), 27427/02, para. 53.
[142] Ibid.
[143] See, for example, *Buckley v. the UK*, ECtHR 29 September 1996, 20348/92; *Chapman v. the UK*, ECtHR (GC) 18 January 2001, 27238/95.
[144] *Dukic v. Bosnia and Herzegovina*, ECtHR 19 January 2012, 4543/09, para. 40.

> does not merely compel the State to abstain from ... interference: in addition to this primarily negative undertaking, there may be positive obligations inherent in an effective respect for private or family life ... These obligations may involve the adoption of measures designed to secure respect for private life even in the sphere of the relations of individuals between themselves.[145]

For the Convention to apply in case the state has failed to take action, there must be 'a direct and immediate link between the measures sought by an applicant and the latter's private life'.[146] This has led to the application of Article 8 in a case concerning the refusal to provide a child with a robotic arm.[147] Such a link has been found to exist, moreover, where requests for alternative housing were concerned – in cases concerning Roma this has led to multiple violations.[148] Environmental pollution, at least once a certain minimum level is attained, also triggers the protection of Article 8.[149] One can think of instances in which polluting fumes or toxic emissions coming from a nearby plant cause health issues,[150] but also concerning airport noise[151] or waste piling up in the streets.[152] Violations have been found in cases of national irregularities, i.e., when national rules have not been respected, or when the decision-making process has not been fair.[153]

The margin granted to the state by the Court may prevent eventual protection on the basis of the right to private life.[154] Nevertheless, it is fair to say that Article 8 forms a vehicle for a broad range of socio-economic guarantees under the Convention.

---

[145] *X and Y v. the Netherlands*, ECtHR 26 March 1985, 8978/80, para. 23.

[146] *Marzari v. Italy*, ECtHR 4 May 1999 (dec.), 36448/97.

[147] *Sentges v. the Netherlands*, ECtHR 8 July 2003 (dec.), 27677/02.

[148] See, for example, *Yordanova a. O. v. Bulgaria*, ECtHR 24 April 2012, 25446/06; *Winterstein a. O. v. France*, ECtHR 17 October 2013, 27013/07.

[149] *Powell and Rayner v. the UK*, ECtHR 21 February 1990, 9310/81; *Fadeyeva v. Russia*, ECtHR 9 June 2005, 55723/00, para. 69.

[150] *López Ostra v. Spain*, ECtHR 9 December 1994, 16798/80; *Guerra a. O. v. Italy*, ECtHR 19 February 1998, 116/1997/735/932.

[151] *Hatton a. O. v. the UK*, ECtHR 2 October 2001, 36022/97; *Hatton a. O. v. the UK*, ECtHR (GC) 8 July 2003, 36022/97.

[152] *Di Sarno a. O. v. Italy*, ECtHR 10 January 2012, 30765/08.

[153] See, for example, *Guerra a. O. v. Italy*, ECtHR 19 February 1998, 116/1997/735/932 and *Taskin a. O. v. Turkey*, ECtHR 10 November 2004, 46117/99, respectively.

[154] Cf. *Hatton a. O. v. the UK*, ECtHR (GC) 8 July 2003, 36022/97.

1.3.4   The Protection of Property (Article 1 Protocol No. 1 ECHR)

Finally, Article 1 of the First Protocol to the ECHR must be mentioned. This provision guarantees the protection of property and reads as follows:

> Every natural or legal person is entitled to the peaceful enjoyment of his possessions. No one shall be deprived of his possessions except in the public interest and subject to the conditions provided for by law and by the general principles of international law.

> The preceding provisions shall not, however, in any way impair the right of a State to enforce such laws as it deems necessary to control the use of property in accordance with the general interest or to secure the payment of taxes or other contributions or penalties.

Like Article 8, Article 1 Protocol No. 1 is interpreted autonomously. When the protection of property is invoked, the crucial question is whether the interest at stake constitutes a 'possession'. This first of all depends on the economic value this interest has or does not have.[155] Moreover, for a property right to be recognized as justiciable under Article 1 Protocol No. 1, it should generally be an existing right.[156] Alternatively, there should be a 'legitimate expectation' of obtaining effective enjoyment of such right.[157] A right to acquire property is not recognized.[158] Over the years, the Court has recognized that company shares[159] and (an application for the registration of) trademarks[160] are covered by the notion of 'possessions', as well as a 'right to a building permit'[161] and economic interests connected with the exploitation of a restaurant.[162] A legitimate expectation based on a court judgment or arbitration award that recognizes a claim against the state can lead to success in Strasbourg as well.[163] Rather than only classic, tangible

---

[155] Van Dijk et al. 2006 (n. 23), 866.

[156] See Van Dijk et al. 2006 (n. 23), 869. The right should be 'sufficiently established to be enforceable' (Stran Greek Refinieries and Stratis Andeadis v. Greece, ECtHR 9 December 1994, 13427/87, para. 59).

[157] Mere hope is not enough. See Prince Hans-Adam II of Liechtenstein v. Germany, ECtHR (GC) 12 July 2001, 42527/98, para. 85.

[158] Van der Mussele v. Belgium, ECtHR 23 November 1983, 8919/80, para. 48.

[159] Bramelid and Malmström v. Sweden, EComHR 12 October 1982 (dec.), 8588/79 and 8589/79.

[160] See Anheuser-Busch Inc. v. Portugal, ECtHR (GC) 11 January 2007, 73049/01, para. 78.

[161] SCEA Ferme de Fresnoy v. France, ECtHR 1 December 2005 (dec.), 61093/00.

[162] Tre Traktörer Aktiebolag v. Sweden, ECtHR 7 July 1989, 10873/84.

[163] See, for example, Stran Greek Refineries and Stratis Andreadis v. Greece, ECtHR 9 December 1994, 13427/87, para. 62.

possessions, thus, Article 1 Protocol No. 1 covers other (legal) entitlements and constructs representing an economic value, too.

The right to protection of property also applies in the field of social security. The Court has held that when contributions have been paid, this gives rise to protection under the Convention.[164] In 2005, moreover, it clarified that

> [i]n the modern, democratic State, many individuals are, for all or part of their lives, completely dependent for survival on social security and welfare benefits. Many domestic legal systems recognize that such individuals require a degree of certainty and security, and provide for benefits to be paid – subject to the fulfilment of the conditions of eligibility – as of right.[165]

According to the ECtHR, the freedom of the state to decide on whether and what kind of social security system it creates is not in any way restricted, but if a benefits scheme is created, regardless of whether this scheme is a contributory or a non-contributory one, 'it must do so in a manner which is compatible with Article 14'.[166] Now, both contributory and non-contributory benefits are protected by the right to property, even when they are not of an allegedly discriminatory nature.[167] This has led to the rapid development of a Strasbourg social security case law. The issues the Court has dealt with concern, for example, access to particular social security systems or the height of a pension.[168] It has also held that where a pension was lawfully revoked because it had been erroneously granted, the protection of property applied.[169] Recently, moreover, it was concluded that a legitimate expectation to receive a disability pension may exist even if the conditions for obtaining this benefit have not been met.[170]

---

[164] See, for example, *X. v. the Netherlands*, EComHR 20 July 1971 (dec.), 4130/69.

[165] *Stec a. O. v. the UK*, ECtHR 6 July 2005 (dec.), 65731/01 and 65900/01, para. 51.

[166] Ibid., paras. 54–55.

[167] See Ingrid Leijten, 'From Stec to Valkov: Possessions and Margins in the Social Security Case Law of the European Court of Human Rights, *Human Rights Law Review*, 13 (2013), pp. 309–349, 326.

[168] See, for example, *Maggio a. O. v. Italy*, ECtHR 31 May 2011, 46286/09, 52851/08, 53727/08, 54486/08 and 56001/08; *Valkov a. O. v. Bulgaria*, ECtHR 25 October 2011, 2033/04, 19125/04, 19475/04, 19490/04, 19495/04, 19497/04, 24729/04, 171/05 and 2041/05.

[169] *Moskal v. Poland*, ECtHR 15 September 2009, 10373/05.

[170] *Bélané Nagy v. Hungary*, ECtHR 10 February 2015, 53080/13; *Bélané Nagy v. Hungary*, ECtHR (GC) 13 December 2016, 53080/13.

Besides in the field of social security, Article 1 Protocol No. 1 has also been applied to housing issues; for example, when someone owns a house, the use of which is restricted by rent laws or other regulations. In these cases, the state is usually granted a wide margin of appreciation, which leads to indirect protection of the tenants benefiting from this legislation.[171] But also when the applicant is a tenant and does not own the house he lives in, the right to protection of property can sometimes be invoked. When a lessee is deprived of the benefit of a renewal option on the lease granted by the local authority, he may rely on the protection of Article 1 Protocol No. 1 against interference with his property.[172] In a like manner, the loss of a specially protected tenancy – although the Court has refrained from answering the question whether this constitutes a 'possession' – can lead to review under Article 1 Proctol No. 1.[173]

The protection of property is violated when an interference with someone's possessions leads to an excessive, individual burden. This can be the case when a landowner is only able to receive a very low level of rent[174] or if someone is not getting any benefit,[175] but also in cases of a partial reduction of a pension[176] or when the requirements of 'good governance' have not been observed.[177] Similar considerations also play a role in the Court's occasional review of tax burdens.[178]

Conclusion

The ECHR is a civil and political rights document, yet the ECtHR also protects socio-economic rights. The Court has recognized that there is no watertight distinction separating the socio-economic sphere from the field protected by the Convention. Several ECHR provisions and the case law generated on the basis thereof illustrate this. Articles 6 and 14, guaranteeing a fair trial and non-discrimination, do not *a priori*

---

[171] See, for example, *James a. O. v. the UK*, ECtHR 21 February 1986, 8793/79; *Mellacher a. O. v. Austria*, ECtHR 19 December 1989, 10522/83, 11011/84 and 11070/84.

[172] *Stretch v. the UK*, ECtHR 24 June 2003, 44277/98.

[173] *Berger-Krall a. O. v. Slovenia*, ECtHR 12 June 2014, 14717/04.

[174] *Hutten-Czapska v. Poland*, ECtHR (GC) 19 July 2006, 35014/97 and *Lindheim a. O. v. Norway*, ECtHR 12 June 2012, 13221/08 and 2139/10.

[175] Cf. *Bélané Nagy v. Hungary*, ECtHR (GC) 13 December 2016, 53080/13.

[176] *Stefanetti a. O. v. Italy*, ECtHR 15 April 2014, 21838/10, 21849/10, 21852/ 10, 21855/10, 21860/10, 21863/10, 21869/10 and 21870/10.

[177] *Moskal v. Poland*, ECtHR 15 September 2009, 10373/05.

[178] See, for example, *N.K.M. v. Hungary*, ECtHR 14 May 2013, 66529/11.

discriminate between civil and political and economic and social rights issues. The right to life and the prohibition of torture, together with the right to private life and the protection of property, have moreover served as the background for numerous complaints concerning housing, health and health care, social security and other related issues.

Besides the ECHR's socio-economic dimension, I presented some background to the Convention, as well as the position and task of the ECtHR. As a supranational fundamental rights protector, this Court should ensure effective, individual guarantees while elucidating what states must do in order to comply with the Convention. At the same time, it must always be mindful of its subsidiary position, showing deference towards decisions made at the national level. This is particularly challenging when socio-economic rights are concerned. How exactly does the Court assess complaints concerning socio-economic rights, and how far can its influence in this field extend? I will turn to these issues in the next chapter, where I will expound upon how the Court's socio-economic dimension has been explained and why the justifications provided do not measure up to the challenges inherent in the Court's socio-economic rights endeavour.

2

Making Sense of the ECtHR's Socio-Economic Protection

It was shown in the previous chapter that the ECtHR has long acknowledged that there is no watertight division separating the socio-economic sphere from the Convention. Yet more can be said on the rationale behind recognizing various (positive) social obligations under the ECHR's procedural, substantive and non-discrimination provisions. Having obtained an image of the ECtHR's socio-economic case law, this chapter proceeds to the doctrinal foundations of this phenomenon. First, however, something must be said on the conceptual distinction between rights norms and interests, which forms the starting point to disentangle the object of this study.

The term 'rights' is often used to refer to the provisions (articles) of a fundamental rights document, as well as to what is protected on the basis thereof. Article 8 ECHR, for example, is known as the 'right to private and family life'. It protects, amongst other things, the right to protection of one's reputation.[1] For grasping the rationales behind the ECHR's socio-economic protection, however, this usage may be confusing. In what follows, a distinction is therefore made between rights 'norms' and 'interests'. The term 'norms' (or 'provisions') is used to refer to the rights as they are written down, whereas the term 'interests' is used for what deserves (or is claimed to deserve) protection through these provisions. This terminology does not involve any value judgment. Norm, on the one hand, is not meant to refer to the moral or normative quality of a provision. Interests, on the other, does not as such refer to an inferior category of individual concerns; they may well – though need not always – overlap with fundamental rights.

Starting from this, a relatively clear distinction can be made between civil and political and socio-economic norms or provisions. Negatively phrased fundamental rights norms generally are an example of the former.

---

[1] *Axel Springer AG v. Germany*, ECtHR (GC) 7 February 2012, 39954/08, para. 83.

When the wording of a provision refers to a right for everyone (individually) and involves a freedom to do or say something or freedom from state interference, this indicates that a first-generation norm is concerned.[2] An example is Article 8(1) ECHR: 'Everyone has the right to respect for his private and family life, his home and his correspondence.' Article 3 ECHR also provides a straightforward example: 'No one shall be subjected to torture or to inhuman or degrading treatment or punishment.' In turn, a provision like Article 12 ICESCR ('The States Parties to the present Covenant recognize the right of everyone to the enjoyment of the highest attainable standard of physical and mental health') can be labelled a socio-economic rights norm. It is plainly addressed at the state and demands action in a typical socio-economic field.[3]

At first glance, some norms seem to be borderline cases. Think of the right to protection of property or the right to education.[4] Yet a look at the exact wording of these rights in the ECHR ('Every natural or legal person is entitled to the peaceful enjoyment of his possessions', and 'No person shall be denied the right to education') shows that these particular provisions are of a classic, rather than a social, kind. More generally, when it comes to the ECHR, the genesis of this treaty suggests that the provisions listed therein can be understood as civil or political.[5]

The distinction between different categories of rights norms must be distinguished from a distinction between protected interests of a civil or political character, and those of a socio-economic nature. Both distinctions do not always match neatly. When the phrasing of a particular provision, according to the explanation given above, can be labelled civil or political, this does not necessarily mean that the interests it protects deserve the same qualification. Consider the provision of health care, which sometimes can be required under Article 3 ECHR. Yet whereas it is generally possible to characterize a specific norm as being *either* civil or political *or* socio-economic, it might be harder to qualify the interests concerned. When an individual complains about garbage piling up in his street and the health damage this might cause, it can be asked whether it

---

[2] See, on the different generations of rights, Christian Tomuschat, *Human Rights: Between Idealism and Realism*, 2nd ed. (Oxford University Press, 2008), 25 ff.

[3] Ida Elisabeth Koch, 'Social Rights as Components in the Civil Right to Personal Liberty – Another Possible Step Forward in the Integrated Human Rights Approach?', *Netherlands Quarterly of Human Rights*, 20 (2002), pp. 29–51, 31, n.4 (speaking of a means-and-end formula, that differs from the if-so formula typical for civil rights).

[4] Arts. 1 and 2 of Protocol No. 1 ECHR. See also Arts. 11(1) and 6(3) ECHR.

[5] See Ch. 1, S. 1.1.1.

is private life, the enjoyment of home, or health, or his interest in a clean environment that is at issue. When an individual's social security benefit is revoked, it can be said that proprietary interests are concerned, but also that his private life or social minimum is at stake.[6]

In any case, it is clear that the issues mentioned could, besides to Article 8 ECHR and Article 1 of Protocol No. 1 ECHR, also be linked to socio-economic norms ensuring a right to health, to a clean environment or to social security.[7] This is an important point: as was already illustrated by the examples in the prior chapter, what is delineated here as the socio-economic case law of the Court is its case law concerning individual complaints that would also, or even most logically, fit a socio-economic rights paradigm.[8]

Why are these distinctions relevant? One could argue that the ECtHR simply grants protection whenever the state fails to do so, and that labels should have nothing to do with this. The problem with this is that it hardly provides any meaningful starting point for assessing the ECtHR's practice, neither in terms of legitimacy or subsidiarity generally, nor in the context of the Court's multidimensional task, its workload or its reasoning in socio-economic cases. Therefore, given also that in daily parlance there is a distinction between what is called 'civil and political' and 'socio-economic', it is appropriate to use the above distinctions in order to get grip on a complex phenomenon like the fundamental rights protection under the ECHR. There is a risk that everything labelled 'socio-economic' in the context of fundamental rights is perceived as second rank or of inferior importance. Awareness of this risk, however, can ensure a more nuanced approach, while the tag 'socio-economic' may trigger a more careful look whenever the character of the Convention, combined with the sensitive nature of socio-economic protection, justifies this.

Altogether, distinguishing first between norms (or provisions) and interests (or matters), while second recognizing that both can be civil or political or economic or social, serves the aim of clarification and

---

[6] Cf. *Di Sarno and Others v. Italy*, ECtHR 10 January 2012, 30765/08.
[7] Depending on the level of abstraction with which they are viewed. Moreover, a right may be classical, the interests it protects socio-economic, but the underlying desire (freedom, ability to participate) again more classical. See Katharine G. Young, *Constituting Socio-Economic Rights* (Oxford University Press, 2012), 34 ff.
[8] Cf. Janneke Gerards, 'Fundamental Rights and Other Interests: Should It Really Make a Difference?' in E. Brems (ed.), *Conflicts between Fundamental Rights* (Antwerp/Oxford/New York: Intersentia, 2008), pp. 655–690, 655, 660 ff.

provides a good starting point for what is to follow. When it is under-stood that the norms of the ECHR are civil and political, yet some of the interests they cover are also, or primarily, socio-economic, an attempt can be made at providing a comprehensive normative explanation for what is going on.[9] The remainder of this chapter presents two different possible understandings of the development of the socio-economic dimension of the Convention. First, the 'effectiveness thesis' emphasizes the effective protection of the civil and political Convention rights (Section 2.1), while, second, the 'indivisibility thesis' draws attention to the inherent importance of economic and social rights (Section 2.2). Both these theses can explain the socio-economic protection that has been offered thus far, but they also bring up questions regarding the direction this development is taking. In Section 2.3, I map out the shortcomings of both theses alongside the criticisms that have been directed at the Court's socio-economic case law, and conclude that it is worth investigating the notion of core rights.

2.1   The Effectiveness Thesis

The first normative justification for the ECHR's socio-economic dimen-sion places the Convention norms in the foreground. According to this view, socio-economic protection is inevitable – not for the sake of fundamental rights protection generally, but in the light of the Conven-tion norms in particular. It can be argued that the effectuation of these civil and political rights norms requires a broad range of guarantees. These secure a variety of interests, some of which are everything but civil or political. In other words, according to the effectiveness thesis, the Court is simply fulfilling its task of interpreting and giving effect to classic rights norms without expressly staying out of the socio-economic sphere.

   In the previous chapter, I explained that several Convention rights do not *a priori* discriminate between the protection of civil and political and socio-economic interests. In this section, the idea of 'effectiveness' will be further elaborated so that it can also shed light on how the ECHR's economic and social dimension has become more significant over the years. This requires that attention be given to the Court's interpretative

---

[9] Ida Elisabeth Koch, 'Economic, Social and Cultural Rights as Components in Civil and Political Rights: A Hermeneutic Perspective', *The International Journal of Human Rights*, 10 (2006), pp. 405–430, 407.

toolbox. A discussion of purposive and autonomous human rights interpretation, as well as of the living instrument character of the Convention, shows that the effectiveness thesis provides a plausible explanation for the ECHR's social dimension and the development thereof.

Fundamental rights are notoriously hard to translate into concrete legal entitlements. Their wording is generally vague, creating room for divergent understandings. Choices made in this regard may stem from the particular legal context, as well as from a preference for an either extensive or more limited role for rights.[10] The Court has often expressed the importance it attaches to the Vienna Convention on the Law of Treaties (VCLT) articles on interpretation.[11] Yet the unique character of the Convention and its enforcement mechanism are considered to allow for distinct interpretive practices, too.[12] In addition to what the VCLT prescribes, thus, the Court has 'developed innovative techniques of interpretation that reflect the substantive nature of the Convention'.[13] For grasping the effectiveness thesis, some of these are of crucial importance.

First, the Court often directly refers to the principle of effectiveness.[14] It, for example, states that '[t]he Convention is intended to guarantee not rights that are theoretical or illusory but rights that are practical and

---

[10] Ch. 3, S. 3.2.

[11] United Nations, Vienna Convention of 23 May 1969 on the Law of Treaties (VCLT), 1155 U.N.T.S. 331 (entry into force 27 January 1980). See in particular Art. 31 VCLT, and Arts. 32 and 33.

[12] Sarah H. Cleveland, Laurence R. Helfer, Gerald L. Neuman, and Diane F. Orentlicher, *Human Rights*, 2nd ed. (Eagan: Thomson Reuters Foundation Press, 2009), 205. See also Franz Matscher 'Methods of Interpretation of the Convention' in R.S.J. Macdonald, F. Matscher, and H. Petzold (eds.), *The European System for the Protection of Human Rights* (Leiden: Martinus Nijhoff Publishers, 1993), pp. 63–81, 66; Steven Greer, *The European Convention on Human Rights* (Cambridge University Press, 2006), 195–196; Paul Mahoney, 'Judicial Activism and Self-Restraint in the European Court of Human Rights', *Human Rights Law Review*, 11 (1990), pp. 57–88, 65; Alastair Mowbray, 'The Creativity of the European Court of Human Rights', *Human Rights Law Review*, 5 (2005), pp. 57–79, 59; Daniel Rietiker, 'The Principle of "Effectiveness" in the Recent Jurisprudence of the European Court of Human Rights: Its Different Dimensions and Its Consistency with Public International Law – No Need for the Concept of Treaty *Sui Generis*', *Nordic Journal of International Law*, 79 (2010), pp. 245–277, 246; Hanneke Senden, *Interpretation of Fundamental Rights in a Multilevel Legal System: An Analysis of the European Court of Human Rights and the Court of Justice of the European Union*, doctoral thesis (Cambridge/Antwerp/Portland: Intersentia, 2011), 73.

[13] Mowbray 2005 (n. 12), 59, arguing that the provisions laid down in the Convention and safeguarded by a supranational and secondary organization, triggered the need for these tailor-made forms of interpretation.

[14] Cf. Rietiker 2010 (n. 12).

effective'.[15] The Court emphasizes the fact that rights that are considered fundamental should not be merely illusive or of symbolic value.[16] These rights are manifested only when individuals' and minorities' most fundamental needs are recognized and actual relief can be provided. This requires some flexibility as regards the kind of interests rights norms 'should' protect. Referring to the principle of effectiveness, the Court has interpreted the ECHR in an extensive manner.[17] Moving beyond formal distinctions, this also entails that – at least prima facie – protection is granted in the socio-economic sphere.[18] Effective protection often demands states to take positive action,[19] and requires that they facilitate the enjoyment of the freedoms protected under the Convention. This holds true regardless of whether such positive action implies a shift towards social guarantees that traditionally were not covered by the Convention.

References to effectiveness are frequently paired with other interpretative techniques. Consider the much-quoted case of *Soering v. the United Kingdom*, where the Court noted that

> the object and purpose of the Convention as an instrument for the protection of individual human beings require that its provisions be interpreted and applied so as to make its safeguards practical and effective . . .. In addition, any interpretation of the rights and freedoms guaranteed has to be consistent with 'the general spirit of the Convention, an instrument designed to maintain and promote the ideals and values of a democratic society'.[20]

The Court here combined the notion of effectiveness with the idea of 'teleological' or 'meta-teleological' interpretation.[21] Several principles and

---

[15] *Airey v. Ireland*, ECtHR 9 October 1979, 6289/73, para. 24.

[16] *Chassagnou and Others v France*, ECtHR (GC) 29 April 1999, 25088/94, 28331/95 and 28443/95, para. 100.

[17] Rietiker 2010 (n. 12), 259; Senden 2011 (n. 12), 76.   [18] Mowbray 2005 (n. 12), 72.

[19] Ibid., 78; Senden 2011 (n. 12), 76.

[20] *Soering v. the UK*, ECtHR 7 July 1989, 14038/88, para. 87.

[21] See Mitchel de S.-O.-l'E Lasser, *Judicial Deliberations: A Comparative Analysis of Judicial Transparency and Legitimacy* (Oxford University Press, 2004), 206 ff.; Janneke Gerards, 'Judicial Deliberations in the European Court of Human Rights' in N. Huls, M. Adams, and J. Bomhoff (eds.), *The Legitimacy of Highest Courts' Rulings. Judicial Deliberations and Beyond* (The Hague: T.M.C. Asser Press, 2009), pp. 407–436, 428–430; Janneke Gerards, 'The European Court of Human Rights and the National Courts: Giving Shape to the Notion of "Shared Responsibility"'in J.H. Gerards and J. Fleuren (eds.), *Implementation of the European Convention on Human Rights and of the Case Law of the ECtHR in National Case Law* (Antwerp/Oxford/New York: Intersentia, 2014), pp. 13–19, 37–39. See also

purposes underlying the Convention provide the necessary starting points for such interpretation.[22] Regularly, the Court refers to the protection of 'democratic values'[23] or 'human dignity'.[24] Also 'personal autonomy'[25] and 'pluralism'[26] play an important role in this regard. Some of these underlying notions lend themselves particularly well to encouraging the protection of economic and social interests. For example, human dignity and personal autonomy are closely intertwined with the provision of adequate health care and a minimum level of subsistence. In *M.S.S. v. Greece and Belgium*, for example, the Court held that

> it has not excluded 'the possibility that the responsibility of the State may be engaged [under Article 3] in respect of treatment where an applicant, who was wholly dependent on State support, found herself faced with official indifference in a situation of serious deprivation or want incompatible with human dignity'.[27]

The *M.S.S.* case concerned an asylum seeker who was deprived of any means of subsistence and was living in extreme poverty. Combining the wording of Article 3 with the principle of human dignity, the Court concluded that there had been a violation. Thus, considering the 'object and purpose' of the Convention, it gave substance to the effective protection of individuals' Article 3 rights. That the protection thereby extended well beyond the sphere of negative civil rights was no reason for the Court to hold differently.

Aharon Barak, *Proportionality: Constitutional Rights and Their Limitations* (Cambridge University Press, 2012), 46. See also Bernadette Rainey, Elizabeth Wicks and Clare Ovey, *Jacobs, White and Ovey: The European Convention on Human Rights*, 6th ed. (Oxford University Press, 2014), 71, where it is held that realizing the objectives of the Convention is of such importance that 'any general presumption that treaty obligations should be interpreted restrictively since they derogate from the sovereignty of States is not applicable . . .'.

[22] See, for example, the ECHR's Preamble. See also Olivier de Schutter en Françoise Tulkens, 'Rights in Conflict: The European Court of Human Rights as a Pragmatic Institution' in E. Brems (ed.), *Conflicts Between Fundamental Rights* (Antwerp/Oxford/New York: Intersentia, 2008), pp. 169–216, 169, 213–5.

[23] See, for example, *Vogt v. Germany*, ECtHR (GC) 26 September 1995, 17851/91; *United Communist Party of Turkey v. Turkey*, ECtHR (GC) 30 January 1998, 19392/92, para. 45.

[24] See, for example, *Pretty v. the UK*, ECtHR 29 April 2002, 2346/02, para. 65. See also François Ost, 'The Original Canons of Interpretation of the European Court of Human Rights' in M. Delmas-Marty and Ch. Chodkiewicz (eds.), *The European Convention for the Protection of Human Rights* (Leiden: Martinus Nijhoff Publishers, 1992), pp. 283–318, 292.

[25] See, for example, *R.R. v. Poland*, ECtHR 26 May 2011, 27617/04, para. 180.

[26] See, for example, *Kokkinakis v. Greece*, ECtHR 25 May 1993, 14307/88, para. 31.

[27] *M.S.S. v. Belgium and Greece*, ECtHR (GC) 21 January 2011, 30696/09, para. 253.

Besides purposive interpretation, the ECtHR's 'autonomous' interpretation also helps explain the Convention's socio-economic dimension as a mere corollary of effective civil and political rights protection. Autonomous interpretation means that Convention terms are granted 'a status of semantic independence: their meaning is not to be equated with the meaning that these very same concepts possess in domestic law'.[28] Letsas has pointed out that autonomous concepts are seemingly inevitable since there is no shared language on the basis of which the Convention must be interpreted.[29] Diverging practices in the member states, combined with the aim of ensuring effective protection in *all* member states, may be reason for the Court to take its own path.[30]

The most clear-cut example of how the Court's autonomous interpretation leads to the adjudication of economic and social cases is the Court's interpretation of the 'possessions' protected by Article 1 of Protocol No. 1 to the ECHR. In the case of *Stec and Others v. the United Kingdom*, the question was raised whether this term also covers noncontributory social benefits. In an earlier case on Article 6(1) ECHR (the right to a fair trial) this provision was held applicable to a dispute over entitlement to non-contributory welfare benefits.[31] This was reason for the Court to interpret the autonomous concept of 'possessions' accordingly.[32] According to the Court, the different funding mechanisms in the member states would make it 'artificial' to only include contributory benefits. This would hinder the provision of equal substantive protection throughout the Council of Europe.[33]

Finally, effective protection allies with the Court's proclamation of the 'living instrument' character of the Convention.[34] In *Tyrer v. the United*

---

[28] George Letsas, 'The Truth in Autonomous Concepts: How to Interpret the ECHR', *European Journal of International Law*, 15 (2004), pp. 279–305, 282.

[29] Ibid., 279; George Letsas, *A Theory of Interpretation of the European Convention on Human Rights* (Oxford University Press, 2007), Ch. 2.

[30] See, for example, *Pellegrin t. France*, ECtHR (GC) 8 December 1999, 28541/95, para. 63.

[31] *Salesi v. Italy*, ECtHR 26 February 1993 13023/87.

[32] *Stec a. O. v. the UK*, ECtHR 6 July 2005 (dec.), 65731/01 and 65900/01, para. 49.

[33] Cf., on this topic, Ingrid Leijten, 'From Stec to Valkov: Possessions and Margins in the Social Security Case Law of the European Court of Human Rights, *Human Rights Law Review*, 13 (2013), pp. 309–349; Ingrid Leijten, 'Social Security as a Fundamental Rights Issue in Europe: Ramaer and Van Willigen and the Development of Property Protection and Non-Discrimination under the ECHR', *Zeitschrift für ausländisches öffentliches Recht und Völkerrecht*, 73 (2013), pp. 177–208.

[34] See Gerards 2008 (n. 8), 663–664. Cf. also Craig Scott, 'Reaching Beyond (Without Abandoning) the Category of Economic, Social and Cultural Rights', *Human Rights Quarterly*, 21 (1999), pp. 633–660, 642 ff.; Ida Elisabeth Koch, *Human Rights as*

Kingdom – dealing with corporal punishment and the question whether this constituted 'degrading treatment' under Article 3 – the Court held that it

> must also recall that the Convention is a living instrument which . . . must be interpreted in the light of present-day conditions. In the case now before it the Court cannot but be influenced by the developments and commonly accepted standards . . . of the member States of the Council of Europe.[35]

It has become clear that the Convention must be interpreted in what is called an 'evolutive and dynamic' manner. This means that new elements within the scope of a Convention right will be recognized 'as soon as it has become clear that such aspects have become accepted throughout the Council of Europe to be part of the notion of "fundamental rights"'.[36] Just like teleological or autonomous interpretation, this approach can also be considered a hallmark of the Court's striving for effectiveness. It allows the Court to ensure that when circumstances or attitudes change, the Convention norms can continue to grant effective protection.

Unsurprisingly, evolutive interpretation has contributed to an increase in socio-economic rights protection.[37] This especially holds true when today's welfare state systems are concerned. Again, the case of *Stec and Others v. the United Kingdom* can be mentioned here, in which noncontributory benefits were considered 'possessions' because

> [i]n the modern, democratic State, many individuals are, for all or part of their lives, completely dependent for survival on social security and welfare benefits. Many domestic legal systems recognize that such individuals require a degree of certainty and security, and provide for benefits to be paid – subject to the fulfilment of the conditions of eligibility – as of right.[38]

Indivisible Rights: The Protection of Socio-Economic Demands under the European Convention on Human Rights (Leiden: Martinus Nijhoff Publishers, 2009), 36.

[35] *Tyrer v. the UK*, ECtHR 25 April 1978, 5856/72, para. 31.

[36] Gerards 2008 (n. 8), 663, referring to S.C. Prebensen, 'Evolutive Interpretation of the European Convention on Human Rights' in P. Mahoney (ed.), *Protecting Human Rights: The European Perspective. Studies in memory of Rolv Ryssdal* (Cologne: Carl Heymanns Verlag, 2000), pp. 1123–1137, 1128.

[37] Ibid., 665–666.

[38] *Stec a. O. v. the UK*, ECtHR 6 July 2005 (dec.), 65731/01 and 65900/01, para. 51.

The case of *Demir and Baykara v. Turkey* also forms a good example. This case concerned a prohibition on the formation of trade unions for civil servants, and the Court referred to international trends for holding that this fell within the scope of Article 11 of the Convention.[39] In turn, when developments are not convincing according to the Court, this may be reason to put a hold on the socialization of the Convention.[40]

Altogether, it is valid to argue that the Court increasingly deals with complaints concerning economic and social interests in order to effectuate precisely the civil and political rights norms enshrined in the ECHR.[41] In the words of Scott:

> [T]he key point is that making rights effective, by way of interpreting rights to have social and economic dimensions that place positive duties on the state, need not proceed from borrowing from rights that already have a recognized legal pedigree as social and economic rights. Instead, effective human rights protection can, and should, be a result of context-ual interpretative analysis of what is needed to make a right truly a right of 'everyone'.[42]

According to the effectiveness thesis, the Court's socio-economic rights protection could be understood as a mere by-product.[43] Socio-economic interests deserve protection simply because they fall within what today must be considered the scope of the Convention. Their protection is unavoidable and serves a good cause, namely the effectuation of the ECHR.[44] However, as I will show next, this is not the only way in which the Court's socio-economic case law can be understood.

---

[39] *Demir and Baykara v. Turkey*, ECtHR 12 November 2008, 34503/97.

[40] See, for example, *Stummer v. Austria*, ECtHR (GC) 7 July 2011, 37452/02.

[41] Ellie Palmer, 'Protecting Socio-Economic Rights through the European Convention on Human Rights: Trends and Developments in the European Court of Human Rights', *Erasmus Law Review*, 2 (2009), pp. 397–425, 402. See also Virginia Mantouvalou, 'Work and Private Life: Sidabras and Dziautas v. Lithuania', *European Law Review*, 30 (2005), pp. 573–585, 574.

[42] Scott 1999 (n. 34), 641 [footnote omitted].

[43] Colm O'Cinneide, 'A Modest Proposal: Destitution, State Responsibility and the European Convention on Human Rights', *European Human Rights Law Review* (2008), pp. 583–605, 587.

[44] Cf. Craig Scott, 'The Interdependence and Permeability of Human Rights Norms: Towards a Partial Fusion of the International Covenants on Human Rights', *Osgoode Hall Law Journal*, 27 (1989), pp. 769–877, 781 (referring to Joseph Raz, 'On the Nature of Rights', *Mind*, 93 (1984), pp. 194–214, 198).

2.2 The Indivisibility Thesis

2.2.1 The Indivisibility of Fundamental Rights

The effectiveness thesis offers an important explanation for the Strasbourg socio-economic case law. It, moreover, shows why this development should not be viewed with suspicion. Nevertheless, it can be argued that the effectiveness thesis does not fully do justice to the importance of economic and social rights in and of themselves, or to the interwoven-type nature of the various human rights traditions. After all, its exclusive focus lies on the ECHR and the norms enumerated therein. This is where a second explanation comes in. The Court's socio-economic case law can also be viewed starting from a broader, integrated[45] perspective on fundamental rights protection. Regarding the Convention as part of a larger whole, the ECtHR's work can be seen as contributing to the realization of all human rights. In human rights jargon, what is referred to here is the indivisibility, interdependence and interrelatedness of fundamental rights.

I will argue that the idea of indivisibility can shed a fresh light on the Court's socio-economic case law. An introduction of this idea, as it is usually understood in the context of international law, will be followed by several examples illustrating the importance of this notion in relation to the case law of the Court. Indivisibility need not be viewed as completely distinct from the idea of effectiveness. Most authors link or conflate the two and hold that a practice that is aimed at effectively protecting particular rights norms contributes to the indivisible protection of human rights more generally. Yet whereas effective protection can indeed have indivisible *effects*, the indivisibility thesis as it is promulgated here concerns an approach grounded on active recognition of (the importance of) socio-economic rights norms.[46] Indivisibility may therefore be understood as a separate rationale underlying the Court's case law, as well as a distinct starting point for assessing the possible future development of the ECHR's social dimension.

Rather than being a recent invention of human rights defenders propagating the justiciability of all human rights norms, the notion of indivisibility can be traced back to when the modern human rights *acquis*

---

[45] The term 'integrated approach' was coined by Scheinin (Martin Scheinin, 'Economic and Social Rights as Legal Rights' in A. Eide et al. (eds.), *Economic, Social and Cultural Rights: A Textbook*, 2nd ed. (Leiden: Martinus Nijhoff Publishers, 2001), pp. 29–54).

[46] Cf. Mantouvalou 2005 (n. 41), 574–575, who uses the term 'substantive integrated approach', distinguishing it from a mere instrumental approach.

came into being.[47] The 1950 United Nations General Assembly Resolution 421 (V) already stated that 'the enjoyment of civic and political freedoms and of economic, social and cultural rights are interconnected and interdependent'.[48] This resolution considered that all rights laid down in the Universal Declaration of Human Rights, i.e., both the civil and political and the economic and social rights, should be taken up in one single international treaty. Although subsequently this idea was abandoned, the notion of interconnectedness did not recede into oblivion. As noted before, it was not that economic and social rights were considered unimportant. Rather, it was the political climate and the perception that these rights were not immediately applicable, that led to the creation of two separate covenants.[49] The Separation Resolution continued to make mention of the idea of indivisibility, stressing that 'when deprived of economic, social and cultural rights, man does not represent the human person whom the Universal Declaration regards as the ideal of the free man'.[50] After the entering into force of the ICESCR, in the Proclamation of Teheran of 1968[51] as well as in more recent documents,[52] the official position of the UN remained that the covenant on civil and political rights and the covenant on economic, social and

---

[47] Koch 2009 (n. 34), 1.

[48] UN General Assembly, Draft International Covenant on Human Rights and Measures of Implementation: Future Work of the Commission on Human Rights, Fifth Session, 4 December 1950, UN Doc. A/RES/421.

[49] Annotations on the Text of the Draft International Covenants on Human Rights, Tenth Session, 1 July 1955, UN Doc. A/2929, 9.

[50] UN General Assembly, Preparation of two Draft International Covenants on Human Rights, 5 February 1952, UN Doc. A/RES/453 (IV). The full citation is as follows: 'Whereas the General Assembly affirmed, in its resolution 421 (V) of 4 December 1950 that "the enjoyment of civic and political freedoms and of economic, social and cultural rights are interconnected and interdependent", and that "when deprived of economic, social and cultural rights, man does not represent the human person whom the Universal Declaration regards as the ideal of the free man"'. This is also the reason why both covenants had 'to contain "as many similar provisions as possible" and to be approved and opened for signature simultaneously, in order to emphasize the unity of purpose'. See, Annotations on the Text of the Draft International Covenants on Human Rights, Tenth Session, 1 July 1955, UN Doc. A/2929, 7.

[51] See, for the text of the Proclamation, United Nations General Assembly Resolution 2442 (XLII), 19 December 1968.

[52] United Nations General Assembly, Vienna Declaration and Programme of Action, 12 July 1993, A/CONF.157/23 (Vienna Declaration), para. 5. See also the Limburg Principles on the Implementation of the International Covenant on Economic, Social and Cultural Rights, UN doc. E/CN.4/1987/17, Annex, reprinted in *Human Rights Quarterly*, 9 (1987), 123.

cultural rights together cover human rights that are all universal, indivisible, interdependent and interrelated.

According to the Limburg Principles, '[a]s human rights and fundamental freedoms are indivisible and interdependent, equal attention and urgent consideration should be given to the implementation, promotion and protection of both civil and political, and economic, social and cultural rights'.[53] The Vienna Declaration (1993) moreover states that '[t]he international community *must treat* human rights globally in a fair and equal manner, on the same footing, and with the same emphasis'.[54] It is thus stressed that indivisibility not only means that an inevitable overlap exists between the civil and the social sphere, but also that (international) actors should act in accordance with this idea. This suggests that they make visible and workable the inseparableness of the different kinds of fundamental rights norms, i.e., comprehend and apply them not in isolation, but in the light of each other.

In Europe, too, the notion of indivisibility has always been subscribed to. On the occasion of the fiftieth anniversary of the UDHR, on 10 December 1998, a declaration was adopted in which the governments of the member states of the Council of Europe reaffirmed 'the need to reinforce the protection of fundamental social and economic rights . . . all of which form an integral part of human rights protection'.[55] What is more, in the Preamble to the Charter of Fundamental Rights of the European Union that entered into force in 2009, reference is made to 'the indivisible, universal values of human dignity, freedom, equality and solidarity'.[56]

The notion of indivisibility ties in with widely shared philosophical accounts of what fundamental rights entail. It is regularly argued in legal and philosophical scholarship that only when positive (social) guarantees are provided, negative freedom can truly be enjoyed. Scholars such as Sen, Nussbaum and Fredman have emphasized elements of positive freedom as being of crucial importance for the fulfilment of human rights.[57] It is clear that '[a]ny form of malnutrition, or fever due to

---

[53] Limburg Principles (n. 52), 123, para. 3.
[54] Vienna Declaration, para. 5 [emphasis added].
[55] Council of Europe, Committee of Ministers, Declaration on the occasion of the 50th anniversary of the Universal Declaration on Human Rights, 10 December 1998.
[56] Charter of Fundamental Rights of the European Union, OJ 18 December 2000 (2000/C 364/01).
[57] See, for example, Amartya Sen, 'The Standard of Living: Lives and Capabilities' in G. Hawthorn (ed.), *The Standard of Living* (Cambridge University Press, 1987),

exposure, that causes severe and irreversible brain damage ... can effect-ively prevent the exercise of any right requiring clear thought'.[58] In turn, '[f]amines have never afflicted any country that is independent, that goes to elections regularly, that has opposition parties to voice criticisms, that permits newspapers to report freely and to question the wisdom of government policy without extensive censorship'.[59] The different cat-egories of rights can thus not be seen as distinct in the sense that one of them can be taken seriously while the other is being disregarded.

Yet regardless of its rational appeal, the idea that human rights must be treated as indivisible is also said to be a 'rhetorical slogan, a sort of mantra that has to be pronounced for the sake of good order, however, having no substantial significance in itself'.[60] According to Cassese, 'this convenient catchphrase serves to dampen the debate while leaving every-thing the way it was'.[61] Koch in this regard makes a helpful distinction between indivisibility as a political notion, and indivisibility in the legal sphere. It is a matter of fact that someone will not survive without food – '[h]uman needs and human activity are not confined to the terms of a treaty' – and this should be considered relevant at least politically. It is a different question, however, whether in a legal context a judge would also hold 'that the right to freedom of expression has been violated because a citizen has not learnt how to read and write'.[62] Albeit being a legal principle, it is clear from the existence of separate international treaties, that indivisibility becomes contentious as soon as judicial protection is concerned. Nevertheless, according to Koch,

pp. 20–38, 36–38.; Amartya Sen, *The Idea of Justice* (Oxford University Press, 2009), 253 ff.; Martha Nussbaum, *Women and Human Development: The Capabilities Approach* (Cambridge University Press, 2000), 5; Martha Nussbaum, *Creating Capabilities: The Human Development Approach* (Oxford University Press, 2011); Sandra Fredman, *Human Rights Transformed: Positive rights and positive duties* (Oxford University Press, 2008). What matters are real opportunities, and a capabilities approach as proposed by Sen and Nussbaum, therefore, 'insists that all entitlements involve an affirmative task for the government: it must actively support people's capabilities, not just fail to set up obstacles. In the absence of action, rights are mere words on paper' (Nussbaum 2011, 65).

[58] Henry Shue, *Basic Rights: Subsistence, Affluence and U.S. Foreign Policy*, 2nd ed. (Prince-ton University Press, 1996), 24–25.

[59] Amartya Sen, 'Freedom and Needs', *New Republic* (January 10 and January 17 1994), pp. 31–38, 34.

[60] Koch 2009 (n. 34), 3. See also Koch 2006 (n. 9), 406.

[61] Antonio Cassese, 'Are Human Rights Truly Universal' in O. Savić (ed.), *The Politics of Human Rights* (London and Brooklyn: Verso Books, 1999), pp. 149–165, 159.

[62] Koch 2006 (n. 9), 407.

case law from human rights treaty bodies confirms that it is possible to talk about, e.g., the right to health care, the right to housing and the right to social security under the conventions on civil and political rights. This is interesting since there is usually no individual petition right under the conventions on economic, social and cultural rights, and it proves that the indivisibility notion does in fact have a legal content.[63]

Human rights obligations can be understood as 'waves of duties', which, as argued by Waldron, means that these rights come with multiple, successive duties requiring commission, omission and other forms of action.[64] Koch holds that in the legal sphere, this idea

> sets free socio-economic and civil-political rights from their separated compartments. It provides a new framework for the understanding of the scope of human rights obligations, and suggests the necessity of a contextual interpretation of human rights conceivably challenging existing text-conformal interpretative traditions.[65]

2.2.2 Indivisibility and the ECtHR

Now how exactly does this tie in with the practice of the ECtHR? Koch notes that the Strasbourg Court 'has been willing to go beyond the wording of the ECHR and read social elements into the civil rights provisions of the Convention even though several of the decisions have implications of a more general character'.[66] Moreover, both Koch and Mantouvalou have delved more deeply into the normative groundings of the notion of indivisibility in relation to the ECtHR's practice. Koch, first,

---

[63] Ibid.

[64] Jeremy Waldron, 'Liberal Rights: Two Sides of the Coin' in Jeremy Waldron, *Liberal Rights: Collected Papers 1981–1991* (Cambridge University Press, 1993), pp. 1–34, 25. See also Koch 2009 (n. 34), 30 (and 25–28); Mantouvalou 2005 (n. 41), 575.

[65] Koch 2009 (n. 34), 30. Koch prefers the idea of 'waves of duties' over the use of the tripartite typology that was introduced by Shue and Eide. See Shue 1996 (n. 58) and see the final report by Eide as Special Rapporteur, *The Right to Adequate Food as a Human Right*, UN Doc. E/CN.4/Sub.2/1987/23, 7 July 1987; Asbjørn Eide, 'Realization of Social and Economic Rights and the Minimum Threshold approach', *Human Rights Law Journal*, 10 (1989), pp. 35–50. Cf. also Ida Elisabeth Koch, 'Dichotomies, Trichotomies or Waves of Duties', *Human Rights Law Review*, 5 (2005), pp. 81–103. In the following discussion of indivisibility and the ECHR, no further reference will be made to this well-known tripartite typology. This is because it is not used by the Court (which instead sometimes refers to a positive-negative dichotomy) and moreover 'does not necessarily bring us further ahead' (Koch 2009 [n. 34], 28).

[66] Ida Elisabeth Koch, 'The Justiciability of Indivisible Rights', *Nordic Law Journal*, 72 (2003), pp. 3–39, 25.

has linked the Court's socio-economic rights protection to the idea of 'obligations to fulfil' and the transition from a state governed by law paradigm to a welfare state paradigm.[67] In later work, she has developed a hermeneutic perspective for explaining this phenomenon.[68] This perspective holds that interpreting a document 'is conceived of as a meeting not only between past and present, but also between text and context, and the interpreter plays an active part in these meetings'.[69] Thus, 'the whole must be understood in terms of the detail and the detail in terms of the whole'.[70] Koch's theory – with references to pre-understanding,[71] and the horizontal and vertical structure of the hermeneutic circle[72] – thereby illuminates the contextual nature of the Court's indivisible approach as well as the development over time thereof.[73]

Second, Mantouvalou's normative justification for the Court's indivisible approach rests in particular on capabilities theory.[74] It develops a positive account of freedom as (ideally) underlying the Court's approach.[75] Focusing in particular on the right to work, Mantouvalou concludes that

> [a] positive account of freedom as capability ... requires the protection of civil and political, and economic and social rights, and can shed light on important principles that are relevant to the protection of labour rights through civil rights documents ... Capabilities theory leads to a better understanding of the notion of freedom and emphasises the collapse of artificial divisions of rights that traditionally placed emphasis on some elements of individual well-being (free expression, for instance), neglecting

---

[67] Ibid.   [68] Koch 2006 (n. 9); Koch 2009 (n. 34), 37.   [69] Koch 2006 (n. 9), 411.

[70] Ibid.; Koch 2009 (n. 34), 41.

[71] Koch 2006 (n. 9), 414–417. 'Pre-understanding' concerns the role and perceptions (and prejudices) of the interpreter. In this regard, Koch points at the changing pre-understandings in the context of socio-economic rights protection in the sense that 'a future horizon will include social rights as justiciable rights to a wider extent' (p. 417). See also Koch 2009 (n. 34), 45–51.

[72] Koch 2006 (n. 9), 417–423; Koch 2009 (n. 34), 51–56. See, for example, Hans-Georg Gadamer, *Truth and Method*, 2nd ed. (London and New York: Continuum International Publishing Group, 1989). In Gadamer's words, 'understanding is always application', or, 'discovering the meaning of a legal text and discovering how to apply it in a particular legal instance are not two separate actions, but one unitary process' (p. 309).

[73] Koch 2009 (n. 34), 37.

[74] See the work of Sen and Nussbaum, for example, Sen 1987 (n. 57); Sen 2009 (n. 57); Nussbaum 2000 (n. 57); Nussbaum 2011 (n. 57).

[75] Virginia Mantouvalou, 'Labour Rights in the European Convention on Human Rights: An Intellectual Justification for an Integrated Approach to Interpretation', *Human Rights Law Review*, 13 (2013), pp. 529–555, 547.

some others (like the right to work) ... In addition, the understanding of freedom as capability enriches the content of human rights by moving their content beyond individualism. Finally, the interpretation of rights in light of this theory is based on values that underlie the Convention, and recognises aspects of them that have been neglected thus far.[76]

Both Koch and Mantouvalou's normative or justificatory theories add to an understanding of the ECtHR's socio-economic rights protection that rests on the idea of indivisibility. Moreover, their theories may go to show that rather than merely allowing certain indivisible effects to occur, what the Court is (or should be) doing is *taking an approach that is inspired by this notion*. Rather than quietly embracing a wide range of interests, this requires some active or explicit engagement with socio-economic norms and the rights these guarantee.

The distinction between what merely boils down to effectuating ECHR norms and a truly indivisible approach resembles the distinction Mantouvalou makes between the 'instrumental' and the 'substantive' aspect of an integrated approach. The former 'sees social rights as means for the effective protection of civil and political rights',[77] whereas the substantive aspect means that the Court should deliberately take *other human rights norms* into account *because* all norms lay down important values and form part of an integrated whole.[78] In the words of Mantouvalou, such an approach 'shows that the notion of indivisibility of rights means something more than the instrumental necessity of one group of rights for the effective protection of another group of rights'.[79]

Some examples may illustrate that the ECHR's socio-economic dimension indeed results from an indivisible approach. The Court's judgments often mention other rights norms than those enshrined in the Convention.[80] First of all, these are cited in the section 'Relevant International Materials'. One of many possible examples is the judgment in *Stummer v. Austria*, where, amongst other norms, Article 1 of the European Social Charter (right to work) is mentioned as being relevant to the issue of prison work.[81] In the pension rights case *Carson and Others v. the United*

---

[76] Ibid., 554.   [77] Mantouvalou 2005 (n. 41), 574.

[78] See, for example, Rainey et al. 2014 (n. 21), 75.   [79] Mantouvalou 2005 (n. 41), 575.

[80] Mantouvalou 2013 (n. 75), 538, links this to the idea of 'cross-fertilization, which is said to take place when a monitoring body is willing to refer to other bodies' jurisprudence'. See on this notion also Laurence R. Helfer and Anne-Marie Slaughter, 'Toward a Theory of Effective Supranational Adjudication', *Yale Law Journal*, 107 (1997), pp. 273–392, 323–326.

[81] *Stummer v. Austria*, ECtHR (GC) 7 July 2011, 37452/02, para. 59.

Kingdom, reference is made to Article 69 of the 1952 International Labour Organization's (ILO) Social Security (Minimum Standards) Convention.[82]

More importantly, however, the Court also frequently refers to socio-economic rights norms in the legal reasoning parts of its judgments ('The Law'). Such references are generally seen as part of the Court's comparative, common ground or consensus method of interpretation.[83] More than merely ensuring the effective application of the Convention rights, it can be seen that these interpretations expressly recognize the social rights norms, decisions or treaty body comments they draw inspiration from. A good example can be found in the case of *Van der Mussele v. Belgium*, in which the Court, only four years after *Airey*, brought up ILO Convention 29 in order to construe the meaning of 'forced and compulsory labour' (Article 4 ECHR).[84]

Probably the best illustration of the Court's indivisible approach, however, is the judgment in *Sidabras and Džiautas v. Lithuania*. In this case, the Court grounded its interpretation on a social rights norm that, at first glance, has no direct (textual) link to the Convention provision at stake. The case concerned two former employees of the former Soviet Security Service (KGB) who were barred from taking up employment in the public and private sectors for ten years. At issue was whether their complaint fell within the scope of Article 8 (private life) read in conjunction with Article 14 ECHR (the non-discrimination principle). The Court held:

> [A] far-reaching ban on taking up private sector employment does affect 'private life'. It attaches particular weight in this respect to the text of Article 1 § 2 of the European Social Charter [ensuring the effective protection of the right of the worker to earn his living in an occupation freely entered upon] and the interpretation given by the European Committee of Social Rights ... and to the texts adopted by the ILO.[85]

Thus, with the help of a particular aspect of the right to work and the way it is explained by the ECSR, it held that the Convention applied. This signals, as Mantouvalou puts it, 'the belief that social entitlements are as

---

[82] *Carson a. O. v. the UK*, ECtHR (GC) 16 March 2010, 42184/05, paras. 49–51.
[83] See, for example, Gerards 2009 (n. 21), 430–435; 74–96; Gerards 2014 (n. 21), 36–37.
[84] *Van der Mussele v. Belgium*, ECtHR 23 November 1983, 8919/80, para. 32.
[85] *Sidabras and Džiautas v. Lithuania*, ECtHR 27 July 2004, 55480/00 and 59330/00, para. 47. See also *Rainys and Gasparavicius v. Lithuania*, ECtHR 7 April 2005, 70665/01 and 74345/01.

intrinsically valuable as fundamental civil and political rights'.[86] Indeed, a case like *Sidabras and Džiautas* can rightfully be called a 'paradigm example of the substantive integrated approach',[87] i.e., of a perspective that considers the ECHR rights to be part of a bigger whole and hence is expressive of the idea of indivisibility. Moreover, rather than only taking account of rules 'applicable in the relations between the parties', the Court has even given weight to rights contained in international instruments that a state party to a case has neither ratified nor signed. In this regard it held that it 'has never considered the provisions of the Convention as the sole framework of reference for the interpretation of the rights and freedoms enshrined therein'.[88] The Court thereby clearly goes further than what Article 31(3)(c) VCLT requires for the harmonious interpretation of international treaty obligations.[89] It values other international human rights,[90] integrating these into what Waldron could call 'a general theory of justice, which will address in a principled way whatever trade-offs and balancing are necessary for institutionalisation in a world characterised by scarcity and conflict'.[91]

2.3 An Incomplete Puzzle

2.3.1 Interpretive Room

The effectiveness and indivisibility theses not only help to explain the development of the socio-economic dimension of the Convention, they also form valid justifications for the Court's active engagement in the socio-economic sphere. Instead of falling prey to the potentially attractive yet artificial idea that civil and political rights norms are only about the protection of civil and political interests, they show that the task of the ECtHR cannot be so limited. At the same time, seen from an indivisible and effective rights protection perspective, the ECtHR's socio-economic rights protection potentially can go very far. That a justificatory explanation can be given for this phenomenon does, therefore, not mean that there are no concerns left.

---

[86] Mantouvalou 2005 (n. 41), 575.
[87] *Ibid.* Cf. also Gerards 2008 (n. 8), 665; Koch 2009 (n. 34), 214–216; Rainey et al. 2014 (n. 21), 75.
[88] *Demir and Baykara v. Turkey*, ECtHR 12 November 2008, 34503/97, para. 67.
[89] See Art. 31 VCLT. [90] Cf. Koch 2006 (n. 9), 408; Rainey et al. 2014 (n. 21), 75.
[91] Waldron 1993 (n. 64), 33.

Consider again the ECtHR's position and role as a supranational rights adjudicator as set out at in the previous chapter. There I explained that the Court is expected to ensure individual justice while providing the necessary guidance with respect to the standards set by the Convention. This means that it is to ensure effective respect of fundamental rights while acknowledging their indivisible character, which may demand a generous interpretation. At the same time, the Court's subsidiary task does not allow for too activist a stance – be it in determining individual cases or when providing objective interpretations. As can be seen from the recent criticism of the Court, this would, moreover, entail the risk that states' willingness to comply with the Convention decreases. The criticism that particularly addresses the ECHR's socio-economic dimension also raises another issue. It has been alleged that the Court's socio-economic protection is inconsistent as well as too incremental. Against the background of issues of legitimacy and subsidiarity, thus, the Court's reasoning in cases concerning economic and social matters is called into question.

Before elaborating on this, I will first say something more about the potential of the ECtHR's socio-economic rights protection. In this regard, it must be assumed that some link between socio-economic rights and the text of the ECHR remains imperative. The provisions laid down in the Convention provide a frame of reference that cannot be ignored. Here the distinction between indivisibility in the political and judicial spheres again becomes relevant. It has been pointed out that 'legal bodies are ... not convinced that philosophical considerations on human rights as a consistent whole will necessarily affect legal dogmatism'.[92] Actors in the legal realm, and in particular courts, remain bound by written rules, legal principles and legitimate interpretations thereof. This may cause 'ceiling effects' in the sense that courts stick to (a limited understanding of) the rights they protect and hold that other (legal) actors are responsible for the protection of other norms. A treaty body's reference to such norms can then serve to limit rather than expand the scope of protection.[93] An example from the Strasbourg case law is the case of *Kyrtatos v. Greece* about environmental pollution. Here the Court considered that '[n]either Article 8 nor any of the other Articles of the Convention are specifically designed to provide general protection of the environment as

---

[92]   Koch 2002 (n. 3), 37–38. See also Koch 2009 (n. 34), 280–281.
[93]   Scott 1999 (n. 34), 638–640; Koch 2002 (n. 3), 36.

such; to that effect, other international instruments and domestic legislation are more pertinent in dealing with this particular aspect'.[94]

Nevertheless, the limitations resulting from the text of the Convention should not be overestimated. It was already shown that the ECHR provisions are generally broad enough to take into account a great variety of socio-economic interests. With the help of the Court's interpretative techniques, these norms can be applied across a broad array of fields. Gerards, in this regard, speaks of the 'prism character' of fundamental rights. Once light falls on a prism, a spectre of colours becomes visible. Gerards holds that '[i]t is relatively easy to recognise "new" hues of colour in the prism of fundamental rights because ... the colours run into one another without logical points of separation'.[95] With the help of analogical reasoning, more and more fundamental interests can be discerned.

The open-endedness of the Court's socio-economic protection can also be illustrated by its doctrine of positive obligations. The relationship between these positive obligations and the socio-economic dimension of the Convention may be obvious.[96] Consider the right to respect for the home (Article 8(1) ECHR): understood in a classical sense, this provision applies to issues involving home searches, and thus the privacy of the applicant, whereas a positive obligation might entail that no eviction of unlawfully residing persons may take place without investigating possibilities for alternative housing.[97] The room for positive obligations appears relatively unlimited. When a negative right is concerned, the state merely has to do one thing, namely refraining from interfering with individual interests. Yet when the question is whether and what action needs to be taken, in order to for example effectively guarantee respect

---

[94] *Kyrtatos v. Greece*, ECtHR 22 May 2003, 41666/98, para. 52. See also *Ivan Atanasov v. Bulgaria*, ECtHR 2 December 2010, 12853/03, para. 77.

[95] Janneke Gerards, 'The Prism of Fundamental Rights', *European Constitutional Law Review*, 8 (2012), pp. 173–202, 180, referring to Malcolm Langford, 'The Justiciability of Social Rights: From Practice to Theory' in M. Langford (ed.), *Social Rights Jurisprudence: Emerging Trends in International and Comparative Law* (Cambridge University Press, 2008), pp. 3–45, 10.

[96] Cf. Heike Krieger, 'Positive Verpflichtungen unter der EMRK: Unentbehrliches Element einer gemeineuropäischen Grundrechtsdogmatik, leeres Versprechen oder Grenze der Justitiabilität?', *Zeitschrift für ausländisches öffentliches Recht und Völkerrecht*, 74 (2014), pp. 187–213.

[97] Cf. *Winterstein a. O. v. France*, ECtHR 17 October 2013, 27013/07 (where the Court went short of recognizing such an obligation, see Ch. 8, S. 8.1.2).

for someone's private life, the list of measures that could be considered necessary seems more or less infinite.[98]

Another example of the potential for further socio-economic protection is offered by Article 1 of Protocol No. 12 to the Convention (P12).[99] Different from Article 14, the applicability of this non-discrimination provision is not dependent on any other substantive provision. In this way P12 aims at 'broadening in a general fashion the field of application of Article 14 ... '.[100] The former may, in particular, expand the already socializing effect of the latter.[101] For example, when an individual is confronted with allegedly discriminatory housing regulations, regardless of whether these have an impact on his private life or property rights, he can invoke his rights under the Convention.[102]

Finally, brief mention can be made of the greater focus on economic and social rights due to the economic and financial crises of the past years. Together with the increased acceptance of socio-economic rights in general, this has led to an increased number of social rights complaints and proceedings. Besides under treaties like the (Revised) European Social Charter, these are also regularly brought under the Convention.[103]

---

[98] Cf. Koch 2002 (n. 3), 33; Mel Cousins, *The European Convention on Human Rights and Social Security Law*, Social Europe Series (Antwerp/Oxford/Portland: Intersentia, 2008), 48; David Feldman, 'The Developing Scope of Article 8 of the European Convention on Human Rights', *European Human Rights Law Review* (1997), pp. 265–274; Colin Warbrick, 'The Structure of Article 8', *European Human Rights Law Review* (1998), pp. 32–44, 34.

[99] Art. 1 P12 reads: '1. The enjoyment of any right set forth by law shall be secured without discrimination on any ground such as sex, race, colour, language, religion, political or other opinion, national or social origin, association with a national minority, property, birth or other status. 2. No one shall be discriminated against by any public authority on any ground such as those mentioned in paragraph 1.'

[100] Explanatory report to Protocol No 12, para. 10, available at www.conventions.coe.int.

[101] Eva Brems, 'Indirect Protection of Social Rights by the European Court of Human Rights' in D. Barak-Erez and A.M. Gross (eds.), *Exploring Social Rights: Between Theory and Practice* (Oxford: Hart Publishing, 2007), pp. 135–167, 162–163; Oddný Mjöll Arnardóttir, 'Discrimination as a Magnifying Lens: Scope and Ambit under Art. 14 and Protocol No. 12' in E. Brems and J.H. Gerards (eds.), *Shaping Rights in the ECHR: The Role of the European Court of Human Rights in Determining the Scope of Human Rights* (Cambridge University Press, 2014), pp. 330–349, 332–334.

[102] Thus far, however, the practical added value of Article 1 P12 has turned out to be limited. Cf. *Sejdic en Finci v. Bosnia and Herzegovina*, ECtHR (GC) 22 December 2009, 27996/06 34836/06, para. 55; *Ramaer and Van Willigen v. the Netherlands*, 23 October 2012 (dec.), 34880/12, para. 28.

[103] See, for example, *Da Conceição Mateus and Santos Januário v. Portugal*, ECtHR 8 October 2013 (dec.), 62235/12 and 57725/12.

Hence in this regard, too, there seems to be room for further expansion of the ECtHR's socio-economic dimension.

2.3.2   Criticism

Due to its (potentially) far-reaching character, it is unsurprising that the Court's socio-economic practice has also been criticized. Brems, for example, holds that '[t]here is an inherent tension between this reality of indivisibility, on the one hand, and, on the other, the need for the Court to draw the line somewhere with regard to its competence to deal with social rights'.[104] In a similar vein, Koch puts the finger on the sore spot when admitting that '[i]t is an open question how far this integrated approach can and should be taken'.[105]

Other, related concerns have been voiced as well, concerning the Court's reasoning and the shortcomings thereof in particular. The ECtHR has often held that the Convention 'does not guarantee, as such, socio-economic rights',[106] while leaving it unclear what socio-economic protection is nevertheless required for compliance with the Convention.[107] Its case law is characterized by incremental, case-by-case reasoning. Such reasoning need not necessarily be viewed as undesirable: it is in line with the judicial role, as commonly understood, to focus on individual redress rather than on general lawmaking.[108] Still, in light of the ECtHR's unique position, a too case-oriented approach may be problematic as this makes it hard for member states to understand from the case law what obligations they have. Illuminating again, is Gerards' prism metaphor. It can be said that '[t]he flowing character of the colours of the fundamental rights prism can . . . easily result in a case-based argumentative approach that is strongly supported by analogical reasoning'.[109] Analogical reasoning can have unintended and undesirable effects, leading courts where they did not intend to go or giving the suggestion of broader developments that

---

[104] Brems 2007 (n. 101), 165.

[105] Koch 2002 (n. 3), 34. Cf. also Krieger 2014 (n. 96), 200.

[106] See, for example, *Pancenko v. Latvia*, ECtHR 28 October 1999 (dec.), 40772/98.

[107] Cf. Ingrid Leijten, 'Defining the Scope of Economic and Social Guarantees in the Case Law of the ECtHR' in E. Brems and J.H. Gerards (eds.), *Shaping Rights in the ECHR: The Role of the European Court of Human Rights in Determining the Scope of Human Rights* (Cambridge University Press, 2014), pp. 109–136.

[108] See, for an argument for incrementalism in social rights adjudication, Jeff King, *Judging Social Rights* (Cambridge University Press, 2012).

[109] Gerards 2012 (n. 95), 180.

are not in fact there.[110] The idea that 'cases make bad law'[111] is especially relevant in a sensitive field like the one central to this study. Rather than merely at the Court's interpretative principles, a critical look should therefore also be had at its incremental approach and analogical reasoning more generally.[112]

Mantouvalou and Palmer also hold that the Court's incremental approach to socio-economic cases is problematic. According to Mantouvalou, a court like the ECtHR should 'tackle social rights issues according to a coherent theory of adjudication, instead of having recourse to case-by-case solutions that lack comprehensive reasoning'.[113] Palmer sees improvement, but also holds that 'in the light of differences between national policies and administrative procedures for the fair distribution of public resources, the incremental approach to the protection of socio-economic rights through the interpretation of Articles 6 and 14 ECHR remains problematic'.[114] A few examples of opaque reasoning can be given from the court's social security case law under Article 1 P1. First, in two similar cases concerning a legislative change with the effect that Italians who had worked in Switzerland obtained lower pensions than expected, the Court reached different conclusions.[115] Yet it failed to adequately clarify why in one case the interference was proportional and in the other it was not. In *Stefanetti and Others. v. Italy,* the applicants lost more than half of what they expected.[116] The Court held that the percentage of the reduction was not decisive, but did conclude on a violation. In *Maggio and Others,* although lower in terms of percentage, the loss was 'reasonable and commensurate', even though Maggio seemed worse off than some applicants in *Stefanetti.*[117] Trying to balance

---

[110]   Ibid., 183. Cf. also Mantouvalou 2005 (n. 41), 583.

[111]   With reference to the context of the Court, see Gerards 2012 (n. 95), 183. In his famous dissenting opinion in *Northern Securities Co. v. United States,* 193 U.S. 197, 400–401 (1904), US Supreme Court Justice Holmes wrote that '[g]reat cases, like hard cases, make bad law'. See also Frederick Schauer, 'Do Cases Make Bad Law?', *The University of Chicago Law Review,* 73 (2006) pp. 883–918; Cass R. Sunstein, *Legal Reasoning and Political Conflict* (Oxford University Press, 1996), 67 and 72. Cf. also the dissenting opinion in the case of *Bélané Nagy v. Hungary,* ECtHR (GC) 13 December 2016, 53080/13, para. 45.

[112]   Gerards 2012 (n. 95), 183.   [113]   Mantouvalou 2005 (n. 41), 584.

[114]   Palmer 2009 (n. 41), 397.   [115]   See also Ch. 8, S. 8.3.3.

[116]   *Stefanetti a. O. v. Italy,* ECtHR 15 April 2014, 21838/10, 21849/10, 21852/ 10, 21855/10, 21860/10, 21863/10, 21869/10 and 21870/10.

[117]   *Maggio a. O. v. Italy,* ECtHR 31 May 2011, 46286/09, 52851/08, 53727/08, 54486/08 and 56001/08.

all the different interests at stake, as the Court often does, it cannot always prevent the impression that the eventual conclusion is somewhat 'random'. At least this generally fails to show why the scale eventually tips one way or the other. Second, the Court has been criticized for providing an interpretation of the 'legitimate expectations' protected under the right to protection of property that, although referring to previous case law, fails to convince. According to Judge Wojtyczek, the way in which the Grand Chamber in *Bélané Nagy v. Hungary* concluded that the applicant had a legitimate expectation to receive a disability benefit despite not meeting the legal conditions ignores the arguments put forward by the dissenters. He holds that the reasoning 'may appear as a step back in the development of the standards of a democratic State ruled by law', which 'makes it difficult for the respondent States to implement the Convention and affects the authority of the Court'.[118] It is obvious that the Grand Chamber aimed at protecting the interests of the applicant who was deprived of entitlement to any social security allowance. The criticism shows, however, that individual protection is not all that is expected.

Another strand of criticism of the Court's socio-economic reasoning is that it tends to promise a lot, while actual protection is not often granted. In more technical terms: the ECtHR's interpretation generally allows prima facie protection of economic and social interests, but eventually these are frequently outbalanced by other (general) interests.[119] In housing or health-related cases under Article 8, for example, the Court often states that 'there may be' positive obligations inherent in effective respect for private life. This is then reason to consider the Convention relevant, albeit actual obligations turn out to be absent.[120] The Court may also refrain from determining why the Convention applies to a socio-economic complaint.[121] At other times, as mentioned previously, it will

---

[118] *Bélané Nagy v. Hungary*, ECtHR (GC) 13 December 2016, 53090/13, concurring opinion, para. 12.

[119] Cf. Leijten 2013 (n. 33).

[120] Cf., for example, *Marzari v. Italy*, ECtHR 4 May 1999 (dec.), 36448/97; *O'Rourke v. the UK*, ECtHR 26 June 2001 (dec.), 39022/97; *Sentges v. the Netherlands*, ECtHR 8 July 2003 (dec.), 27677/02.

[121] See, for example, *Valkov a. O. v. Bulgaria*, ECtHR 25 October 2011, 2033/04, 19125/04, 19475/04, 19490/04, 19495/04, 19497/04, 24729/04, 171/05 and 2041/05, paras. 87 and 113; *Berger-Krall a. O. v. Slovenia*, ECtHR 12 June 2014, 14717/04, para. 135. See also Janneke Gerards and Hanneke Senden, 'The structure of fundamental rights and the European Court of Human Rights', *International Journal of Constitutional Law*, 7 (2009), pp. 619–653, 630–632.

emphasize that the Convention 'does not guarantee, as such, socio-economic rights'.[122] Krieger in this regard speaks of *ein leeres Verspre-chen* (an empty promise).[123] It is self-evident that fundamental rights do not work as trumps in the socio-economic sphere. The way a state shapes its welfare policies lies at the heart of its democratic prerogatives, and involves a plethora of budgetary and other interests. In the light of this, however, it must be asked whether it is always appropriate to hold the Convention applicable in the first place. A promise of fundamental rights protection is not worth much when the Court mostly defers to the position of the national authorities. For example, there is an infinite list of socio-economic interests that can be linked to an individual's private life. The question is, however, whether all of these should trigger review when only few stand a chance against the general interests involved.[124]

Also relevant here is the Court's use of the margin of appreciation. Developed to ensure deference to decisions of the national authorities in line with the Court's subsidiary task, this doctrine has become one of the scapegoats of those who critically analyze the Strasbourg fundamental rights system. It is said that the margin 'has become slippery and elusive as an eel' and seems to be used 'as a substitute for coherent and legal analysis of the issues at stake'.[125] In this regard Palmer notes that the 'variable use of the malleable margin of appreciation' undermines the development of a more coherent approach to socio-economic protec-tion.[126] From the Court's case law, however, it follows that in the context of general measures of economic and social strategy, the margin is considered to be a wide one.[127] It thus does not have much explanatory

---

[122] See, for example, *Pancenko v. Latvia*, ECtHR 28 October 1999 (dec.), 40772/98.

[123] Krieger 2014 (n. 96), 191–193 (with further examples).

[124] See David J. Harris, Michael O'Boyle, Edward P. Bates, and Carla M. Buckley, *Harris, O'Boyle and Warbrick: Law of the European Convention on Human Rights*, 2nd ed. (Oxford University Press, 2009), 365–366. Cf. also Gerards 2012 (n. 95), 187 ff. (on delineating fundamental rights); David J. Harris, Michael O'Boyle, Edward P. Bates, and Carla M. Buckley, *Harris, O'Boyle and Warbrick: Law of the European Convention on Human Rights*, 3rd ed. (Oxford University Press, 2014), 531.

[125] Lord Lester of Herne Hill, 'Universality versus Subsidiarity: A Reply', *European Human Rights Law Review* (1998), pp. 73–81, 76. See, for criticism on this doctrine, also, for example, Jan Kratochvíl, 'The Inflation of the Margin of Appreciation by the European Court of Human Rights', *Netherlands Quarterly of Human Rights*, 29 (2011), pp. 324–357.

[126] Palmer 2009 (n. 41), 399. See also Krieger 2014 (n. 96), 209, 212.

[127] See, for example, *Stec a. O. v. the UK*, ECtHR (GC) 12 April 2006, 65731/01 and 65900/01, para. 52; *Stummer v. Austria*, ECtHR (GC) 7 July 2011, 37452/02, para. 89; *Taskin a.*

value for the violations that are nevertheless found. In addition, it can be unclear what role the margin plays in relation to the eventual test.[128]

Altogether, according to Palmer, the Court's approach 'has been flawed by a deep-seated reluctance ... to define appropriately the parameters of its own adjudicative role in shaping the normative content of resource-intensive rights through the development of values and principles embodied in the ECHR'.[129] Step by step, the Court has created protection for socio-economic rights, without, however, developing 'a position on socio-economic rights as such'.[130] So whereas the potential of the ECHR's socio-economic dimension is obvious, it appears much less clear how the Court has to deal with the room for socio-economic rights protection that has been created.

It is crucial that whereas the notions of effectiveness and indivisibility help to understand the socio-economic practice of the Court, neither really shows how it can be given shape. On the one hand, the aim of effectuating ECHR rights, combined with the interpretative canons of the ECHR, allows for very far-reaching interpretations, especially in relation to notions such as private life. On the other hand, providing indivisible protection by incorporating socio-economic rights can also go far beyond what is already visible in the Strasbourg case law. Hence, although the theses presented in this chapter allow for comprehending the developments thus far, they arguably cannot do much more than that. Obviously, both ideas serve well as a starting point for ensuring individual protection, which is what the Court should focus on. At the same time, they cannot tell a full story: besides individual protection the Court should, after all, also show deference to national (democratic) decisions while providing guidance on the obligations stemming from the Convention. Reliance on only the notions of effectiveness and indivisibility can therefore not, as such, ensure that the Court's socio-economic case law strikes the right balance between individual, subsidiary and standard-setting protection.

O. v. Turkey, ECtHR 10 November 2004, 46117/99, paras.116–117; *Fadeyeva v. Russia*, ECtHR 9 June 2005, 55723/00, para. 104.

[128] Cf. *Giacomelli v. Italy*, ECtHR 2 November 2006, 59909/00, paras. 80 and 97; *Yordanova a. O. v. Bulgaria*, ECtHR 24 April 2012, 25446/06, para. 118; *Winterstein a. O. v. France*, ECtHR 17 October 2013, 27013/07, para. 148. See also Oddný Mjöll Arnardóttir, 'The "Procedural Turn" under the European Convention on Human Rights and Presumptions of Convention Compliance', *International Journal of Constitutional Law*, 15 (2017), pp. 9–35. See Ch. 8, S. 8.1.2.

[129] Palmer 2009 (n. 41), 399–400.   [130] Brems 2007 (n. 101), 164.

The same goes for the normative justifications that according to Koch and Mantouvalou underlie the Court's indivisible approach. A hermeneutic approach allowing rights norms to be interpreted in their broader context can ensure protection that is not constrained by traditional labels.[131] Similarly, using 'freedom' as a normative starting point for providing indivisible protection may lead to a protective mechanism that captures both classic and social claims, and negative and positive ones.[132] Yet both ideas focus on creating interpretative space rather than on how this space should be dealt with. They fail to illuminate the way in which the Court, in its reasoning, can combine socio-economic protection with showing respect for national decisions and practices. Proportionality and the margin provide little solace here: as I mentioned, the way these doctrines are used forms part of the reason why an explanation for the Court's socio-economic practice is needed in the first place.

Effective and indivisible rights protection is at most a partial answer to the challenges the Court is facing. A complete understanding that can provide sufficient guidance for the further development of the ECHR's socio-economic dimension requires something more. As I will argue in this book, the idea of core rights protection forms the missing piece of the puzzle. It is this idea that, when properly understood, adds to an understanding of the socio-economic protection by the ECtHR that is conscious of this Court's institutional position and the different roles it is expected to fulfil. It is capable of completing the explanation and justification the ECHR's socio-economic dimension requires, while not being blind to the challenges accompanying it and the problems still left to solve in this regard.

Conclusion

Although the ECHR norms can be labelled civil and political, the interests they protect may be of a socio-economic kind. I presented two explanations for this phenomenon: the effectiveness thesis, which stresses the need for effective protection of the rights enshrined in the ECHR, and the indivisibility thesis, which instead focuses on the importance of socio-economic rights.

In line with this, Koch and Mantouvalou explain the socio-economic dimension of the ECtHR by referring to the idea of a hermeneutic

---

[131] Koch 2006 (n. 9); Koch 2009 (n. 34).   [132] Mantouvalou 2013 (n. 75).

interpretation and freedom as a normative starting point, respectively. Their theories provide a justification for the Court's broad interpretation of the ECHR, but leave open the question of how exactly the Court should assess complaints of a socio-economic nature. The Court's socio-economic case law is criticized for being too ad hoc and incremental. Moreover, while being prima facie covered by the Convention, it remains unclear under what exact circumstances socio-economic protection must be granted. What seems lacking, thus, is a specific structure for reasoning indivisible rights, or in other words, a comprehensive explanation for the ECtHR's socio-economic practice that not only does justice to its multidimensional task, but also shows the way forward. Before addressing the question of how the idea of core rights can fill this gap, however, I first have to say something more on fundamental rights reasoning and, in particular, the stages of fundamental rights adjudication.

3

The Stages of Fundamental Rights Adjudication

The previous chapter has set the baseline for understanding the development of the socio-economic dimension of the ECHR. It is the aim of this book to look at this development through the lens of a core rights perspective. But before the idea of core rights can be explored, some further stage-setting needs to be done. The effectiveness and indivisibility theses provide insufficient guidance in regard to the way the Court should deal with socio-economic rights. This is particularly relevant in regard to the perceived shortcomings in the Court's reasoning. To assess the potential of core rights protection, thus, it must first be clarified what room for manoeuvre the Court has in this regard.

In fundamental rights adjudication, different stages can be distinguished that together form the framework for a court's reasoning. These stages and the ways in which they can be approached will be outlined in this chapter. This reveals the different tasks inherent to the adjudicative process, the fulfilment of which may help to structure the eventual judgment. In this way, this chapter prepares the ground for grasping the idea of core rights protection. Moreover, it presents various arguments for valuing the potential of this notion for the Strasbourg practice.[1]

The two main stages of fundamental rights adjudication distinguished here are the determination of the scope of a right and the review of the justification given for interfering with that right.[2] This distinction follows on from the structure of fundamental rights, as well as serving a number of practical aims. Although this book concentrates on the ECtHR, this chapter refers to 'courts' more generally. Taking the Strasbourg practice as the starting point would run the risk of overlooking alternative approaches that might prove valuable later on. At the same time,

---

[1] Part III.

[2] As a third stage, the remedy stage could be mentioned, which however is beyond the scope of this book. Cf. Aharon Barak, *Proportionality: Constitutional Rights and Their Limitations* (Cambridge University Press, 2012), 26–27.

there is no need to provide an exhaustive overview of all the shapes fundamental rights adjudication can take. In order to reflect on the reasoning of the ECtHR, the possibilities presented should be sufficiently relevant to this court's problematic.

In what follows, I will first say something on the structure of fundamental rights and how this structure relates to the stages of fundamental rights adjudication. Section 3.1 illuminates the rationales behind differentiating between the interpretation of rights and the review of limitations. Section 3.2 zooms in on the interpretation stage, and I show that courts can choose amongst different approaches when determining the scope of a right. Section 3.3 concerns the judicial review of limitations of rights. This section deals with the role of proportionality and balancing, as well as briefly discussing the intensity of a court's review.

3.1 The Structure of Fundamental Rights

It might seem natural that when talking about fundamental rights adjudication, a distinction is made between the determination of scope and the review of the justification.[3] Illustrative is a comment by former ECtHR Judge Fitzmaurice, who stated in his dissenting opinion in the case of *Marckx v. Belgium* that the two main stages distinguished here 'are elementary, standard propositions which should not need stating because they are such as everyone would assent to in principle'.[4] Still, it is worth explaining in some detail why this distinction is so central to the adjudication of fundamental rights cases.[5]

---

[3] See, for example, David L. Faigman, 'Reconciling Individual Rights and Government Interests: Madisonian Principles versus Supreme Court Practice', *Virginia Law Review*, 78 (1992), pp. 1521–1580, 1522–1523; Robert Alexy, *A Theory of Constitutional Rights*, transl. Julian Rivers (Oxford University Press, 2002), 196 ff. (also 84–86, 178 ff.); Gerhard van der Schyff, *Limitation of Rights: A Study of the European Convention and the South African Bill of Right* (Nijmegen: Wolf Legal Publishers, 2005), 11; Janneke Gerards and Hanneke Senden, 'The structure of fundamental rights and the European Court of Human Rights', *International Journal of Constitutional Law*, 7 (2009), pp. 619–653, 620; Moshe Cohen-Eliya and Iddo Porat, 'American Balancing and German Proportionality: The Historical Origins', *International Constitutional Law Journal*, 2 (2010), pp. 263–286, 263; Barak 2012 (n. 2). Many high courts around the world have adopted this distinction, see Stephen Gardbaum, 'Limiting Constitutional Rights', *UCLA Law Review*, 54 (2007), pp. 798–854, 806–807; Kai Möller, *The Global Model of Constitutional Rights* (Oxford University Press, 2012), 23.

[4] *Marckx v. Belgium*, ECtHR 13 June 1979, 6833/74, dissenting opinion paras. 3–5.

[5] Not in the least because some authors do question the relevance of the distinction, or at least do not refer to it, especially when it comes to human rights issues. See, for example,

In legal scholarship, the distinction between determining the scope of rights and assessing their limitations is something that is generally recognized. It stems from the idea that most fundamental rights are not absolutes. Individual rights alone do not suffice to meet the needs of society, and there can be countervailing (legal) interests that under certain circumstances take precedence. Alexy, in his famous *Theorie der Grundrechte*,[6] explains the existence of limits to constitutional rights by linking it to the differentiated structure of fundamental rights. The concept of a limit to a right signals that there are two things connected by a 'relation of limitation'. First, there is the *right in itself*, which is not limited, and second, there is what is left over when the limit has been applied, i.e., the *right as limited*.[7] A differentiation is thus made between the *scope* of a right, and the room for limitation – or the extent of *protection*.[8] Phrased in this way, the structure of rights is relevant not only conceptually but also for the practice of courts. It implies that they must distinguish between the right and its scope on the one hand, and the question of to what extent this right deserves protection on the other. First, a court interprets the relevant right in order to see whether a complaint falls within its scope.[9] Only when this preliminary question has been answered in the affirmative, will a court review the justification adduced for the impugned measure and decide whether the individual right will eventually be protected or not.

An example can clarify this. Article 11 ECHR, which contains the 'freedom of assembly and association', reads as follows:

George Letsas, *A Theory of Interpretation of the European Convention on Human Rights* (Oxford University Press, 2007); Steven Greer, *The European Convention on Human Rights* (Cambridge University Press, 2006); Bradley W. Miller, 'Justification and Rights Limitations' in G. Huscroft (ed.), *Expounding the Constitution: Essays in Constitutional Theory* (Cambridge University Press, 2008); Grégoire Webber, *The Negotiable Constitution: On the Limitation of Rights* (Cambridge University Press, 2009); András Jakab, 'Re-Defining Principles as "Important Rules" A Critique of Robert Alexy' in M. Borowski (ed.), *On the Nature of Legal Principles* (Proceedings of the Special Workshop 'The Principles Theory' held at the 23rd World Congress of the International Association for Philosophy of Law and Social Science (IVR), Kraków, 2007) (Stuttgart: Franz Steiner Verlag/Baden-Baden: Nomos, 2010), pp. 145–160; George Letsas, 'The Scope and Balancing of Rights: Diagnostic or Constitutive?' in E. Brems and J.H. Gerards (eds.), *Shaping Rights in the ECHR: The Role of the European Court of Human Rights in Determining the Scope of Human Rights* (Cambridge University Press, 2014), pp. 38–64.

[6] Robert Alexy, *Theorie der Grundrechte* (Baden-Baden: Nomos, 1985); Alexy 2002 (n. 3).

[7] Alexy 2002 (n. 3), 178–179.   [8] Barak 2012 (n. 2), 19. See also Alexy 2002 (n. 3), 196.

[9] This can be called the threshold question. See Faigman 1992 (n. 3), 1522–1523.

1. Everyone has the right to freedom of peaceful assembly and to freedom of association with others, including the right to form and to join trade unions for the protection of his interests.
2. No restrictions shall be placed on the exercise of these rights other than such as are prescribed by law and are necessary in a democratic society in the interests of national security or public safety, for the prevention of disorder or crime, for the protection of health or morals or for the protection of the rights and freedoms of others. This Article shall not prevent the imposition of lawful restrictions on the exercise of these rights by members of the armed forces, of the police or of the administration of the State.

The first paragraph makes clear that everyone enjoys the right to freedom of peaceful assembly, etc. In order to know when this right applies, it must be determined what 'peaceful assembly' means exactly, as well as 'association with others, including the right to form and join trade unions for the protection of his interests'. In other words, the right's scope needs to be identified. Paragraph 2, then, indicates that in certain circumstances limitations of the freedom of assembly and association can be justified. For this to be the case, the limitation must be prescribed by law.[10] Moreover, it must be 'necessary in a democratic society', i.e., meet the requirements of proportionality, while fulfilling at least one of the purposes mentioned. The phrasing of this fundamental rights norm thus clearly supports the idea of a division between scope and limitation. Whereas paragraph 1 states the prima facie right, paragraph 2 contains the 'limitation clause'.[11] The same goes for a number of other ECHR norms, such as Article 8 (right to respect for private and family life), Article 9 (freedom of thought, conscience and religion) and Article 10 ECHR (freedom of expression). Also Article 1 of Protocol No. 1 to the ECHR (protection of property) communicates a clear division.

An express distinction in the wording of a provision is not required for a two-stage approach. Sometimes the conditions for limitation can rather be found in a general limitation clause.[12] Such clauses generally are taken up in a fundamental rights document immediately after the norms to

---

[10] The ECtHR has explained the term 'law' autonomously and in a substantive way. *Sunday Times v. the UK*, ECtHR 26 April 1979, 6538/74, para. 47.

[11] Alexy 2002 (n. 3), 185. See, for a different view, Barak 2012 (n. 2), 33.

[12] See, for example, Art. 1 of the Canadian Charter of Rights and Freedoms: 'The Canadian Charter of Rights and Freedoms guarantees the rights and freedoms set out in it subject only to such reasonable limits prescribed by law as can be demonstrably justified in a free

which they apply. Moreover, there are fundamental rights norms that neither have their own limitation clause, nor are subject to a general one, but for which an 'unwritten limitation clause' applies.[13] The possibility for limitation is then implied and can only be seen from its application in practice.[14] Finally, there is the category of 'absolute rights'.[15] Absolute rights are 'non-derogable' in the sense that they cannot be limited. When absolute rights are interfered with, they are also violated, which in turn means that '[t]he extent of their protection or realization is equal to their scope as their limitation cannot be justified'.[16] Although the twofold structure of scope and limitation does not seem relevant to these rights, they also need to be adjudicated in a logical manner. Just like 'relative' fundamental rights, they require interpretation, i.e., the scope of what is absolutely protected needs to be identified. Article 3 ECHR provides a good example:[17] 'No one shall be subjected to torture or to inhuman or degrading treatment or punishment'. To decide whether the protection of Article 3 is triggered, it must thus be clarified what 'torture' or 'inhuman or degrading treatment or punishment' means.

The distinction between scope and limitations fits well with an understanding of rights as principles. According to Alexy, derogable fundamental rights have a 'double aspect', and contain both rules and principles. The right as stated can be perceived as the 'rule', but it is not a complete rule as it does not allow for solving cases by mere subsumption. There is room for competing interests, and thus a balance needs to be struck between the right and one or more of these interests. In this regard, the constitutional right can be perceived as a principle, or, in Alexy's

---

and democratic society'. See also Art. 36(1) of the South African constitution; Art. 52(1) of the Charter of Fundamental Rights of the European Union.

[13] Alexy 2002 (n. 3), 185, 188.   [14] See, for example, Gardbaum 2007 (n. 3), 789.

[15] These are also called unqualified rights, see Aileen Kavanagh, *Constitutional Review under the UK Human Rights Act* (Cambridge University Press, 2009), 257.

[16] Barak 2012 (n. 2), 27.

[17] See *Ramirez Sanchez v. France*, ECtHR (GC) 4 June 2006, 59450/00, para. 115. However, there is discussion on the absolute character of Article 3, see, for example, Stijn Smet, 'The "Absolute" Prohibition of Torture and Inhuman or Degrading Treatment in Article 3 ECHR: Truly a Question of Scope Only?' in E. Brems and J.H. Gerards (eds.), *Shaping Rights in the ECHR: The Role of the European Court of Human Rights in Determining the Scope of Human Rights* (Cambridge University Press, 2014), pp. 273–293 (with further references) and Gerhard van der Schyff, 'Interpreting the Protection Guaranteed by Two-Stage Rights in the European Convention on Human Rights: The Case for Wide Interpretation' in E. Brems and J.H. Gerards (eds.), *Shaping Rights in the ECHR: The Role of the European Court of Human Rights in Determining the Scope of Human Rights* (Cambridge University Press, 2014), pp. 65–83, 68.

terminology, as an 'optimization requirement'.[18] It states what is prima facie protected while leaving it up to the court to decide whether the fundamental rights principle, or rather the principle with which it collides (the competing interest), prevails.[19]

This is not to say that a bifurcated approach requires that rights be conceived of as principles . Alexy's theory implies that whenever a conflict between a fundamental rights principle and another principle occurs, neither will enjoy 'precedence *per se*'.[20] It thus does not prioritize fundamental rights over other interests. But rights can also be perceived as particularly important, *a priori* weighty rules. This need not mean that they are seen as 'trumps'[21] that forbid any interference whatsoever, but merely implies that rights have a special status conferred upon them.[22] Barak, for example, clearly distinguishes between 'constitutional rights' and 'public interest' concerns. The reason he does not use the term 'prima facie rights' is because in his view, when a fundamental right is limited this

---

[18] 'Principles are *optimization requirements*, characterized by the fact that they can be satisfied to varying degrees, and that the appropriate degree of satisfaction depends not on what is factually possible but also on what is legally possible. The scope of the legally possible is determined by opposing principles and rules' (Alexy 2002 [n. 3], 47–48).

[19] Ibid., 50–57.   [20] Ibid., 51.

[21] Ronald Dworkin, 'Rights as Trumps' in J. Waldron (ed.), *Theories of Rights* (Oxford University Press, 1984), pp. 153–167. Dworkin's notion of trumps and the related distinction between principles and policies (Ronald Dworkin, *Taking Rights Seriously* [Cambridge, MA: Harvard University Press, 1977], Ronald Dworkin, *A Matter of Principle* [Cambridge, MA: Harvard University Press, 1985]); cf. also Rawls' priority of the right over the good, John Rawls, *Political Liberalism* [New York: Columbia University Press, 1993], 173) present an image of rights as blocking any potentially overriding powers or interests. In its pure form, however, this idea has been criticized. Mattias Kumm ('Constitutional Rights as Principles: On the Structure and Domain of Constitutional Justice', *International Journal of Constitutional Law*, 2 (2004), pp. 574–596, 592), for example, points out that the category of these absolute rights would be mainly empty, or, that this asks for a definition of rights that includes 'only the reasons against which the rights-holder enjoys categorical protection'. The possible exception given by authors defending the trumps theory is in case of genuine catastrophe. However, as Frederick Schauer ('A Comment on the Structure of Rights', *Georgia Law Review*, 27 (1993), pp. 415–434, 424) points out, this does not explain 'the possibility that deontologically conceived rights may have to be overridden when interests would otherwise have to be sacrificed to a very large, but short of catastrophic, extent'. See, on the idea of 'soft trumping', Matthias Klatt and Moritz Meister, *The Constitutional Structure of Proportionality* (Oxford University Press, 2012).

[22] See, for a critical response to Alexy in this regard, for example, Jürgen Habermas, *Between Facts and Norms. Contributions to a Discourse Theory of Law and Democracy* (Cambridge, MA: MIT Press, 1996), 203 ff.

does not alter its scope at the constitutional level.[23] He accords special status to the right as it is initially stated, which then influences a court's review of limitations. In a similar vein, Weinrib recognizes the elevated character of rights while emphasizing that 'competing specifications of the ideal of public justice' may require necessary limitations.[24] Thus, although Alexy's is probably the most sophisticated explanation of the structure of rights, a two-stage approach does not require that rights are perceived as principles that need (merely) to be optimized.

At the same time, several authors who do not see rights as principles explicitly reject a bifurcated approach.[25] Sceptics of the idea of distinguishing between interpretation and review hold that this distinction is of inferior concern, if anything.[26] What counts where constitutional or human rights are concerned, after all, is the end result. It is not necessary to speak of prima facie application since, in the words of Jakab, 'provisions protecting fundamental rights (... [like] the freedom of speech) do not prohibit a restriction ... of the freedom of expression, only its breach'.[27] The latter point is correct, yet it does not follow from this that there is no reason for determining prima facie rights at all.

Next to the structure of rights, there is more that argues in favour of distinguishing between interpretation and review. First, this distinction helps to make visible in a given (legal) culture what is considered fundamental. It requires rights to be delineated as recognizable individual guarantees before they are shaped by majority concerns. Whilst majority decisions may impart presumptive validity to limitations of rights, they should not conceal what these rights are about in the first place.[28] Determining prima facie rights includes ensuring that individuals can know when they can invoke their rights, and identifying government responsibilities. When a legislative or executive act interferes with something belonging to the realm of fundamental rights, the least intrusive measures need to be chosen and a sufficient justification must be provided.[29] Second, a two-stage approach is also important for the

---

[23] Barak 2012 (n. 2), 37–42.

[24] Jacob Weinrib, *Dimensions of Dignity. The Theory and Practice of Modern Constitutional Law* (Cambridge University Press, 2016), 222, 239.

[25] See, for example, Miller 2008 (n. 5); Webber 2009 (n. 5).

[26] It is moreover argued that rights and other interests are conceptually interconnected or interdependent. See Richard H. Fallon Jr., 'Individual Rights and the Powers of Government', *Georgia Law Review*, 27 (1993), pp. 343–390, and critically Schauer 1993 (n. 21).

[27] Jakab 2010 (n. 5), 150.   [28] Cf. Faigman 1992 (n. 3), 1525–1526

[29] See, for a discussion of proportionality review, S. 3.3.2.

identification of judicial competences. The distinction between interpretation and application is helpful because it enables the demarcation of the judicial task. Interpreting rights at a separate, preliminary stage urges a court to explain why its jurisdiction does or does not extend to the case at hand. Only when it convincingly argues that a claim is prima facie covered by a right it is tasked to protect, is a court competent to review the matter.

Particularly in the context of the ECtHR, it is important to appreciate the distinction between scope and limitations. Several Convention rights contain express limitation clauses and hence require the adoption of a two-stage approach.[30] But also the unique role and position of the ECtHR, as outlined in Chapter 1, emphasizes the need for bifurcated rights adjudication.[31] The subsidiary task of the ECtHR is limited to adjudication on the basis of the provisions listed in the Convention. In order to not encroach upon state powers more than its mandate allows for, the Court should clarify why a complaint can be considered to fall within the scope of one or more of the Convention rights, and thus allows for Strasbourg review. Besides, whereas ensuring effective, individual protection is an essential aspect of the ECtHR's task, its case law also has a guiding function serving as an important source of information for states wanting to comply with the Convention. Clarity on when a Convention right applies and a justification is required can help to achieve this aim. Thus, given the subsidiary position and multidimensional task of courts like the ECtHR, an undifferentiated adjudicative approach seems unsatisfying.

3.2   Determining the Scope of a Right

3.2.1   *Interpreting Fundamental Rights*

As a preliminary, it must be stressed that determining the scope of a right does not mean that a court clarifies in the abstract what is covered by this right. It rather decides whether in a particular case the individual interest can be subsumed under the invoked right's header. For example, if an individual invokes his or her right to freedom of religion, can what he or she claims deserves protection actually be seen as an exercise of this right? This can be decided in different ways, and the measure of leeway a court has in choosing amongst the various options varies from one legal

---

[30] See, in particular, Arts. 8–11 ECHR.   [31] See Ch. 1, S. 1.1.2.

culture to the other.[32] In any case, deciding on the scope of a right is a matter of interpretation. Doctrines of constitutional and human rights interpretation have been discussed in much depth elsewhere.[33] In Chapter 2, moreover, I introduced the interpretative methods most relevant for the ECtHR.[34] Nevertheless, it is worth stressing that the interpretive methods a court can use are manifold and that the choices made in this regard can have far-reaching consequences for the protection offered by specific rights.

Several methods of interpretation explicitly focus on the relevant fundamental rights provision, while others rely on more dynamic sources and ideas not necessarily captured in the provision itself. Examples of the former are textual and originalist interpretation. Textual interpretation is concerned with the wording used and results in an interpretation that is in accordance with what the text prescribes, while originalist interpretation focuses on the subjective intent of those who drafted a particular rights provision. Both methods are often combined in the sense that what is sought after is what the founding fathers of a constitution or rights treaty thought they were writing down.[35] The other set of interpretative methods include purposive, or teleological, interpretation, as well as comparative interpretation. Purposive interpretation refers to the aim behind a provision, or to the overarching objectives of the document in which it is found.[36] This implies that the interpreter moves beyond the subjective purpose, and instead looks at the broader aim behind the

---

[32] Barak 2012 (n. 2), 63–64.

[33] With regard to the ECtHR's interpretive practice, see, for example, Janneke Gerards, 'Judicial Deliberations in the European Court of Human Rights' in N. Huls, M. Adams, and J. Bomhoff (eds.), *The Legitimacy of Highest Courts' Rulings. Judicial Deliberations and Beyond* (The Hague: T.M.C. Asser Press, 2009), pp. 407–436; Hanneke Senden, *Interpretation of Fundamental Rights in a Multilevel Legal System: An Analysis of the European Court of Human Rights and the Court of Justice of the European Union*, doctoral thesis (Antwerp/Oxford/New York: Intersentia, 2011).

[34] See Ch. 2, S. 2.1.

[35] Both are especially present in the U.S. Constitutional debate, see, for example, Robert W. Bennett and Lawrence Solum, *Constitutional Originalism: A Debate* (Ithaca: Cornell University Press, 2011).

[36] Cf. Barak 2012 (n. 2), 45 ff. See, with regard to the ECtHR, Gerards 2009 (n. 33), 428–430; Janneke Gerards, 'The European Court of Human Rights and the National Courts: Giving Shape to the Notion of "Shared Responsibility"'in J.H. Gerards and J. Fleuren (eds.), *Implementation of the European Convention on Human Rights and of the Case Law of the ECHR in National Case Law* (Antwerp/Oxford/New York: Intersentia, 2014), pp. 13–93, 37–39.

provision or the system as a whole (objective purpose).[37] Comparative interpretation on the other hand, uses comparative information for delineating prima facie rights.[38] The idea is that many jurisdictions share basic fundamental understandings and that comparative insights hence provide arguments for why something should, or should not, be included in the scope of a right. Especially relevant also for international and supranational courts, comparative interpretation forms an enticing alternative. It can aid in navigating between the Scylla of too much restraint and the Charybdis of activism, when the way states understand particular rights is taken to guide the delineation of rights at the supranational level. When national understandings develop, this may be reason to adjust an interpretation accordingly. Sometimes consensus amongst member states seems required, while at other times a clear trend appears convincing enough, too.[39]

What particular method(s) of interpretation a court opts for indeed partly depends on the relevant adjudicative context. It was already mentioned in the previous chapter that a teleological but also a comparative method of interpretation play an important role in the Strasbourg practice.[40] These can be linked to the idea of evolutive interpretation, according to which interpretations of rights are not carved in stone but evolve over time.[41] When a court values rights protection that keeps pace with societal changes, it is less likely that it opts for a textual interpretation compared to a comparative or a teleological interpretation. In order to ensure actual protection, the ECtHR also regularly refers to the principle of autonomous interpretation.[42] This means that it does not look at how certain (legal) notions are understood at the national level, as this may obstruct actual and equal protection throughout the Council of Europe. Also the idea of autonomous interpretation may thus provide the

---

[37] Barak 2012 (n. 2), 48.

[38] See, in relation to the ECtHR, Gerards 2009 (n. 33), 430-35; Gerards 2014 (n. 36), 36–37.

[39] Cf. Senden 2011 (n. 33), 245–255.   [40] See Ch. 2, S. 2.1 and 2.2.2.

[41] See, in relation to the ECtHR, George Letsas, 'The ECHR as a Living Instrument: Its Meaning and Legitimacy' in Geir Ulfstein, Andreas Follesdal and Birgit Peters (eds), *Constituting Europe: The European Court of Human Rights in a National, European and Global Context* (Cambridge University Press, 2013), pp. 106–141; Janneke Gerards, 'Fundamental Rights and Other Interests: Should It Really Make a Difference?' in E. Brems (ed.), *Conflicts between Fundamental Rights* Antwerp/Oxford/New York: Intersentia, 2008), pp. 655–690, 663–664; Barak 2012 (n. 2), 65; Gerards 2014 (n. 36), 36–37.

[42] See, on autonomous interpretation and the ECtHR, George Letsas, 'The Truth in Autonomous Concepts: How to Interpret the ECHR', *European Journal of International Law*, 15 (2004), pp. 279–305; Gerards 2009 (n. 33), 430–435; Gerards 2014 (n. 36), 39–40.

necessary guidance in determining the way in which a particular rights norm is to be interpreted.

It is generally agreed that once a specific interpretation has been given, it acquires a certain permanence.[43] Gardbaum, who describes the determination of a right's scope as the determination of its internal limits, holds that 'once [these are] specified, they always apply so that, where triggered, there simply is no constitutional right to be infringed'.[44] In turn, what is covered by a rights norm will continue to be understood as prima facie protected in future cases. Thus, even though the scope of a right is determined in relation to the facts of a case, a court's interpretation needs to be consistent. This is not to say that interpretations of a right can never be adjusted. Several interpretive starting points just discussed allow for developing a right's scope over time, albeit in a transparent manner. It does mean that a right must be interpreted while keeping in mind that an interpretation will be meaningful beyond the context of the specific case. Closely related to the issue of consistency is the idea of analogical reasoning, holding that a decision on whether or not a particular interest falls within the scope of a right is made by comparing the case to earlier cases. On the basis of analogies and differences found, it can be concluded whether prima facie protection must be granted.[45]

3.2.2   Broad and Narrow Scope, Negative and Positive Obligations

Most fundamental rights norms contain vague wording that is open to different understandings. One can think of the 'freedom of expression' or the 'right to private life', both of which can be explained as covering less or more individual interests. The former, for example, can be interpreted to include a prima facie right to offend or stigmatize, but this could also be considered to fall outside of the right's scope. It is the interpreter's outlook on the desired inclusiveness of a right that can influence the shape these rights will obtain in practice. In other words, besides the different interpretative methods just mentioned, also a court's – or a given legal culture's – preference for a broad or a narrow understanding of the concept of fundamental rights can play a role in the determination of

---

[43] Barak 2012 (n. 2), 23.   [44] Gardbaum 2007 (n. 3), 803.

[45] Cf., on the case law of the ECtHR, Janneke Gerards, 'The Prism of Fundamental Rights', *European Constitutional Law Review*, 8 (2012), pp. 173–202. But see, for the link between analogical reasoning and a (too) incremental approach, Ch. 2, S. 2.3.2.

scope. A distinction between these two approaches is clearly visible in legal thinking, as well as in legal practice. Usually the two strains of thought not only inform the scope of rights, but also the accompanying room for limitations.[46] On one hand, it is argued that both should be defined in a broad manner. The idea is that once a fundamental right is interpreted extensively, there should be ample room for justifiably interfering with this right. On the other hand, fundamental rights can be defined more narrowly. Incorporating only few, particularly fundamental interests, leaves less room for limitations. In this section I expound on the reasons for choosing either approach to the extent that they concern the first stage of fundamental rights adjudication.

Alexy is a clear proponent of a broad definition of fundamental rights. He holds that '[a] wide conception of scope is one in which everything which the relevant constitutional principle suggests should be protected falls within the scope of protection'.[47] According to Alexy, a narrow interpretation is problematic because the conclusions it prescribes do not ally with the permissive character of the norms enumerated in the constitution.[48] Excluding certain modes of exercising a right 'means that acts which have the characteristics set out in the scope of constitutional permissive norms do not enjoy constitutional protection if they have further characteristics which are to be classified as unspecific modes of exercise'.[49] A rightsholder is consequently left with a liberty without the right to decide on the manner he wants to make use of it.

Alexy's conception generates space for constitutional courts functioning as forums for principled justification.[50] Rather than playing the 'counter-majoritarian difficulty card' by asking why there should be room for review by non-elected judges, it asks what justifies a legislative or executive decision.[51] This ties in with the idea of a 'culture of justification'.[52] Also Möller, in expounding his 'global model of constitutional

---

[46] See, for example, Alexy 2002 (n. 3), 201; Kumm 2004 (n. 21); Mattias Kumm, 'Who Is Afraid of the Total Constitution? Constitutional Rights as Principles and the Constitutionalization of Private Law', *German Law Journal*, 7 (2006), pp. 341–369; Gerards and Senden 2009 (n. 3).

[47] Alexy 2002 (n. 3), 210. Cf., in relation to the ECHR, Van der Schyff 2014 (n. 19).

[48] Alexy 2002 (n. 3), 205.   [49] Ibid., 205.   [50] Kumm 2004 (n. 21), 584.

[51] Ibid., 589.

[52] See, for example, Etienne Mureinik, 'A Bridge to Where? Introducing the Interim Bill of Rights', *South African Journal on Human Rights*, 10 (1994), pp. 31–48; David Dyzenhaus, 'Law as Justification: Etienne Mureinik's Conception of Legal Culture', *South African Journal on Human Rights*, 14 (1998), pp. 11–37; Moshe Cohen-Eliya and Iddo Porat, 'Proportionality and the Culture of Justification', *American Journal of Comparative Law*,

rights', links a broad interpretation of rights to the idea of justification. For him, 'the point of rights ... is not to single out certain especially important interests for heightened protection'.[53] Rather than setting up some kind of threshold, 'the scope of freedom protected by rights must extend to everything which is in the interest of a person's autonomy'.[54] A broad scope provides individuals with a possibility to demand reasons for majority decisions, even when this often – and especially when more trivial interests are concerned – does not lead to the finding of a violation. It does, however, prevent cases deserving of eventual protection from being overlooked.

What, then, would argue in favour of a more narrow definition of scope? According to a narrow conception 'rights cover only a *limited domain* by protecting only certain *especially important* interests of individuals'.[55] Only individual interests that are particularly qualified enjoy protection, so that instead of encompassing '[s]uch mundane matters as the prima facie right to ride horses in public woods or to feed pigeons in public squares', a right to liberty would, for example, be limited to its more essential features.[56] Instead of covering everything that has some link with 'private life', only fundamental interests could trigger the protection of *a justiciable right to* private life.

Generally, two sets of reasons have been given for opting for a narrow understanding of the scope of rights. First, there are the arguments that focus on the role of courts in relation to the other powers. Supporters hold that a broad definition of fundamental rights creates too much room for courts to interfere with the choices made by the legislature.[57] A broad scope would 'disable the legislature in favor of the courts, which would be empowered, in many cases, to strike down unfavorable legislation that might interfere with individual rights'.[58] Even if a court does not have the power to invalidate legislative acts, it can be doubted whether it should have a (final) say on virtually every thinkable conflict of interests – in terms of fundamental human or constitutional rights, that is. Other

59 (2011), pp. 463–490; Moshe Cohen-Eliya and Iddo Porat, 'Proportionality and Justification' (Article Review: Aharon Barak, *Proportionality: Constitutional Rights and Their Limitations*, Cambridge University Press 2012), *University of Toronto Law Journal* (2013), pp. 458–477. See also Barak 2012 (n. 2), 22.

53 Möller 2012 (n. 3), 87   54 Ibid., 77, 95.   55 Ibid., 2.
56 Kumm 2004 (n. 21), 584 (referring to the German cases BVerfGE 39, 1 and BVerfGE 88, 203), 583, 589.
57 Cf. Alexy 2002 (n. 3), 211; Van der Schyff 2005 (n. 3), 213 (with references).
58 Gerards and Senden 2009 (n. 3), 626.

legal rules and principles may be enacted allowing (national) courts to judge a broad range of conflicts on the basis of other standards. Second, and related to this, reasons for a narrow scope are based on a preferred understanding of rights as foundational norms rather than as principles that do not have special status. According to this line of argument, it is undesirable to frame every conceivable individual interest in terms of fundamental rights, as this inflates this concept as well as leads to the constitutionalization or juridification of society.[59] In line with this, 'a premature rhetoric of rights can inflate expectations while masking a lack of claimable entitlements'.[60] It can 'lead first to delusion and then to frustration', since much of what seems to be guaranteed is subsequently excluded from protection by means of legitimate limitations.[61] As I showed in the previous chapter, this is also the criticism that has been directed at the ECtHR's socio-economic rights protection.[62]

More generally, to the extent that the arguments in favour of a limited understanding of prima facie guarantees focus on the appropriate role for courts in the broader web of public authority, they arguably gain particular significance in the context of supranational rights adjudication. At the national, constitutional level there may be good reason for holding government accountable for all its action (and inaction) based on constitutional rights. Public authority is then counterbalanced by constitutional accountability. Yet the role of supranational courts, like the ECtHR, appears to be a different one. The deference – or distance towards national balances of power – associated with international or supranational courts suggests that not every exercise of power or lack thereof should be subject to their jurisdiction.[63] The task of the Strasbourg Court is limited to the protection of the rights written down in the European Convention. And even though effective protection may require these

---

[59] Cf. Alexy 2002 (n. 3), 213; Möller 2012 (n. 3). See also Gerards and Senden 2009 (n. 3), 626 ff.; Gerards 2012 (n. 45); Janneke Gerards, 'The Scope of ECHR Rights and Institutional Concerns: The Relationship between Proliferation of Rights and the Case Load of the ECHR' in E. Brems and J.H. Gerards (eds.), *Shaping Rights in the ECHR: The Role of the European Court of Human Rights in Determining the Scope of Human Rights* (Cambridge University Press, 2014), pp. 84–105.

[60] Onora O'Neill, *Towards Justice and Virtue* (Cambridge University Press, 1996), 133.

[61] Alexy 2002 (n. 3), 345 (on the criticism directed at his two-stage approach).

[62] See Ch. 2, S. 2.3.2.

[63] See, however, for the argument that constitutional rights cannot be distinguished from human rights in this regard, Kai Möller, 'From Constitutional to Human Rights: On the Moral Structure of International Human Rights', *Global Constitutionalism*, 3 (2014), pp. 373–403.

rights to be interpreted in a purposive manner, it seems hardly plausible to say that the ECtHR should extend its review to every case in which an individual interest was interfered with.[64]

The wide-narrow distinction is not a matter of either-or. A wide scope can be opted for with regard to the interpretation of one rights provision, while a court decides in favour of a more narrow approach in regard to another – provided it has good reasons for doing so. Moreover, a wide scope need not be limitless in the sense that the interpretation question no longer plays a meaningful role.[65] In turn, 'narrowness' does not necessarily imply that a prima facie right covers only a very limited number of interests, or that a right's scope cannot develop over time. A court like the ECtHR, thus, can ensure effective human rights protection without falling prey to the idea that ECHR rights and individual interests are one and the same thing.

One final issue must be addressed in regard to the interpretation of fundamental rights. Generally, courts must determine the scope of a right only having regard to the right itself. Governmental interests should not be considered in defining what actually constitutes a fundamental right. For example, listing 'freedom of speech' in a constitution or fundamental rights catalogue does not suffice for guaranteeing this right. In order to prevent rights and freedoms from becoming meaningless, it must be ensured that their interpretation occurs independently of majority interests. Thus, what speech *in concreto* means should not be for the government to decide.[66] The need for an independent interpretation of prima facie rights forms an important reason for distinguishing between interpretation and review in the first place.

Now it is not an easy task to interpret a rights norm only having regard to the right itself.[67] It is difficult to perceive of a right in isolation from specific (state) traditions and practices. Any delineation, therefore, runs the risk of being at least indirectly influenced by a balancing of individual and general interests. In this regard, the desirability of an anti-majoritarian scope may well form another ground for a broad interpretation of rights. After all, the more the prima facie understanding of a

---

[64] Gerards and Senden 2009 (n. 3), 629; See also Gerards 2014 (n. 59).

[65] Barak, who clearly prefers a broad interpretation, in this regard says the following: 'The interpretation of the constitutional text should not include, as per its proper interpretation, tenuously related issues not reflecting the reasons for which it was made' (Barak 2012 (n. 2), 71).

[66] Faigman 1992 (n. 3), 1528.   [67] See, for example, Fallon 1993 (n. 26), 344.

right encompasses, the less likely it is that minority interests are insufficiently taken into account. Where appropriate, the general interest may still prevail at the review stage.

Yet whereas such an approach may seem harmless in the context of negative freedoms, it appears somewhat more problematic when omissions by the state are concerned. It is argued that in cases concerning positive claims, the interpretation can proceed in the same way as when negative aspects of rights are concerned.[68] For defining prima facie positive guarantees, it is likewise desirable to refrain from taking state interests into account. One could thus say that the interpretation of a right's positive scope should take place in a generous manner. But is giving a broad, independent interpretation to positive (aspects of) rights really this straightforward? The scope of a right determines a court's competences, but it also informs the other branches about when a fundamental right is at stake. Although an interference with a prima facie right does not automatically entail a breach of this right, a 'rights statement' can thus serve to show that there are certain obligations which can only remain unfulfilled once there is a sufficient justification. Now, there is an important difference between negative and positive rights in this respect. In the case of negative guarantees, prima facie protection means that the authorities need to *refrain from doing something*, i.e., do nothing unless there is a satisfactory reason for acting. However, in the case of positive rights, *action needs to be taken*, except when the authorities can adduce a sufficient justification for failing to fulfil the relevant right.

If rights statements are taken at least somewhat seriously, thus, a very broad interpretation of positive rights and obligations is not always without problems. Think of cases where a court holds that a complaint about a lack of adequate housing is prima facie protected, or that in principle someone has a right to certain medication. Particularly when such prima facie positive (socio-economic) guarantees are inferred from negative, classic rights provisions, a court may overstep the boundaries of its legitimate task. General theories arguing for broad possibilities for rights protection may overlook the fact that courts are still bound to particular rights provisions. Consider the right to protection of property of Article 1 P1 ECHR that may be seen to include social benefits, *but only to the extent that these can be linked to the concept of 'possessions'*

---

[68] Gerards and Senden 2009 (n. 3), 644; Barak 2012 (n. 2), 429–430.

protected under this norm.[69] A broad (positive) interpretation cannot always convincingly be linked to the provision concerned. It may result in the court skipping the interpretation phase altogether and resorting to an overall test of whether the omission of the state was justified. In the light of the importance of a bifurcated approach, such a practice seems questionable.[70]

3.3   Reviewing the Limitation of a Right

3.3.1   Room for Limitations

At the review stage it is decided whether the prima facie right, or rather the interest allegedly justifying its limitation, prevails. The reasons for interfering with a right are crucially important at this point in the adjudicatory process.[71] This ensures 'an institutional dialogue about rights between the three arms of government, in contrast to representative or judicial monologues about rights'.[72] It is in accordance with a traditional understanding of the separation of powers that the legislature, first, decides on the distribution of freedom by means of generally applicable laws. Only thereafter can a court judge upon individualized claims, *in the light of* this democratically legitimized legal framework.[73]

Just like the scope of rights, the possibilities for limitation can be understood either more broadly or more narrowly. The interpretation and the review stage interrelate on this point, and the reasons for preferring one approach to the other are similar to the ones discussed previously. First, when fundamental rights are understood broadly, a great number of conflicts concerning individual interests can be perceived as involving such rights. From this it follows that there should be ample room for limitations, as most of these conflicts do not entail a breach of a fundamental right. The combination of a broad scope and a

---

[69] See Ch. 1, S. 1.3.4; Ch. 8, S. 8.3.3.

[70] Cf. Ingrid Leijten, 'Defining the Scope of Economic and Social Guarantees in the Case Law of the ECtHR' in E. Brems and J.H. Gerards (eds.), *Shaping Rights in the ECHR: The Role of the European Court of Human Rights in Determining the Scope of Human Rights* (Cambridge University Press, 2014), pp. 109–136.

[71] See, for example, Gerards and Senden 2009 (n. 3), 624; Barak 2012 (n. 2), 76.

[72] Julie Debeljak, 'Balancing Rights in a Democracy: The Problems with Limitations and Overrides of Rights under the Victorian Charter of Human Rights and Responsibilities Act 2006', *Melbourne University Law Review*, 32 (2008), pp. 422–469, 423.

[73] Cf., for example, Christoph Möllers, *The Three Branches: A Comparative Model of Separation of Powers* (Oxford University Press, 2013).

broad understanding of justifiable limitations corresponds with the idea of a 'culture of justification'.[74] This requires that a state provides reasons for its actions or omissions in a broad array of fields, and then it is for the courts to assess these. The interim conclusion that an impugned measure infringes upon a fundamental right is then not a very informative one. 'Having a right' does not confer much on an individual,[75] except for the possibility of having his case reviewed.

Second, according to a more narrow approach, only interests that are qualified, in that they can be considered to stand out from individual interests more generally, fall within the category of fundamental consti-tutional or human rights. In turn, this means that there is less room for legitimate interferences. A narrow understanding of rights and limita-tions allies with a more limited understanding of the role ascribed to courts: rather than having the competence to review complaints concern-ing a great deal of the conflicts that occur in modern society, the fundamental rights protecting role of courts only comprises the power to conclude on issues which are truly fundamental. Since rights are considered a special category, the interests for and ways in which they are limited must also be qualified.[76] In this way, the mere fact that an interest falls within a right's scope has some predictive value as to what the final outcome might be. The same argument applies to cases con-cerning positive obligations: when only a limited range of positive claims is perceived to be prima facie protected, it will be more difficult to justify an omission.

Especially when combined with an individual complaints mechanism, like in the case of the ECHR, one of the purposes of a fundamental rights catalogue is to detect those instances in which the authorities have gone too far or, alternatively, have done too little. This may argue in favour of broad possibilities of review, as long as democratically supported reasons for interferences or omissions are taken seriously. At the same time, the institutional setting of a court like the ECtHR can form an argument for not giving a too wide interpretation to both scope and limitations. After all, it can be questioned whether supranational courts are always equipped for reviewing a wide range of national issues. Rather than providing a safety net in case a state violates fundamental human rights, these courts then turn into 'forums for principled justification' no matter what exactly is at stake. In Chapter 1, I explained that the ECtHR needs

---

[74] See n. 52.   [75] Kumm 2004 (n. 21), 582.
[76] See, for example, Weinrib 2016 (n. 24), 239.

to provide for effective individual protection, but that it is also expected to outline a clear rights standard providing the necessary guidance to the CoE member states. Due to these different and often conflicting aims, an over-broad approach does not seem appropriate. Sometimes, at least, a middle way between a broad and a narrow approach is preferred.

3.3.2   Proportionality, Balancing and Categorical Review

Besides as a matter of broad and narrow possibilities for limitations, the way in which a court reviews a justification can also be described along the lines of the criteria it uses. Courts can rely on proportionality review and ad hoc balancing exercises, or revert to more categorical modes of testing.[77] It is these approaches that I discuss in this section, while again focussing on what is or could be relevant for the Strasbourg practice of rights protection.

The measure by which the extent of the realization of a right is measured is often that of proportionality. Put simply: 'Proportionate limitations of rights are justifiable; disproportionate ones are not'.[78] Proportionality entails more than the question of whether there is a proper relationship between the aims of the limitation and the means used. Instead, the proportionality of an interference is reviewed in the light of the importance of the right concerned. It can only be justified when the benefit of realizing the purpose of the limitation is greater than the costs associated with the limitation of the right.[79] The popularity of proportionality review is mirrored in the fact that many constitutions and other bills of rights either more or less directly prescribe this test.[80] Several articles of the ECHR, for example, require that an interference with a right is 'necessary in a democratic society'.[81] This is generally reviewed by means of a proportionality test. Moreover, the threefold requirement of the right to freedom enumerated in Article 2(1) of the

---

[77] See, on the US discussion on both approaches, for example, Pierre Schlag, 'Rules and Standards', *UCLA Law Review,* 33 (1985), pp. 379–429; T. Alexander Aleinikoff, 'Constitutional Law in the Age of Balancing', *Yale Law Journal,* 96 (1987), pp. 943–1005; Richard H. Pildes, 'Avoiding Balancing: The Role of Exclusionary Reasons in Constitutional Law', *Hastings Law Journal,* 45 (1994), pp. 711–751.

[78] Julian Rivers, 'Proportionality and Variable Intensity of Review', *Cambridge Law Journal,* 65 (2006), pp. 174–207, 174.

[79] Barak 2012 (n. 2), 132.

[80] See, for example, Art. 52(1) Charter of Fundamental Rights of the European Union.

[81] Arts. 8–11 ECHR.

German *Grundgesetz* ('Every person has the right to free development of their personality, to the extent that they do not infringe the rights of others or offend against the constitutional order or public morals') is translated into demands of proportionality.[82] The same in some cases holds true for the requirement of 'reasonableness'.[83]

Now this does not mean that there is only one proportionality test.[84] Generally, however, the principle of proportionality is concretized into four sub-principles or tests.[85] First, a limitation of a right should serve a *legitimate aim*. Second, it should meet the requirement of *suitability* for achieving the desired (legitimate) objective. This means that the law or measure that affects the right at stake should realize or at least advance the (legitimate) aim of that law or measure. When this is not the case, the interference is disproportional. Third, there is the principle of *necessity*, which requires infringing measures to go no further than is necessary to achieve their objective. The availability of alternative, less-intrusive measures implies that the right concerned has been breached. Finally, there is the aspect of *proportionality in the narrow sense*, or proportionality *stricto sensu*, i.e., the requirement of a proper relation between the fulfilment of the purpose and the harm done to the right at stake. The mode of assessment used to determine the latter is what Alexy, and with him many others, has termed 'balancing'.[86]

The sequence of the different prongs of the proportionality test is important. According to Weinrib it must first be asked whether a conflict with a right is possible (which depends on the objective of the impugned law); second, whether it is actual (only when the measure is suitable and meets the minimal impairment requirement); and *only* when both conditions are met, whether the impugned measure is proportional in the strict sense.[87] Yet it is not for nothing that we speak of an 'age of balancing'.[88] Regardless of the importance of the lawfulness, the

---

[82] Cf. Kumm 2006 (n. 46), 348.

[83] Cf. Art. 1 of the Canadian Charter of Rights and Freedoms. For the link between proportionality and reasonableness, see, Möller 2012 (n. 3), 200–207. Cf. also Katherine G. Young, 'Proportionality, Reasonableness, and Socio-Economic Rights' (20 January 2017) in V.C. Jackson and M. Tushnet (eds.) *Proportionality: New Frontiers, New Challenges* (Cambridge University Press, forthcoming 2017); Boston College Law School Legal Studies Research Paper No. 430. Available at SSRN: https://ssrn.com/abstract= 2892707.

[84] Cf. Jacco Bomhoff, *Balancing Constitutional Rights: The Origins and Meanings of Postwar Legal Discourse* (Cambridge University Press, 2014).

[85] Cf. for example, Barak 2012 (n. 2), 131.   [86] Alexy 2002 (n. 3), 100.

[87] Weinrib 2016 (n. 24), 223.   [88] Aleinikoff 1987 (n. 77).

suitability and the necessity test, it is clearly the idea of balancing that is omnipresent in today's legal thinking and practice. In the words of Pildes:

> Contemporary constitutional law presents most constitutional conflicts as ones between individual rights and state interests. The central role that metaphors of judicial balancing play in modern constitutional decision making emerges from organizing constitutional conflicts in these terms. When rights and state interests, each with their claim to legitimacy, are perceived to be in collision, we are compelled toward 'weighing' the 'strength' of state interests against the 'degree' of intrusion on individual rights. 'Balancing' becomes the principle technique of judicial decision.[89]

What is more, it is said that in the case of positive and socio-economic claims, the eventual balancing test is not only the most prominent, but in fact the only meaningful aspect of proportionality review. In the words of Möller:

> The statement that constitutional rights law is all about proportionality must be qualified slightly because proportionality is generally applied only with regard to negative civil and political rights ... It does not make much sense with regard to, in particular, socio-economic rights and positive obligations because in almost all circumstances the realization of those rights requires scare resources; therefore any limitation will always further the legitimate goal of saving resources and will always be suitable and necessary to the achievement of that goal. The only meaningful test would be the balancing stage.[90]

A few things must be noted in this regard. Importantly, also the fulfilment of negative rights may bring along significant costs, so according to this logic the protection of these rights may also result in a mere balancing of interests. Whether a multiple-prong proportionality test can be applied depends not on the kind of right at stake, but on the level of abstractness of the pursued aim. Rather than for 'saving resources', it is conceivable that a limitation of a positive or socio-economic right is not suitable or necessary for the achievement of any more specific goal. In this regard, I think that the problem rather lies in the fact that when government inaction is concerned, 'not taking a measure' is not really directed at any aim at all.[91] Möller's remarks tie in with Young's understanding of

---

[89] Pildes 1994 (n. 77), 711.   [90] Möller 2012 (n. 3), 179.

[91] However, this also depends on the definition of prima facie positive rights. When the government is aware of the fact that, as a matter of right, everyone should have access to basic housing, the non-fulfillment of this right must be duly justified, starting with having a legitimate aim for not doing so.

proportionality in the context of economic and social rights. Rather than as a structured doctrine, she shows, instead, that proportionality as a principle infuses the reasonableness standard that plays a dominant role there.[92] It directs the attention to the gravity of the need and vulnerability of the rights-holder, without translating into a multi-pronged test. Yet in this reasonableness approach, 'the interpretation of the right's content is collapsed in an incremental, and context-driven inquiry', which is why it does not amount to a two-stage approach.[93]

According to Aleinikoff, balancing is 'uncontroversial today because of its resonance with current conceptions of law and notions of rational decisionmaking'.[94] He holds that the balancing metaphor takes two distinct forms: first, a court can be guided by the fact that one interest 'outweighs' the other; and second, a court may conclude its test by stating that a 'fair balance' was struck. Both conceptions have in common the idea that constitutional law concerns disputes regarding competing interests, and the 'claimed ability to identify and place a value on those interests'.[95]

Alexy embraces the idea that constitutional conflicts have to do with the dynamics of individual rights versus state interests. At the same time, he argues that '[s]uch interests and requirements cannot have weight in any quantifiable sense'.[96] According to his 'Law of Competing Principles', in the case of a conflict between an individual right and a state interest, neither of these enjoys precedence per se over the other. Both have equal weight in the abstract, but one principle can be more important in a concrete case. The relation of precedence of one principle over the other is hence a conditional one: 'The circumstances under which one principle takes precedence over another constitute the conditions of a rule which has the same legal consequences as the principle taking precedence.'[97] Alexy's theory is famous for the fact that it deduces the necessity of a balancing act from constitutional rights norms in their capacity as principles.[98] As was mentioned previously, principles require optimization to the extent legally and factually possible. The requirement of balancing is derived from what is legally possible. Thus, confronted with a conflict between principles, it is imperative that the Law of Competing Principles be applied, according to Alexy.[99]

---

[92] Young 2017 (n. 83). [93] Ibid., 20. [94] Aleinikoff 1987 (n. 77), 944.
[95] Ibid., 946. [96] Alexy 2002 (n. 3), 52. [97] Ibid., 54. [98] Ibid., 66–69.
[99] Ibid., (n. 3), 67. Rather than a logical necessity, Barak considers proportionality review the best manner possible for dealing with conflicts involving rights (Barak 2012 [n. 2], 243).

Regardless of these justifications, however, balancing is often criticized for giving too much leeway to the court in charge of the balancing exercise. Consider, for example, the criticism propelled by Habermas concerning the Alexy-inspired case law of the Federal Constitutional Court of Germany. Habermas considers the *Wertordnungslehre* according to which fundamental rights are value-laden principles that are to be optimized to be an expression of wrong self-image of this court.[100] Balancing does not always lead to one necessary outcome, yet Alexy argues that it should not be regarded as a non-rational or irrational procedure for that reason. The rationality of balancing, indeed, is not derived from the decision-making process leading to conditional preferences on the basis of the Law of Competing Principles, but instead from the *justification* of this statement of precedence. It is hence the rationality of the established statement that is important, which comes about by using 'all the arguments available in constitutional argumentation generally'.[101] The constitutive role for balancing exercises leads to the Law of Balancing that can be phrased as follows: 'The greater the degree of non-satisfaction of, or detriment to, one principle, the greater must be the importance of satisfying the other.'[102]

Albeit demanding a rationalized response, Alexy's *formal* structure of balancing is said not to solve the problem of incommensurability.[103] In order to have a common criterion for assessing the relative degree of the interference or satisfaction of the different elements, according to Weinrib, proportionality must be understood as a *moral* doctrine instead.[104] He acknowledges the priority of rights over competing considerations bringing along a presumption of invalidity of infringing acts. Not every objective can legitimate rights' limitations, and 'government must demonstrate that the law limiting a constitutional right is necessitated by the very normative ideal that the right instantiates'.[105] In his conception, this ideal is human dignity; rather than resolving conflicts between competing

---

[100] See Habermas 1996 (n. 21), 205–207, who distinguishes between values and norms (and considers fundamental rights to belong to the second category). For further criticism, see, for example, Stavros Taskyrakis, 'Proportionality: An Assault on Human Rights?, *International Journal of Constitutional Law*, 7 (2009), pp. 468–493; Francisco J. Urbina, 'A Critique of Proportionality', *American Journal of Jurisprudence*, 57 (2012), pp. 49–80, Ariel L. Bendor and Tal Sela, 'How proportional is proportionality', *International Journal of Constitutional Law*, 13 (2015), pp. 530–544.

[101] Alexy 2002 (n. 3), 101.   [102] Ibid., 102.

[103] See, for example, Webber 2009 (n. 5), 90.   [104] Weinrib 2016 (n. 24), 239.

[105] Ibid., 241.

particulars, this allows balancing to address (commensurate) determinations of a single underlying norm.[106]

It appears that in Weinrib's understanding, fundamental rights cannot easily or entirely be 'balanced away'.[107] His theory is presented as having a 'categorical core' and can indeed be linked to more categorical approaches to resolving conflicts involving rights. Such approaches use rule-like tools in the sense that they rely on legal categories that allow for classifying circumstances, thereby determining the legal outcome without having to weigh the relevant rights and interests against each other.[108] An example is the use of 'exclusionary reasons',[109] which Pildes has defined as 'reasons not to act'.[110] These are reasons which a state by definition cannot invoke as justification for limiting rights: '[E]xclusionary reasons are preemptive, in that they categorically rule out the reasons they exclude. Thus, exclusionary reasons are not weighed against the reasons they exclude; rather they prevail in such conflicts.'[111] When an interference with a fundamental right is grounded on an exclusionary reason, a court will conclude that the individual right concerned has been breached.[112] Categorization may result in the identification of different kinds of 'rules' for different (aspects of) rights. Even with such differentiation, relative predictability can be

---

[106] Ibid., 244.

[107] See, for this argument against balancing, for example Jochen von Bernstorff, 'Kerngehaltsschutz durch den UN-Menschenrechtsausschuss und den EGMR: vom Wert Kategorialer Argumentationsformen', *Der Staat*, 50 (2011), pp. 165–190, 167. See also Jochen von Bernstorff, 'Proportionality Without Balancing: Why Judicial Ad Hoc Balancing in Unnecessary and Potentially Detrimental to the Realisation of Individual and Collective Self-Determination' in L. Lazarus, Ch. McCrudden, and N. Bowles (eds.), *Reasoning Rights: Comparative Judicial Engagement* (Oxford: Hart Publishing, 2014), pp. 63–86.

[108] See, for example, Kathleen M. Sullivan, 'Post-Liberal Judging: The Roles of Categorization and Balancing', *University of Colorado Law Review*, 63 (1992), pp. 293–317, who speaks of brightline boundaries. See also Niels Petersen, 'How to Compare the Length of Lines to the Weight of Stones', *German Law Journal*, 14 (2013), pp. 1387–1408. The difference between the two modes of thinking is well visible in the historical distinction between the German value-based '*Interessenjurisprudenz*' and more systematic '*Begriffsjurisprudenz*'. See Barak 2012 (n. 2), 503–504, as well as Frederick Schauer, 'Categories and the First Amendment: A Play in Three Acts', *Vanderbilt Law Review*, 34 (1981), pp. 265–307. See also Pildes 1994 (n. 77) (on avoiding balancing).

[109] Joseph Raz, *Practical Reasons and Norms*, 2nd ed. (Oxford University Press, 1990), 190; Pildes 1994 (n. 77). For criticism, see, for example, William Edmundson, 'Rethinking Exclusionary Reasons: A Second Edition of Joseph Raz's Practical Reason and Norms', *Law and Philosophy*, 12 (1993), pp. 329–343.

[110] Pildes 1994 (n. 77), 712.   [111] Ibid.

[112] See also Weinrib's understanding of the obligatory objective criterion (2016 (n. 24), 224–226).

provided as categories apply to more than one case only. In this way, categorization addresses another point of criticism directed at proportionality and balancing: namely that these techniques are too ad hoc and that outcomes are much too focused on the particularities of a specific case.

Categorization in turn is considered problematic when it comes to the formation of appropriate legal categories. When the applicable category determines the outcome of a case, but also when it merely informs the strictness of the test, the definition of the category, or the 'rule', becomes of crucial importance. A categorical approach is thus likely to lead to a body of case law concentrating on the creation of new categories or the modification of already existing ones. In this way, categorical approaches seem to entail a degree of creativity and case-based analogy reasoning as well.[113] It is the task of the court to employ this creativity in an adequate manner to guarantee consistency and predictability, which does not necessarily form less of a challenge than the task it faces when resorting to a balancing approach. As I will show in the next part of this book, core rights reasoning – which can also be understood as a form of categorization – has been subject to similar criticism.

As Weinrib's understanding of proportionality already demonstrates, proportionality and categorization need not be fully separated. While the latter may involve some kind of (definitional) balancing,[114] the former may use rule-like considerations. In this way, categorization can influence the how of balancing, as well as of proportionality review more generally. In respect to (one or all of) the respective tests, regard can be had to certain pre-fixed, or incrementally developed, 'rules' or considerations. For example, the different requirements could be applied more strictly in a case in which a very important right is concerned. Barak, in this regard, distinguishes between 'high level' or 'fundamental' rights, and 'all the other rights'.[115] What right is concerned makes a difference in terms of the threshold for the proper purpose requirement. It could also serve to strengthen the suitability or rational connection requirement by requiring a 'substantial', or rather a 'reasonable', probability of fulfilling the legitimate aim. After the necessity test, Barak then suggests a 'principled balancing formula' reflecting 'a general legal norm which sets a

---

[113] Barak 2012 (n. 2), 504–505.

[114] See, for example, Alec Stone-Sweet and Jud Mathews, 'All Things in Proportion? American Rights Doctrine and the Problem of Balancing', *Emory Law Journal*, 60 (2011), pp. 711–751.

[115] Barak 2012 (n. 2), 531.

constitutional principle that applies on a set of similar circumstances'.[116] Altogether, his approach overcomes and prevents an all too dominant focus on the ad hoc character of the balancing test.[117]

3.3.3   Intensity of the Review

In fundamental rights adjudication, courts may vary the intensity of their review according to what exactly is at stake. Deference is usually linked to a court's review, rather than to its interpretation of the scope of rights. This has to do with the fact that interpretation should proceed on the basis of the right itself. Instead, at the second adjudicational stage, a court is confronted with a conflict between the state and an individual.[118] Rights are limited by means of Acts of Parliament or other authoritative rules and decisions that cannot be considered lightly. While there must be room for individualized review of (the effects of) majority decisions, it remains the prerogative of authorities with (indirect) democratic legitimacy to balance individual and other concerns.[119] In order to position themselves in relation to these authorities and their decision-making powers, it is appropriate for courts to take a deferential stance.

Especially in the context of *supranational* rights adjudication, moreover, courts cannot automatically opt for strict review. Even more so than for national (constitutional) courts, it can be said that a supranational courts' task is of a subsidiary nature, and thereby inherently

---

[116] Ibid., 544.

[117] See, for other suggestions with regard to the necessity test, for example, Janneke Gerards, 'How to Improve the Necessity Test of the European Court of Human Rights', *International Journal of Constitutional Law*, 11 (2013), pp. 466–490, 'Necessity and Proportionality: Towards A Balanced Approach' in L. Lazarus, Ch. McCrudden and N. Bowles (eds.), *Reasoning Rights: Comparative Judicial Engagement* (Oxford: Hart Publishing, 2014), pp. 41–62; Von Bernstorff 2014 (n. 105).

[118] But think of the horizontal effect (*Drittwirkung*) of fundamental rights (for example, Möller 2012 (n. 3), 10). In the context of the ECtHR, however, only the state can be held accountable for failing to provide horizontal protection. David J. Harris, Michael O'Boyle, Edward P. Bates, and Carla M. Buckley, *Harris, O'Boyle and Warbrick: Law of the European Convention on Human Rights*, 3rd ed. (Oxford University Press, 2014), 23–24, speak of the misleading use of the term *Drittwirkung* in this regard.

[119] The counter-majoritarian difficulty (cf. Alexander Bickel, *The Least Dangerous Branch: The Supreme Court at the Bar of Politics* [Yale University Press, 1986]) concerns the problem that unelected judges overrule the decision-making of elected officials. See also Jeremy Waldron, 'The Core of the Case against Judicial Review', *Yale Law Journal*, 155 (2006), pp. 1346–1406. See however John Hart Ely, *Democracy and Distrust: A Theory of Judicial Review* (Harvard University Press, 1980).

limited. Whereas the former are tasked with counterbalancing decisions taken by the legislature or the executive, and can with relative ease engage in a dialogue with the other branches, the position of the latter is more complex. Lacking the power to strike down national laws, the success of supranational adjudication is primarily dependent on acceptance at the national level. In line with this, a supranational court, like the ECtHR, will often be 'too far away' to assume the authority to closely scrutinize what has occurred nationally.[120] This holds true especially when it comes to culturally or politically sensitive matters.

Now this does not mean that a (supranational) court *always* needs to opt for (very) deferential review. This has to do with the rationale of fundamental rights protection. Regardless of the position of courts, the importance of these rights sometimes requires close scrutiny. It was already illustrated that fundamental rights norms can be interpreted very broadly.[121] They can cover environmental nuisances or claims for higher pensions, but also instances of torture or serious interferences with a person's privacy. Not all of the issues covered by rights norms can be considered equally fundamental: whereas there is often ample room for the authorities to decide on how to protect (and limit) a right, in the case of especially important interests a stricter stance seems appropriate.[122] Hence, the intensity of review may require a decision in the light of the individual circumstances and the more specific room to manoeuvre that should be accorded to the state.

The different possible approaches to varying the intensity of the review can roughly be placed under two distinct headings. There are approaches characterized by fluid degrees of deference, whereas models with more strictly separated levels of intensity can also be identified.[123] A preference for the latter, more categorical approach is especially visible in the United States. Outside the United States, and indeed also in the Strasbourg case law, a less tangible degree of deference usually characterizes the applicable test.[124] I will say a bit more on both types of approaches.

---

[120] See, for example, *James and others v. the United Kingdom*, ECtHR 21 February 1986, 8793/79, para. 46.

[121] See, for example, Janneke Gerards, 'Intensity of Judicial Review in Equal Treatment Cases', *Netherlands International Law Review*, 51 (2004), pp. 135–183, 139; Janneke Gerards, *Judicial Review in Equal Treatment Cases* (Leiden: Martinus Nijhoff Publishers, 2005), 79–81.

[122] Cf. Rivers 2006 (n. 78).   [123] See, for this distinction, also Gerards 2004 (n. 121).

[124] See, on the doctrine of the margin of appreciation, for example, Yukata Arai-Takahashi, *The margin of appreciation doctrine and the principle of proportionality in the*

First, deference can be understood as the competence of a court to conclude on a violation only if any reasonable person could see that the measure taken was not appropriate or unreasonable. It can also be asked whether the measure is 'arbitrary', 'clearly excesses the bounds of discretion' or is based on a 'manifest error'. A 'narrow margin of appreciation', on the other hand, demands a detailed and thorough investigation of the justification adduced for the limitation. Now whereas these outer extremes are quite clear in the sense that when applied it is either more or less likely that a violation will be found, a 'degree of deference' approach generally is not particularly transparent. This is especially true when 'in-between degrees' are concerned, such as 'a certain margin of appreciation'.[125] The exact implications of such a degree of deference remain unclear and hence lack predictive value.

Second, a court may use more categorical 'levels of intensity'. According to Barak, in the United States 'the categorical attributes of the right determines the level of constitutional scrutiny; that level of scrutiny, in turn, determines the limitations that may be placed on the rights at issue'.[126] Traditionally, US black-letter law distinguishes three basic standards of review:[127] the weakest form is labelled the 'rational basis test' and will be passed if the state's action was rationally related to a legitimate government purpose.[128] The burden of proof lies on the individual complaining of an alleged fundamental rights violation, and thereby the instances in which his interests prevail are rare. At the other end of the spectrum, 'strict scrutiny' implies that state action has to be necessary (narrowly tailored) for achieving a compelling government purpose.[129] It is up to the government to show that there is no less intruding alternative, and this test is famous for being 'strict in theory,

---

jurisprudence of the ECHR (Antwerp/Oxford/New York: Intersentia, 2002); Letsas 2006 (n. 5); Janneke Gerards, 'Pluralism, Deference, and the Margin of Appreciation Doctrine', *European Law Journal*, 17 (2011), pp. 80–120; Jan Kratochvíl, 'The Inflation of the Margin of Appreciation by the European Court of Human Rights', *Netherlands Quarterly of Human Rights*, 29 (2011), pp. 324–357; Dean Spielmann, 'Wither the Margin of Appreciation', *Current Legal Problems*, 67 (2014), pp. 49–65.

[125] Cf. Gerards 2004 (n. 121), 141.   [126] Barak 2012 (n. 2), 506.

[127] Although it is generally recognized that there are in fact more levels that have been developed in judicial practice. See, for example, Cass R. Sunstein, *Legal Reasoning and Political Conflict* (Oxford University Press, 1996), 77.

[128] 485 U.S. 1, 14 (1988); 449 U.S. 166, 175, 177 (1980); 385 U.S. 522, 527 (1959).

[129] 466 U.S. 429, 432 (1984).

but fatal in fact'.[130] Finally, there is an in-between tier labelled 'inter-mediate scrutiny', which requires that the impugned law must be 'substantially related to an important government purpose'.[131] Neither the government's purpose needs to be compelling, nor do the means have to be necessary. However, the burden of proof shifts from the individual applicant contending a breach of his fundamental right, to the state.

Different to a more flexible sliding scale approach, categorical tiers of scrutiny clearly indicate what is demanded for justifying an interference with a right. Yet this still leaves open the question of how a choice is made for one of the different levels of scrutiny – or indeed degrees of deference. In the United States, the applicable level of scrutiny depends on the right that is concerned. The alleged justification must always pass the rational basis test, but when specific rights are at stake, stricter tests will be applied. Intermediate scrutiny, for example, is applied in cases concerning gender discrimination and discrimination against non-marital children. Strict scrutiny is used when alleged discrimination based on race or national origin is evaluated.[132]

Especially when linked to concrete levels of scrutiny, a rights-based approach seems attractive from the perspective of clarity and predictability. It may bring up the question, however, whether a court should look to the general right (for example the right to life or the right to privacy) or rather to the more specific aspect thereof that is at stake in a particular case. Besides this issue of the level of abstractness, there is the problem of how to determine which rights deserve more or less intensive review. As in categorical approaches, more generally, creating rules for solving individual cases is not an easy task.

It is also possible for a court to not only focus on the individual right concerned, but instead also on the nature and level of intrusiveness of the impugned measure. The Strasbourg margin of appreciation, for example, 'will vary according to circumstances, subject matter and background'.[133] Although such an approach is more flexible and can respond to the particularities of a case, it is equally vulnerable to criticism – albeit for different reasons. Which factors exactly are considered relevant, and how

---

[130] Gerald Gunther, 'The Supreme Court, 1971 Term – Foreword: In Search of Evolving Doctrine on a Changing Court: A Model for a Newer Equal Protection', *Harvard Law Review*, 86 (1972), pp. 1–48, 8.

[131] 429 U.S. 190, 197 (1976); 463 U.S. 248, 266 (1983).

[132] See, for example, 515 U.S. 200 (1995).

[133] See, for example, *Petrovic v Austria*, ECtHR 27 March 1990, 20458/92, para. 38.

are they weighed in order to determine the applicable level of scrutiny or degree of deference? When taking all circumstances into account, the court may forestall the eventual review rather than merely determining the intensity with which it should take place.

The connection between the intensity of the review and the review itself is an intricate one. Or, in the words of Rivers: 'Confusion about the role of discretion is caused in no small part by confusion about the nature of proportionality itself'.[134] I will not try to deal with this issue here, but instead conclude with some remarks on the practice of the Strasbourg Court.

The ECtHR's margin of appreciation doctrine is criticized both for its unclear content and for its unclear relation to the Court's review.[135] At the same time, it is heralded as an indispensable characteristic of its subsidiary task. The ECtHR is expected to leave some decisions to the national authorities and is cautious to interfere, especially in cases where these authorities are better placed to make determinations. In line with this, in the literature, two concepts of the margin of appreciation have been identified: one is labelled 'structural' while the other is called 'substantive'.[136] The former relates to the Court's deferential stance on institutional grounds, while the second concerns the leeway there is in deciding conflicts between individual freedoms and collective aims. Recently, the margin has been related to the Court's increasingly procedural review. Rather than engaging in a normative assessment, the Court now more frequently asks whether the decision-making procedure at the national level was sufficient.[137] Whether or not this is the case may be decisive for the outcome of a case, or rather inform the 'width' of the margin of appreciation. In any case, what this underscores is that the intensity of the ECtHR's review mostly not only depends on the right concerned, but on multiple considerations.

---

[134] Rivers 2006 (n. 78), 176.

[135] Cf. Lord Lester of Herne Hill, 'Universality versus Subsidiarity: A Reply', *European Human Rights Law Review* (1998), pp. 73–81, 76; Kratochvíl 2011 (n. 124), and more generally the sources mentioned in n. 124.

[136] Letsas 2006 (n. 5).

[137] See, for example, Oddný Mjöll Arnardóttir, 'The "Procedural Turn" under the European Convention on Human Rights and Presumptions of Convention Compliance', *International Journal of Constitutional Law*, 15 (2017), pp. 9–35; Patricia Popelier and Catherine Van de Heyning, 'Subsidiarity Post-Brighton: Procedural Rationality as Answer', *Leiden Journal of International Law*, 30 (2017), pp. 5–23; Janneke Gerards and Eva Brems (eds.), *Procedural Review in European Fundamental Rights Cases* (Cambridge University Press, 2017).

Conclusion

In this chapter I argued that when adjudicating conflicts between rights and interests, courts should adhere to a two-stage approach. At least, that is, when this is demanded by the structure of a right. Besides the structure of rights, more pragmatic reasons for differentiating between the interpretation of a right and the review of a limitation thereof concern the demarcation of the judicial task and clarity on the scope of fundamental rights. Especially in the context of supranational rights adjudication, a bifurcated approach is therefore appropriate.

This does not mean that interpreting rights and reviewing limitations are straightforward tasks. It was my aim in this chapter to show that both often involve difficult choices. When defining the scope of a right, courts can opt for a broad, generous view, or rather a more narrow interpretation. There is a lot to say for a broad interpretation of rights, although the relevant rights norm should not be lost out of sight. Moreover, in the case of positive obligations or socio-economic rights, broad interpretations may prima facie demand too much – in which case it is tempting for courts to skip the definition phase altogether.

The review stage corresponds with the interpretation stage in the sense that a broader scope allows for more justifiable limitations, and vice versa. At this stage, state interests are taken into account, which is often done by applying a proportionality or balancing test. Whereas the rationalizing potential of structured proportionality review is sometimes overstated, categorical alternatives do not form a problem-free solution either. Nevertheless, rule-like considerations can be considered for making proportionality more transparent. Fundamental rights review is characterized by a variable margin of appreciation, i.e., a court can vary the degree of deference granted according to what is at stake. It can do so in an ad hoc manner, but also by relying on clear levels of intensity related to the right concerned. In the next part, I explore how the idea of core rights relates to the various possibilities a court adjudicating fundamental rights has at its disposal.

PART II

Core Rights Protection

4

Core Rights as Limits to Limitations

In the first two chapters of this book, I introduced the socio-economic dimension of the ECHR. I showed that the notions of effectiveness and indivisibility go a long way in explaining this phenomenon, but that they cannot provide a complete normative justification for it. Effectiveness and indivisibility both focus on the room that has been created for the protection of socio-economic rights under the Convention, but they fail to show how this room should be used. This issue cannot be tackled easily, especially given the Court's complex position and multidimensional task. In particular, the Court's efforts at reasoning socio-economic cases have been criticized. It is the central tenet of this book that the idea of core rights protection has something to add here. Not only does it allow for a more complete understanding of the protection offered thus far, it also highlights ways in which the Court's reasoning in socio-economic cases can be improved.

Several authors have hinted at the possible role of core rights in relation to the EHCR's socio-economic dimension. Koch, for example, has asked whether the ECHR guarantees 'a minimum core right to social cash benefits',[1] while Palmer speaks of 'developing core responsibilities for socio-economic provision' under the Convention.[2] However,

---

[1] Ida Elisabeth Koch, *Human Rights as Indivisible Rights: The Protection of Socio-Economic Demands under the European Convention on Human Rights* (Leiden: Martinus Nijhoff Publishers, 2009), 181.

[2] Ellie Palmer, 'Protecting Socio-Economic Rights through the European Convention on Human Rights: Trends and Developments in the European Court of Human Rights', *Erasmus Law Review*, 2 (2009), pp. 397–425, 408 (speaking of 'developing core responsibilities for socio-economic provision' in relation to Arts. 2, 3 and 8 ECHR). See also Eva Brems, 'Indirect Protection of Social Rights by the European Court of Human Rights' in D. Barak-Erez and A.M. Gross (eds.), *Exploring Social Rights: Between Theory and Practice* (Oxford: Hart Publishing, 2007), pp. 135–167, 167 ('[T]he Court might want to examine which benefits it can draw from the work accomplished by the social rights experts of other entities. In addition to defining the essence of each right, the UN General Comments have,

in order to see how exactly core rights protection can be helpful in understanding and guiding the ECtHR's socio-economic protection, this notion must be considered in depth. It is to this exercise that I will now turn.

Chapter 3 introduced the different stages of fundamental rights adjudication and the possibilities a court has in this regard. Against this background, Part II provides an overview of what core rights protection is and how courts can deploy it. Drawing from constitutional and international law theory and practice, it shows what core rights protection entails at the different stages of rights adjudication i.e., when reviewing the limitation of a right, but also when determining a right's scope. At the outset, it can be noted that the ECtHR from time to time refers to the 'essence' of the rights it protects. I will elaborate on this later.[3] For now it suffices to say that the Court's use of this notion is confusing and that to grasp the potential of a core rights perspective, we should rather look elsewhere.

This chapter starts by discussing core rights as limits to limitations. For this purpose, it builds foremost on German constitutional law and especially the *Wesensgehaltsgarantie* (the guarantee of the essence of rights) that can be found in Article 19(2) of the German Basic Law (*Grundgesetz*, GG). Section 4.1 introduces the idea of limits to limitations, while Section 4.2 outlines the addressees and scope of the *Wesensgehaltsgarantie* that may serve as inspiration for the use of core rights elsewhere. Finally, Section 4.3 addresses the debate between those who rely on an absolute, and those who argue for a relative understanding of the essential aspects of rights.

---

in particular, emphasized issues of availability . . . , acceptability and quality.'); Ida Elisabeth Koch, 'Social Rights as Components in the Civil Right to Personal Liberty - Another Possible Step Forward in the Integrated Human Rights Approach?', *Netherlands Quarterly of Human Rights*, 20 (2002), pp. 29–51, 46 (speaking of '[t]he existence of minimum core standards?'); Ida Elisabeth Koch, 'The Justiciability of Indivisible Rights', *Nordic Law Journal*, 72 (2003), pp. 3–39, 23 (asking 'whether the Court has established a not very well defined minimum core right to treatment for dying patient[s] without anyone to take care of them'); Cf. also Janneke Gerards, 'Fundamental Rights and Other Interests: Should It Really Make a Difference?' in E. Brems (ed.), *Conflicts between Fundamental Rights* (Antwerp/Oxford/New York: Intersentia, 2008), pp. 655–690, 688–689; Janneke Gerards, 'The Prism of Fundamental Rights', *European Constitutional Law Review*, 8 (2012), pp. 173–202, 195 (concerning the practice of the ECtHR in general).

[3] Ch. 8, S. 8.3.3.

4.1   A Traditional Understanding of Core Rights Protection

Core rights are generally thought of as parts of fundamental rights that cannot be interfered with. In the case of relative rights, which can be limited for legitimate government purposes, the limitation may only go so far as to keep intact the core of the right. To explain this further, we can look at the genesis of the German *Wesensgehaltsgarantie*. Article 19, Section 2, of the German Basic Law of 1949 reads as follows: '*In keinem Falle darf ein Grundrecht in seinem Wesensgehalt angetastet werden*' ('In no case may the core content of a constitutional right be infringed'). The provision is often described as an 'original creation'.[4] A predecessor of the *Wesensgehaltsgarantie* cannot be found, at least not in German constitutional history.[5] This can be explained by the fact that the *Wesensgehalt*, as it is generally understood, assumes a positively defined sphere of individual liberty. It builds upon the idea that a separate sphere of self-realization exists that is independent from the aims and purposes of the state and that has to be respected by the legislature as well. At the time of the Weimar Republic, the legislature had the power to limit fundamental rights to the extent that practically nothing remained. These rights were therefore sometimes characterized as *leerlaufend* (running idle).[6]

Even though, at the time, the idea of a separate, protected individual sphere had not yet led to a distinct understanding of the relation between constitutional rights and ordinary legislation securing these rights, this idea started to develop and it was debated whether the power of the legislature should not be more restrained. In line with this, it was discussed whether fundamental rights should not have an 'unchangeable core'.[7] This development partly explains why after the Second World War core rights guarantees entered German constitutional law. Obviously, moreover, the disrespect of constitutional rights by the Nazi regime also

---

[4] Barbara Remmert, 'Art. 19' in Theodor Maunz and Günther Dürig, *Grundgesetz* (Munich, Verlag C.H. Beck, 2012), no. 2; Horst Dreier, 'Art. 19 II' in H. Dreier (ed.), *Grundgesetz Kommentar*, Band I, 3rd ed. (Tübingen: Mohr Siebeck Verlag, 2013), no. 1; Ernst Zivier, *Der Wesensgehalt der Grundrechte* (Berlin: Ernst Reuter Gesellschaft der Förderer und Freunde der Freien Universität e.v., 1960), 1.

[5] Cf. Claudia Drews, *Die Wesensgehaltsgarantie des Art. 19 II GG*, Diss. (Baden-Baden: Nomos, 2005), 28, n. 31.

[6] Ibid., 26.

[7] See, for example, Dreier 2013 (n. 4), no. 1; Christoph Brüning, 'Art. 19' in Klaus Stern and Florian Becker (eds.), *Grundrechte-Kommentar. Die Grundrechte des Grundgesetzes mit ihren europäischen Bezügen* (Cologne: Carl Heymanns Verlag, 2010), no. 2.

played a significant role in the creation of specific guarantees to prevent fundamental rights being too easily, or even entirely, ignored.[8]

A first proposed reading of the core rights guarantee that was to be taken up in the post-war German Constitution held that limitations of rights would have to leave untouched 'the constitutional right as such' (*'das Grundrecht als solches'*).[9] Another proposal, made by the then Parliamentary Council, was somewhat more concrete and stressed that it was in fact an interference with the *Wesen*, the 'core' of a right, that had to be forbidden.[10] Eventually the *Wesensgehaltsgarantie* was given its present wording, and was grouped together with several other requirements in one single provision.

Even though the difficulty of determining the inviolable substance of a right had been put on the table during the drafting period, it was not discussed at any length.[11] The most important insight that can be inferred from the provision's genesis is that it resulted from an awareness that fundamental rights could become meaningless – especially through acts of the legislature. The *Wesensgehaltsgarantie* conceives of the idea of core rights as a positive, defensive idea that underlines the importance of rights as a category of fundamental guarantees, the essence of which deserves special protection. It presents a traditional understanding of the notion of core rights, namely as the starting point for a protective mechanism against overly extensive interferences with fundamental rights. The *Wesensgehaltsgarantie* is often characterized as a *Schranken-Schranke*, (a limit to limitations).[12] Whereas it is common ground that rights may be interfered with, the idea of fundamental rights is considered incompatible with an unlimited possibility to do so.

---

[8] Remmert 2012 (n. 4), no. 4; Klaus Stern, *Das Staatsrecht der Bundesrepublik Deutschland. Band III/2. Allgemeine Lehren der Grundrechte* (Munich: Verlag C.H. Beck, 1994), 864; Dreier 2013 (n. 4), No. 2; Zivier 1960 (n. 4), 74; Georg Herbert, 'Der Wesensgehalt der Grundrechte', *Europäische Grundrechte-Zeitschrift*, 12 (1985), pp. 321–335, 322; Drews 2005 (n. 5), 28.

[9] Art. 21(4) Verfassungsentwurfs von Herrenchiemsee. Remmert 2012 (n. 4), no. 5, points out that it is remarkable that in this reading, not only *Einschränkungen* (limitations) but also *Ausgestaltungen durch Gesetz* (definitions, explications through law) are mentioned. This implies that, next to when a right is limited, the core must be protected also when the right is interpreted.

[10] 'In so far as a fundamental right can be limited in accordance with the provisions of this Constitution, its core must not be touched upon.'

[11] Remmert 2012 (n. 4), nos. 8, 10; Dreier 2013 (n. 4), no. 2.

[12] See, for example, Dreier 2013 (n. 4), no. 7; Stern 1994 (n. 8), 865.

The German doctrine is not the only example that can be given of a core rights doctrine dealing with the permissibility of limitations. Several states have followed the German example. The Constitution of Colombia of 1991, for example, holds that '[i]n no case shall the essential core of a right be affected',[13] while the 2010 Kenyan Constitution states that '[a] provision in legislation limiting a right or fundamental freedom ... shall not limit the right or fundamental freedom so far as to derogate from its core or essential content'.[14] At the European level, too, the idea of core rights is considered relevant: under the title 'Scope of Guaranteed Rights', the Charter of Fundamental Rights of the European Union (CFR), which entered into force in 2009, states that '[a]ny limitation on the exercise of the rights and freedoms recognised by this Charter must ... respect the essence of those rights and freedoms'.[15]

Moreover, at the international level, the idea of core rights protection has taken root in the context of economic and social human rights. The concept of the 'minimum core' was developed by the Committee on Economic, Social and Cultural Rights (CESCR), the body entrusted with the task of monitoring compliance with the International Covenant on Economic, Social and Cultural Rights (ICESCR). The ICESCR provides for an extensive list of economic and social fundamental rights member states must comply with. At the same time, however, it also enshrines the principle of 'progressive realization'.[16] This means that the various rights need not be realized entirely immediately, but that, given the available resources, states should work towards full compliance progressively. The progressive realization requirement is in line with practical realities, yet also makes it difficult to monitor states' compliance.

To overcome this problem, the CESCR, in its 1990 General Comment No. 3, has made clear that 'a minimum core obligation to ensure the satisfaction of, at the very least, minimum essential levels of each of the rights is incumbent upon every State party'.[17] Hence, states are not allowed to decide for themselves how they will use their resources for the purposes of complying with the Covenant, but are required first and foremost to ensure its core guarantees.

---

[13] Art. 334 of the Colombian Constitution of 1991.
[14] Art. 24(2)(c) of the Constitution of Kenya of 2010.   [15] Art. 52(1) CFR.
[16] Art. 2(1) ICESCR.
[17] CESCR, General Comment No. 3: The Nature of States Parties' Obligations (Art. 2(1) of the Covenant), 14 December 1990, E/1991/23, para. 10.

The ICESCR's minimum core obligations – the content of which has been outlined by the CESCR in further General Comments[18] – could also be understood as a means of controlling interferences with rights. Yet since this notion was developed for the purposes of state monitoring rather than for adjudicating alleged individual breaches of socio-economic rights, relatively little can be learned from it in this regard. The ICESCR example is not primarily concerned with the justification of *limitations*, but rather with what needs to be strived for in the first place. One could therefore say it elaborates on the *definition* of rights and not so much the possibility of constraints. I will further explain this in the following chapter, where the doctrine of minimum core obligations will be discussed in more length. The South African debate on core rights, which also can be seen to concern the content rather than (the limits to) the limitation of socio-economic rights, will also feature in that chapter.

4.2   The *Wesensgehaltsgarantie*: Protecting the Essence of Rights

4.2.1   One Guarantee, Three Branches

The practical role of the German *Wesensgehaltsgarantie* in constitutional adjudication has always remained limited. Hence it is discussed in this book mainly for the inspiration that can be found in its theoretical features. The scholarly debate that has taken place over the past sixty years and more on the meaning of the *Wesensgehaltsgarantie* is highly interesting. Besides presenting insights on the applicability of a core rights doctrine, it also deals with the relation between core rights protection and proportionality review. I will first turn to the former, and leave the discussion of core rights and proportionality for the final part of this chapter.

Article 19(2) GG is designated *Sicherung des Wesengehalts*,[19] *Garantie des Wesensgehalts*,[20] or simply *Wesensgehaltsgarantie* (core content guarantee).[21] These labels show the provision's two most important aspects: it first concerns the *Wesen*, i.e., the *core* or *essence* of constitutional

---

[18] See also Ch. 6, S. 6.2.

[19] Hans D. Jarass, 'Art. 19' in Hans D. Jarass and Bodo Pieroth (eds.), *GG. Grundgesetz für die Bundesrepublik Deutschland. Kommentar*, 14th ed. (Munich: Verlag C.H. Beck, 2016), no. 8 ff.

[20] Michael Sachs, 'Art. 19' in Michael Sachs (ed.), *GG. Grundgesetz Kommentar*, 7th ed. (Munich: Verlag C.H. Beck, 2014), no. 33 ff.

[21] See, for example, Christoph Enders, 'Art. 19' in Volker Epping and Christian Hillgruber (eds.), *Beck'scher Online-Kommentar GG*, 16th ed. (Munich: Verlag C.H. Beck, 2012).

rights; and second, it aims at the *assurance* or *guarantee* thereof. Article 19 GG is said to form part of a general fundamental rights doctrine. The different sections of this provision do not contain self-standing fundamental rights, but requirements for protecting the rights taken up elsewhere.[22] At the same time, when an interference with a fundamental right is in breach of Article 19(2) GG, this means that the corresponding constitutional right is likewise violated.[23] Thus, a failure to keep intact the core content of a fundamental right means that a limitation of this right went too far and thereby constitutes its violation. The law or act concerned is then unconstitutional, and must be regarded as null and void.[24]

The text of Article 19(2) GG does not indicate a particular addressee. But as was just mentioned, it was created in response to the danger that legislative acts would render fundamental rights meaningless. Usually, after all, it is the legislature that is involved in the regulation and limitation of rights.[25] There is, moreover, something to say for the view that the *Wesensgehaltsgarantie* exclusively binds the legislature, at least when it is considered that Section 2 of Article 19 GG must be read in conjunction with the first section of that provision. The requirements listed in Section 1 are exclusively directed at the legislative branch, obliging it to refrain from creating limitations to fundamental rights that only apply to a single case and to always cite the article that is being limited. Stretching this logic, it can be argued that the same goes for the *Wesensgehaltsgarantie*.[26]

Nevertheless, the arguments for holding that all three powers, i.e., the legislature as well as the executive and the judiciary, are bound by the *Wesensgehaltsgarantie* appear more convincing.[27] Besides the fact that there must have been a reason for not including the *Wesensgehaltsgaratie* in Article 19(1), the provision's wording speaks in favour of such interpretation. Unlike Section 1, it does not speak of *Gesetz* (statute), but explicitly stresses that *in keinem Falle*, in no case, can the core of a right be infringed upon. The very rationale of including a core

---

[22] See, for example, Drews 2005 (n. 5), 16; BVerfGE 1, 264 (280); BVerfGE 117, 302 (310).

[23] Remmert 2012 (n. 4), no. 4.

[24] See, for example, ibid., no. 48. BVerfGE 22, 180 (219f.).

[25] Cf. Drews 2005 (n. 5), 23–24.

[26] See, for example, Hartmut Jäckel, *Grundrechtsgeltung und Grundrechtssicherung – eine rechtsdogmatische Studie zu Artikel 19 Abs. 2 GG* (Berlin: Duncker & Humblot, 1967), 44.

[27] Cf. Drews 2005 (n. 5), 24.

rights provision was the protection against the possible nullification of fundamental rights. From that perspective, regarding the legislature as the only addressee would limit its effectiveness in an undesirable manner.[28] Finally, this reading finds support in the text of Article 1(3) GG. There, at the beginning of the German fundamental rights catalogue, it can be read that '[t]he following constitutional rights bind the legislature, the executive, and the judiciary as directly applicable law'. When the *Wesensgehaltsgarantie* is understood as an elaboration of what these fundamental rights require, in line with Article 1(3) GG it should bind all three branches of government.[29]

Regardless of this conclusion, it can still be accepted that the legislature is primarily addressed. The legislature is most likely to be confronted with a situation in which decisions must be made regarding the scope and depth of (general) limitations of rights.[30] The extent to which the other branches are bound by the *Wesensgehaltsgarantie* depends on whether their decisions can also have limiting effects. Generally, acts of the executive have the potential to 'hollow out' rights when they decide on the basis of vague legal terms or when they have wide discretionary powers that can be used in such a way that the core of a right is infringed upon.[31] Something similar goes for the judiciary: when a court has latitude in dealing with a statute that is in itself constitutional and core avoiding, it is obliged to act in conformity with Article 19(2) GG.[32] Article 18, second sentence GG, illustrates this. According to this provision, the extent to which rights can be forfeited is to be determined by the German Federal Constitutional Court. In making this determination, the core of the right at stake should be protected.

Thus, to determine the addressees of the *Wesensgehaltsgarantie*, the aim of preventing fundamental rights from becoming futile is decisive. It therefore binds all national branches whenever they place the essence of these rights at risk. This starting point resembles the basic thought behind the (judicial) protection of human rights. In the Strasbourg context,

---

[28] Brüning 2010 (n. 7), no. 36. See also Zivier 1960 (n. 4), 85; Jäckel 1967 (n. 26), 44; Drews 2005 (n. 5), 28 ff; Sachs 2014 (n. 20), no. 33.

[29] Drews 2005 (n. 5), 28–29. See also Jäckel 1967 (n. 26), 44, n. 2; Ludwig Schneider, *Der Schutz des Wesensgehalts von Grundrechten nach Art. 19 Abs. 2 GG* (Berlin: Dunkler & Humblot, 1983), 37.

[30] Cf. Enders 2012 (n. 21), no. 25.

[31] Remmert 2012 (n. 4), no. 27. See also, Stern 1994 (n. 8), 881; Sachs 2014 (n. 20), nos. 36; Schneider 1983 (n. 29), 32 ff.

[32] Drews 2005 (n. 5), 32, 296.

too, the aim of protecting fundamental rights leaves no room for distinguishing between different branches: the ECtHR judges whether the state, in its entirety, has violated one or more of the Convention rights. Whether the legislature, the executive or the national court was responsible for the impugned measure is of inferior importance.

4.2.2 Scope of Applicability

Besides the addressees, something can also be said on the object of the *Wesensgehaltsgarantie*. What can be understood by *Grundrecht* (constitutional right), or when exactly does Article 19(2) apply? This discussion at first might seem irrelevant for our current purposes, since it is specifically tied to the German Constitution. But as the central question is to what kind of rights the *Wesensgehaltsgarantie* can apply, the conclusions reached are important for the potential of core rights more generally.

Assuming that a reading of Article 19(2) that links it to Article 19(1) is not imperative and looking again at the aim of this provision, namely to protect fundamental rights from substantively running idle, it makes sense to apply the *Wesensgehaltsgarantie* to all fundamental rights that can be hollowed out by the state.[33] In other words, the term 'constitutional right' should be understood to cover as many rights guarantees as possible.[34] The reason why one cannot simply speak of all fundamental rights is that protecting the core of a right should at least be logically possible.[35] This is not a problem as far as negatively formulated fundamental freedoms are concerned. Regardless of whether these contain a specific limitation clause or not, interferences can be forbidden when they fail to leave the essence of the right intact.[36]

Likewise, it is possible that the state disrespects the core of a right when it does nothing, or does too little. Positively formulated guarantees can also run the risk of becoming futile and thus require the protection of Article 19(2) GG.[37] The German Basic Law contains only few positively formulated guarantees, yet there is also a category of positive obligations that do not follow directly from the Constitution's text, but that have been

---

[33] Remmert 2012 (n. 4), no. 22.   [34] Cf. Drews 2005 (n. 5), 48.   [35] Ibid., 45.

[36] Ibid., 46–48. Cf. also Dreier 2013 (n. 4), no. 10; Herbert 1985 (n. 8), 331; Jäckel 1967 (n. 26), 45; Herbert Krüger, 'Der Wesensgehalt der Grundrechte i.S. des Art. 19 GG', *Die Öffentliche Verwaltung*, 8 (1955), pp. 597–602, 599; Remmert 2012 (n. 4), no. 23; Stern 1994 (n. 8), 878; Zivier 1960 (n. 4), 85; Brüning 2010 (n. 9), no. 36.

[37] Drews 2005 (n. 5), 56–57; Remmert 2012 (n. 4), nos. 23, 45.

inferred from negatively formulated rights norms. A reason for this is the development from a liberal to a social *Rechtsstaat*, and the growing importance of the idea that the state needs to create and secure the conditions for enabling individuals to make use of their fundamental freedoms.[38] Core rights protection may thus require positive protection, at least to a certain minimum degree, regardless of whether positive rights have been written down expressly.[39] Indeed, this could be relevant in regard to the ECtHR's doctrine of positive obligations, at least when the Court adheres to the different stages of rights adjudication, i.e., to a model based on prima facie rights and the limited possibility of limitations.[40]

When it comes to equality rights, views are more divided. On the one hand, it is considered that such rights have a distinct structure. Equality guarantees do not generally include a specific possibility for limitation, which suggests that it is in any case forbidden to constrain them.[41] On the other hand, when it is argued that the interference model also applies to fundamental equality norms and limitations are hence possible, the *Wesensgehaltsgarantie* could become relevant.[42] Such a structure seems apparent from the protection against discrimination under the ECHR. A distinction is, after all, made between differential treatment (triggering prima facie protection) and discrimination (which violates the Convention).[43] In this regard, the idea of core rights could, at least theoretically, be helpful in determining when treatment is not only differential, but also discriminatory.

4.3 Absolute and Relative Core Rights Protection

4.3.1 *Objective versus Subjective Protection*

According to Drews, there are only two things about the *Wesensgehaltsgarantie* that are really beyond dispute.[44] First, it is not a self-standing fundamental right, while second, it is clear that an interference with a fundamental right in breach of Article 19(2) GG is unconstitutional. Yet how to determine whether the core of a right is touched upon is

---

[38] Cf. Drews 2005 (n. 5), 54; BVerfGE 33, 303 (331).

[39] Cf. also Peter Häberle, *Die Wesensgehaltsgarantie des Art. 19 II GG – zugleich ein Beitrag zum institutionellen Verständnis der Grundrecht und zur Lehre vom Gesetzesvorbehalt*, 3rd ed. (Heidelberg: C.F. Müller, 1983), 369 ff., 422 ff.

[40] Ch. 3.

[41] Dreier 2013 (n. 4), no. 9; Enders 2012 (n. 8), no. 21. In this regard the protection against discrimination can be understood as essential, per se. Cf. Ch. 5, S. 5.1.2 (Ch. 6, S. 6.2, 6.3).

[42] Cf. Enders 2012 (n. 21), no. 22; Remmert 2012 (n. 4), no. 24; Drews 2005 (n. 5), 59.

[43] Cf. Ch. 1, S. 1.2.2. See also Ch. 7, 7.2.   [44] Drews 2005 (n. 5), 16–17.

a highly controversial matter.[45] The *Wesensgehaltsgarantie* has been described as the least-contoured norm of the Constitution,[46] but also as the central guarantee against hollowing out rights' content.[47] In any case, the ongoing discussion on the content it is concerned with provides important insights not just on core rights protection, but on judicial review of rights' limitations more generally.

In this section, the German debate will be outlined from an observer's point of view, laying bare the different positions taken therein and the approach to rights reasoning these reflect. The debate on the meaning of the *Wesensgehaltsgarantie* deals with two separate issues: the first is whether its protection is objective or rather subjective in kind, while the second concerns the conflict between absolute and relative theories of core rights. Let me start by briefly addressing the former.

The objective-subjective discussion centres on the question of whether the term fundamental right in Article 19(2) GG refers to the subjective right of each individual, or instead to an objective right, i.e., to the meaning of a fundamental right for society in general.[48] The latter implies that the focus lies not on individual protection, but instead on the fundamental rights norm as such. According to the objective theory, the *Wesensgehaltsgarantie* forbids any interference with a fundamental rights norm that has the effect of nullifying this norm in the constitutional order. In an individual case, someone can then be deprived of his right entirely. As long as the right concerned remains meaningful in a more objective sense, a breach of Article 19(2) GG will not occur.[49]

The objective theory relates to the guarantee of particular *Einrichtungen* (institutions) that can be deduced from constitutional provisions. Examples are marriage or personal property, which have to be guaranteed in a general fashion.[50] Because a narrow interpretation would unduly limit the application of the *Wesensgehaltsgarantie*, the notion of 'institutions' is usually understood in a broader sense to include fundamental

---

[45] Ibid., 59 ff.

[46] Günter Dürig, 'Der Grundrechtssatz von der Menschenwürde. Entwurf eines praktikablen Wertsystems der Grundrechte aus Art. 1 Abs. I in Verbindung mit Art. 19 Abs. II des Grundgesetzes', *Archiv des öffentlichen Rechts*, 81 (1956), pp. 117–157, 133.

[47] Schneider 1983 (n. 29), 17.

[48] Cf. BVerfGE 2, 266 (285). This question was answered differently in different cases, see Sachs 2014 (n. 20), no. 45. See also Jäckel 1967 (n. 26), 57 ff.

[49] See, for example, Jarass 2016 (n. 19), no. 9; Dreier 2013 (n. 4), no. 13; Herbert 1985 (n. 8), 324. Cf. BVerfGE 100, 313 (376).

[50] Drews 2005 (n. 5) 80 ff.

rights generally.[51] The objective view could be referred to as a social theory. Such an interpretation emphasizes the importance of a fundamental rights norm for the entire constitutional order – its meaning for social life in its entirety, rather than for the position of an individual.[52]

In turn, the subjective view holds that in every individual instance, the *Wesen* of a right must be protected.[53] This view is grounded on the aim of Article 19(2) GG in particular, as well as that of fundamental rights protection more broadly speaking. Dürig, for example, holds that the rationale of the *Wesensgehaltsgarantie* is that the rightsholder should not become the object of state action.[54] It is thus to be read as referring to individual, subjective rights.[55] Additionally, it is held that the historical background and aims of the *Grundgesetz* point at the protection of individuals and their isolated legal positions.[56]

Indeed, the objective theory may seem to be at odds with the *raison d'être* behind fundamental rights, including those enshrined in the European Convention. The fact that it nevertheless finds significant support merely results from the desire to give the *Wesensgehaltsgarantie* a workable meaning.[57] There are instances in which fundamental rights are taken away completely.[58] To make sure that Article 19(2) GG is not devoid of meaning, it is then argued that this provision concerns not so much the subjective, but rather the objective importance of rights' cores. Various authors, however, do not perceive this matter as an either/or question. They contend, at least implicitly, that the *Wesensgehaltsgarantie* can have both an objective and a subjective meaning.[59]

The objective-subjective and the absolute-relative discussion are inherently related.[60] When the first is resolved in favour of a subjective

[51] Ibid., 81.

[52] See, for example, Joachim Chlosta, *Der Wesensgehalt der Eigentumsgewährleistung. Unter besonderer Berücksichtigung der Mitbestimmungsproblematik* (Berlin: Duncker & Humblot, 1975), 40.

[53] See, with references, Drews 2005 (n. 5), 299.   [54] Dürig 1956 (n. 46), 136.

[55] See, for example, Eike von Hippel, *Grenzen und Wesensgehalt der Grundrechte* (Berlin: Duncker & Humblot, 1965), 48, fn. 4; Herbert 1985 (n. 8), 324, 332, 334–335.

[56] See, for example, Chlosta 1975 (n. 52), 41 ff.

[57] Remmert 2012 (n. 4), nos. 20, 37; Brüning 2010 (n. 7), no. 42; Jarass 2016 (n. 22), no. 9; Dreier 2013 (n. 4), no. 14.

[58] Cf. BVerfGE 45, 187 (270f.); BVerfGE 109, 133 (156); BVerfGE 115, 118 (165).

[59] See, for example, Dreier 2013 (n. 4), nos. 13–14; Brüning 2010 (n. 7), no. 42; Enders 2012 (n. 21), nos. 27–28; Martin Borowski, *Grundrechte als Prinzipien*, 2nd ed. (Baden-Baden: Nomos, 2007), 287.

[60] Drews 2005 (n. 5), 60–61.

interpretation, it is likely that the meaning of the *Wesensgehalt* is considered to be circumstantial or relative. Inversely, when the *Wesensgehalt* is perceived to be absolute, an objective interpretation may be preferred. As will be seen, the relative theory seems to be the easier one to work with, although the appeal of absolute core rights protection cannot be ignored either.

4.3.2   Absolute Theories

The absolute-relative debate is crucial for understanding core rights protection as a matter of rights reasoning. The essential question here is whether the *Wesensgehalt* of a right implies an absolute or rather a relative boundary.[61] Does every fundamental right have a substantive core that may never be curtailed and is absolutely protected against state interference? Or can the essence of a fundamental right only be determined in the context of a specific case, through balancing the different interests involved?

According to various absolute theories,[62] the *Wesensgehaltsgarantie* absolutely protects those aspects of a constitutional right, without which one can no longer speak of that right.[63] These aspects form the actual *Kern* (core), or alternatively the substance or heart of a fundamental right.[64] Absolute theories are founded on a spatial understanding of fundamental rights. They view fundamental rights as structures consisting of two parts: namely an inner core, in which the state may not interfere, and a core-surrounding part, the limitation of which is not by definition precluded.[65] Such limitation is constitutional when the requirements of proportionality (*Verhältnismäßigkeit*) are met, which require that a limitation is suitable, necessary and proportional in the narrow sense.[66] In turn, when it comes to the core area of a right, the requirement of proportionality does not apply.[67] There can be no justification for interfering with the *Wesen* of a

---

[61] Ibid., 60. See also 62 ff.

[62] See, generally, ibid., 62 ff. Commentators/authors that (explicitly) favour an absolute view are, for example, Jarass 2016 (n. 19), no. 9; Chlosta 1975 (n. 52); Dürig 1956 (n. 46); Enders 2012 (n. 21), no. 31; Herbert 1985 (n. 8); Jäckel 1967 (n. 26); Krüger 1955 (n. 36); Bernhard Schlink, *Abwägung im Verfassungsrecht* (Berlin: Duncker & Humblot, 1976); Stern 1994 (n. 10), 865 ff.

[63] Drews 2005 (n. 5), 62.   [64] See, for example, Krüger 1955 (n. 36), 599.

[65] Drews 2005 (n. 5), 63.

[66] See, on the requirement of proportionality, also Ch. 3, S. 3.3.2.

[67] Dreier 2013 (n. 4), no. 16.

constitutional right, i.e., there are no higher-ranking goods that would allow such interference.[68] The protection of a right's core is unqualified and thus not balanced against the gains of the impugned measure.

In an early comment on the *Wesensgehaltsgarantie*, Krüger argues that even though limits to fundamental rights are necessary, the Constitution grants absolute priority to citizens' autonomy: in the end it is up to the citizen to decide whether and how to make use of core rights.[69] This conclusion aligns with the wording 'in no case', which suggests that there is no room for legitimate interferences. Moreover, the *Bundesverfassungsgericht* has held that, because of this wording, '[t]he question, under which circumstances such an interference can exceptionally be accepted, is of no relevance'.[70] At the same time, it appears that balancing exercises are not always avoided.[71] Authors point out that the German Constitutional Court's case law is neither consistent, nor clear on this matter.

Absolute protection would imply that not even for the protection of the rights of others can an individual be limited in the exercise of his core rights.[72] Herbert, however, contends that in the case of conflicts between (core) fundamental rights, protection is sometimes necessarily merely relative.[73] In his view, the guarantee will apply only if there is no such conflict, i.e., if a limitation serves public aims that do not directly relate to fundamental rights.

Although most authors appear to favour an absolute understanding of core rights, little is said on what exactly the *Wesen* of the different fundamental rights enshrined in the German Constitution consist of. It is agreed that the *Wesensgehalt*, in any case, is interfered with when any 'right to fend off interferences is annulled substantively or its efficient invocation is procedurally precluded'.[74] What follows from the case law, as well, is that the content of the *Wesensgehalt* should be determined for each fundamental right separately.[75] Moreover, if a fundamental right provides for multiple obligations, directions of protection and functions, the *Wesensgehalt* will have to be interpreted for these different aspects separately.[76]

Herbert nevertheless attempts to provide some overarching insights on the core content of fundamental rights. He does not equal the *Wesensgehalt* with the protection that is left over after a proportionality test has

[68] See Stern 1994 (n. 8), 867; Brüning 2010 (n. 7), no. 40; Sachs 2014 (n. 20), no. 41.
[69] Krüger 1955 (n. 36), 597.   [70] BVerfGE 7, 377 (411).
[71] See, for example, BVerfGE 80, 367 (373).   [72] Krüger 1955 (n. 36), 599.
[73] Herbert 1985 (n. 8), 333.   [74] BVerfGE 61, 82 (113).
[75] BVerfGE 22, 180 (219) and BVerfGE 109, 133 (156).   [76] Remmert 2012 (n. 4), no. 40.

taken place. Instead, he argues for a positive understanding, which can play a guiding role when reviewing to which extent a substantive aspect of a fundamental right deserves to be protected.[77] This guiding principle determines whether or not a proportionality test is necessary in the first place. The starting point must be the material scope of a right, from which the *Wesensgehalt* can be inferred.[78]

A few more guidelines Herbert identifies are the following:[79] first of all, the character and function of fundamental rights provides some guidance. Fundamental rights belong to individuals, and as such they primarily serve to guarantee self-determination in fields typically imperilled by state powers, as well as secure the conditions and possibilities for the self-development, participation and contribution of the individual in the community. The more the freedom of the individual concerns a social relation or function, the broader the authority of the legislature can be understood. This does however not mean that the *Wesensgehalt* is limited to aspects of the private sphere. Various individual freedoms move beyond this sphere and concern, for example, public speech, or association and assembly.

Second, human dignity also forms a guiding principle that ensures a minimal level of individual autonomy and social dignity.[80] It is regularly held that the *Wesensgehaltsgarantie* is comparable to the guarantee of human dignity that is listed in Article 1(1) GG ('Human dignity shall be inviolable').[81] The point that this would render Article 19(2) GG redundant can be reason to hold differently.[82] Herbert in this regard suggests that the core of a right at least includes the aspects of this right that concern human dignity, but that these do not exhaust the *Wesensgehalt*. It however remains unclear whether the additional aspects of the *Wesensgehalt* should also be determined through the lens of human dignity. What comes closest to human dignity is what potentially should be protected as core elements as well.

Third, Herbert argues that comparative insights can be helpful in determining the *Wesensgehalt* of a right. This means that other bodies of law or legal obligations may help in clarifying the contours of a right's core. One could think of prohibitions following from the ECHR or *ius cogens*,

---

[77] Herbert 1985 (n. 7), 333.   [78] Ibid., 331.   [79] Ibid., 332.   [80] Ibid.
[81] Brüning 2010 (n. 9), no. 41; Sachs 2014 (n. 20), no. 43; Borowski 2007 (n. 59), 288; Stern 1994 (n. 8), 873 f.; Jarass 2016 (n. 19), no. 9.
[82] Brüning 2010 (n. 7), no. 41. Cf. also Enders 2012 (n. 21), no. 28.

though these arguably present an absolute minimum that mostly does not reach the level of protection that is or should be granted by Article 19(2) GG.[83] However, since his article was written, international legal standard setting – not in the least by the ECtHR – has expanded significantly. Nonetheless, comparative insights can form the stepping-stones for carving out the minimum protected by Article 19(2) GG.[84]

Altogether, absolute theories do not merely imply that a core is absolutely protected, but also that the meaning of this core is 'absolute', i.e., established in an abstract, case-independent fashion. They hold that there needs to be a predetermined area that the legislature, as well as the executive and the judiciary, cannot touch upon. This need not mean that the core of a right can never change. Even when it is not dependent on the particular circumstances of an individual case, a right's core can be considered dynamic and can change over time.[85] If it is understood that fundamental rights relate to social realities that are subject to constant change, the same can be said of these rights and – at least to some extent – their essential aspects.[86] In this way, the strictness of the absolute theory can be nuanced.

4.3.3   Core Protection as Proportionality

According to a relative understanding of the *Wesensgehaltsgarantie*, the essence of a right does not constitute an absolute, predetermined boundary to limitations to the exercise of that right. Rather, it is something that needs to be determined in the context of a specific case by balancing the different interests.[87] A relative *Wesensgehalt* does not preclude a proportionality test; the *Wesen* of a right is in fact that what is left over once such a test has been performed.

---

[83] Herbert 1985 (n. 8), 332–333.   [84] See also Ch. 5, S. 5.2.2; Ch. 6, S. 6.1.2.
[85] Drews 2005 (n. 5), 65–66.   [86] Herbert 1985 (n. 8), 334.
[87] See, generally, Drews 2005 (n. 5), 66 ff.; Remmert 2012 (n. 4), no. 36 ff.; Stern 1994 (n. 8), 867–868; Borowski 2007 (n. 59), 287f.; Sachs 2014 (n. 20), nos. 42.; Enders 2012 (n. 21), no. 29 ff.; Jarass 2016 (n. 19), no. 9; Dreier 2013 (n. 4), nos. 17–8; Brüning 2010 (n. 7), nos. 40f. For some supporters of a relative theory, see Von Hippel 1965 (n. 55); Zivier 1960 (n. 4); Walter Hamel, *Die Bedeutung der Grundrechte im sozialen Rechtsstaat. Eine Kritik an Gesetzgebung und Rechtsprechung* (Berlin: Duncker & Humblot, 1957); Robert Alexy, *A Theory of Constitutional Rights*, transl. Julian Rivers (Oxford University Press, 2002); Häberle 1983 (n. 39); Arthur Kaufmann, 'Über den "Wesensgehalt" der Grund- und Menschenrechte', *Archiv für Rechts- und Sozialphilosophie*, 70 (1984), pp. 384–399; Borowski 2007 (n. 59).

In this regard, a relative understanding of the *Wesensgehalt* implies that Article 19(2) GG *de facto* equals the German *Verhältnismäßigkeitsgrundsatz* (principle of proportionality).[88] According to Von Hippel, every fundamental rights norm can only be effectuated, if and to the extent there are no higher-ranking conflicting interests.[89] Limitations of fundamental rights are, according to this view, always allowed, as long as they serve interests that outbalance the individual fundamental right at stake.[90] When general (societal) interests prevail, the *Wesensgehalt* of the individual right is by definition not interfered with.[91] Instead, this signals that the limitation is actually in compliance with Article 19(2) GG. Only when it is decided whether a measure is proportional does it become clear what the *Wesensgehalt* could entail in the first place.

Zivier also considers the *Wesensgehaltsgarantie* to be redundant. He mentions three crucial starting points for rendering rights definitive. First of all, attention has to be paid to the fundamental rights norm itself. Second, account must be taken of the possibility to limit this right, and, third, of the relation between this possibility and the fundamental rights norm.[92] From this he infers that the core content of a right can only be determined when both the right and the limitation are considered. And this, according to Zivier, is only possible with the help of the principle of proportionality.[93]

Alexy also sees a close relation between core rights protection and proportionality. This ties in with his idea of fundamental rights as principles,[94] meaning that fundamental rights are optimization requirements that can be fulfilled to different degrees depending on the legal and factual possibilities. When a fundamental right conflicts with another principle, neither takes precedence per se. Rather, their relation is determined by the principle of proportionality.[95] Alexy's theory implies that even when a very important individual interest is at stake, this alone cannot be reason to have it prevail.[96] The prima facie rights that follow

---

[88] Von Hippel 1965 (n. 55); Hamel (n. 87) 1957; Zivier 1960 (n. 4). See further Drews 2005 (n. 5), 67–68. Cf. also Dreier 2013 (n. 4), nos. 17–18.; Sachs 2014 (n. 20), no. 42; Brüning 2010 (n. 7), no. 40. See on the requirement of proportionality, Ch. 3, S. 3.3.2.

[89] Von Hippel 1965 (n. 55), 25–26. Cf. also 47.

[90] Indeed, it is not necessary that the countervailing interests are of a fundamental (rights) nature. Cf. Herbert 1985 (n. 8), 333, who instead holds that *only* when this is the case, a core right can be relative.

[91] Von Hippel 1965 (n. 55), 47.   [92] Zivier 1960 (n. 4), 76 ff.   [93] Ibid., 79.

[94] Alexy 2002 (n. 87). See Ch. 3, S. 3.1. See also Borowski 2007 (n. 59), 287–8.

[95] Alexy 2002 (n. 87), 65.

[96] This follows from the 'Law of Balancing', see ibid., 102; Ch. 3, S. 3.3.2.

from constitutional provisions can always – depending on the concrete circumstances – be outbalanced. What matters is the relation between the degree of interference and the importance of satisfying the competing interest.

Alexy by no means denies that there are limits to limitations of fundamental rights.[97] These limits however cannot be determined at the outset, but are always dependent on the requirement of *Angemessenheit*, i.e., proportionality in the narrow sense. Referring to the *Wesensgehaltsgarantie* in particular, Alexy holds that '[t]he absolute theory goes too far in saying that there are legal positions such that no possible legal reason can ever restrict them'.[98] He does not deny that there are conditions under which it is very likely that there is no conflicting principle that can ever take precedence. When this is the case, essential cores become visible. Such a conclusion is, however, still something relative; it is grounded on a specific relation between the different principles at stake, and a possibility always remains that competing principles do take precedence in case the facts are different.[99] Borowski concurs with Alexy's interpretation: he holds that even though what follows from the proportionality test is a 'rule-like core', this rule nevertheless remains dependent on a rights-principle being balanced against conflicting principles. The upshot is hence that the *Wesensgehaltsgarantie* has no self-standing significance, and that there cannot be an authoritative definition of an absolute core.[100]

And still, the conclusion that a right's core can never be affected as long as other interests are of higher importance remains somewhat counterintuitive. After all, fundamental rights secure interests against the will of the majority, and should therefore not be entirely dependent on countervailing state interests. Hamel attempts to provide a solution by referring to the 'social aspect' of fundamental rights.[101] He holds that the constitutional-political meaning of fundamental rights comprises a socio-political one. Individual rights inherently relate to human coexistence. They do not only concern individual freedoms, but duties as well.[102] Referring to the freedom of profession, as well as to the protection of property and the freedom of association, Hamel stresses that rights (and their cores) must be understood in the light of their purpose in a social *Rechtsstaat*.[103] It is the task of the state to develop the values of

---

[97] Ibid., 192.   [98] Ibid., 195   [99] Ibid., 195–6.   [100] Borowski 2007 (n. 59), 290.
[101] Hamel 1957 (n. 87), 23–24, 38–39.   [102] Ibid., 23–24.   [103] Ibid., 39.

human coexistence. Limitations of fundamental rights that are necessary to serve this goal cannot be said to interfere with the *Wesen* of these rights.[104] Indeed, the *Wesen* of a right cannot be determined without considering such limitations.

Häberle's theory argues against the *Eingriffs- und Schrankendenkens*, i.e., the idea of prima facie rights and their limitations that is predominant in German constitutional law.[105] He does not regard freedom, and the constitutional rights that protect individual freedoms, as 'areas of individual discretion' that are independent from legislative practice.[106] According to this interpretation, rights are understood as boundless, at least before they are restricted 'from outwards'.[107] Häberle instead focuses on the interrelatedness of freedom and law.[108] He argues that it is generally misconceived that freedom and law refer to each other, which in the context of fundamental rights implies that these rights form a system of 'regulated freedom'. Fundamental rights are not limited by the legislature, but instead have immanent boundaries. They are not only defensive, but belong to the state instead, and have the aim to protect incorporated citizens rather than purely autonomous ones.[109] The task of the legislature is therefore to identify the boundaries of fundamental rights in the sense that every limitation is in fact a determination of the content of a right.[110]

For the *Wesensgehaltsgarantie* this means that the core of a right is not something that can be determined independently from the Constitution as a whole, including interests other than fundamental rights.[111] Also Häberle sees a role for the requirement of proportionality as enabling the demarcation of rights.[112] In this regard, his relative theory does not depart from the other relative views outlined here. Nevertheless, whereas Alexy, amongst others, builds his relative theory on the idea that individuals have broad, prima facie rights that should be upheld to the greatest extent possible, Häberle does not distinguish between a prior fundamental right and a right as limited. In fact, he does not recognize something like a right's prima facie scope, as rights and their cores can only exist in context.

Kaufmann, finally, explicitly rejects an institutional characterization of fundamental rights. He is sceptical when it comes to the *Wesensgehalt* as

---

[104] Ibid., 41 ff.   [105] Häberle 1983 (n. 39), 3.   [106] Ibid., 152.
[107] Ibid., 51 ff., 126 ff. Cf. Ch. 3, S. 3.1.   [108] Ibid., 152, 161, 225.   [109] Ibid., 19.
[110] Ibid., 180.   [111] Ibid., 58.   [112] Ibid., 31, 51, 58. Cf. also 125.

it is commonly understood, namely in a substance-ontological sense.[113] From his point of view, the search for a substantial *Wesensgehalt* is useless. Law, according to Kaufmann, is relational, rather than substantive. Rights cannot be understood in a meaningful way other than in relation to other rights and rights bearers; law exists by virtue of an adequate relation between these.[114] Although Kaufmann avoids the term *Wesensgehalt*, as he believes there cannot be such a thing,[115] he, in fact, does the same as the other relativists, namely determining the limits to limitations with the help of a circumstantial proportionality test.[116]

The different relative theories have in common that they emphasize the interdependence of rights and other goods. They do not recognize a core that is determined in advance and plays a guiding role in the adjudicative process by defending a particular area of freedom against interferences. Rather, they state that what can be considered the *Wesen* of a right always has to be determined by taking into account countervailing interests. This *Wesen* might still be considered to be absolutely protected in the sense that it cannot be interfered with, which is in fact what Article 19(2) GG dictates. It is, however, relative because what the core is cannot be determined in an absolute way. The main difference between the different relative theories, then, is that some focus on the technical impossibility of avoiding a balancing test for determining whether an interference with a prima facie right is justified (e.g., Alexy, Borowski), whereas others stress the socio-political or institutional character of fundamental rights (e.g., Hamel, Häberle). The latter thereby abolish the idea of a bifurcated approach and determining a prima facie right in the first place. Such an approach, I argued in Chapter 3, is not desirable in the context of supranational fundamental rights protection.

Conclusion

Core rights are generally understood to place a limit on rights' limitations. They find their genesis in the idea that fundamental rights guarantee a sphere of individual liberty in which the power of the legislature is not unlimited. In other words, even though it is accepted that most fundamental rights can be limited, their cores must remain intact. The idea of limits to limitations has found expression in the German Basic Law. Article 19, Section 2, of Germany's post-war Constitution holds that

---

[113] Kaufmann 1984 (n. 87), 390 ff.   [114] Ibid., 393.   [115] Ibid., 392.
[116] Drews 2005 (n. 5), 70–71.

'In no case, can the core of a right be infringed upon'. While not understood to be a self-standing fundamental right, a failure to comply with this *Wesensgehaltsgarantie* is unconstitutional. The intricate doctrinal debate that has resulted from this provision provides insights on core rights protection more generally. Important for the purposes of this study is that the core of a right can also be interfered with in the context of positive rights, i.e., when 'too little' has been done by the legislature or in fact by any of the other branches, as the importance of the *Wesensgehaltsgarantie* suggests that all of these are bound.

The more precise content of the *Wesen* of fundamental rights is controversial. I explained that the debate centres first on the question of whether Art. 19(2) GG ensures objective or subjective protection. The former understanding allows for circumventing the problems associated with core rights protection in individual cases, while it must be admitted that the latter best fits the purpose of constitutional rights as we know it. The *Wesensgehaltsgarantie* hardly finds any explicit mention in the case law of the German *Bundesverfassungsgericht*. This can be explained by the second debate, in which many authors prefer a relative over an absolute understanding of rights' cores. That is to say, they equal the *Wesensgehaltsgarantie* with the requirement of proportionality, holding that there can be no absolute determination of core content but only a case-specific consideration of whether the core has been successfully avoided.

5

Minimum Cores and the Scope of
Fundamental Rights

Core rights not only function as limits to limitations. Especially in the context of economic and social fundamental rights, they may perform other roles, too. This chapter is reserved for a discussion of core rights in relation to the scope of rights. Where socio-economic rights are concerned, the issue is often not whether and to what extent these rights may be infringed upon, but what socio-economic arrangements are required qua rights in the first place. Here, core rights may aid in translating broadly phrased socio-economic rights norms into concrete legal entitlements.

The examples presented in this chapter will be drawn from the protection of socio-economic rights at the international and constitutional levels. Because of this focus, the core rights lessons they offer are of particular relevance for this study. In order to comprehend the potential role of core rights for the protection of socio-economic rights under the ECHR, besides the particularities of the European Convention system, the specific character of these rights must be taken into account. When socio-economic rights are concerned, the term used is generally that of 'minimum cores' or 'minimum core obligations'. This refers to the recognition of core aspects that constitute the most basic guarantees or obligations connected to a particular socio-economic right.

The chapter starts with a discussion of the minimum core obligations recognized in relation to the International Covenant on Economic, Social and Cultural Rights (ICESCR) (Section 5.1). There, the concept of core rights has been developed as a response to the challenge of monitoring compliance with rights that are subject to the requirement of progressive realization. Another example of the potential of minimum core protection is set against the backdrop of South Africa's transformative Constitution. On the basis of this model Constitution for the protection of economic and social rights, the Constitutional Court of South Africa (CC) has developed a reasonableness standard that is frequently cited. As I show in Section 5.2, however, this has not silenced the debate on the use of the minimum core for socio-economic rights adjudication, and more specifically for giving content to these rights. A final, again constitutional, example of minimum socio-economic protection comes from Germany in Section 5.3. The right to an *Existenzminimum* (subsistence minimum) follows from the guarantee of human dignity in conjunction with the social state principle. It corroborates the insights central to this chapter, and allows for connecting them more directly to the practice of the ECtHR.

5.1   The ICESCR and Minimum Core Obligations

5.1.1   The Requirement of Progressive Realization

The idea of minimum core obligations in the field of economic and social rights is generally considered to be introduced by the United Nations Committee on Economic, Social and Cultural Rights (CESCR), the body responsible for monitoring the implementation of the ICESCR. The notion has its genesis in this Committee's General Comment No. 3 from 1990 on the nature of states parties' obligations.[1] Yet only by taking a broader look at the international protection of economic and social rights can the idea and purpose of minimum core obligations be fully traced.

In Chapter 1, it was already mentioned that the 1948 Universal Declaration of Human Rights (UDHR) contains a nearly complete range of fundamental rights.[2] However, the UDHR is merely a declaratory document and the rights it contains had to be listed in a binding international bill of rights in order to arrange actual legal effect. As the result of extensive discussions, and under pressure from the Western-dominated United Nations Commission on Human Rights, the United Nations General Assembly eventually agreed to create not one such bill, but to divide the rights into two separate covenants.[3] Those favouring this separation 'argued that civil and political rights were enforceable, or justiciable, or of an "absolute" character, while the economic, social and

---

[1]   CESCR, General Comment No. 3: The Nature of States Parties' Obligations (Art. 2(1) of the Covenant), 14 December 1990, E/1991/23, para. 10 (General Comment No.3).

[2]   See Ch. 1, S. 1.1.1.

[3]   See the analysis, prepared by the United Nations, of the drafting process: Annotations on the Text of the Draft International Covenants on Human Rights, Tenth Session, 1 July 1995, UN Doc. A/2929, 7. See also Matthew C. R. Craven, *The International Covenant on Economic, Social and Cultural Rights* (Oxford University Press, 1995), 17–20.

cultural rights were not or might not be'.[4] The latter rights were regarded as not truly individual and as requiring the state to take positive action.[5]

When devising the two separate covenants, it was stressed that they had to resemble each other to the greatest possible extent.[6] Yet even a superficial glance at both treaties reveals that their set-up and wording differs in significant respects. Whereas the International Covenant on Civil and Political Rights (ICCPR) generally uses terms as 'everyone has the right to … ', or 'no one shall … ', the ICESCR instead speaks of 'states parties' that 'recognize the right of everyone to … '. A crucial difference, moreover, follows from Article 2(1) ICESCR. Laying out the obligations of states, and thus forming the keystone of the Covenant, this article stipulates that:

> Each State Party to the present Covenant undertakes to take steps, individually and through international assistance and co-operation, especially economic and technical, *to the maximum of its available resources*, with a view to *achieving progressively* the full realization of the rights recognized in the present Covenant by all appropriate means, including particularly the adoption of legislative measures.[7]

In other words, the extent to which ICESCR rights – such as the right to work, social security or the highest attainable standard of health – must be guaranteed is not necessarily the same for all states, but subject to the resources available. Moreover, the standard of implementation of the ICESCR is that of 'progressive realization'. This means that its rights can be realized to various degrees.[8] There are no such qualifications in the ICCPR, which contains obligations of result prohibiting interferences with rights unless there is an adequate justification.

---

[4] Annotations on the Text of the Draft International Covenants on Human Rights, 8. Cf. also Asbjørn Eide, 'Economic, Social and Cultural Rights as Human Rights' in A. Eide, C. Krause and A. Rosas (eds.), *Economic, Social and Cultural Rights: A Textbook*, second revised edn (Leiden: Martinus Nijhoff Publishers, 2001), pp. 9–28, 10.

[5] Annotations on the Text of the Draft International Covenants on Human Rights, 8.

[6] Ibid., 7.

[7] Art. 2(1) ICESCR [emphasis added]. Art. 2(1) of the ICCPR instead establishes the obligation of each State Party 'to respect and ensure' the rights recognized therein.

[8] See, for an elaborate discussion of this requirement, Ben Saul, David Kinley and Jacqueline Mowbray, *The International Covenant on Economic, Social and Cultural Rights: Commentary, Cases, and Materials* (Oxford University Press, 2014), Ch. 3, and in particular 151–157. Cf. also Craven 1995 (n. 3), 129–134; Philip Alston and Gerard Quinn, 'The Nature and Scope of States Parties' Obligations under the International Covenant on Economic, Social and Cultural Rights', *Human Rights Quarterly*, 9 (1987), pp. 156–229, 172–177.

Even though Article 2(1) is in line with practical realities and the perceived differences between the two types of human rights, the progressive realization standard is said to have hindered the conceptualization as well as the monitoring of ICESCR rights.[9] On one hand, it acknowledges that the obligations under the ICESCR may be so onerous that not every state will be able to comply with them straightaway.[10] Rather than resigning to the fact that a right would then simply not be guaranteed at all, the obligation is meant to ensure that at least best efforts are being made. The non-fulfilment of a right in its entirety should not stand in the way of guaranteeing it to the extent the available resources allow. On the other hand, it can be asked whether this exception does justice to the importance of socio-economic rights and the fact that the difference between these rights and their civil and political counterparts is, at least to some extent, artificial. The realization of civil and political rights can, after all, also be costly and difficult. Moreover, the requirement of progressive realization arguably provides 'a loophole large enough in practical terms to nullify the Covenant's guarantees: the possibility that states will claim lack of resources as the reason they have not met their obligations'.[11] Particularly in the light of the 'availability of resources' phrasing, the obligation to progressively guarantee economic and social rights can become empty.[12] Theoretically speaking, a state can always claim that at a particular moment in time, due to a lack of resources, it simply could not comply with one or more aspects of an ICESCR right. Because the available resources differ from state to state, the progressive realization standard recognizes an element of subjectivity that entails that obligations are not uniform or universal, and that may obscure evaluating compliance with the Covenant.[13]

---

[9] Audrey R. Chapman and Sage Russell, 'Introduction' in A.R. Chapman and S. Russell (eds.), *Core Obligations: Building a Framework for Economic, Social and Cultural Rights* (Antwerp/Oxford/New York: Intersentia, 2002), pp. 1–19, 4.

[10] Ibid., 5–6. However, even though realization may vary in different contexts, the requirement of progressive realization is understood as in principle prohibiting retrogressive measures. See, for example, CESCR, General Comment No. 3, para. 9.

[11] Ibid., 5.

[12] Henry J. Steiner, Philip Alston and Ryan Goodman, *International Human Rights in Context: Law, Politics, Morals*, 3rd ed. (Oxford University Press, 2007), 275. But cf. the Limburg Principles on the Implementation of the International Covenant on Economic, Social and Cultural Rights, UN doc. E/CN.4/1987/17, Annex, reprinted in *Human Rights Quarterly*, 9 (1987), 125, para. 21.

[13] Cf. Audrey R. Chapman, 'A "Violations Approach" for Monitoring the International Covenant on Economic, Social and Cultural Rights', *Human Rights Quarterly*, 18 (1996), pp. 23–66.

It is a challenge, per se, to identify effective approaches to the implementation of ICESCR rights. In May 2013, the Optional Protocol to the ICESCR entered into force, allowing for individual and collective communications. At the beginning of 2017, however, only twenty-two states have ratified this protocol and only few communications have yet been considered.[14] Primarily, the CESCR supervises the implementation of the Covenant on the basis of regular reports by the States Parties. But supervising whether states comply with the requirement of progressive realization in the light of their particular resource constraints brings significant methodological challenges. Only on the basis of correct and precise information is it possible to assess whether states are indeed using all means available for moving expeditiously towards full implementation of the ICESCR rights.[15] Thus, no matter how sensible the obligations defined in Article 2(1) may appear at first glance, they have significantly complicated the CESCR's monitoring efforts. The possibilities of the requirement of progressive realization in the light of available resources to improve the ICESCR's effectiveness have proven limited – at least, that is, when taken on their own.

5.1.2   Immediate Core Obligations

Even with plenty of data available it remains difficult to determine what progressively moving towards full implementation of ICESCR rights *in concreto* entails. The requirement does not clarify whether it suffices to spend the available resources on whatever states think is relevant for complying with the Covenant, as long as it can be considered as a step towards complete realization, or whether more specific action is required. When the need to specify the ICESCR's content and actual obligations became more pressing, it was therefore recognized that there are certain elements of the Covenant that need to be fulfilled immediately. In 1986, a group of experts convened by the International Commission of Jurists came together in the province of Limburg in the Netherlands. They

---

[14] See United Nations General Assembly, Optional Protocol to the International Covenant on Economic, Social and Cultural Rights: Resolution/Adopted by the General Assembly, 5 March 2009, A/RES/63/117, and for ratifications, indicators.ohchr.org.

[15] See, for example, Audrey R. Chapman and Sage Russell (eds.), *Core Obligations: Building a Framework for Economic, Social and Cultural Rights* (Antwerp/Oxford/New York: Intersentia, 2002), 5; Chapman 1996 (n. 13), 29 ff. See also Sandra Fredman, *Human Rights Transformed: Positive Rights and Positive Duties* (Oxford University Press, 2008), 82; Saul et al. 2014 (n. 8), 143–144.

elaborated on state obligations belonging to economic and social rights, which resulted in the Limburg Principles.[16] Paragraph 8 of these Principles holds that '[a]lthough the full realization of the rights recognized in the Covenant is to be attained progressively, the application of some rights can be made justiciable immediately while other rights can become justiciable over time'.[17] A distinction was thus made between duties that have to be satisfied instantaneously and requirements that – should the available resources not allow for their immediate satisfaction – could be fulfilled at a later point. Some of the immediate duties could be inferred directly from the text of the ICESCR. Article 2(2) of the Covenant, for example, holds that states must undertake 'to guarantee that the rights enunciated in the present Covenant will be exercised without discrimination of any kind ... '. It was considered that this requirement is of such importance that immediate realization is warranted.[18]

Next to pinpointing certain ICESCR provisions that require full compliance from the outset, a second way of identifying immediate obligations was proposed consisting of highlighting the importance of certain particular aspects of ICESCR rights. In 1987, Philip Alston, then Rapporteur of the Committee, wrote about its endeavours to clarify the normative content of these rights.[19] Stating that 'each right must ... give rise to a minimum entitlement, in the absence of which a state party is in violation of its obligations',[20] he propelled the idea that every economic and social right contains specific (substantive) elements that should be fulfilled forthwith.

Consider, for example, the right to health (Article 12(1) ICESCR)[21] or to social security (Article 9 ICESCR).[22] These rights are phrased in vague terms such as 'the highest attainable standard of physical and mental

---

[16] These principles have also been called the 'best guide available to state obligations under the CESCR' (Eide 2001 (n. 4), 25).

[17] Limburg Principles, 124, para. 8.

[18] See, for example, Chapman and Russell 2002 (n. 15), 6. The non-discrimination requirement is further emphasized in Article 3 ICESCR. See also the Limburg Principles, 125, paras. 22 and 35.

[19] Philip Alston, 'Out of the Abyss: The Challenges Confronting the New UN Committee on Economic, Social and Cultural Rights', *Human Rights Quarterly*, 9 (1987), pp. 332–381, 352 ff.

[20] Ibid., 353. Cf. also the Limburg Principles, 126, para. 25, para. 28.

[21] 'The States Parties to the present Covenant recognize the right of everyone to the enjoyment of the highest attainable standard of physical and mental health.'

[22] 'The States Parties to the Present Covenant recognize the right of everyone to social security, including social insurance.'

health', thereby allowing for a very broad interpretation, including very costly and far-reaching obligations. Alston admitted that in most cases it is impossible to fulfil these rights immediately.[23] However, this should not mean that there are no aspects of these rights that should be fulfilled first and foremost. Pointing out the 'core elements' of the different rights norms, Alston suggested, could help make them more workable and effective. As Bilchitz later put it: 'The notion of progressive realisation must thus be read to include as a base-line the provision of minimum essential levels of a right which the state is then required to build upon'.[24]

Three years after Alston's article was published, the CESCR endorsed the idea of 'minimum core obligations' when adopting its third General Comment, entitled *The Nature of States Parties Obligations*. Paragraph 10 states that:

> On the basis of the extensive experience gained by the Committee, as well as by the body that preceded it, over a period of more than a decade of examining States parties' reports the Committee is of the view that *a minimum core obligation to ensure the satisfaction of, at the very least, minimum essential levels of each of the rights is incumbent upon every State party*. Thus, for example, a State party in which any significant number of individuals is deprived of essential foodstuffs, of essential primary health care, of basic shelter and housing, or of the most basic forms of education is, prima facie, failing to discharge its obligations under the Covenant. If the Covenant were to be read in such a way as not to establish such a minimum core obligation, it would be largely deprived of its raison d'être. By the same token, it must be noted that any assessment as to whether a State has discharged its minimum core obligation must also take account of resource constraints applying within the country concerned. Article 2 (1) obligates each State party to take the necessary steps 'to the maximum of its available resources'. In order for a State party to be able to attribute its failure to meet at least its minimum core obligations to a lack of available resources it must demonstrate that every effort has been made to use all resources that are at its disposition in an effort to satisfy, as a matter of priority, those minimum obligations.[25]

The Committee thus differentiated between guaranteeing the core elements of a right and ensuring full compliance. Even though account can

---

[23] Alston 1987 (n. 19), 352.

[24] David Bilchitz, 'Towards a Reasonable Approach to the Minimum Core: Laying the Foundations for Future Socio-Economic Rights Jurisprudence', *South African Journal on Human Rights*, 19 (2003), pp. 1–26, 12. Cf. also Fredman 2008 (n. 15), 84.

[25] CESCR, General Comment No. 3. para. 10 [emphasis added].

still be had to possible resource constraints,[26] such constraints do not relieve states of their duty to guarantee the minimum core of a right. If a minimum core obligation has not been complied with, it is up to the state to demonstrate that every effort has been made to use its limited resources in order to meet the most basic requirements of the Covenant.[27] Implicit herein is the obligation that even when resources are limited, the distribution thereof should be adjusted so as to enable the fulfilment of at least minimum essential levels of the ICESCR rights, i.e., those aspects that are considered to belong to these rights' core.

The minimum core can be said to narrow down the problematically wide scope of the economic and social rights listed in the ICESCR. As Alston explained: 'The fact that there must exist such a core (which to a limited extent might nevertheless be potentially subject to derogation or limitations in accordance with the relevant provisions of the Covenant) would seem to be a logical implication of the use of the terminology of rights'.[28] The normative content of rights cannot be so indeterminate as to give a rightsholder 'no particular entitlement to anything'.[29] When no further differentiation within the potential reach of socio-economic rights is made, the result may be that any thinkable claim can become a trivial one. With the help of minimum cores, a rather vague notion of what these rights *in concreto* require is replaced by the clear-cut expectation that at least their core must be respected. The minimum core guides the way in which a state should move towards full realization by pointing out what should be done first. In turn, this makes it easier to monitor their achievements, and it may prevent states from arguing that scarce resources were used for other purposes as a means towards full compliance.

A possible point of criticism is that working with minimum cores creates the danger that expectations as well as achievements will not rise above a certain minimum level. It might threaten the broader goals of protecting economic and social rights.[30] Nevertheless, it can also be

---

[26] This is evidenced by the fact that this leads to a prima facie failure of the state to discharge its obligations (ibid.).

[27] Cf. Fredman 2008 (n. 16), 85.   [28] Alston 1987 (n. 19), 352.

[29] Ibid., 353. Cf. also Fredman 2008 (n. 15), 70 ff; Craig Scott and Philip Alston, 'Adjudicating Constitutional Priorities in a Transnational Context: A Comment on *Soobramoney*'s Legacy and *Grootboom*'s promise', *South African Journal on Human Rights*, 16 (2000), pp. 206–268, 227.

[30] Fredman 2008 (n. 15), 84 ff.; Katharine G. Young, *Constituting Socio-Economic Rights* (Oxford University Press, 2012), 69–71.

argued that a less inclusive definition of rights actually enhances their workability and effectiveness, too. According to Young, this

> reflects a 'minimalist' rights strategy, which implies that maximum gains are made by minimizing goals. It also trades rights-inflation for rights ambition, channeling the attention of advocates towards the severest cases of material deprivation and treating these as violations by states towards their own citizens or even to those outside their territorial reach.[31]

The mere requirement of progressive realization provides states with an argument as to why certain aims could not have been achieved. At the same time, it fails to provide an answer to the problem that it is difficult, if not impossible, to control whether all available means were at least spent on furthering the increase of the standard of protection in the first place. Minimum cores prevent states from using their limited resources in the way they see fit. They guarantee that attention is directed to the fulfilment of basic guarantees, i.e., to ensuring minimum levels of the various socio-economic rights.[32] When these are not complied with, there is a prima facie breach of the Covenant. It is then up to the state to adduce evidence for the fact that it could not allocate its (scarce) resources so that at least the minimum core would be guaranteed. Thus, rather than showing what limitations are allowed for, core socio-economic rights conceptually clarify what should be guaranteed qua rights in the first place. When determining prima facie rights, in other words, the idea of core rights allows for differentiating between core and other obligations. This mitigates expectations while setting standards that cannot be considered lightly. As I will explain later, in a similar vein core rights may also help the ECtHR in determining what the ECHR prima facie requires in terms of socio-economic protection.[33]

5.2   Core Rights and Reasonableness: The South African Debate

5.2.1   Adjudicating Socio-Economic Rights

This chapter aims to set out how core rights can be used for determining the scope of rights. The example of the ICESCR, however, fails to show

---

[31] Katharine G. Young, 'The Minimum Core of Economic and Social Rights: A Concept in Search of Content', *Yale Journal of International Law*, 33 (2008), pp. 113–175, 113–114. See also Young 2012 (n. 30), 66, fn. 3.

[32] See, for a further discussion on the content of the minimum core, Ch. 6, S. 6.1.

[33] Ch. 7, S. 7.2 and 7.3.1; Ch. 8.

what this means in the context of individual legal positions. Although this might change with the Optional Protocol, at the UN level there is not yet an elaborate body of case law in which the implications of minimum core obligations have been fleshed out.[34] Used primarily for monitoring purposes, this example thus leaves open the question what the effect of the minimum core can be in terms of subjective entitlements, and remains silent on the role of courts and case-based adjudication in this regard. The South African example makes up for this lacuna. The South African Constitution is famous for enumerating individual socio-economic rights that have been rendered explicitly justiciable. Courts are given 'the power to interpret these rights and to resolve disputes on their basis'.[35] Because of this, and because the development of this competence has gone hand in hand with a lively debate on the use of minimum core rights, the South African experience provides a particularly valuable source for this study.

In what follows, I will explore the potential of core rights protection for the adjudication of economic and social rights claims by presenting the South African debate on this issue, including the stance taken by the South African Constitutional Court (CC). I will outline several early landmark cases and the choice these cases presented between reasonableness review and core rights protection. The academic debate that followed, however, has been able to overcome this dichotomy, illuminating, amongst other things, the possibility of a less rigid minimum core approach. In order to grasp all this, however, something must first be said on the South African Constitution.

During the negotiations on the drafting of the post-apartheid Constitution of South Africa (Constitution) of 1996,[36] a vigorous debate took place on whether economic and social rights had to be

---

[34] ICESCR, An Evaluation of the Obligation to take Steps to the 'Maximum of Available Resources' under an Optional Protocol to the Covenant, 10 May 2007, E/C.12/2007/1 (indicating the potential role of the minimum core for considering communications under the OP). Views have thus far been adopted in a *M.A. López Rodríguez v. Spain*, Communication No. 1/2013 and *I.D.G. v. Spain*, Communication No. 2/2014. See Ch. 6, S. 6.2.

[35] Danie Brand, 'Socio-Economic Rights and the Courts in South Africa: Justiciability on a Sliding Scale' in F. Coomans (ed.) *Justiciability of Ecnomic and Social Rights: Experiences from Domestic Systems* (Antwerp/Oxford/New York: Intersentia, 2006), pp. 207–236, 208; see S. 38, 167, 169, and 172 of the South African Constitution.

[36] The Constitution of the Republic of South Africa (Act no. 108, 1996). Entered into force on 4 February 1997.

included.[37] The aim of the new Constitution was to facilitate the transformation of South African society, i.e., 'the dismantling of racist and sexist laws and institutions, redressing their legacy, healing the divisions of the past and building a new society committed to social justice and the improvement in the quality of people's lives'.[38] In the light of this, most political parties agreed on, and civil society organizations were clearly in favour of, incorporating justiciable economic and social rights norms.[39] Objections that the inclusion of socio-economic rights was in breach of the doctrine of separation of powers, and the budgetary and policymaking prerogatives of the nonjudicial branches, could not counteract this sentiment.[40] When the CC had to judge on the first draft of the new Constitution, it held that '[i]t cannot be said that by including socio-economic rights within a bill of rights, a task is conferred upon the courts so different from that ordinarily conferred upon them by a bill of rights that it results in a breach of the separation of powers'.[41] Moreover, the CC noted that economic and social rights were 'at least to some extent, justiciable',[42] leaving nothing standing in the way of their eventual incorporation.[43]

---

[37] See, for example, Nicholas Haysom, 'Constitutionalism, Majoritarian Democracy and Socio-Economic rights', *South African Journal on Human Rights*, 8 (1992), pp. 451–463; Etienne Mureinik, 'Beyond a Charter of Luxuries: Economic Rights in the Constitution', *South African Journal on Human Rights*, 8 (1992), pp. 464–474; Dennis Davis, 'The Case against the Inclusion of Socio-Economic Demands in a Bill of Rights Except as Directive Principles', *South African Journal on Human Rights*, 8 (1992), pp. 475–490.

[38] Sandra Liebenberg, 'South Africa: Adjudicating Social Rights Under a Transformative Constitution' in M. Longford (ed.), *Social Rights Jurisprudence: Emerging Trends in International and Comparative Law* (Cambridge University Press, 2008), pp. 75–101, 76 [footnote omitted].

[39] Ibid. Cf. also Cass R. Sunstein, *Designing Democracy: What Constitutions Do* (Oxford University Press, 2001), 224.

[40] See, for example, Liebenberg 2008 (n. 38), 77; Paul O'Connell, *Vindicating Socio-Economic Rights: International Standards and Comparative Experiences* (London: Routledge, 2012), 50–51.

[41] *Ex parte Chairperson of the Constitutional Assembly: In re Certification of the Constitution of the Republic of South Africa 1996* (First Certification judgment) 1996 (4) SA 744 (CC), para. 77.

[42] Ibid., para 78.

[43] The Constitutional Court subsequently approved of the revised Constitution, see *Ex parte Chairperson of the Constitutional Assembly: In re Certification of the Amended Text of the Constitution of the Republic of South Africa 1996* (Second Certification judgment) 1997 (2) SA 97 (CC).

The economic and social rights norms taken up in the 1996 Constitution illuminate the character of these rights. Section 26, first of all, covers the right to access to adequate housing:

1. Everyone has the right to have access to adequate housing.
2. The state must take reasonable legislative and other measures, within its available resources, to achieve the progressive realisation of this right.
3. No one may be evicted from their home, or have their home demolished, without an order of court made after considering all the relevant circumstances. No legislation may permit arbitrary evictions.

Section 27 deals with health care, food, water and social security:

1. Everyone has the right to have access to
   (a) health care services, including reproductive health care;
   (b) sufficient food and water; and
   (c) social security, including, if they are unable to support themselves and their dependants, appropriate social assistance.
2. The state must take reasonable legislative and other measures, within its available resources, to achieve the progressive realisation of each of these rights.
3. No one may be refused emergency medical treatment.

Both provisions contain 'internal limitations',[44] i.e., the second paragraphs of the respective sections indicate that the rights should be realized progressively, while taking account of the available resources. They resemble Article 2(1) ICESCR and signal that complete, immediate fulfilment is not expected.

Besides Sections 26 and 27, Sections 28, 29 and 35(2)(e) can be mentioned, covering children's rights, educational rights and the socioeconomic rights of detained prisoners, respectively.[45] The right to education contains, amongst other things, 'the right ... to further education, which the state, through reasonable measures, must make progressively available and accessible'.[46] But except for this clause, these rights do not

---

[44] Cf. Pierre de Vos, 'Pious Wishes or Directly Enforceable Human Rights? Social and Economic Rights in South Africa's 1996 Constitution', *South African Journal on Human Rights*, 13 (1997), pp. 67–101, 92 ff.
[45] Moreover, in S. 24 rights related to the environment are taken up.
[46] S. 29(1)(b) of the Constitution.

contain internal limitations. However, Section 36 of the Constitution provides for a 'general limitation clause', which reads as follows:

> (1) The rights in the Bill of Rights may be limited only in terms of law of general application to the extent that the limitation is reasonable and justifiable in an open and democratic society based on human dignity, equality and freedom, taking into account all relevant factors, including
> (a) the nature of the right;
> (b) the importance of the purpose of the limitation;
> (c) the nature and extent of the limitation;
> (d) the relation between the limitation and its purpose; and
> (e) less restrictive means to achieve the purpose.
> (2) Except as provided in subsection (1) or in any other provision of the Constitution, no law may limit any right entrenched in the Bill of Rights.

All socio-economic rights, thus, may be justifiably limited – given that the criteria mentioned in Section 36 are met. Together with the internal limitation clauses, this qualification sets the stage for the adjudication of these rights, as well as for the potential of core rights therein.[47] Paradoxically, though, like in the CESCR context, this potential does not so much center on the determination of justifiable limits to limitations, but rather on the scope, or content, of socio-economic rights before such limitations come into play.

The transformative character of the Constitution places a particular onus on the judiciary, vesting in it the power to adjudicate socio-economic rights claims and thereby contribute to the country's development.[48] Some early landmark cases show how it embarked on this task, employing the different provisions to develop its renowned standard of socio-economic rights review. Shortly after the enactment of the Constitution, the Constitutional Court had to decide on the case of *Soobramoney v.*

---

[47] Cf. De Vos 1997 (n. 44), 95.

[48] O'Connell 2012 (n. 40), 54. See also Dikgang Moseneke, 'Transformative Adjudication', *South African Journal on Human Rights*, 18 (2002), pp. 309–319, 316; Pius Langa, 'The Vision of the Constitution', *South African Law Journal*, 120 (2003), pp. 670–679, 671–672; Geoff Budlender, 'The Role of the Courts in Achieving the Transformative Potential of Socio-Economic Rights', *ESR Review*, 8 (2007), pp. 9–11, 9; Craig Scott, 'Towards a Principled, Pragmatic Judicial Role', *ESR Review*, 1 (1999), pp. 4–7, 4; Sandra Liebenberg, *Socio-Economic Rights: Adjudication under a Transformative Constitution* (Cape Town: Juta and Company, 2010), Ch. 2.

Minister of Health, KwaZula-Natal.[49] The applicant, Mr Soobramoney, suffered from irreversible kidney failure, but was not admitted to a dialysis programme as he did not qualify under the terms of the hospital's policy. Lacking the money needed to go to a private clinic, the refusal of treatment in a public hospital meant that he was going to die. The applicant relied on Section 11 (right to life) and Section 27(3) (the right to emergency medical treatment) of the Constitution, seeking a positive order to provide him with ongoing treatment and admit him to the renal unit of the hospital. The Constitutional Court, however, did not grant him such order. If it would decide in favour of Soobramoney, and thus in favour of numerous others in a similar position, so the Court argued, this would have unbearable consequences for the health care budget. It would be to the detriment of other people's care and other needs in general.[50] In reaching this conclusion, the Court applied a deferential method of review, stating that 'a court will be slow to interfere with rational decisions taken in good faith by the political organs and medical authorities whose responsibility it is to deal with such matters'.[51]

Legal scholars initially received the *Soobramoney* judgment as an anti-climax.[52] Hopes, after all, were high with regard to the Court's new, transformative role in the area of economic and social rights protection. And yet, as Scott and Alston noted, *Soobramoney* turned out to be a first careful step into this new field rather than a predictor of a forever reluctant approach.[53] In the following landmark case, the CC did find a violation of a socio-economic right. In *Government of the Republic of South Africa v. Grootboom and Others*,[54] the question was whether the state's housing program was in accordance with Section 26 of the

---

[49] Soobramoney v. Minister of Health, KwaZula-Natal, 1997 (12) BCLR 1696 (CC) (*Soobramoney*).

[50] Ibid., para. 28. Cf. Lon L. Fuller, 'The Forms and Limits of Adjudication', *Harvard Law Review*, 92 (1978), pp. 353–394, 371 ff., who describes the problem of 'polycentricity in adjudication' of which this is a typical example. See also Davis 1992 (n. 37), 477–478; Scott and Alston 2000 (n. 29), 252–253.

[51] *Soobramoney*, para. 29. See, for example, Darrel Moellendorf, 'Reasoning about Resources: Soobramoney and the Future of Socio-Economic Rights Claims', *South African Journal on Human Rights*, 14 (1998), pp. 327–333; Fredman 2008 (n. 165, 116 (characterizing the Court's test as a 'rationality test'); Mantouvalou, in Conor Gearty and Virginia Mantouvalou, *Debating Social Rights* (Oxford: Hart Publishing, 2011), 144–145.

[52] See, for example, O'Connell 2012 (n. 40), 56; Moellendorf 1998 (n. 51), 327.

[53] Scott and Alston 2000 (n. 29), 241.

[54] Government of the Republic of South Africa v. Grootboom & Others 2001 (1) SA 46 (CC) (*Grootboom*).

Constitution (the right to access to adequate housing). Mrs Grootboom and the other applicants had for a long time lived in shacks on a recognized settlement called Wallecedence. The living conditions there were intolerable; there was no water or sewage, and hardly any electricity. Some applicants had applied for subsidized low-cost housing, but had been on a waiting list for seven years. Finally, the applicants left Wallecedence and moved to private land, which they occupied unlawfully and from which they were subsequently evicted for that reason. Because they had nowhere else to go, they asked the Constitutional Court for an order that would direct the state to provide them with 'adequate basic temporary shelter or housing . . . pending their obtaining permanent accommodation'.[55] The CC did not grant such an order because it considered that Section 26 did not entitle the applicants to immediate housing or shelter.[56] Nevertheless, it did find that the state's housing program was unconstitutional. The reason for this was that the program did not sufficiently accommodate any short-term housing needs of vulnerable groups. According to the Court '[a] program that excludes a significant segment of society cannot be said to be reasonable'.[57]

Compared to *Soobramoney*, the CC in *Grootboom* articulated a more nuanced approach characterized by 'reasonableness review'.[58] Rather than recognizing a self-standing right on the basis of this provision, it asked 'whether the measures taken by the state to realise the right afforded by section 26 are reasonable'.[59] In so doing, 'the Court laid the foundations for its future adjudication of socio-economic rights'.[60] I now turn to the debate on whether the choice for reasonableness, and against the minimum core, provides a sufficient starting point for socio-economic rights adjudication.

5.2.2   Debating the Minimum Core

While some applauded the outcome of *Grootboom* and the promise of the 'administrative law approach' it signalled,[61] others regretted that the

---

[55] Ibid., para. 57.   [56] Ibid., para. 86.   [57] Ibid., para. 43.

[58] See, for example, O'Connell 2012 (n. 40), 57.

[59] *Grootboom*, para. 33. Cf. also para. 41.

[60] Murray Wesson, '*Grootboom* and Beyond': Reassessing the Socio-Economic Jurisprudence of the South African Constitutional Court', *South African Journal on Human Rights*, 20 (2004), pp. 284–308, 285.

[61] Cf. Sandra Liebenberg, 'The Right to Social Assistance: The Implications of *Grootboom* for Policy Reform in South Africa', *South African Journal on Human Rights*, 17 (2001),

Court had opted for a reasonableness test.[62] They would have favoured an alternative approach that had been suggested to the Constitutional Court. In *Grootboom, amici curiae* had invited the Court to give content to the right at stake by identifying the 'core' of the obligations it imposed on the state.[63] Under the heading 'The content of the positive obligations imposed by social and economic rights', they suggested that it, in line with the CESCR, determine a concrete, immediate entitlement: 'The "core" provides a level of minimum compliance, to which resources have to be devoted as a matter of priority. This duty clearly has to be balanced with the obligation to put into operation programmes aimed at full realisation of the right, and to move progressively towards full realisation'.[64] The *amici* were not of the opinion that only core socio-economic rights could be subject to review by a court. Rather, they tried to convince the CC that in order to provide genuine protection, there had to be an obligation 'to provide for the core of immediate absolutely basic human needs – which will result in special attention being given to the most vulnerable and those living in most unfavourable conditions'.[65] Yet the Court was not willing to come up with a minimum core definition of what Article 26 requires. It held that such a definition would be problematic as needs and opportunities of different individuals may vary significantly.[66] Whereas '[t]he committee [the CESCR] developed the concept of minimum core over many years of examining reports by reporting states', the CC claimed that it did not have sufficient information to do the same.[67] Explaining why reasonableness review was the preferred way of approaching socio-economic rights claims, Justice Yacoob noted that 'a wide range of possible measures could be adopted by the state to meet its obligations'. Reasonableness review means that a court does not enquire whether 'more desirable or favourable measures'

---

pp. 232–357; Pierre de Vos, '*Grootboom*, The Right of Access to Housing and Substantive Equality as Contextual Fairness', *South African Journal on Human Rights*, 17 (2001), pp. 258–276; Cass R. Sunstein, 'Social and Economic Rights? Lessons from South Africa', *Constitutional Forum*, 11 (2000–2001), pp. 123–132, 123, 130–132.

[62] David Bilchitz, *Poverty and Fundamental Rights: The Justification and Enforcement of Socio-Economic Rights* (Oxford University Press, 2007), 139 ff.; Marius Pieterse, 'Resuscitating Socio-Economic Rights: Constitutional Entitlements to Health Care Services', *South African Journal on Human Rights*, 22 (2006), pp. 473–502, 475; Theunis Roux, 'Understanding *Grootboom* – A Response to Cass R. Sunstein', *Constitutional Forum*, 12 (2002), pp. 41–51.

[63] *Grootboom*, Heads of the argument on behalf of the *amici curiae*.   [64] Ibid., para. 27.

[65] Ibid., para. 29. See Liebenberg 2010 (n. 48), 149.   [66] *Grootboom*, para. 33.

[67] Ibid., para. 32.

were available, or 'whether public money could have been better spent'.[68] It leaves prioritization to the state,[69] merely asking if the government policy is reasonable. In *Grootboom*, the government was directed to make 'reasonable provision within its available resources for people ... with no access to land, no roof over their heads, and who were living in intolerable situations'.[70] The Constitutional Court did not require it, however, to make provision for these groups as a matter of priority before spending its resources elsewhere. It did not directly engage with the individual right protected by Section 26, but rather chose to place the leeway of the government in the foreground.

The reasonableness approach was further consolidated in *Minister of Health & Others v. Treatment Action Campaign & Others (TAC)*.[71] The CC held here that 'determinations of reasonableness may in fact have budgetary implications, but are not in themselves directed at rearranging budgets'.[72] The case concerned the government's refusal to provide Nevirapine to HIV-positive pregnant women.[73] Because the efficacy and possible side effects of the drug were being carefully monitored, Nevirapine was only available at designated test sites. This limitation was held to be unreasonable, and for that reason unconstitutional. In the Court's view, the cost implications of providing the drug were negligible, and there was no serious doubt about the safety of Nevirapine. The CC therefore ordered the removal of any restrictions on the availability of Nevirapine and instructed the government to dispense it.[74]

Notwithstanding the fact that the CC's standard of review led to finding a violation, the *TAC* judgment has been criticized for not giving content to what should have been central to the case, namely the right to health care enshrined in Article 27(1)(a).[75] Again *amici curiae* had argued that the CC should identify a minimum core, but it expressly rejected this suggestion, holding that 'it is impossible to give everyone access even to a core service immediately. All that is possible and all that

---

[68] Ibid., para. 41.

[69] But see Sunstein 2000–2001 (n. 61), 127; Roux (2002, (n. 62) 46–47).

[70] *Grootboom*, para. 99.

[71] Minister of Health & Others v. Treatment Action Campaign & Others 2001 (5) SA 721 (CC) (*TAC*).

[72] *Ibid.*, para. 38.

[73] Nevirapine is an antiretroviral drug of which a tablet has to be given to mothers at the onset of labour, and a few drops to a just-born baby, in order to prevent mother-child transmission of HIV.

[74] *TAC*, para. 135.   [75] Bilchitz 2003 (n. 24), 8.

can be expected of the state, is that it act reasonably to provide access to the socio-economic rights ... on a progressive basis'.[76] In line with this, it reasoned that

> [i]t should be borne in mind that in dealing with such matters the courts are not institutionally equipped to make the wide-ranging factual and political enquiries necessary for determining what the minimum-core standards call for ... The Constitution contemplates rather a restrained and focused role for the courts, namely to require the state to take measures to meet its constitutional obligations and to subject the reasonableness of these measures to evaluation.[77]

In the years after *Soobramoney*, *Grootboom* and *TAC*, the CC has shown that it is sometimes willing to take a less distant stance towards the government. In *Khosa and Mahlaule v. Minister for Social Development*, for example, it rejected the government's resource defence regarding the exclusion of social welfare grants to non–South African citizens and linked the overarching concepts of dignity and equality to the socio-economic rights at stake.[78] More recent cases have, however, not altered its conclusion that there is no room for determining minimum cores. A reasonableness standard, although being infused by substantive requirements giving it the necessary 'bite',[79] remains the hallmark of the Constitutional Court's overall applauded socio-economic rights review.

The Court's deferential review of a complaint concerning the right to water combined with a rejection of its minimum core in the 2010 case of *Mazibuko and Others v. City of Johannesburg*, however, has been severely criticized.[80] More generally, the Court's determination has not prevented

---

[76] *TAC*, para. 35.   [77] Ibid., paras. 37–38.

[78] Khosa v. Minister of Social Development, 2004 (6) BCLR 569 (CC). See, for example, also Rail Commuters Action Group v. Transnet Ltd., 2005 (4) BCLR 301 (CC), para. 88; See O'Connell 2012 (n. 40), 62 ff.

[79] Cf. Katharine G. Young, 'Proportionality, Reasonableness, and Socio-Economic Rights' (20 January 2017) in V.C. Jackson and M. Tushnet (eds.) *Proportionality: New Frontiers, New Challenges* (Cambridge University Press, forthcoming 2017); Boston College Law School Legal Studies Research Paper No. 430. Available at SSRN: https://ssrn.com/abstract=2892707 (on proportionality infused reasonableness).

[80] Mazibuko and others v. City of Johannesburg, 2010 (4) SA 1 (CC). According to David Bilchitz, 'Socio-Economic Rights, Economic Crisis, and Legal Doctrine', *International Journal of Constitutional Law*, 12 (2014), pp. 710–739, 727, it exemplifies the fact that '[t]he underlying rationale behind the reasonableness approach appears to be that it requires the government to provide justifications for its actions'. It was held in this case that 'social and economic rights enable citizens to hold government to account for the manner in which it seeks to pursue the achievement of social and economic rights' (para. 59). In doing so, however, the Court failed to identify a minimum core standard,

a continuing debate on the 'core rights alternative'. Both structural and substantive arguments have been fleshed out in favour of, as well as against, ameliorating judicial socio-economic rights protection with the help of core rights. First of all, supporters of the minimum core stress that reasonableness review, without first elaborating upon what exactly is protected by the different rights, immediately shifts the attention to Sections 26(2) and 27(2), and thus to the conduct of the state. This fails to do justice to the two-stage approach to fundamental rights adjudication, the benefits of which I have outlined earlier in this book.[81] Speaking of the South African case law, Liebenberg holds that

> [t]he two-stage approach entails an initial principled focus on the nature and scope of the relevant right and whether the impugned legislation or conduct infringes the right. Thereafter the burden is placed on the respondent to establish that limitations to the right are reasonable and justifiable according to the stringent requirements of the general limitations clause (s 36).[82]

Because the first step is missing, what is left, in Liebenberg's view, is a disproportionate focus on the state's justificatory arguments.[83] In line with this, Bilchitz asserts that the CC's approach in *TAC* 'is guilty of failing to integrate ss 27(2) and 27(1): it focuses the whole enquiry on s 27(2) without providing a role for s 27(1)'.[84] Thereby, it 'deflects the focus of constitutional enquiry from the urgent interests at stake ... and allows these to be overshadowed by a general balancing of multiple considerations'.[85]

It is argued that a minimum core approach could ensure that individual rights obtain a space apart from resource constraints and other reasons for the government not to meet socio-economic needs. Bilchitz in this regard does not agree with the *amici* in *TAC* who argued that two causes of action could follow from Section 27.[86] They held that the first paragraph stated a free-standing individual right containing a minimum core that could be requested immediately. The second paragraph, which

---

as it did not clarify what the right to 'sufficient water' entails. See David Bilchitz, 'Does Sandra Liebenberg's New Book Provide a Viable Approach to Adjudication Socio-Economic Rights?', *South African Journal on Human Rights*, 27 (2011), pp. 546–557, 554.

[81] Ch. 3, S. 3.1.   [82] Liebenberg 2010 (n. 48), 141.   [83] Ibid., 139, 146.

[84] Bilchitz 2003 (n. 24), 9; Bilchitz 2007 (n. 63), 159.

[85] Bilchitz 2007 (n. 62), 176. See also Marius Pieterse, 'Coming to Terms with Judicial Enforcement of Socio-Economic Rights', *South African Journal on Human Rights*, 20 (2004), pp. 383–417, 410–411.

[86] Bilchitz 2003 (n. 24), 5–6; Bilchitz 2007 (n. 62), 156.

holds that reasonable legislative and other measures must be taken to progressively achieve these rights within the available resources, would, according to the *amici*, have to be read as separately conferring positive obligations on the state.[87] The Court was right, according to Bilchitz, to hold that rather than being independent from one another both paragraphs of the rights' norm are intrinsically linked. However, claiming that the obligations in the second paragraph are related to the rights in 26 (1) and 27(1) implies that measures the state adopts must be assessed in the light of these rights.[88] In order for a court to do so, it cannot simply rely on the rights norms as these are stated: because of their broad wording and the fact that they need not be fulfilled entirely immediately, Sections 26(1) and 27(1) cannot as such provide a standard against which the reasonableness of the measures taken by the government can be tested.[89]

According to Bilchitz, having an end in mind against which the measures taken can be reviewed requires the recognition of certain aspects of socio-economic rights as containing immediate, core obligations. Lacking clarity on the core and non-core content of a right would make reasonableness 'stand in for whatever the Court regards as desirable features of state policy'.[90] Moreover, it would leave the other branches of government with an amorphous standard from which to judge their own conduct.[91] These points, indeed, very much resemble the reasons for introducing the minimum core in the context of the ICESCR.[92] Yet here, case-based adjudication is concerned. The minimum core enables a court to 'provide clear reasons for its involvement in these cases, and a clear statement of the important interests involved which would demarcate the scope of its own decision-making powers'.[93]

This leads to the second point, namely that core rights do not merely highlight some aspects of rights, but rather their most important aspects. '[W]hen there are interests protected by a right that differ in their degree of importance for human beings',[94] it makes sense to secure that some of these are prioritized.[95] In the words of Liebenberg:

---

[87] Amicus Brief *TAC*, para. 14.
[88] Bilchitz 2003 (n. 264), 10. See also Bilchitz 2007 (n. 62), 156–157.
[89] Cf. also Sunstein 2001 (n. 61), 132.   [90] Bilchitz 2003 (n. 24), 10.
[91] Ibid.; Bilchitz 2007 (n. 62), 162.   [92] S. 5.1.2.   [93] Bilchitz 2003 (n. 24), 10.
[94] Ibid., 14.
[95] Ibid., 11–12; Bilchitz 2007 (n. 62), 187 ff. Cf. also Scott and Alston 2000 (n. 29), 250–251.

> [T]he meeting of minimum core obligations should enjoy prioritized consideration in social policymaking and in the judicial enforcement of these rights, due to the urgency of the interests they protect. Without the meeting of the minimum essential needs which people require to survive, the State's obligation to progressively achieve the full realization of the rights becomes meaningless.[96]

In the view of its proponents, a minimum core approach can direct resources to where they are most needed, thereby fulfilling the purpose of socio-economic rights. It ensures that the notion of progressive realization does not exempt the state from immediately – or at least as a matter of priority – protecting its population's most basic interests.[97]

Others have, however, sympathized with the Constitutional Court's rejection of the minimum core. The Court's practical point that minimum core protection is unrealistic since it is 'impossible to give everyone access even to a 'core' service immediately'[98] has been corroborated by the elaboration of more normative arguments endorsing the choice for a reasonableness-based approach.[99] First of all, it is argued that 'the Court's circumspection avoids an escalation of separation of powers and other tensions'.[100] Were the Court to engage in defining and enforcing core rights, it might usurp the policy-making tasks of the government.[101]

---

[96] Liebenberg 2010 (n. 48), 164.

[97] Ibid.; Bilchitz 2003 (n. 24), 12; Bilchitz 2007 (n. 62), 193–194, giving the example of the progressive realization of the right to housing as involving two components.

[98] TAC, para. 35.

[99] See, for example, Albie Sachs, 'The Judicial Enforcement of Socio-Economic Rights', Current Legal Problems, 56 (2003), pp. 579–601; Paul Nolette, 'Lessons learned from the South African Constitutional Court: toward a Third Way of Judicial Enforcement of Socio-Economic Rights', Michigan State Journal of International Law, 12 (2003), pp. 91–119, 116–118; Mark S. Kende, 'The South African Constitutional Court's Embrace of Socio-Economic Rights: A Comparative Perspective', Chapman Law Review, 6 (2003), pp. 137–160, 153; Mark S. Kende, 'The South African Constitutional Court's Construction of Socio-Economic Rights: A Response to the Critics', Connecticut Journal of International Law, 19 (2004), pp. 617–629; Wesson 2004 (n. 61); Bruce Porter, 'The Crisis of Economic, Social and Cultural Rights and Strategies for Addressing it' in J. Squires, M. Langford and B. Thiele (eds.), The Road to a Remedy: Current Issues in the Litigation of Economic, Social and Cultural Rights (Australian Human Rights Centre in collaboration with the Centre for Housing Rights and Evictions, 2005), pp. 43–69, 48–55; Carol Steinberg, 'Can Reasonableness Protect the Poor? A Review of South Africa's Socio-Economic Rights Jurisprudence', South African Law Journal, 123 (2006), pp. 264–284; Karin Lehmann, 'In Defense of the Constitutional Court: Litigating Socio-Economic Rights and the Myth of the Minimum Core', American University International Law Review, 22 (2006), pp. 163–197.

[100] Kende 2004 (n. 99), 618.   [101] See on this argument Liebenberg 2010 (n. 48), 165.

Courts are seen as institutionally ill-equipped for making the enquiries necessary to determine enforceable minimum standards. Controlling for reasonableness, instead, enables the 'judicial, legislative and executive functions [to] achieve appropriate constitutional balance'.[102] Now that its institutions of constitutionalism and judicial review are still relatively young, such constitutional balance is considered a delicate issue in South Africa.[103] The CC's authority and the acceptance of its judgments are said to root 'as much in its ability to insinuate itself institutionally in conflicts over the separation and distribution of powers as ... in its defence of rights'.[104] Judicial activism thus needs to be avoided.[105]

The second, related branch of criticism of the minimum core builds on the virtues of institutional dialogue. Whereas the separation of powers argument underscores the distinct tasks of the different powers, the dialogue argument articulates the ideal of cooperation between them.[106] Dixon, for example, has recognized the important role of courts in helping to improve socio-economic rights by pointing out 'blind spots' and omissions to the legislature.[107] In her view, it is for the legislature to respond to such findings. In the dialogue argument, the minimum core idea represents an 'intrusive, rule-based' approach.[108] Aiming at defining an essence for economic and social rights that is incontestable, it leads to closure and obstructs any form of conversation between the legislator and the judiciary that could provide for better outcomes, both in terms of institutional cooperation and effective protection.[109] Yet Dixon differentiates between 'relying on a truly cosmopolitan, or international understanding of the minimum core' and 'borrowing the conceptual apparatus of the minimum core as an independent basis for interpreting sections 26 and 27 of the South African Constitution at the domestic level'.[110] The former

---

[102] *TAC*, para. 38.
[103] Cf., for example, Steinberg 2006 (n. 99), 274; Fredman 2008 (n. 15), 114.
[104] Heinz Klug, *Constituting Democracy: Law, Globalism and South Africa's Political Reconstruction* (Cambridge University Press 2000), 159.
[105] Cf. Kende 2004 (n. 99).
[106] See, for example, Craig Scott, 'Reaching Beyond (Without Abandoning) the Category of Economic, Social and Cultural Rights', *Human Rights Quarterly*, 21 (1999), pp. 633–660; Steinberg 2006 (n. 99); Rosalind Dixon, 'Creating Dialogue about Socio-Economic Rights: Strong Form Versus Weak-Form Judicial Review Revisited', *International Journal of Constitutional Law*, 5 (2007), pp. 391–418.
[107] Dixon 2007 (n. 106), 404–405.   [108] Steinberg 2006 (n. 99), 274.
[109] Cf. Dixon 2007 (n. 106), 407; Liebenberg 2010 (n. 48), 167–168; Young 2008 (n. 31), 138–140.
[110] Dixon 2007 (n. 106), 415–416.

approach – using the minimum cores identified by the CESCR – is less problematic: because the CESCR explicitly looks at consensus amongst states, this approach signals cooperation rather than foreclosing it.[111]

In fact, according to Dixon, only the second type of approach is questionable. This approach encourages courts to use the abstract concept of the minimum core to provide it with content in a subjective manner. It would enable the South African Constitutional Court to unilaterally develop a domesticated understanding of socio-economic rights' most important aspects, creating obligations that have to be enforced in every conceivable case. This would require the CC to ignore the scope of existing and future disagreement on the nature and prioritization of, as well as the values underpinning, socio-economic rights.[112]

Underlying the scepticism towards (domestic) minimum core protection is the assumption that it is difficult, if not impossible, to objectively identify the core of rights.[113] If socio-economic policy choices are to be made, they should be executed by the legislature or the executive. Courts should refrain from determining what they cannot determine, and avoid the minimum core. A normative approach towards defining the minimum core is often based on a single metric. This can be the idea of basic needs or biological survival, the notion of freedom or that of the inviolability or sanctity of human life. Liebenberg notes that this type of principle unavoidably leads to the definition of minimum cores that are either overinclusive or underinclusive.[114] It can be argued, for example, that the most essential aspect of the right to access to housing is fulfilled once someone is not sleeping on the streets. Yet in some contexts, this may be unnecessarily minimalistic as it is feasible for a higher standard to be required. On the other hand, in the case of the right to health, for example, a survival-based core might require the provision of expensive, tertiary health care, even where this is impossible. Moreover, no matter what definition of a core right is chosen, it will necessarily overlook other needs and interests.[115] Guaranteeing a minimum core can be to the detriment of rights of others that might seem less crucial if looked at in isolation or from a single point of view – but that can, in fact, be just as important.[116] If a minimum core doctrine were used at all, therefore, it

---

[111] Cf. CESCR, General Comment No. 3. para. 10.   [112] Dixon 2007 (n. 108), 416–417.
[113] Cf. Lehmann 2006 (n. 99), 185.
[114] Liebenberg 2010 (n. 48), 168. See also Ch. 6, S. 6.3.1.   [115] Ibid., 169–170.
[116] Ibid., 170.

seems that this core should be determined by taking account of the particular context, i.e., in a case-by-case fashion.[117]

5.2.3   Beyond a Core Rights/Reasonableness Dichotomy

A closer look at the arguments of those who are critical of the Constitutional Court's reasonableness approach shows that reasonableness and core rights protection are not poles apart. At least, that is, when the minimum core is not perceived as setting an absolute, inflexible standard. In the final part of this section, I discuss two comprehensive suggestions for improving the South African Constitutional Court's socio-economic rights review. Both give an idea of how the minimum can infuse such review without completely taking over.

Liebenberg, to start with, has been one of the most active contributors to the debate on the development of South Africa's socio-economic rights protection. In her 2010 book *Socio-Economic Rights: Adjudication under a Transformative Constitution*, she presents an approach characterized by 'democratic deliberation in the ongoing processes of transforming the current status quo'.[118] Her proposal for improving socio-economic rights adjudication starts from the CC's reasonableness test. She considers this test appropriate as it places the burden on the government to explain that the measures it has taken were reasonable. As a result, it 'avoids closure and creates the ongoing possibility of challenging various forms of socio-economic deprivations in a wide range of different contexts'.[119] Nevertheless, Liebenberg admits that reasonableness review can be problematic when it 'conflates the two-stage approach to constitutional analysis'.[120] In her view, 'until some understanding is developed of the content of the right, the assessment of whether the measures adopted by the state are reasonably capable of facilitating its realization takes place in a normative vacuum'.[121]

Liebenberg asks how the model of reasonableness review 'can be developed so as to ensure a more substantive engagement with the purposes and underlying values of socio-economic rights'.[122] She opines

---

[117] See, for example, Danie Brand, 'The Minimum Core Content of the Right to Food in Context: A Response to Rolf Künneman' in D. Brand and S. Russell (eds.), *Exploring the Core Content of Economic and Social Rights: South African and International Perspectives* (Pretoria: Protea Book House, 2002), pp. 99–108, 101 ff.

[118] Liebenberg 2010 (n. 48), 29.   [119] Ibid., 173–174.   [120] Ibid., 175.

[121] Ibid., 176, referring to Bilchitz 2007 (n. 62), 143.   [122] Liebenberg 2010 (n. 48), 179.

that courts should be required 'to make a conscious effort to develop the normative content of the various socio-economic rights'.[123] This would prevent reasonableness review from degenerating into an overly marginal or unprincipled method of review.

Liebenberg rejects a strict minimum core approach not only because it might lead to closure, but also because it is based on a single metric and cannot respond to the facts of the case at hand.[124] Besides the idea of dialogue, the importance of context, as well as that of value pluralism, underlies her approach. The task of developing the normative content of rights, in her view, 'should be approached by considering the purposes and values which the rights seek to promote in the light of their historical and current socio-economic context'.[125] In this regard, she does see a small role for the minimum core doctrine, namely in determining the burden of justification that lies on the state, as well as in directing priority attention to people's basic needs.[126] Liebenberg thus argues in favour of a minimum core that cannot be equalled to the content of a right, but rather is one of the factors that colours the reasonableness test.[127] The fact that a core right is at stake should be one of the considerations relevant to determining whether the governments' conduct was reasonable, rather than a decisive standard that, when failed to comply with, results in a violation. This minimum core in her view should not be determined on the basis of a single normative starting point. Instead, the enquiry of what it entails

> should be primarily guided by a context-sensitive assessment of the impact of the deprivation on the particular group. In assessing the severity of the impact, the courts should consider the implications of the lack of access to the resource or service in question for other intersecting rights and values such as the rights to life, freedom and security of the person, equality and human dignity. This accords with an interpretive approach which embraces the interdependence between various constitutional rights and values.[128]

---

[123] Ibid., 180.   [124] See, for her various critical points, ibid., 163–173.   [125] Ibid., 180.

[126] Ibid., 184–185.

[127] Ibid., 173: '[T]he minimum core concept need not be located within a rigid, two-tier approach to the adjudication of socio-economic rights but can . . . play an important role in the evaluation of the reasonableness of the State's measures in realising socio-economic rights.' And at 184: 'The valuable contribution of the concept of minimum core obligations . . . should be incorporated in the reasonableness analysis by placing a particularly heavy burden of justification on the State in circumstances where a person or group lacks access to a basic socio-economic service or resource corresponding to the rights in ss 26 and 27.'

[128] Ibid., 185. Cf. also 173.

Thus, as long there is no conclusive prioritization of some aspects of a right over others and the minimum core is grounded on a variety of important values, thereby being relative or at least context-sensitive, Liebenberg does not completely oppose the idea of the minimum core. Byrne has held in this regard that

> Liebenberg's advocacy of having a more substantive minimum interpret- ation that will actually address the socio-economic situation of the most marginalized seems at odds with her opposition to attempts to define progressively and expansively the minimum core for many of the sub- stantive rights. As jurisprudence continues to develop both domestically and internationally (the imminent coming into force of the complaints mechanism to the International Covenant on Economic, Social and Cul- tural Rights could make a significant difference to our understanding of the minimum core) one senses that the anti-minimum core arguments will be less persuasive over time.[129]

In line with this, Liebenberg's cautious inclusion of the minimum core in 'substantive reasonableness review' can be seen as clearing the way for a more comprehensive role giving content to socio-economic rights. Nevertheless, it is still something other than acceptance of the minimum core as a self-standing instrument for defining the content of the right at the first stage of fundamental rights review. For this we must turn to Bilchitz, whose more fully developed minimum core approach is however more nuanced than the understanding which opponents of the concept – including the South African Constitutional Court – generally rely on.[130]

With regard to Liebenberg's approach, Bilchitz holds that 'one cannot have it both ways': Liebenberg wants substantive content *and* flexibility, but Bilchitz argues that 'the more content that is given to a right by a court, the less it remains open for contestation and determination in the future; the more open it remains, the less content it has and the less it provides individuals and communities with the concrete entitlements to enforce in the future'.[131] Fixed content, according to Bilchitz, need not be avoided. Rather, 'it is the very stuff of law that makes rights meaningful'.[132]

In his *Poverty and Fundamental Rights: The Justification and Enforce- ment of Socio-Economic Rights* (2007), Bilchitz indeed does not shy away

---

[129] Iain Byrne, 'Sandra Liebenberg, *Socio-Economic Rights: Adjudication under a Trans- formative Constitution*' (Book review), *Human Rights Law Review*, 12 (2012), pp. 183–186, 185.
[130] Bilchitz 2007 (n. 62).   [131] Bilchitz 2011 (n. 80), 549.   [132] Ibid., 550.

from fixed content. What he attempts to show is that a robust statement on the content of a right, in the form of the recognition of a minimum core, is indispensable for the proper adjudication of the socio-economic rights enshrined in South Africa's Constitution. Bilchitz criticizes the CC's failure to give content to the rights the Constitution protects by focusing on the requirement of reasonableness in the light of the constitutionally mandated ends. These ends, in his view, 'cannot themselves be determined by the reasonableness enquiry and, thus, the approach on its own fails to generate any useful conclusions'.[133] Rather than reasoning purely on a case-by-case basis, moreover, 'it will be necessary for ... [a court] to provide a certain amount of general content to a right that will enable it to reach the decision it does in that case. For it may be questioned how decisions are to be made in a particular context without some general principles to guide the decision-making'.[134]

In determining the general, principled content of rights, Bilchitz considers it important to take account of the 'different levels of individual need'.[135] More concretely, he distinguishes two thresholds of interests. Referring also to the CESCR's approach, the first is said to be

> the most urgent interest in being free from general threats to one's survival. This interest is of greatest urgency, as the inability to survive wipes out all possibility for realizing the sources of value in the life of a being. I shall refer to this in what follows as the first threshold of provision or the minimum core. In this context, the threshold would amount to having at least minimal shelter from the elements such that one's health and thus one's ability to survive are not compromised.[136]

Yet this is not all that is protected by the relevant rights. Since the aim of the South African Constitution is to '[i]mprove the quality of life for all citizens and free the potential of each person',[137] the eventual goal is also to meet the second threshold, which is to allow people to not only survive but to flourish and achieve their goals.[138] In this regard, '[w]hilst the realization of the maximal second interest is a medium- to long-term goal, the urgency of the first interest strongly justifies an unconditional

---

[133] Ibid., 160.

[134] Ibid. Even a contextual determination of reasonableness presupposes some a-contextual standards. Moreover, this clarifies the scope of a court's decision-making powers as well as the state's obligations (161–162).

[135] Ibid., Ch. 1, 180.   [136] Ibid., 187.

[137] Preamble to the Constitution of the Republic of South Africa.

[138] Bilchitz 2007 (n. 62), 188.

obligation to realize it as a matter of priority'.[139] It does not make sense to hold that there is an obligation to meet the second threshold but not the first, as in order to reach the second level the realization of the first is presupposed.

The determination of a core rights standard through these two thresholds is helpful in the context of 'progressive realization', i.e., when there is a lack of a general standard or full compliance with such a standard cannot be expected immediately. By addressing urgent matters first, the right to progressively achieve certain bigger aims can actually become a right of everyone.[140]

Bilchitz explains that the minimum core is not so context-dependent as is often argued, because the 'common human interests' that exist in different situations are the same.[141] Moreover, he underlines that the minimum core need not be rigid and absolutist.[142] Such rigidity and absoluteness is often seen as one of the most problematic features of cores of rights, as it simply is 'impossible to give everyone access even to a "core" service immediately'.[143] Bilchitz rebuts this criticism by stating, first, that 'priority' in his account does not mean 'lexical priority' in the sense that all efforts and sources must be spent on complying with minimum core rights before attention can be paid to further realization: 'Such a policy would be short-sighted and fail to invest in any long-term solutions for the situations that people find themselves in'.[144] Rather, cores should obtain weighed priority. This relates to the fact that 'those interests which have priority are those which we have particularly strong reasons to value and which require strong countervailing considerations to outweigh them'.[145] A justification for not realizing the minimum core could, for example, be that such realization would be impossible in the light of the scarcity of resources. Not meeting core obligations can also be justified when this requires a disproportionately vast amount of resources, does not leave at least some room for reaching the higher threshold that allows individuals to 'realize their aims and achieve positive experiences' or prevents the realization of other rights' cores.[146]

To those who are not convinced that it makes sense to define individual rights standards that simply cannot always be met, Bilchitz responds that rather than including resource considerations and other state interests in the determination of the content of constitutional rights, it is

---

[139] Ibid., 189.   [140] Ibid., 193.   [141] Ibid., 200–202, responding to Brand 2002 (n. 117).
[142] Bilchitz 2007 (n. 62), 214.   [143] TAC, para. 35.   [144] Bilchitz 2007 (n. 62), 210.
[145] Ibid., 211   [146] Ibid., 212.

important to state conditional rights. Independent minimum core rights must be recognized, Bilchitz argues, for otherwise 'the failure to meet basic needs under conditions of scarcity does not violate any claim people have'.[147] In other words, '[p]eople have rights by virtue of being creatures of a certain type with certain interests and not by virtue of having control over a certain quantity of resources'.[148] Indeed, the identification of minimum core entitlements can steer government behaviour in the desired direction;[149] while it does not imply that as soon as a minimum threshold is not yet reached, the Constitution is breached. As Bilchitz notes, the minimum core should be rigid in one respect only: it should be strict to the extent that it recognizes that 'it is simply unacceptable for any human being to live without sufficient resources to maintain their survival'.[150] Otherwise, it can indeed be said to be a heavily weighing, yet prima facie requirement.

In brief, it can be said that both Liebenberg and Bilchitz try to bridge the gap between reasonableness and minimum core protection. Whereas Liebenberg starts from the former, yet includes a small role for the minimum core, Bilchitz gives content to socio-economic rights with the help of the minimum core, while sometimes allowing for justifiable interferences due to resource constraints or, indeed, reasonableness. Liebenberg's core rights notion can be described as 'relative' for taking into account the specific context of a case. In Bilchitz's view, only the protection offered by the core (rather than the core itself) is relative, as it allows for some exceptions.[151] Bilchitz's less-rigid minimum core approach shows us an important alternative. It provides something to hold on to, without the inflexibility usually associated with core rights. Core rights can play a guiding role in the practice of courts even when it is recognized that they cannot always be fulfilled immediately.

5.3   The Right to a Subsistence Minimum in Germany

The use of minimum cores can highlight aspects of rights that require some kind of prioritization. It may also distinguish certain (prima facie) rights from the broader range of interests that could potentially fall within the scope of broadly phrased rights norms. Moreover, even if the provisions a court has at its disposal are of a classical kind, core

---

[147] Ibid., 217; Bilchitz 2003 (n. 24), 19–20, and 22.   [148] Bilchitz 2003 (n. 24), 20.
[149] Bilchitz 2007 (n. 62), 219.   [150] Bilchitz 2003 (n. 24), 15.
[151] See further Ch. 7, S. 7.1.1.

socio-economic rights can inform the scope of these provisions. This is illustrated by the right to an *Existenzminimum* (subsistence minimum) that has been recognized on the basis of the German Basic Law.[152] Even though the German Federal Constitutional Court does not speak of 'core rights protection', this minimum socio-economic right can be linked to the examples outlined in this chapter so far. Because of the lack of explicit socio-economic rights norms combined with an approach that grants essential social protection, the right to a subsistence minimum provides valuable insights for our discussion of the ECtHR.[153]

The right to a subsistence minimum has nothing to do with the *Wesensgehaltsgarantie* discussed in Chapter 4.[154] Rather than the limitation of constitutional rights, it concerns the interpretation of the principle of human dignity – hence its inclusion in this chapter. The *Existenzminimum* is not a recent legal phenomenon in Germany. For a long time now, the duty to provide for such a minimum has been considered to follow from Article 20(1) GG.[155] This provision holds that '[t]he Federal Republic of Germany is a democratic and federal social state' and is known as the 'social state principle'. Article 20 does not fall under the header of basic rights, but forms the start of the chapter of the *Grundgesetz* on 'The Federation and the Länder': it hence was considered a duty for the state and not a subjective, individual constitutional right. The state had to provide for tolerable living conditions on the basis of statutory entitlements in the law.[156] Yet individuals could not go to court claiming a breach of their fundamental rights when it failed to do so.

On the basis of two landmark cases dating from 2010 and 2012, this has now changed.[157] In the *Hartz IV* judgment, as well as later in the *Asylbewerberleistungsgesetz* (*Asylum Seekers Benefits*) judgment, the

---

[152] BVerfGE 125, 175, 1 BvL 1/09 of 9 February 2010 (*Hartz IV*), para. 133 ff.
[153] Cf. Ingrid Leijten, 'The German Right to an *Existenzminimum*, Human Dignity, and the Possibility of Minimum Core Socioeconomic Rights Protection', *German Law Journal*, 16 (2015), pp. 23–48.
[154] See however Georg Herbert, 'Der Wesensgehalt der Grundrechte', *Europäische Grundrechte-Zeitschrift*, 12 (1985), pp. 321–335, 334.
[155] BVerfGE 1, 97 (104). See, for example, Claudia Bittner, 'Casenote – Human Dignity as a Matter of Legislative Consistency in an Ideal World: The Fundamental Right to Guarantee a Subsistence Minimum in the German Federal Constitutional Court's Judgment of 9 February 2010', *German Law Journal*, 12 (2011), pp. 1941–1960, 1942.
[156] See, for example, BVerfGE 1, 159 (161).
[157] *Hartz IV* and BVerfGE 132, 134, BvL 10/10, of 18 July 2012 (*Asylum Seekers Benefits*), respectively.

German Constitutional Court has clarified that the *Existenzminimum* is in fact an individual, constitutional right.[158] The *Hartz IV* case concerned the constitutionality of social assistance benefits paid under federal legislation. As of 2005, the Second Book of the German Code of Social Law arranges for basic provisions for employable persons either with no income or earning low wages. The payments are not linked to prior wages and are completely tax-funded. They include, besides a standard benefit, benefits for accommodation and heating, and became known as *Hartz IV*. With regard to these benefits, the *Bundesverfassungsgericht* held that Article 1 GG (the guarantee of human dignity), in combination with Article 20(1), confers on individuals a right to a dignified minimum existence.[159] This right, according to the FCC,

> *only* covers those means which are vital to maintain an existence that is in line with human dignity. It guarantees the whole subsistence minimum by a uniform fundamental rights guarantee which encompasses both the physical existence of the individual, that is food, clothing, household goods, housing, heating, hygiene and health . . ., and ensuring the possibility to maintain inter-human relationships and a minimum of participation in social, cultural and political life.[160]

The 2012 *Asylum Seekers Benefits* judgment, on the other hand, concerned benefits paid under the Asylum Seekers Benefits Act 1993 (AsylbLG). This statute provided a separate rule for social benefits in the sense that asylum seekers were not covered by arrangements made in the Second (including *Hartz IV*) and Twelfth Book of the Code of Social Law, but by this statute. The benefits granted under the AsylbLG were adjusted to the needs of people only staying in Germany for a short time and were significantly lower. Over time, however, the arrangements of the AsylbLG were also applied to people who remained in Germany for a significant period due

---

[158] Bittner 2011 (n. 155), 1944. See, on this development, Christian Seiler, 'Das Grundrecht auf ein menschenwürdiges Existenzminimum: Zum Urteil des Bundesverfassungsgerichts vom 9.2.2010', *Juristenzeitung* (2010), pp. 500–505; Thorsten Kingreen, 'Schätzungen "ins Blaue hinein"': Zu den Auswirkungen des Hartz IV-Urteils des Bundesverfassungsgerichts auf das Asylbewerberleistungsgesetz', *Neue Zeitschrift für Verwaltungsrecht* (2010), pp. 558–562; Matthias Schnath, 'Auswirkungen des neuen Grundrechts auf Gewährleistung des Existenzminimums auf die besonderen Hilfen nach dem Zwölften Sozialgesetzbuches (SGB XII)', *Sozialrecht aktuell* (2010), pp. 173–176 Jens-Hendrik Hörmann, *Rechtsprobleme des Grundrechts auf Gewährleistung eines menschenwürdigen Existenzminimums. Zu den Auswirkungen des 'Regelleistungsurteils' auf die 'Hartz IV'-Gesetzgebung und andere Sozialgesetze* (Hamburg: Verlag Dr. Kovac, 2012).

[159] *Hartz IV*, para. 133 ff.   [160] Ibid., para. 135 [emphasis added].

to humanitarian reasons (e.g., war refugees); they received the lower benefits for up to four years. Moreover, the rate of the benefits had not been increased since 1993, when the statute entered into force.

The *Bundesverfassungsgericht*, asked to decide upon the constitutionality of section 3(2)(2) and (3) in conjunction with section 3(1)(4) of the AsylbLG, held in this case that

> [w]hen people lack the material means to guarantee a life in dignity ... the state is – in accordance with its responsibility to protect human dignity and in compliance with its general social state mandate – obliged to ensure that the material conditions are provided to those in need. *As a human right, this fundamental right is granted to Germans as well as foreigners residing in Germany alike.* This objective obligation inferred from Article 1 S. 1 GG corresponds with an individual entitlement to state action, because the fundamental right protects the dignity of every single person ... and in circumstances of economic distress it can only be guaranteed through material support.[161]

Thus, it was clarified that the right to a subsistence minimum applies to all persons, regardless of their residential status, in Germany.[162]

Why can the protection of a right to an *Existenzminimum* be understood as a kind of core rights protection?[163] This is the case because it holds that a minimum level of socio-economic protection at all times must be guaranteed. Rather than implying a right to material prerequisites and means of subsistence generally, the right to an *Existenzminimum* protects the core of the guarantee of human dignity in combination with the *Sozialstaatsprinzip*.[164] It does not entail a right to the full range of possibilities of participating in social, cultural and political life, but guarantees that there should always be an essential level thereof.

The right to a subsistence minimum is absolutely protected: it is based on the guarantee of human dignity (Article 1 GG), which does not allow for any exceptions. At the same time, what is protected in an absolute manner is stated in relatively vague terms. In the *Hartz IV* case, after concluding that there was an individual right to an *Existenzminimum*, the FCC held that the Constitution does not permit for determining the precise shape of this right.[165] What the right *in concreto* means is

---

[161] *Asylum Seekers Benefits*, para. 63 [emphasis added].   [162] Ibid., para. 94.

[163] Cf. Stefanie Egidy, 'Casenote – The Fundamental Right to the Guarantee of a Subsistence Minimum in the Hartz IV Decision of the German Federal Constitutional Court', *German Law Journal*, 12 (2011), pp. 1961–1982, 1972.

[164] Cf. *Hartz IV*, para. 135. See also *Asylum Seekers Benefits*, para. 90.

[165] *Hartz IV*, para. 142.

eventually left to the legislature to decide. No wonder, therefore, that scholars have called the right to an *Existenzminimum* 'relative in nature'.[166] According to this view, there are still no exceptions possible, yet it is the content of the minimum that is not entirely predetermined, and thereby is considered relative.

The impossibility of defining its exact contours, however, does not mean that compliance with the right to a subsistence minimum cannot be meaningfully assessed. First of all, the FCC has stressed that the leeway of the legislature ends where the subsistence minimum provided is 'evidently insufficient'.[167] Within this leeway, it can moreover review the basis and methods of calculation of the benefits, even if it cannot set any quantified requirements. In the words of the FCC:

> The protection of the fundamental right therefore also covers the proced-
> ure to ascertain the subsistence minimum because a review of results can
> only be carried out to a restricted degree by the standard of this funda-
> mental right. In order to ensure the traceability of the extent of the
> statutory assistance as commensurate with the significance of the funda-
> mental right, as well as to ensure the review of the benefits by the courts,
> the assessment of the benefits must be clearly justifiable on the basis of
> reliable figures and plausible methods of calculation.[168]

More concretely, the *Bundesverfassungsgericht* held that four criteria need to be complied with:

1) the legislature needs to cover and describe the objective of ensuring an existence in line with Article 1(1) in conjunction with Article 20(1);
2) it needs to select – within its margin of appreciation – a procedure of calculation fundamentally suited to an assessment of the subsistence minimum;
3) in essence, the necessary facts must be completely and correctly ascertained; and
4) the legislature needs to stay within the bounds of what is justifiable within the chosen method and its structural principles at all steps of the calculation process.[169]

---

[166] Seiler 2010 (n. 158), 504. See also Volker Neumann, 'Menschenwürde und Existenzminimum', *Neue Zeitschrift für Verwaltungsrecht* (1995), pp. 426–432, 429; Bittner 2011
(n. 155), 1953.
[167] *Hartz IV*, para. 141.   [168] Ibid., para. 142.
[169] Ibid., para. 143. These can be translated into the rationale, transparency and consistency
requirement, see Bittner 2011 (n. 155), 1948.

In the *Hartz IV* case, the conclusion was that the benefits granted were not evidently insufficient. However, since the calculation of the subsistence minimum did not fully consider some expenditures and deductions had been estimated randomly, the fourth requirement, which is essentially one of consistency, had not been fulfilled.[170] This was reason to conclude that there had been a breach of Article 1(1) in conjunction with Article 20(1) GG.[171] In turn, in the *Asylum Seekers Benefits* case, the FCC added that if the legislature, in protecting a subsistence minimum, uses different methods of calculation for different groups, this must be objectively justified.[172] Besides holding that the asylum seeker benefits in this regard did not meet the different procedural requirements, it considered them to be evidently insufficient.[173] This was because the level of the payments had not changed since 1993 to take into account the considerable inflation since that time, even though the statute provided for regular adjustments.[174]

The approach taken by the *Bundesverfassungsgericht* is an interesting one that allows for some valuable insights. First, it is often argued that it is not suitable or possible for a court to identify core rights, at least not without duly considering the circumstances of a particular case and the general interests at stake therein. The *Bundesverfassungsgericht* has solved this by opting for a quite abstract guarantee of a subsistence minimum that is hardly objectionable and, moreover, fits the aims and development of the *Grundgesetz*. It thus shows that a court is capable of defining core guarantees independent from the case at hand. Second, although one could argue that its definition is meaningless, so long as the subsistence minimum's precise content is left to the legislature to determine, the FCC has found an interesting way to give the abstract core requirement and the fact that it cannot be interfered with 'bite'. It has opted for a second step, namely the specification of the right to a subsistence minimum with the help of specific 'procedural' conditions the method used by the legislature needs to be in line with. Considering the sensitive field of social policy, it has thereby refrained from determining a quantitative minimum, which is indeed not the task of a judicial body. Nevertheless, the FCC has provided for a clear standard that can guide the legislative, as well as the adjudicative practice. This standard is, first, quite vague, and, second, procedural. Whereas it avoids the sensitive

---

[170] *Hartz IV*, para. 171. See Bittner 2011 (n. 155), 1949–1950.
[171] *Hartz IV*, para. 144, 210.   [172] *Asylum Seekers Benefits*, para. 97. See also para. 99.
[173] Ibid., paras. 106–115.   [174] Ibid., paras. 108–111.

issue of precise socio-economic core content, this combination allows effective judicial protection.

Conclusion

I have shown that core rights can do more than form a limit to rights' limitations. The idea that certain socio-economic guarantees are particularly urgent and need to be ensured as a matter of priority may also help to determine the justiciable scope of socio-economic rights. This can be seen in the context of the ICESCR, where the requirement of progressive realization in the light of the available resources failed to provide a touchstone that was sufficiently concrete to direct socio-economic efforts. Minimum core obligations were added to the broad norms of the Covenant in order to render them more workable. In socio-economic rights adjudication, reasonableness review is considered an appropriate approach to decide whether an impugned act or omission is justified. Yet the overall test this results in, according to some, fails to give content to rights and thereby the claims people have. Core rights in this regard allow for bifurcated rights review by identifying a standard against which the reasonableness or proportionality of a measure can be reviewed. According to Bilchitz, this standard does not have to be rigid: even when a failure to guarantee core rights can be justified, it still makes sense to clarify what is expected.

The example of the right to an *Existenzminimum* on the basis of the German Constitution has shown two more things: First, minimum guarantees can also be used to determine the socio-economic scope of norms that were not designed to ensure individual protection in this field. Second, courts may leave the precise interpretation of this standard to the other branches and resort to procedural type review in order to check for compliance. In other words, the minimum required need not be prescribed in much detail in order to form the starting point for the review of individual cases. Nevertheless, I will elaborate on the issue of determining core socio-economic content in the following chapter.

6

Core Socio-Economic Content

Outlining the potential role of core rights to determine whether a limitation of a right is allowed or whether a rights claim exists in the first place is one thing. It is yet another thing to define the content of core rights. In the previous chapters, several hints have been given as to the content of minimum cores. This endeavour, however, has thus far been incomplete. The issue of the content of the core cannot be ignored or only dealt with superficially. At the same time, my conclusion will be that judicial engagement with core content need not require a meticulous definition of essential guarantees.

This chapter deals exclusively with core socio-economic content. The reason for this is that the gist of my argument is that the idea of core rights is helpful for understanding and improving the socio-economic case law of the ECtHR. The Strasbourg Court's task is connected to the civil and political rights norms enshrined in the Convention. Nevertheless, I argue that it is the core of economic and social rights that may guide the fulfilment of this task in an effective and indivisible manner without overstretching the Court's legitimate role. Moreover, the content of the core appears less contentious when socio-economic, rather than civil and political rights, are concerned. I will return to this at a later point.[1]

First, a methodological issue is addressed. Section 6.1 discusses different answers to the question of where and how core content is found. After that, a brief overview is given of the minimum core obligations that have been determined by the CESCR.[2] In order to draw parallels with the

---

[1] See, Ch. 7, S. 7.1.2.

[2] See, for extensive discussions on the ICESCR's core obligations, Audrey R. Chapman and Sage Russell (eds.), *Core Obligations: Building a Framework for Economic, Social and Cultural Rights* (Antwerp/Oxford/New York: Intersentia, 2002); Danie Brand and Sage Russell (eds.), *Exploring the Core Content of Economic and Social Rights: South African and International Perspectives* (Pretoria: Protea Book House, 2002). Cf. also Ben Saul, David Kinley and Jacqueline Mowbray, *The International Covenant on Economic, Social and Cultural Rights: Commentary, Cases, and Materials* (Oxford University Press, 2014).

case law of the Court, the discussion of which focuses on rights to housing, health, and social security, it is the minimum core of these rights that is presented in Section 6.2. An overview of the relevant General Comments illustrates that the Committee, over the years, has compiled an extensive list of essential guarantees, thereby showing that the argument that core rights are indeterminable – at least from a pragmatic point of view – is void. Section 6.3 then lays bare the red threads that run through the different cores and that allow for a more general picture of their socio-economic content.

6.1   Determining Core Socio-Economic Rights

6.1.1   Intrinsic Core Rights

In the debate on core rights, broadly two methods are identified for the determination of core content. First, the minimum core of a right can be determined by looking at the right itself. The question is then what is the most essential part of this right. In other words, this approach searches for what Coomans calls 'the intrinsic value of each human right', or the elements 'essential for the very existence of that right as a human right'.[3] Using the same term as the CESCR, Örücü in this regard speaks of the 'unrelinquishable nucleus [that] is the *raison d'être* of the basic legal norm, essential to its definition, and surrounded by the less securely guarded elements'.[4]

It is often argued that rights do not have such an intrinsic core.[5] Cores of rights are not 'out there' in the sense that when looking closely at a particular right, an incontestable essence can be found. Nevertheless, attempts at delineating a right's most important aspects can be made with the help of a normative starting point that provides for the necessary focus. Young has explained, for example, that the recognition of a normative core can proceed from a foundational norm or idea on the basis of which certain aspects are considered more important than others. Foundational principles such as survival (needs), freedom, or

---

[3] Fons Coomans, 'In Search of the Core Content of the Right to Education' in D. Brand and S. Russell (eds.), *Exploring the Core Content of Economic and Social Rights: South African and International Perspectives* (Pretoria: Protea Book House, 2002), pp. 159–182, 166–167.

[4] Esin Örücü, 'The Core of Rights and Freedoms: The Limits of Limits' in Tom Campbell et al. (eds.), *Human Rights: From Rhetoric to Reality* (Oxford: Basil Blackwell, 1986), pp. 37–59, 52 [emphasis added].

[5] See the discussion in Ch. 4, S. 4.3.2, and Ch. 5, S. 5.2.2.

dignity (values), can help pinpoint core elements. Moreover, the advantage of grounding core obligations explicitly on such principles is that the minimum core becomes less arbitrary, as a moral reason is directly provided in justification of the weight of the minimum core.[6]

At the same time, Young points out that the normative essence approach forms a risky enterprise. Relying on specific background reasons could prevent broad acceptance by states, other actors and individuals.[7] To substantiate this, Young explains:

> [T]he Essence Approach mimics the structure of foundational linear arguments common to rights, which move from the deepest or most basic propositions for the interests underlying rights, through a series of derivative concerns, each one supported by and more concrete than the last. The 'core' of the right is thus its most basic feature, which relies on no other foundations for justification.[8]

However,

> the resemblance between justificatory reasoning and the Essence approach is a strained one, because the implication of a 'minimum' core can narrow the range of foundations, rather than enlarge them. And it is precisely this minimalism that upsets the foundational support, so that the base point of the right is also its narrowest. This puts into question the ability of the core to accommodate contrasting normative foundations.[9]

The minimum core is a narrow concept, which is said to decrease its chances of broad acceptance. Young presents the examples of a core derived from the idea that economic and social rights should first and foremost promote survival, and of a core that is grounded on the value of human flourishing. These two accounts would 'lead in very different directions, thwarting efforts at giving a certain, determinate meaning to the minimum core'.[10] Whereas the former justification would focus on the right to life and the provision of basic needs as belonging to the essence of socio-economic rights, the latter would stress such notions as dignity, equality and freedom, which seem to demand something other than minimum nutritional requirements or some basic form of shelter to be protected against the elements. Being entirely dependent on (minimum) state support arguably does not correspond with living a dignified life in freedom. However, it can be asked whether the different underlying

---

[6] Katharine G. Young, 'The Minimum Core of Economic and Social Rights: A Concept in Search of Content', *Yale Journal of International Law*, 33 (2008), pp. 113–175, 126 ff.
[7] Ibid., 127, 138–139.   [8] Ibid., 126 [footnote omitted].   [9] Ibid., 127.   [10] Ibid.

justifications truly point in 'very different directions', or that, rather than in kind, the different cores they suggest in fact merely differ in degree.[11]

The hardest thing about identifying a minimum core, it can be argued, is deciding how far exactly it should go. Most likely those who think a minimum core must be based on the idea of biological survival, as well as those who consider living a human life to be the guiding value, will reason that the core of a right to housing includes that nobody has to sleep on the streets. However, whereas from the perspective of biological survival a roof that protects against the elements might suffice, 'living a human life' might call for facilities such as sewage and electricity to also be included in what should minimally be provided. Does the minimum core of the right to food only entail the provision of a package of calories, or does it require more, such as the possibility to independently grow or buy food not just for immediate use, but also for long-term purposes? What the idea of intrinsic cores of socio-economic rights reveals is that such cores are prone to point in the same direction, but that there will be a difference of degree in their inclusiveness.

To agree, then, on a particular level of inclusiveness, what might be needed is some kind of 'incompletely theorized agreement'. Sunstein's idea holds that even when people cannot agree on theories, they can still agree on practices, or outcomes.[12] When disagreements on underlying normative theories are put aside – which does not mean they need to be abolished altogether – broad acceptance could be possible. Some form of basic socio-economic protection will then resonate with different groups without there being a need to determine its foundation.

Looking at the CESCR, it appears that what it considers the *raison d'être* of the Covenant relates to the provision of 'essential foodstuffs, . . . essential primary health care, . . . basic shelter and housing, . . . [and] the

---

[11] Cf. Ibid., 138–139. In later work, Young holds that 'interpreting the minimum of economic and social rights is compatible with ethical pluralism' (Katharine G. Young, *Constituting Socio-Economic Rights* [Oxford University Press, 2012], 66). Quoting Michael Ignatieff, 'Human Rights as Ideology' in M. Ignatieff (A. Gutmann [ed.]), *Human Rights as Politics and Idolatry* [Princeton University Press, 2001], 56), she states that 'people from different cultures may continue to disagree about what is good, but nevertheless agree about what is insufferably, unarguably wrong'.

[12] See, for example, Cass R. Sunstein, 'Incompletely Theorized Agreements', *Harvard Law Review*, 108 (1995), pp. 1733–1772; Cass R. Sunstein, 'Incompletely Theorized Agreements in Constitutional Law', *Social Research*, 74 (2007), pp. 1–24. Cf. also Cass R. Sunstein 'Incompletely Theorized Agreements', *Harvard Law Review*, 108 (1995), pp. 1733–1772, 1737.

most basic forms of education'.[13] In the different General Comments, it emphasizes that there must be access to a minimum essential level of benefits, minimum essential food and basic shelter, housing and sanitation.[14] Indeed, these core elements comply with a basic needs paradigm, albeit their degree of inclusiveness is arguably high as they demand more than what is needed for mere survival. The CESCR does not cling to a specific normative justification for these core obligations. Nevertheless, or perhaps for that reason, the focus on basic, minimum provisions in the context of socio-economic rights seems defensible. It ties in with the different thresholds of interests identified by Bilchitz, who also makes clear that intrinsically these rights must entail at least a minimum level of protection, which can then be built upon.[15]

6.1.2 Consensus and Expert Information

A second approach to determining minimum cores does not merely rely on the characteristics of the right itself, but rather on external sources. This could, for example, be consensus amongst states on minimum socio-economic guarantees, or an expert organization's authoritative determination of certain basic standards.

An example is provided by the Committee's General Comment on the right to the highest attainable standard of health. This states that the core obligations related to this right include the obligation '[t]o provide essential drugs, as from time to time defined under the WHO Action Programme on Essential Drugs'.[16] By referring to this World Health Organization (WHO) standard, the CESCR has specified a core obligation that is based on, as well as evolves with, external information. But one could also think of the mention that is made of states parties reports in General Comment No. 3.[17] In clarifying the right to housing, the CESCR made use of various reports and other documentation on this

---

[13] CESCR, General Comment No. 3, para. 10.

[14] See, for example, CESCR, General Comment No. 14, para. 43(a)(b)(c); CESCR, General Comment No. 15, para. 37(a); CESCR, General Comment No. 19, para. 59(a).

[15] Cf. David Bilchitz, *Poverty and Fundamental Rights: The Justification and Enforcement of Socio-Economic Rights* (Oxford University Press, 2007), 187 ff. See also Sandra Fredman, *Human Rights Transformed: Positive rights and positive duties* (Oxford University Press, 2008), 86.

[16] CESCR, General Comment No. 14, para. 43(d).

[17] CESCR, General Comment No. 3, para. 10.

topic,[18] whereas in a similar vein, it referred to the Programme of Action of the International Conference on Population and Development and the Alma-Ata Declaration in its General Comment on the right to health.[19]

Young speaks of a similar approach characterized by broad agreement. The minimum consensus approach relies on consensus that has already been established.[20] Taking this perspective, she holds that '[t]he minimum core content is the right's agreed-upon nucleus, whereas elements outside core translate to the plurality of meanings and disagreement surrounding the right'.[21] Minimum consensus could be inferred from a 'synthesis of jurisprudence',[22] or from what states have been doing so far. In this way questions of normative content can be avoided. In the words of Young,

> the Consensus Approach ... explicitly addresses two central challenges to the Essence Approach: that resolving disagreement by an abstract, overlapping consensus of reasonable political theories does not resolve the problems of representation and voice, and that even broad ethical agreements may not resonate enough with social facts to constitute law.[23]

Two things are made clear here: first, an agreed upon understanding of the minimum core allows for the 'voice' of the various stakeholders to be included. This is important especially in complex, political and international settings like that of the ICESCR – but also the ECtHR. It, moreover, allies with what Alston wrote in the 1990s on the definition of economic and social rights norms, namely that: '[t]he approaches adopted by States themselves in their internal arrangements ... will shed light upon the norms, while the dialogue between the State and the Committee will contribute further to deepening the understanding'.[24] An approach to the minimum core that explicitly takes notice of national arrangements can mitigate concerns about international interference with states' socio-economic policies. For that reason, it might be preferred over

---

[18] CESCR, General Comment No. 4, para. 2. Cf. also Scott Leckie, 'The Human Right to Adequate Housing' in A. Eide, C. Krause and A. Rosas (eds.), *Economic, Social and Cultural Rights: A Textbook*, 2nd rev. ed. (Leiden: Martinus Nijhoff Publishers, 2001), pp. 149–168, 155.

[19] CESCR, General Comment No. 14, para 43.   [20] Young 2008 (n. 6), 140 ff.

[21] Ibid., 140. Cf. Hart's distinction between 'a core of certainty and a penumbera of doubt' (H.L.A. Hart, *The Concept of Law* [Oxford: Clarendon Press, 1994], 123).

[22] Leckie 2001 (n. 18), 155.   [23] Young 2008 (n. 6), 141 [footnote omitted].

[24] Philip Alston, 'The Committee on Economic, Social and Cultural Rights' in Philip Alston (ed.), *The United Nations and Human Rights: A Critical Appraisal* (Oxford: Clarendon Press, 1992), pp. 473–508, 491.

a purely normatively determined core. Second, the inclusion of social facts ensures that the minimum core does not drift away too far from reality. Special attention is thereby paid to legal facts such constitutions, laws, and case law: 'Through comparative analysis of sociolegal equivalents, a converging set of principles regarding socioeconomic protection is empirically "uncovered" rather than deductively "discovered".'[25]

Now this does not mean that a consensus-based approach is not normative at all. Consensus itself is a value that can be debated or put into question, just like freedom or equality, for example.[26] Although it fits in nicely with international legal thinking, tension also exists with regard to the very idea of fundamental rights. As was explicated in Chapter 3, fundamental rights serve to protect minorities, and they should, therefore, not be made dependent on what the majority considers to belong to a right in the first place.[27] A counterargument could be that, especially in a multilevel legal context, the interpretation of economic and social rights necessarily takes state concerns to some extent into account. When choices are made on how significant portions of the budget should be spent, relying on states' expertise and experience and granting some degree of deference to what they consider important is defensible.

A practical issue related to the idea of consensus is the question whose consensus, exactly, is needed, and when is the agreement broad enough. Even if a solution is agreed upon, such agreement is often informed by compromise rather than reason.[28] And when account is taken of (international) expert bodies' statements or standards, the state support underlying these often has an indirect and incomplete character. In fact, 'consensus' cannot be taken too literally; 'drawing inspiration' from facts and figures probably is more in line with reality.

One final point of criticism is that an approach for determining the minimum core that relies on what is already there lacks ambition. Young notes that this is a problem especially in the field of economic and social fundamental rights, as these still need to be developed further.[29] And yet, especially when combined with expert opinions, the chances that a consensus-oriented core turns out to be too unambitious are relatively small. After all, standards set by expert bodies entail desirable aims rather than pessimistic expectations. At the same time, in the light of what was already said on the relation between international instruments and national decision-making, some modesty is needed for the furtherance

---

[25] Young 2008 (n. 6), 142.   [26] Ibid., 144.   [27] See Ch. 3, S. 3.2.2.
[28] Young 2008 (n. 6), 149.   [29] Ibid., 147–148.

of economic and social protection at the supranational level. Which is not to say that states cannot also be held accountable to international legal standards in the field of human rights they have willingly agreed to comply with. Thus, the ECtHR could, besides from state practices and expert opinions, learn from the standards set by the European Committee of Social Rights (ECSR) in relation to the (Revised) European Social Charter ((R)ESC), and especially the baseline obligations that could be identified. The same can be said for the minimum cores developed in the context of the CESCR, the general elaboration of which will now be looked at more closely.

6.2   Minimum Core Content

6.2.1   The Right to Adequate Housing (Article 11(1) ICESCR)

When a closer look is had at General Comment No. 3, it becomes clear that besides introducing the idea of minimum core obligations, the Committee does not address the more precise content thereof. It is mentioned that a state will not, prima facie, comply with its obligations under the Covenant when 'any significant number of individuals is deprived of essential foodstuffs, of essential primary health care, of basic shelter and housing, or of the most basic forms of education'.[30] On the rights other than those concerning food, health, housing and education, it remains completely silent.

Only some years after the adoption of General Comment No. 3, the CESCR started giving some more clarity in this regard. The first General Comment that exclusively deals with a particular ICESCR right is the 1991 Comment on the right to adequate housing (Article 11(1) ICESCR).[31] In General Comment No. 4, the Committee does not explicitly refer to the notion of minimum core obligations, as it does in subsequent General Comments. Nevertheless, this Comment, together with General Comment No. 7 on forced evictions, has been of vital

---

[30] CESCR, General Comment No. 3: The Nature of States Parties' Obligations (Art. 2(1) of the Covenant), 14 December 1990, E/1991/23 (General Comment No. 3), para. 10.

[31] CESCR, General Comment No. 4: The Right to Adequate Housing (Art. 11(1) of the Covenant), 13 December 1991, E/1992/23 No. 4 (General Comment No. 4). Art. 11(1) ICESCR reads: 'The States Parties to the present Covenant recognize the right of everyone to an adequate standard of living for himself and his family, including adequate food, clothing and housing, and to the continuous improvement of living conditions. The States Parties will take appropriate steps to ensure the realization of this right, recognizing to this effect the essential importance of international co-operation based on free consent.'

importance in defining the scope and content of the right to housing, hence showing how this right's essence is to be understood.[32]

The right to housing is ranked amongst the most important of the rights enumerated in the ICESCR. This is the case partly because housing is intimately linked to the enjoyment of many other rights.[33] Its significance is moreover reflected in the fact that before Comment No. 4 was adopted, the CESCR had already been able to 'accumulate a large amount of information pertaining to this right'.[34] With the help of this information, stemming from state reports as well as international materials, it could now provide for clarification on what the right to housing exactly entails. According to the CESCR, 'the right to housing should not be interpreted in a narrow or restrictive sense which equates it with, for example, the shelter provided by merely having a roof over one's head or views shelter exclusively as a commodity'.[35] It also established seven factors determining what constitutes adequate housing. First of all, there must be legal security of tenure, i.e., legal protection against forced eviction, harassment and other threats.[36] Moreover, a house must contain certain facilities, like access to natural and common resources, energy for cooking, sanitation, etc., and it should be affordable, habitable, accessible and culturally adequate.[37] Finally, the requirement of 'location' implies that 'adequate housing must be in a location which allows access to employment options, health-care services, schools, child care centres and other social facilities'.[38] The right to housing requires certain steps to be taken immediately:

> As recognized in the Global Strategy for Shelter and in other international analyses, many of the measures required to promote the right to housing would only require the abstention by the Government from certain practices and a commitment to facilitating 'self-help' by affected groups.[39]

Moreover, the Committee clarified that due priority must be given to those social groups living in unfavourable conditions,[40] that a national housing strategy needs to be adopted[41] and that the housing situation in a state needs to be monitored.[42]

---

[32] Cf. Saul et al. 2014 (n. 2), 928.
[33] CESCR, General Comment No. 4, para. 1. There also is an obvious link with the right to privacy, see Matthew C.R. Craven, *The International Covenant on Economic, Social and Cultural Rights* (Oxford University Press, 1995), 330.
[34] CESCR, General Comment No. 4, para. 2.   [35] Ibid., para. 7.   [36] Ibid., para. 8(a).
[37] Ibid., para. 8(b, c, d, e, and g).   [38] Ibid., para. 8(f).   [39] Ibid., para. 10.
[40] Ibid., para. 11.   [41] Ibid., para. 12.   [42] Ibid., para. 13.

As already indicated, the various clarifications were not explicitly presented as the minimum core of the right to housing. However, they do serve to narrow down and make the potentially very broad scope of this right more specific. In this connection, it may be inferred that the right to housing does not entail the task of the state to ensure the provision of housing.[43] Moreover, the negative obligation to abstain from certain practices, and the duty to commit to facilitating self-help, can be understood as providing a baseline from which further, progressive realization can be achieved.

Reflecting the importance of legal security of tenure, in 1997 another General Comment related to the right to housing was adopted.[44] On the specific matter of forced evictions, the CESCR held that 'legislation against forced evictions is an essential basis upon which to build a system of effective protection'.[45] More precisely, this should include 'measures which (a) provide the greatest possible security of tenure to occupiers of houses and land, (b) conform to the Covenant and (c) are designed to control strictly the circumstances under which evictions may be carried out'.[46] The Committee acknowledged that there are situations in which forced evictions can be justified, but emphasized that they should always take place in compliance with certain important conditions. For example, measures must be taken 'to ensure that no form of discrimination is involved'.[47] Moreover, a number of procedural guarantees must be in place, including the provision of legal remedies,[48] and the eviction should be carried out 'in accordance with general principles of reasonableness and proportionality'.[49] According to the CESCR:

> Appropriate procedural protection and due process are essential aspects of all human rights but are especially pertinent in relation to a matter such as forced evictions which directly invokes a large number of the rights recognized in both the International Covenants on Human Rights. The Committee considers that the procedural protections which should be applied in relation to forced evictions include: (a) an opportunity for genuine consultation with those affected; (b) adequate and reasonable notice for all affected persons prior to the scheduled date of eviction; (c) information on the proposed evictions, and, where applicable, on the alternative purpose for which the land or housing is to be used, to be made available in reasonable time to all those affected; (d) especially where groups of people are involved, government officials or their representatives to be present during an

---

[43] Saul et al. 2014 (n. 2), 931.

[44] CESCR, General Comment No. 7: The right to adequate housing (Art.11(1)): forced evictions, 20 May 1997, E/1998/22 (General Comment No. 7).

[45] Ibid., para. 9.   [46] Ibid.   [47] Ibid., para. 10.   [48] Ibid., para. 13.

[49] Ibid., para. 14.

eviction; (e) all persons carrying out the eviction to be properly identified; (f) evictions not to take place in particularly bad weather or at night unless the affected persons consent otherwise; (g) provision of legal remedies; and (h) provision, where possible, of legal aid to persons who are in need of it to seek redress from the courts.[50]

Finally, moreover,

> evictions should not result in individuals being rendered homeless or vulnerable to the violation of other human rights. Where those affected are unable to provide for themselves, the State party must take all appropriate measures, to the maximum of its available resources, to ensure that adequate alternative housing, resettlement or access to productive land, as the case may be, is available.'[51]

The requirements related to forced evictions are also not explicitly phrased as core obligations. They are, in fact, rather extensive, and may, for that reason, be considered to entail more than just minimum protection. However, the requirements do create a specific focus, and point out that especially procedural protection and protection against discrimination are of crucial importance. Moreover, the fact that an entire Comment is dedicated to the topic of forced evictions – as an important aspect of security of tenancy, which in turn is an aspect of the right to adequate housing – can be seen to imply that protection against such evictions must be considered of essential importance for compliance with Article 11(1) ICESCR.

6.2.2 The Right to the Highest Attainable Standard of Health (Article 12 ICESCR)

The right to the highest attainable standard of health (Article 12 ICESCR)[52] is notoriously hard to define.[53] The full realization of this

---

[50] Ibid., para. 15.   [51] Ibid., para. 16.

[52] Art. 12 ICESCR reads: '1. The States Parties to the present Covenant recognize the right of everyone to the enjoyment of the highest attainable standard of physical and mental health. 2. The steps to be taken by the States Parties to the present Covenant to achieve the full realization of this right shall include those necessary for: (a) The provision for the reduction of the stillbirth-rate and of infant mortality and for the healthy development of the child; (b) The improvement of all aspects of environmental and industrial hygiene; (c) The prevention, treatment and control of epidemic, endemic, occupational and other diseases; (d) The creation of conditions which would assure to all medical service and medical attention in the event of sickness.'

[53] Cf. Brigit Toebes, *The Right to Health as a Human Right in International Law* (Antwerp/ Oxford/New York: Intersentia/Oxford: Hart Publishing, 1999), 16–26. See also Saul et al. 2014 (n. 2), 979–981.

right requires extensive and costly measures. In General Comment No. 14 (2000), the CESCR underlined that the right to health is interpreted as

> an inclusive right extending not only to timely and appropriate health care but also to the underlying determinants of health, such as access to safe and potable water and adequate sanitation, an adequate supply of safe food, nutrition and housing, healthy occupational and environmental conditions, and access to health-related education and information, including on sexual and reproductive health. A further important aspect is the participation of the population in all health-related decision-making at the community, national and international levels.[54]

By explicitly referring to the core obligations that stem from the right to health, Comment No. 14 also indicates which guarantees must be considered as a matter of priority. The announcement of these minimum cores is preceded by various references to other international legal documents. The Comment mentions the Programme of Action of the International Conference on Population and Development and the Alma-Ata Declaration as 'providing compelling guidance on the core obligations arising from article 12'.[55] These obligations are:

(a) To ensure the right of access to health facilities, goods and services on a non-discriminatory basis, especially for vulnerable or marginalized groups;

(b) To ensure access to the minimum essential food which is nutritionally adequate and safe, to ensure freedom from hunger to everyone;

(c) To ensure access to basic shelter, housing and sanitation, and an adequate supply of safe and potable water;

(d) To provide essential drugs, as from time to time defined under the WHO Action Programme on Essential Drugs;

(e) To ensure equitable distribution of all health facilities, goods and services;

(f) To adopt and implement a national public health strategy and plan of action, on the basis of epidemiological evidence, addressing the health concerns of the whole population; the strategy and plan of action shall be devised, and periodically reviewed, on the basis of a participatory and transparent process; they shall include methods,

---

[54] CESCR, General Comment No. 14: The Right to the Highest Attainable Standard of Health (Art. 12 of the Covenant), 11 August 2000, E/C.12/2000/4 (General Comment No. 14), para. 11.

[55] Ibid., para. 43.

such as right to health indicators and benchmarks, by which progress can be closely monitored; the process by which the strategy and plan of action are devised, as well as their content, shall give particular attention to all vulnerable or marginalized groups.[56]

What the Committee considers to be of 'comparative priority', moreover, is this:

(a) To ensure reproductive, maternal (pre-natal as well as post-natal) and child health care;

(b) To provide immunization against the major infectious diseases occurring in the community;

(c) To take measures to prevent, treat and control epidemic and endemic diseases;

(d) To provide education and access to information concerning the main health problems in the community, including methods of preventing and controlling them;

(e) To provide appropriate training for health personnel, including education on health and human rights.[57]

It has been argued that it is unreasonable to oblige poor countries to comply with the core obligations recognized under the right to health. These obligations require 'an activist, committed state party, with a carefully honed set of public policies related to the right to health', including a national public health strategy and plan of action.[58] But only few countries can be said to live up to this image. Apart from this, however, the different minimum cores signal some interesting points. First of all, besides at the outset of the document, where it refers to international documents and expert guidelines, the CESCR also mentions expert information in listing the core obligations, namely the WHO Action Programme on Essential Drugs. It thereby explicitly relies on international expertise for determining the essential aspects of the right to health.[59] Second, just like in the context of the right to housing, particular attention must be paid to discrimination and to 'vulnerable and marginalised groups'. It is also interesting that the cores of the right to health clearly show overlap with other minimum cores. Amongst

---

[56] Ibid., para. 43.   [57] Ibid., para. 44.

[58] Audrey R. Chapman, 'Core Obligations Related to the Right to Health' in Audrey Chapman and Sage Russell (eds.), *Core Obligations: Building a Framework for Economic, Social and Cultural Rights* (Antwerp: Intersentia, 2002), pp. 185–215, 205.

[59] See further S. 6.3.2.

them, a right to 'minimum essential food' and 'basic shelter, housing and sanitation' can be found, which underlines the interrelatedness of the different economic and social rights.[60] More particularly, this seems to show that economic and social rights are not only connected with respect to their more peripheral aspects, but also when it comes to the very core of these rights – at least in the way these are explicated by the CESCR.

6.2.3   The Right to Social Security (Article 9 ICESCR)

Article 9 ICESCR holds that 'The States Parties to the present Covenant recognise the right of everyone to social security, including social assistance'. Its brief phrasing cannot easily be translated into clear content.[61] According to General Comment No. 19 (2008),[62] '[t]he right to social security is of central importance in guaranteeing human dignity for all persons when they are faced with circumstances that deprive them of their capacity to fully realize their Covenant rights'.[63] Important in this respect are availability, (the coverage of) social risks and contingencies (e.g., health care, sickness, old age, unemployment, employment injury, family and child support and maternity), adequacy and accessibility.[64] The Comment also underlined the importance of the relation between the right to social security and other rights.[65] Moreover, 'States parties have a core obligation to ensure the satisfaction of, at the very least, minimum essential levels of each of the rights enunciated in the Covenant'. In the case of social security, this requires a state:

> (a) To ensure access to a social security scheme that provides a minimum essential level of benefits to all individuals and families that will enable them to acquire at least essential health care, basic shelter and housing, water and sanitation, foodstuffs, and the most basic forms of education. If a State party cannot provide this minimum level for all risks and contingencies within its maximum available

---

[60] Cf. Toebes 1999 (n. 53), 259–272.

[61] Its meaning, though, can at least to some extent be clarified by reference to ILO standards on this topic, which can arguably be seen as the right's *lex specialis*. See Saul et al. 2014 (n. 2), 618.

[62] CESCR, General Comment No. 19: The right to social security (Art. 9 of the Covenant), 4 February 2008, E/C.12/GC/19 (General Comment No. 19).

[63] Ibid., para. 1.   [64] Ibid., paras. 10–27.   [65] Ibid., para. 28.

resources, the Committee recommends that the State party, after a wide process of consultation, select a core group of social risks and contingencies;

(b) To ensure the right of access to social security systems or schemes on a non-discriminatory basis, especially for disadvantaged and marginalized individuals and groups;

(c) To respect existing social security schemes and protect them from unreasonable interference;

(d) To adopt and implement a national social security strategy and plan of action;

(e) To take targeted steps to implement social security schemes, particularly those that protect disadvantaged and marginalized individuals and groups;

(f) To monitor the extent of the realization of the right to social security.[66]

Evident from obligation (a) is again that the essential aspects are intimately connected to the realization of the other (core) ICESCR rights. Moreover, here too the importance of non-discrimination and the targeting of especially disadvantaged and marginalized individuals and groups is emphasized.[67] Also noticeable is the negative core obligation to respect social security schemes that are in place, and protect them from unreasonable interferences. This signals that authorities need not necessarily do much to ensure basic guarantees. However, according to Saul et al.,

> [t]he core obligations ... identified nevertheless remain slippery. On the one hand, the CESCR requires states to provide the benefits necessary to guarantee basic subsistence rights (at paragraph 59(a) above), but in the next sentence allows for states which cannot provide a 'minimum essential level of benefits' to 'select a core group of social risks and contingencies' after consulting widely. There is thus an ill-defined lower minimum within a better defined higher minimum – even though the higher minimum itself is pegged at a very low level, namely the provision of subsistence rights (plus basic education).[68]

---

[66] Ibid., para. 59 [footnotes omitted].

[67] See also, ibid., paras. 29–30. This is also considered to be an 'obligation of immediate effect', see para. 40, just like ensuring equal rights of men and women. See also Saul et al. 2014 (n. 2), 654–694.

[68] Saul et al. 2014 (n. 2), 645.

This may demonstrate the following things: First, the problem of allowing the state to choose amongst different possible courses for the realization of core obligations mirrors the 'progressive realization loophole' outlined in the previous chapter – the procedural requirement of a wide process of consultation however offers some solace in this regard. Second, an ill-defined lower minimum can be trickier than a more general, higher standard, because the latter is unambiguous as to what should be strived for.

6.3   Minimum Protection for All

It was mentioned in the previous chapter that according to Bilchitz, 'fixed content' need not be avoided, because 'it is the very stuff of law that makes rights meaningful'.[69] The idea of minimum cores enables the clarification of socio-economic rights' most important content, i.e., the aspects thereof that need to be fulfilled first and foremost. It allows for narrowing down the problematic, nebulous scope of full economic and social rights. The CESCR has succeeded in listing minimum core obligations that follow from the rights enshrined in the ICESCR. Starting from the initial notion of minimum essential levels in General Comment No. 3, it has spelled out tasks and aims for states to prioritize.

I already hinted at the fact that there is a certain overlap between the different minimum cores. They can be grouped into different categories, and as such provide valuable information on the types of guarantees that are considered to form the essential core of socio-economic rights. Before saying something more on this overlap, however, it should be mentioned that there are differences as well. These relate to the famous trichotomy of respecting, protecting and fulfilling socio-economic rights. This tripartite typology was introduced by Eide in 1987 as showing different levels of obligations.[70] At the primary level, states must 'respect the freedom

---

[69] David Bilchitz, 'Does Sandra Liebenberg's New Book Provide a Viable Approach to Adjudication Socio-Economic Rights?', *South African Journal on Human Rights*, 27 (2011), pp. 546–557, 550.

[70] See, for example, the final report on The Right to Adequate Food as a Human Right by Eide as Special Rapporteur E/CN.4/Sub.2/1987/23, 7 July 1987; Asbjørn Eide, 'Realization of Social and Economic Rights and the Minimum Threshold approach', *Human Rights Law Journal*, 10 (1989), pp. 35–50. Over the years Eide has developed his approach and added the obligation to facilitate, see Asbjørn Eide, 'Economic, Social and Cultural Rights as Human Rights' in A. Eide, C. Krause and A. Rosas (eds.), *Economic, Social and Cultural Rights: A Textbook*, 2nd rev. ed. (Leiden: Martinus Nijhoff Publishers, 2001), pp. 9–28.

of individuals to take the necessary actions and use the necessary resources'.[71] At the secondary and tertiary level, they need to protect 'the freedom of action and the use of resources as against other, more assertive or aggressive subjects', and fulfil the expectations of all with regard to the enjoyment of their rights, respectively.[72] Now this could give the impression that the obligation to respect needs to be prioritized,[73] and that minimum core obligations are thus obligations to respect. At the same time, rights to health, housing, social security, etc., have not been recognized merely to protect existing arrangements. They serve the aim of improving of the status quo with regard to socio-economic needs.[74] For this reason, it would make sense if socio-economic core rights mainly concern obligations to fulfil or at least protect socio-economic needs.

The minimum cores listed in the various General Comments, however, comprise obligations of all three kinds. They concern active duties: to take (targeted) steps; to provide, to adopt and implement; and to monitor. Other minimum cores are of a negative kind: the state must show 'respect' by avoiding certain practices in the housing field,[75] and with regard to the social security schemes that are in place[76] – but also when it comes to the free choice of education.[77] This shows that, first, the tripartite typology cannot be used to determine the content of core rights. Second, regardless of the 'typically' positive character of socio-economic rights, ensuring negative obligations in this field can be considered of key importance as well.[78]

Turning to the overlap of the different core obligations, then, it can be said that this takes two forms: first, there is actual overlap in the sense that the core obligations recognized under one right, resemble or correspond to what is identified as a core aspect of another right. For example, the right to social security demands access to social security schemes so that individuals can afford essential health care,[79] while the right to

---

[71] Eide 1989 (n. 70), 39.   [72] Ibid., 40.   [73] Cf. Bilchitz 2007 (n. 15), 195.

[74] Cf. Rolf Künnemann, 'The Right to Adequate Food: Violations to Its Minimum core Content' in A.R. Chapman and S. Russell (eds.), *Core Obligations: Building a Framework for Economic, Social and Cultural Rights* (Antwerp/Oxford/New York: Intersentia, 2002), pp. 163–183, 172.

[75] CESCR, General Comment No. 4, para. 10.

[76] CESCR, General Comment No. 19, para. 59(c).

[77] CESCR, General Comment No. 13: The Right to Education (Art. 13 of the Covenant), 8 December 1999, E/C.12/1999/10 (General Comment No. 13), para. 57.

[78] Katharine G. Young, *Constituting Socio-Economic Rights* (Oxford University Press, 2012), 74–75.

[79] CESCR, General Comment No. 19, para. 59(a).

health requires access to health facilities, goods and services.[80] The right to health, moreover, requires as a core obligation access to minimum essential food to ensure freedom from hunger,[81] while the right to food, unsurprisingly, also entails a core obligation to mitigate and alleviate hunger.[82] This signals that not only socio-economic rights in general but also their essential aspects coincide in important respects.

Second, besides in substance, the different minimum core obligations resemble each other in kind. At least four categories can be identified: first, there is the category of non-discrimination. Whatever exactly states do, or provide for, in terms of socio-economic rights, this must be done in a non-discriminatory manner. The immediate obligation to ensure non-discrimination echoes in the various core obligations that deal with the task of the state to prevent unequal treatment or access.[83] Whether in regard to access to social security or foodstuffs or protection against forced evictions, it should always be ensured that rights are conferred on individuals in a non-discriminatory manner. A second category of core obligations is inherently linked to this issue and concerns the protection of disadvantaged and marginalized individuals and groups.[84] Together with the recognition of basic guarantees in terms of food, health care, etc., this allows for the conclusion that minimum core obligations concern a basic standard of living conditions for all. The state should focus its attention and resources on those vulnerable individuals and groups that cannot assure such a living standard by themselves.

Third and fourth, there are the strategic and procedural minimum cores. Strategic obligations entail that states are at the very least required to adopt and implement a strategy and plan of action in the different

---

[80] CESCR, General Comment No. 14, para. 43(a).   [81] Ibid., para. 43(b).

[82] CESCR, General Comment No. 12: The Right to Adequate Food (Art. 11 of the Covenant), 12 May 1999, E/C.12/1999/5 (General Comment No. 12), para. 6.

[83] See, for example, CESCR, General Comment No. 13, para. 57; CESCR, General Comment No. 14, para. 43(a); CESCR, General Comment No. 15: The Right to Water (Arts. 11 and 12 of the Covenant), 20 January 2003, E/C.12/2002/11 (General Comment No. 15), para. 37(b); CESCR, General Comment No. 18: The Right to Work (Art. 6 of the Covenant), 6 February 2006, E/C.12/GC/18 (General Comment No. 18), para. 31(b); CESCR, General Comment No. 19, para. 59(b). See, on the requirement of non-discrimination, also CESCR, General Comment No. 20: Non-discrimination in economic, social and cultural rights (Art. 2, para. 2, of the International Covenant on Economic, Social and Cultural Rights), 2 July 2009, E/C.12/GC/20 (General Comment No. 20), especially para. 7.

[84] See, for example, CESCR, General Comment No. 14, para. 43(a); CESCR, General Comment No. 18, para. 31(a); CESCR, General Comment No. 19, para. 59(b).

socio-economic fields, to implement schemes and to monitor the extent of the realization of the rights.[85] They hence focus on the means for working towards the fulfilment of the material aims of (core) socio-economic rights. These obligations are of crucial importance in the context of state monitoring, suggesting ways for general improvement. Yet they are arguably hard to translate into core rights protection in individual cases. This is less so when it comes to procedural cores. Procedural obligations are especially highlighted in General Comment No. 7,[86] concerning forced evictions. They do not require a certain (substantive) end result, leaving room for state choices and practices. Rather, they aim at equitable, fair outcomes, also in individual cases. In a fair procedure, the needs of vulnerable individuals and groups are taken into account and discrimination can be addressed.

Together, thus, the different core obligations present a relatively coherent story. This is a story of equality, of minimum guarantees, and of the means for achieving these. In short, states have a duty to provide a subsistence minimum for all.[87] This standard may appear vague, for it is a matter of discussion what such a minimum exactly entails. Nonetheless, recognizing a right to a subsistence minimum may, even without precise specification, form the starting point not only for monitoring purposes but also for dealing with individual complaints. In this regard, it is worth briefly mentioning some of the first views adopted by the Committee on a communication filed under the Optional Protocol. In *López Rodríguez v. Spain* the CESCR did not conclude on a violation of the right to social security under the ICESCR. Material was that the reduction of a non-contributory disability benefit of a prisoner could not be seen to impair his basic needs: '[A] non-contributory benefit cannot, in principle, be withdrawn, reduced or suspended as a consequence of the deprivation of liberty of the beneficiary, unless the measure is provided by law, is reasonable and proportionate, and guarantees at least a minimum level of benefits'.[88] That reliance on a relatively vague minimum may be useful

---

[85] See, for example, CESCR, General Comment No. 14, para. 43(f); CESCR, General Comment No. 15, para. 37(f)(g)(h); CESCR, General Comment No. 18, para. 31(c); CESCR, General Comment No. 19, para. 59(d)(e)(f).

[86] CESCR, General Comment No. 7, para. 15.

[87] CESCR, General Comment No. 14, para. 43(b)(c); CESCR, General Comment No. 15, para. 37(a); CESCR, General Comment No. 19, para. 59(a).

[88] *M.A. López Rodríguez v. Spain*, Communication No. 1/2013, Views of the CESCR under the OP to the ICESCR (fifty-fifth session) (22 February–4 March 2016), UN doc. E/C.12/57/D/1/2013. In *I.D.G. v. Spain* (Communication No. 2/2014, Views of the CESCR under

also followed from the discussion of the right to a subsistence minimum in Germany.[89] This arguably holds true in particular when protection on the basis of classical rights norms is concerned. There, the idea of protecting a social minimum presents a middle path between an unlimited interpretation and excluding social protection altogether.

Conclusion

The content of core socio-economic rights and obligations is not beyond contestation. The idea that it is impossible to objectively identify such content is one of the obvious grounds to jettison the concept of core rights. In this chapter, my aim was to argue against this conclusion. Not by proclaiming that there is a deontological core to each right, but by clarifying a few things. First, there are different approaches to determine core content. Core rights may be determined based on the right in question, or rather with the help of broader agreement or expert information on what is essential in terms of rights. These approaches are mutually enhancing in the sense that whereas there are good reasons for interpreting rights independently, in order to avoid a court-centred understanding or closure more generally, other sources may prove valuable as well. Further, it is clear from the practice of the CESCR that it is possible to determine minimum core obligations. The different, relatively detailed core obligations it has recognized are perhaps not incontrovertible, yet they have played their role in theory and practice – even if by evoking criticism and thus keeping alive an important debate on socio-economic rights. I showed that the cores that have been recognized are both negative and positive. Yet they resemble each other regardless of the precise socio-economic right or rights norm that lies at their origin.

---

the OP to the ICESCR (fifty-fifth session) (1–19 June 2015), UN doc. E/C.12/55/D/2/ 2014) the Court found a violation focusing on the procedural guarantees related to the right to housing (cf. S. 6.2.1).

[89] See Ch. 5, S. 5.3.

PART III

Core Socio-Economic Rights and the ECtHR

7

A Core Rights Perspective for the ECtHR

By now, a broad but also diffuse picture of core rights protection has emerged. In the previous chapters, different core rights doctrines have been brought to the fore. Core rights, in the sense of particularly import-ant aspects of rights, serve as a reminder of the fact that there are limits to limitations of rights, but they can also be used for specifying the scope and content of socio-economic rights. In other words, core rights can play a role at both stages of fundamental rights adjudication, i.e., when interpreting a rights norm but also when reviewing whether an infringe-ment was justified. Part II has not given an exhaustive overview of today's theory and practice related to the notion of core rights.[1] It has, however, presented the most important features thereof. Ranging from the inter-national monitoring context to constitutional adjudication, from Europe to South Africa, and from classical guarantees to socio-economic rights, it must be concluded that the notion of core rights is in many ways widespread.

It is now time to return to the ECtHR and its socio-economic protec-tion. After summarizing some of the findings from the previous chapters, I will outline the way in which these can add to a better understanding of the Strasbourg socio-economic case law, as well as serve to improve the Court's reasoning in this field. The core rights perspective I develop builds on different core rights experiences, but is tailored to the Stras-bourg context. It ties in with the ECtHR's current practice while providing a blueprint moving forward. Compared to a mere focus on effectiveness

---

[1] Interesting links could, for example, be made to the protection of a right to a vital minimum in Colombian constitutional law. See David Landau, 'The Promise of a Min-imum Core Approach: The Colombian Model for Judicial Review of Austerity Measures' in A. Nolan (ed), *Economic and Social Rights after the Global Crisis* (Cambridge University Press, 2015), pp. 276–298. Relying on the idea of the social state in combination with human dignity, the targeted approach Landau describes shows similarities with the protection of the *Existenzminimum* in Germany (Ch. 5. S. 5.3).

and indivisibility, adding a core rights perspective results in a better fit for the ECtHR's socio-economic protection – keeping in mind the exemplary role of this Court as a supranational individual rights protector, as well as its sensitive position in a Europe that, in many ways, appears to be in turmoil.

Section 7.1 summarizes several important core rights-related insights. Starting from the insight that core rights can be used at the interpretation stage, as well as at the review stage, it is shown that the role of core rights protection in rights adjudication can take roughly four forms. Moreover, I recapitulate the point that core rights can be indeterminable and workable at the same time, and that courts using core rights do not necessarily overstep their powers. Section 7.2 will then explain which understanding of core socio-economic rights protection best suits the practice of the ECtHR. Finally, in Section 7.3, I clarify how a core rights perspective is integrated in the Court's reasoning, i.e., in defining the scope of the ECHR rights as well as in deciding upon individual applications. The Court's review is often characterized by a proportionality or balancing test, and the question is therefore how core socio-economic rights protection sheds a different light on this test.

7.1   Core Rights Revisited

7.1.1   From Absolute-Absolute to Relative-Relative Core Rights

There are several persistent perceptions of core rights protection. One of the most important of these is the idea that core rights are absolute. Core rights are often thought of as being decisive for the outcome of a case. For example: if the right to emergency medication belongs to the core of the right to health, any failure to guarantee this core is thought to constitute this right's breach. It is also often assumed that core rights need to be determined in the abstract and are everlasting. Partly because of these assumptions, determining core rights is perceived as an extremely difficult or even impossible task. When left to a court, moreover, the determination of core rights may be considered to confer too much power on the judiciary. Combined with the idea that core guarantees preclude broader rights protection, this easily leads to the conclusion that a core rights approach can better be avoided.

Yet these perceptions only partly coincide with reality, or at least lack nuance. Of course, the German *Wesensgehalt* doctrine shows that a core right can be perceived as an absolute *Schranken-Schranke* (limit to limitations).[2] Moreover, generally applicable core rights have been determined by, for example, the UN Committee on Economic, Social and Cultural Rights (CESCR) in its General Comments.[3] But this does not mean that the identified cores present unassailable truths concerning the meaning and importance of specific rights, nor does it mean that exceptions to or alterations over time of core guarantees are necessarily precluded. Similarly, the fact that a court (or other non-democratic body) identifies and applies core rights does not in itself justify the conclusion that it thereby oversteps the boundaries of its competences.

If there is one thing the previous chapters have shown, it is that core rights theory and practice is diverse. Ingrained ideas on the concept of core rights can be confronted with alternative understandings that seem less inherently problematic. If we are willing to move beyond a narrow understanding of what rights' cores are and what they can be used for, a richer picture emerges that allows for informed deliberation on the possible added value of this notion for legal contexts, like that of the ECtHR. For this purpose, I will start this chapter by bringing some order to the chaos by redefining the absolute-relative dichotomy so that it incorporates the existing variety of core rights possibilities.

The idea that cores are by definition absolutes is a common reason for criticizing the concept of the minimum core. When understood as inflexible rules predetermining the outcome of cases, core rights protection can indeed be problematic. First, there is the issue of conflicting cores. If two or more absolute cores conflict, obviously no rational solution can be found. Second, the absolute protection of essential aspects of rights may seem utopian in the light of practical possibilities. This holds true especially in the context of positive and socio-economic rights. After all, it is fair to say that resources and means will not always suffice to guarantee even individuals' most basic needs. And third, underlying the distrust of absolute cores is the thought that it is profoundly difficult to identify the core of a right. This seems especially problematic when the core will prevail over any imaginable and future conflicting interest.

All this seems reason for jettisoning the idea of core rights protection altogether. This is what the opponents of core rights protection in the South African debate, as well as the South African Constitutional Court

---

[2] See Ch. 4, S. 4.3.1.
[3] See the General Comments on the various ICESCR rights and Ch. 5, S. 5.1 and Ch. 6, S. 6.1.

itself, have indeed favoured.[4] In the German context, however, this solution is less obvious, since a norm protecting the core of rights has been included in Article 19(2) of the *Grundgesetz*. This provision cannot simply be ignored, which is why alternative understandings of core rights protection have been suggested. On one hand, there are those who have proposed an objective reading of the *Wesensgehaltsgarantie*, according to which Article 19(2) guarantees that the core of every fundamental right is preserved for society in general.[5] On the other hand, it has been suggested that rights' cores are relative in the sense that they always hinge upon the particularities of a specific case.[6] According to this understanding, the core of a right can become visible only by means of the outcome of a balancing test – when it turns out that a measure was proportional, the core of the right at stake was not interfered with.

However, it is not necessary to either ignore the concept entirely or resort to an objective or purely circumstantial understanding of rights' cores in order to overcome the downsides of absolute core protection. When going through the different core rights approaches, it appears that there are more than strictly absolute and completely case-dependent cores. This has to do with the fact that both the absolute and the relative attributes of cores can be understood in two different ways, resulting in a catalogue of no less than four different core rights possibilities.

The different understandings relate to the different stages of rights reasoning, and are hence relevant for the adjudicative context. 'Absolute' can refer to absolute *content*, i.e., to the definition of a core that is

---

[4] In the case of *Grootboom* (Government of the Republic of South Africa v. Grootboom & Others 2001 (1) SA 46 (CC) (S. Afr.), the South African Constitutional Court amongst other things held that it lacks the necessary information to determine minimum cores and that needs diverge to such extent that no core entitlements follow from the Constitution (paras. 32–42). In *TAC* (Minister of Health & Others v. Treatment Action Campaign & Others 2001 (5) SA 721 (CC)) it held that it is 'impossible to give everyone access even to a 'core' service immediately' (para. 35). According to Young, the concept of the core is being jettisoned even by those who are otherwise committed to the economic and social rights framework (Katharine G. Young, 'The Minimum Core of Economic and Social Rights: A Concept in Search of Content', *Yale Journal of International Law*, 33 (2008), pp. 113–175, 115–116). Cf. Ch. 5, S. 5.2.2.

[5] Cf. Claudia Drews, *Die Wesensgehaltgarantie des Art. 19 II GG*, Diss. (Baden-Baden: Nomos, 2005), 77–82. See Ch. 4, S. 4.3.1.

[6] Ibid., 66–75. Cf. Peter Häberle, *Die Wesensgehaltgarantie des Art. 19 II GG – zugleich ein Beitrag zum institutionellen Verständnis der Grundrecht und zur Lehre vom Gesetzesvorbehalt*, 3rd ed. (Heidelberg: C.F. Müller, 1983), Robert Alexy, *A Theory of Constitutional Rights*, transl. Julian Rivers (Oxford University Press, 2002), and Martin Borowski, *Grundrechte als Prinzipien*, 2nd ed. (Baden-Baden: Nomos, 2007). See Ch. 4, S. 4.3.3.

independent of the circumstances of a particular case, as well as to absolute *protection*, which implies that when the core of a right is touched upon, this automatically results in a violation of the relevant rights norm. 'Relative' core rights protection, in turn, can either mean that the *core itself* is relative, because it can only be determined in the context of the specific case at hand, or that it is *protected* in a relative manner, meaning that there is some room for justifying an interference with the core of a right.

The first combined possibility that follows from this is absolute-absolute core rights protection. This is the idea that cores of rights are determined independently from the particular facts of a case and are absolutely protected. It can be found in the German constitutional law debate. Because the *Wesensgehaltsgarantie* states, '*In no case* may the core content of a constitutional right be infringed', relative protection seems precluded. Those who, moreover, consider the content of the core to be something absolute, start from the idea that there are certain, case-independent aspects of fundamental rights that are so important they cannot be interfered with.[7] The concrete definition of these aspects, also in the German debate, is however often left open.[8]

The German right to an *Existenzminimum* (subsistence minimum) may also be considered an absolute-absolute core guarantee. The *Bundesverfassungsgericht* has indicated, albeit in open terms, what this minimum entails.[9] In addition, because it is inferred from the absolute protection of human dignity, when the state does not live up to the minimum, the Constitution has automatically been violated.[10] Finally, in the debate on economic and social rights protection in South Africa, opponents of the incorporation of minimum cores in the Constitutional Court's socio-economic practice use arguments against absolute-absolute

---

[7] Ibid., 62–66, and Ch. 4, S. 4.3.2.

[8] But see Georg Herbert, 'Der Wesensgehalt der Grundrechte', *Europäische Grundrechte-Zeitschrift*, 12 (1985), pp. 321–335. He refers, amongst other things, to the character and function of fundamental rights, human dignity and comparative insights.

[9] See BVerfGE 125, 175, 1 BvL 1/09 of 9 February 2010 (*Hartz IV*) and BVerfGE 132, 134, 1 BvL 10/10, of 18 July 2012 (*Asylum Seekers Benefits*). It 'guarantees the whole subsistence minimum by a uniform fundamental rights guarantee which encompasses both the physical existence of the individual, that is food, clothing, household goods, housing, heating, hygiene and health . . . , and ensuring the possibility to maintain inter-human relationships and a minimum of participation in social, cultural and political life' (*Hartz IV*, para. 135).

[10] Art. 1(1) GG. Read in conjunction with the *Sozialstaatsprinzip* of Art. 20(1) GG, this provision is understood to include a right to a subsistence minimum. See Ch. 5, S. 5.3.

cores – holding that these cannot be objectively determined and, more-over, cannot be met in practice.[11] The Constitutional Court has con-cluded against using core rights, on the basis of what seems to be the same strict understanding.[12]

In the second possibility, core rights can be understood in an absolute-relative way. Like their absolute-absolute counterparts, the content of such cores is something absolute, i.e., not contingent on the circum-stances of the case. However, the *protection* of these cores is to some extent case-dependent, which means that in certain instances an inter-ference with an essential aspect of a right can be justified. This possibility thereby acknowledges that resource constraints or other very weighty considerations can stand in the way of securing even the very core of a right, without implying that the content of the core itself cannot be determined except for in the light of these constraints.

A first example is the minimum core approach as it has been developed by the CESCR in relation to economic and social rights. Although minimum core obligations must be prioritized, the CESCR has accepted that non-compliance with a minimum core may result only in a prima facie violation of the ICESCR. Such a violation entails a heavy burden of justification, and it is up to the state to prove that all resources have in fact been spent. Yet, it is not imperative that a failure to fulfil a core obligation leads to a breach of the ICESCR.[13] Bilchitz's contribution to the South African debate can be placed under the same header. He argues for a less rigid minimum core that allows for limited exceptions.[14]

---

[11] Ch. 5, S. 5.2.2.   [12] See n. 4.

[13] According to the CESCR, 'a State party in which any significant number of individuals is deprived of essential foodstuffs, of essential primary health care, of basic shelter and housing, or of the most basic forms of education is, prima facie, failing to discharge its obligations under the Covenant ... In order for a State party to be able to attribute its failure to meet at least its minimum core obligations to a lack of available resources it must demonstrate that every effort has been made to use all resources that are at its disposition in an effort to satisfy, as a matter of priority, those minimum obligations' (CESCR, General Comment No. 3: The Nature of States Parties' Obligations (Art. 2(1) of the Covenant), 14 December 1990, E/1991/23, para. 10).

[14] David Bilchitz, 'Towards a Reasonable Approach to the Minimum Core: Laying the Foundations for Future Socio-Economic Rights Jurisprudence', *South African Journal on Human Rights*, 19 (2003), pp. 1–26; David Bilchitz, *Poverty and Fundamental Rights: The Justification and Enforcement of Socio-Economic Rights* (Oxford University Press, 2007). See Ch. 5, S. 5.2.3. These exceptions relate to scarcity of resources, but also recognize that when the fulfilment of a core requires a disproportionally vast amount of resources, or leaves no room for the realization of other rights and aims, not meeting core obligations can be justified (ibid., 212).

According to Bilchitz, the minimum core should be rigid in one respect only: namely, to the extent that 'it is simply unacceptable for any human being to live without sufficient resources to maintain their survival'.[15] Core rights must therefore be determined independent from resources and other state concerns, because otherwise 'the failure to meet basic needs under conditions of scarcity does not violate any claim people have'.[16] Core rights are thus a matter of content per se, while countervailing interests may obstruct their eventual manifestation. The advantage of recognizing absolute-relative cores is that it offers clarity on what should be strived for in terms of rights protection. Absolute-relative cores provide for standards that can guide adjudicational practice, indicating what should obtain weighed priority and is thus more difficult to be outbalanced by other interests.

The third alternative is a relative-absolute understanding of rights' cores. A first question is whether this is possible in the first place: how can something relative, the content of which is thus not determined beforehand, be absolutely protected? It is the gist of the relative-absolute perception of core rights that what these rights entail exactly cannot be determined *a priori*, but only in a contextual manner. At the same time, the protection afforded is absolute in the sense that interferences with the core of a right are unacceptable. To make this work, it must be accepted that the core of a right can only become apparent when a specific rights claim is reviewed. When an interference is considered to be justified given the circumstances of a case, this means that the core has not been interfered with. In turn, when a violation is found, this could mean that the absolutely protected core has been touched upon.

A clear example is the German *Wesensgehaltsgarantie* as explained by those who support a relative theory. This theory purports that the core of a right is determined on the basis of a proportionality analysis or balancing test, which allows taking into account of specific facts and circumstances. Such an approach is in keeping with Alexy's optimization thesis, according to which a balancing exercise is necessary for securing an optimal manifestation of rights given the concrete legal and factual possibilities.[17] Indeed, for some relativists, core rights only appear when prima facie rights are turned into eventual entitlements.[18] Others, however, do not seem to distinguish between the right in itself and the right as limited, but hold that rights – and so their cores – are always carved

---

[15] Bilchitz 2003 (n. 14), 15. [16] Bilchitz 2007 (n. 14), 217.
[17] Ch. 4, S. 4.3.3. See Alexy 2002 (n. 6). [18] Ibid.; Borowski 2007 (n. 6).

out in the light of all relevant factors.[19] They renounce the idea of prima facie rights, and thereby a two-stage approach to rights adjudication.

Next to the *Wesensgehaltsgarantie*, the German right to a subsistence minimum could, instead of as an absolute-absolute guarantee, also be understood as a relative-absolute one – albeit in a somewhat different way. Since the right to a subsistence minimum, as it has been formulated by the *Bundesverfassungsgericht* (namely in a qualitative manner),[20] leaves room for further (quantitative) interpretation by the legislator, it has been said that this right is 'by nature relative'.[21] Yet once the FCC holds that the right to a subsistence minimum has not been complied with, the constitution is violated. However, the idea that the *content* of the minimum subsistence guarantee is relative is not entirely convincing. The FCC has, after all, set important parameters for what it entails,[22] and it seems natural that rights statements leave some room for further interpretation. Compared to a relative understanding of the *Wesensgehaltsgarantie*, a somewhat indistinct core rights interpretation can nevertheless form the starting point for social rights adjudication.

Unsurprisingly, the final possibility is relative-relative core rights protection. But what is left of the pronounced role of core rights when both their content and protection are not absolute? It seems that when the content of a core is contingent on the circumstances of a case, and this core allows for justifiable interferences, the notion of core rights protection *de facto* becomes meaningless. Still, Liebenberg's proposal for improving the reasonableness test of the South African Constitutional Court signals that cores that are relative both in terms of their content and protection can have some – though admittedly limited – added value.[23] She holds that minimum cores could play a role in reasonableness review, though not as a general standard determining the content of

---

[19] Cf. Häberle 1983 (n. 6).   [20] See n. 9.

[21] Christian Seiler, 'Das Grundrecht auf ein menschenwürdiges Existenzminimum: Zum Urteil des Bundesverfassungsgerichts vom 9.2.2010', *JuristenZeitung*, 65 (2010), pp. 500–505, 504.

[22] These parameters take the shape of procedural requirements, thereby acknowledging the fact that it is not for the courts to determine a quantitative subsistence minimum (see Ch. 5, S. 5.3).

[23] Sandra Liebenberg, *Socio-Economic Rights: Adjudication under a Transformative Constitution* (Cape Town: Juta and Company, 2010). See Ch. 5, S. 5.2.3. Since Liebenberg does not want to give fixed content to rights, according to David Bilchitz, 'Does Sandra Liebenberg's New Book Provide a Viable Approach to Adjudication Socio-Economic Rights?', *South African Journal on Human Rights*, 27 (2011), pp. 546–557, her approach fails to set the necessary standard.

the right that ought to be protected. Instead, what constitutes the core of a right needs to be determined on the basis of the multiplicity of intersectional aspects that together determine the individual interest concerned.[24] Because these aspects differ from case to case, so must cores. Furthermore, core rights alone cannot be decisive for whether an interference or omission was reasonable or not. They instead constitute one factor amongst many that need to be taken into account, and 'can be incorporated in the reasonableness analysis by placing a particularly heavy burden of justification on the state in circumstances where a person or group lacks access to a basic socio-economic service or resource'.[25] Liebenberg's proposal thus aims at distinguishing levels of interferences and omissions. This clarifies that some individual claims deserve more protection than others, yet because of the contextual focus does not provide for a standard that can be applied in other cases as well.

Relative-relative cores can thus affect the strictness of the test. Rather than varying 'according to the circumstances, subject matter and background',[26] relying on core rights implies that the individual interest is placed on the foreground when deciding on the intensity of the review.[27] Similarly, according to an absolute-relative approach, noncompliance with the core of a right may be justified – but only if very strong reasons are provided. However, what this overview of core rights possibilities has underscored is that core rights do not only play a role at the review stage. They may function as a decisive test, or indicate a heavy burden of justification, but also are a matter of rights' scope. Cores may be used to determine whether a particular interest is covered by a rights norm in the first place and can thus form the starting point for an admissible claim.[28]

---

[24] Liebenberg 2010 (n. 23), 184–185.   [25] Ibid., 184 [footnote omitted].

[26] Cf. the ECtHR's margin of appreciation, see, for example, *Petrovic v. Austria*, ECtHR 27 March 1990, 20458/92, para. 38. See Ch. 3, S. 3.3.3.

[27] Katharine G. Young, 'Proportionality, Reasonableness, and Socio-Economic Rights' (20 January 2017) in V.C. Jackson and M. Tushnet (eds.) *Proportionality: New Frontiers, New Challenges* (Cambridge University Press, forthcoming 2017); Boston College Law School Legal Studies Research Paper No. 430. Available at SSRN: https://ssrn.com/abstract=2892707.

[28] Cf. Ida Elisabeth Koch, *Human Rights as Indivisible Rights: The Protection of Socio-Economic Demands under the European Convention on Human Rights* (Leiden: Martinus Nijhoff Publishers, 2009), 288, speaking of 'a minimum core approach to justiciability'; Bruce Porter, 'The Crisis of Economic, Social and Cultural Rights and Strategies for Addressing it' in J. Squires, M. Langford and B. Thiele (eds.), *The Road to a Remedy: Current Issues in the Litigation of Economic, Social and Cultural Rights* (Australian Human Rights Centre in collaboration with the Centre for Housing Rights and Evictions, 2005), pp. 43–69, 52.

This can be done in an absolute, general manner, or rather on a case-by-case basis. Minimum cores can be used as 'the appropriate vehicle for courts' to help set certain priorities and delineate the states' prima facie obligations.[29] In line with this, the CESCR, for example, suggests that incorporation of the ICESCR in national legal orders 'enables courts to adjudicate violations of the right to health, *or at least its core obligations, by direct reference to the Covenant*'.[30] As I will further explain in this chapter, the double role of core rights is also relevant in the practice of the ECtHR. Whereas the content of socio-economic cores enables a more transparent interpretation of ECHR rights, their protection informs the standard of review at the application stage.

7.1.2   Indeterminable but Workable

Sceptical attitudes towards the idea of core rights protection are often grounded in the belief that the core of a right is indeterminable. German legal writers, for example, have argued that the *Wesensgehaltsgarantie* really adds nothing to the requirement of proportionality. Apart from that, the *Wesen* of a right is empty or non-existent.[31] The issue of indeterminacy is also brought up in the South African debate. It is argued that there is no essential element that can be distilled from a right that cannot somehow be contested or repudiated. Cores, then, only exist by virtue of subjective interpretations, hence it is better not to identify them in the first place.[32]

The critics are largely right. It seems impossible to know what the essence of a fundamental right really is. At least, that is, when what is sought after is an unassailable, irrefutable truth.[33] In the same vein, it is

---

[29] Katherine G. Young, *Constituting Socio-Economic Rights* (Oxford University Press, 2012), 79.

[30] CESCR, General Comment No. 14: The Right to the Highest Attainable Standard of Health (Art. 12 of the Covenant), 11 August 2000, E/C.12/2000/4, para. 60 [emphasis added].

[31] See, for example, Arthur Kaufmann, 'Über den "Wesensgehalt" der Grund- und Menschenrechte', *Archiv für Rechts- und Sozialphilosopie*, 70 (1984), pp. 384–399, 391–392.

[32] See, Ch. 5, S. 5.2.2.

[33] Cf. Jochen von Bernstorff, 'Proportionality Without Balancing: Why Judicial Ad Hoc Balancing in Unnecessary and Potentially Detrimental to the Realisation of Individual and Collective Self-Determination' in L. Lazarus, Ch. McCrudden and N. Bowles (eds.), *Reasoning Rights: Comparative Judicial Engagement* (Oxford: Hart Publishing, 2014), pp. 63–86, 83.

obvious that completely objective criteria for identifying the essential aspects of a right cannot be found either. Foundational principles pointing at particular cores may be repudiated, whereas consensus as a basis to determine cores can be contested as well. Nevertheless, this indeterminacy is not reason for jettisoning the concept of core rights altogether in all legal contexts. First, when the content of cores or the protection they offer is understood in a relative manner, the issue of the determination of the core becomes somewhat less critical. When its content is flexible or can be developed over time, or when an interference with a core of a right does not automatically lead a breach of this right, it seems less problematic that there is an element of subjectivity involved.

Moreover, it can be worth using the concept of core rights when the practical advantages outweigh the possible downsides. In the context of the ICESCR, for example, the notion of minimum cores evolved from the need to solve a concrete practical problem. The requirement of progressive realization leaves unanswered the question of what needs to be achieved as a matter of priority. The notion of core rights was introduced as the missing piece of the puzzle: it enabled the CESCR to monitor whether states used their available resources to progressively realize the rights enshrined in the ICESCR by concentrating on certain very important guarantees.[34] The cores identified by the CESCR are perhaps not incontestable. However, they do serve the aim of clarifying the immediate content of the ICESCR norms, thereby increasing their workability and thus playing an important role.

In addition to the fact that the use of core rights can serve practical purposes, let me make two more points. First, the disagreement on core content – either potential or real – must not be overstated. Here we can learn from Sunstein's 'incompletely theorized agreements'[35] and the notion of overlapping consensus.[36] It can be said that 'people from different cultures may continue to disagree about what is good, but nevertheless agree about what is insufferably, unarguably wrong'.[37] This

---

[34] See, Ch. 5, S. 5.1.

[35] See, for example, Cass R. Sunstein, 'Incompletely Theorized Agreements', *Harvard Law Review,* 108 (1995), pp. 1733–1772, Cass R. Sunstein, 'Incompletely Theorized Agreements in Constitutional Law', *Social Research,* 74 (2007), pp. 1–24.

[36] John Rawls, *A Theory of Justice* (Cambridge, MA: Harvard University Press, 1971) (1999); John Rawls, *Political Liberalism* (New York: Columbia University Press, 1993).

[37] Michael Ignatieff, 'Human Rights as Ideology' in M. Ignatieff (A. Gutmann (ed.)), *Human Rights as Politics and Idolatry* (Princeton University Press, 2001), 56. See also Young 2012 (n. 29), 66.

is especially true where social rights are concerned. What people think should be protected at minimum by socio-economic rights norms can be the same regardless of different principled starting points. For example, a roof over one's head and access to basic social assistance will normally be understood as crucially important aspects of the right to housing and the right to social security, respectively.

Second, determining socio-economic cores for the purposes of adjudication need not involve much detail. It is true that there can be doubt as to the exact degree of protection core rights should entail. Whereas the focus of the core might be relatively unequivocal, in other words, it can still be a matter of controversy what basic housing or social security precisely entails. That this issue need not be solved entirely is illustrated by the German FCC's interpretation of the right to a subsistence minimum.[38] Phrasing this minimum right in relatively abstract, non-quantifiable terms, the FCC has left some room for the legislator to determine the exact content of the subsistence minimum and the way in which it is provided. It merely, but unambiguously, clarified that *minimum* social rights are to be protected as a matter of human dignity. Thereby it underscored the importance of basic individual, social protection, while demarcating the judicial role in this regard – a point on which I will now say something more.

7.1.3   Core Rights and Courts

It is often suggested that by pinpointing cores, a court transgresses the boundaries of its adjudicative task. It would lead courts to engage in decisions on the general distribution of rights and freedoms. This can be considered problematic from the perspective of separation of powers, since courts would thereby usurp policy-making tasks belonging to the government. This problem is even more obvious when positive and socio-economic rights are concerned. Choices in the field of social policy are usually politically and ideologically laden and are closely intertwined with budgetary constraints. One may consider fields like housing, health care or social security, where the means that can be spent on costly measures are scarce. In this context, the judiciary's determination of core issues that deserve priority will easily circumscribe the democratic *Spielraum* of the other branches.

---

[38] See Ch. 5, S. 5.3.

A related concern is that judges lack the expertise to make choices amongst the different policy and budgetary options.[39] Does the immediate requirement to grant access to low-cost housing to marginalized groups serve the desired aims better than any long-term housing policy directed at the population at large? And would a core requirement in the field of health care not impede the achievement of health aims more generally, or leave too little room for improvement in the field of housing? It seems plausible to argue that courts do not have the necessary data required to calculate what works best towards the realization of broader socio-economic rights. What they can do is ask whether a given policy was reasonable or the measures taken proportional – but they lack the competences needed for setting policy priorities.

Again, it can be said that when core rights are considered to be (in some way) relative, the impact on the leeway of the other branches is less far-reaching and hence less contentious. When it is merely determined that minimum social protection must be granted, moreover, it is difficult to hold that this is a subjective determination that could have just as well turned out differently. When the concrete measures are left to be decided by nonjudicial actors, 'usurpation of powers' may seem to be an overstatement.

Besides, it is doubtful whether the identification of core guarantees by definition increases the power of courts as opposed to the other branches. It is true that the definition and application of cores confers on courts an important and difficult task. But at the same time, a core rights approach also limits and structures their competences. First of all, using a core rights perspective for determining the justiciable scope of a right requires a court to engage with the scope of its authority. In this way, the minimum core could help a court to 'provide clear reasons for its involvement in . . . [socio-economic] cases, and a clear statement of the important interests involved which would demarcate the scope of its own decision-making powers'.[40] A court's review will subsequently be guided by this core, which means that once it is held that a core right is at stake, the argumentative leeway of the court is confined. When core rights are

---

[39] The South African Constitutional Court, for example, has held in the case of *Grootboom* ((n. 4), para. 33) that it could only determine minimum cores when 'sufficient information is placed before a court to enable it to determine the minimum core in any given context'. This it considered not to be the case.

[40] Bilchitz 2003 (n. 14), 10.

absolutely protected, courts have no choice but to conclude that there has been a violation. As such, the core rule binds the court while simultaneously enhancing the predictability of the case law. Also, when cores are perceived as important indicators rather than absolute rule-like guarantees, they cannot be ignored. An interference with a core right can require that the onus of proof be shifted to the state, or demand that a particularly compelling justification is provided. Although this still leaves room for different outcomes, the room for reaching a subjective conclusion is hereby clearly reduced and more limited than when a court conducts an opaque balancing test. In fact, it can be that a proportionality or reasonableness test becomes more structured with the help of core rights, namely by adding a component that affects the – generally very ad hoc – way these tests are being conducted.[41]

The fact that core rights may actually direct and constrain the judicial power could also be considered a disadvantage. This is the case when it is considered that courts dealing with fundamental rights should remain flexible enough to grant individual protection when needed, without being barred by narrow definitions or core-periphery distinctions. Yet a focus on core rights need not minimize rights protection, while flexibility does not always seem appropriate regardless of the particular legal context. It is said that core rights protection 'trades rights inflation for rights ambition': rather than offering prima facie protection to a great variety of interests that might be only tentatively connected to the rights norm concerned, it channels the attention towards more specific guarantees.[42] This does not only fit a more limited understanding of the courts' role in the socio-economic area, but can also ensure meaningful, actual protection. The risk that such a targeted approach, securing the needs of certain claimants, is to the detriment of the achievement of more general socio-economic protection seems minimal because the constraints it places on the flexibility of courts do not imply that there is no room for context-sensitive protection. Especially for a supranational human rights protector like the ECtHR, bound by the civil and political norms of the ECHR, core socio-economic rights protection may therefore be a fitting approach.

---

[41] Cf. Von Bernstorff 2014 (n. 33), especially 83–84; Liebenberg 2010 (n. 23), 184–185. See also Ch. 3, S. 3.3.2 (on the [potential] role of categorical rules in proportionality review).
[42] Young 2012 (n. 29), 67.

7.2   Minimum Core Socio-Economic Protection under the ECHR

Core rights protection is inherent in the idea of fundamental rights protection. That fundamental rights are no trumps and can often justifiably be limited is generally accepted, but so is the idea that rights should not be sacrificed entirely. References to core rights in constitutions and human rights practices worldwide embrace the importance of especially protecting rights' most essential aspects. In the context of the ICESCR, for example, minimum cores were identified not just because it was thought that the focus should be on a few, more tangible socio-economic guarantees, but also because particular aspects of socio-economic rights were considered especially urgent and important.[43] It can be added that the idea of core rights is particularly relevant in times of rights proliferation.[44] There is today a clear preference for qualifying a great number of interests as fundamental rights, as this creates a forum for justification.[45] Whether prima facie rights are rendered definitive then depends on the conflicting interests at issue.[46] The expansion of rights has been described in a somewhat condemning way as resulting in 'rights inflation'.[47] Yet regardless of how this development is assessed, it makes clear that, both in theory and in practice, fundamental rights are not, or are no longer, guarantees applying only to a limited array of narrowly circumscribed individual freedoms. In turn, this means that it is

---

[43] Cf. CESCR, General Comment No. 3, para. 10, stating that '[i]f the Covenant were to be read in such a way as not to establish such a minimum core obligation, it would be largely deprived of its raison d'être'.

[44] In Möller's theory (Kai Möller, *The Global Model of Constitutional Rights* [Oxford University Press, 2012]), this is an important element of the 'global model of constitutional rights'. See, in relation to the ECtHR, Janneke Gerards, 'Fundamental Rights and Other Interests: Should It Really Make a Difference?' in E. Brems (ed.), *Conflicts between Fundamental Rights* (Antwerp/Oxford/New York: Intersentia, 2008), pp. 655–690, 659 ff. (cf. also Janneke Gerards, 'The Prism of Fundamental Rights', *European Constitutional Law Review*, 8 [2012], pp. 173–202).

[45] See, for example, Alexy 2002 (n. 6); Mattias Kumm, 'Constitutional Rights as Principles: On the Structure and Domain of Constitutional Justice', *International Journal of Constitutional Law*, 2 (2004), pp. 574–596; Aharon Barak, *Proportionality: Constitutional Rights and Their Limitations* (Cambridge University Press, 2012); Möller 2012 (n. 44), and Ch. 3, S. 3.2.2.

[46] Alexy 2002 (n. 6), 178–179.

[47] Möller 2012 (n. 44), 3, who holds that '[e]specially in Europe a development has been observed which is sometimes pejoratively called "rights inflation"'. He however uses this term 'in a neutral sense as referring to the increasing protection of relatively trivial interests as (prima facie) rights'.

possible – or indeed necessary – to differentiate within the (potential) scope of rights.[48]

Chapter 1 and Chapter 2 have introduced the subject and problem that triggered this study. I have shown that a broad interpretation of ECHR rights has led the court to engage in the field of socio-economic rights protection. Explanations for this development have focused on the interpretative room for positive, social protection rather than on how the Court should deal with this leeway. Together with the criticism directed at the Court's proportionality review and margin of appreciation, this has left a vacuum in the justification of its socio-economic practice, as well as in guiding the way forward. Having delved into the idea of core rights protection, it can now be explained exactly why and how this idea suits the socio-economic protection offered by the Strasbourg Court. We have seen that core rights protection can take different forms, so the first question is which of these is most promising in this regard.

The ECtHR is a unique court. Established in 1950 to secure the collective enforcement of certain of the rights stated in the UDHR, its practice has turned into the most effective example of supranational fundamental rights protection worldwide. The task of the Court is characterized by various tensions. As a human rights court, it aims to ensure individual rights protection. At the same time, as a supranational court, the ECtHR is required to show deference to member states' policies and practices, interfering only when its subsidiary role requires it to do so. In this connection, the Court also needs to provide a certain level of clarity on what the ECHR rights require.[49] It follows from the margin of appreciation that there is room for states to determine what must be done to comply with the Convention, yet given that the Court's interpretation has *res interpretata* effect and *de facto* functions as a signpost for member states devising policies and practices, some guidance is nevertheless required. That is, the Court needs to reason in a convincing and transparent manner, ensuring individual protection while elucidating the standards of the Convention.[50]

The tensions inherent in the Court's multidimensional task are especially apparent in its protection of socio-economic rights. The socio-economic sphere cannot be distinguished from the sphere protected by the Convention altogether. At the same time, stretching the civil and

---

[48] Cf. Barak 2012 (n. 45), 531.   [49] Ch. 1, S. 1.1.2.   [50] Ch. 2, S. 2.3.2.

political norms of the Convention to include positive social protection can easily be criticized. For example, if a right to protection of property is understood as granting a right to acquire property rights in the form of social security benefits, the Court's sphere of influence is expanded enormously.[51] On the other hand, once socio-economic interests are prima facie protected, automatically granting a wide margin of appreciation leaves one to wonder why the Convention was held applicable in the first place.[52]

The idea of core rights protection accommodates the aim of ensuring robust individual rights protection, while also adhering to a plausible interpretation of ECHR rights. The core rights notion envisaged here is not an absolute one, i.e., core socio-economic rights protection under the Convention should leave some room for justifiable limitations. This guarantees the flexibility necessary for a Court like the ECtHR to sometimes step back, even if important social guarantees are at stake. After all, socio-economic rights have not explicitly been taken up in the Convention, and especially when positive protection is concerned the Court's possibilities are limited. In addition, even though most Council of Europe member states are relatively affluent, there may be reasons for (temporarily) not complying even with basic social rights. The recent economic and financial crises have been a case in point. Even if it can be argued that in times of crisis states are not allowed to depart from ensuring a minimum level of social rights, if at least this is factually possible, it is another thing to hold that a court like the ECtHR should automatically find a violation in these circumstances.

When it comes to the determination of core content, however, a core rights approach tailored to the socio-economic practice of the ECtHR is more absolute. Whereas the issue of whether a core socio-economic right is violated hinges upon the circumstances of the case to some extent, the question of whether such a core is at stake should be answered in a more general fashion. In line with this, as is required according to a two-stage approach to rights adjudication, the Court should determine the scope of a right before reviewing a limitation thereof. In doing so, core socio-economic rights help clarify the prima facie contours of Convention

---

[51] Cf. *Bélané Nagy v. Hungary*, ECtHR (GC) 13 December 2016, 53080/13, which will be discussed in Ch. 8, S. 8.3.3.

[52] Cf. Young 2017 (n. 27), for the argument that in a (deferential) proportionality analysis, socio-economic rights are easily 'balanced away'.

rights.[53] That is, core social protection, both negative and positive, can plausibly be linked to several of the norms enshrined in the Convention. Different to an overbroad or non-existing interpretation, a core socio-economic rights oriented interpretation moreover ensures that there is an identifiable standard against which the proportionality of an act or omission can be judged.[54] A focus on core rights resulting in a limited interpretation of the scope of ECHR rights, at least where it concerns the socio-economic dimension thereof,[55] is defensible given the limited role and task of the Court in the socio-economic field and is in keeping with the idea that the ECtHR should not become the final arbiter in every issue concerning individual interests. This would, after all, demand choices a supranational judicial body – and in particular one that has not been explicitly charged with the task to adjudicate social rights – is not well placed to make.

Thus, the core rights perspective that may add to our understanding of, as well as guide further development of the socio-economic case law of the Court holds that core socio-economic rights can be seen to fall within the prima facie scope of the Convention, while deserving strong, though not absolute, protection.

This core rights perspective, as should be clear from the above explanation, falls within the absolute-relative category. Before tackling in more detail its relation to the Court's interpretative practice and proportionality review, let me briefly explain why the other forms of core rights have less potential. First, for reasons already stated, the idea of absolute-absolute cores is too demanding. Laying down hard rules to which no exceptions are thinkable seems unfitting for the supranational ECtHR, especially in the socio-economic field. An exception, though, would be Article 3 ECHR, which is an absolute rights norm, yet should accommodate a (very) minimal level of social protection. Second, a relative-absolute understanding of core rights would not add much. It holds that cores cannot be determined *a priori*, but instead depend on all the circumstances of the case. What this requires is in fact nothing more than using proportionality review and balancing the various interests.[56]

---

[53] Bilchitz 2003 (n. 14); Bilchitz 2007 (n. 14). It is important to state the content of core rights as this is what their importance demands. Even if this implies that core rights are conditional, this at least ensures that the basic claims people have are determined apart from budgetary and other concerns.

[54] Bilchitz 2007 (n. 14). See Ch. 5, S. 5.2.2 and 5.2.3.   [55] See, further, S. 7.3.1.

[56] Alexy 2002 (n. 6), 196.

When an interference is considered proportional, then the core of the right invoked was not interfered with. When there has been a violation, this might instead imply that the absolutely protected essence of the right was touched upon. Relative-absolute cores are merely the end result, rather than something that can be taken into account when arguing a case. Finally, a relative-relative core rights approach to the protection of socio-economic rights is not ambitious enough either. Because it is flexible as to both content and protection,[57] it is likely to be used as a mere rhetorical tool whenever the Court is looking for reasons to find a breach of the Convention. Of course, though, identifying relative cores in the light of the circumstances of the case allows for differentiating between aspects of rights. If an individual core right is concerned, this could, for example, result in a narrower margin of appreciation. Over time, moreover, relative core content could develop into a more general impression of what core socio-economic rights are protected under the Convention. This shows that a relative-relative approach, although indeed somewhat unenterprising, may form a first step towards a more solid core rights perspective. I will show in the final chapter of this book that this is also how some of the Court's current case law can be understood.

How then, exactly, does the ECtHR determine the core socio-economic content of the rights enshrined in the ECHR? In Chapter 6, I showed that core rights seem either to be inferred from the right itself, from consensus amongst states or from expert opinions. The first option looks for intrinsic cores, or for their 'unrelinquishable nucleus', without which one could no longer speak of that right.[58] In the context of socio-economic rights, this has led to a focus on minimum essential levels of these rights. In regard to the right to social security, for example, it can be said that the *raison d'être* of such a right is to ensure at least a subsistence minimum, i.e., the means necessary for acquiring essential health care, food, education, etc. Although the inclusiveness of the minimum core can be a matter of discussion, the direction in which it points is clear: basic provisions form the very essence of socio-economic rights, while without these there is nothing to build a higher level of socio-economic protection upon.[59]

---

[57] Cf. Liebenberg 2010 (n. 23), 184–185.   [58] Ch. 6, S. 6.1.1.

[59] Cf. Bilchitz 2007 (n. 14), 187, who refers to different levels of individual need, the first of which is said to be 'the most urgent interest in being free form general threats to one's survival. This interest is of greatest urgency, as the inability to survive wipes out all possibility for realizing the sources of value in the life of a being'. See also 189.

Comparative or other external sources can be used when the right itself does not pinpoint a certain minimum, or when other insights and experiences appear relevant for the definition of (additional) cores.[60] This mitigates concerns about subjective, judicial definitions of core rights that bar broader dialogue about the meaning of socio-economic rights.[61] It allows reflection on a broader agreement amongst nonjudicial bodies and branches, as well as the development thereof.

For the ECtHR, it cannot be said which of the two approaches should be favoured. A combination instead seems most promising. First, looking for the *raison d'être* of fundamental rights means asking why a particular rights norm exists and what at least is required to ensure that this right is meaningful for those who can rely on it. This implies a teleological approach to interpretation that takes into account a norm's objective and purpose, as well as 'the general spirit of the Convention, an instrument designed to maintain and promote the ideals and values of a democratic society'.[62] In applying such an approach, the ECtHR would first look at the rights norms enshrined in the ECHR, and more particularly at the aims and intrinsic values underlying these.[63] Now that it is understood to encompass positive obligations, the right to respect for private life (Article 8 ECHR) can, for example, be linked to the importance of having a place to stay and to find shelter, and to have some privacy without being interrupted by others. When the active connotation of the term 'treatment' is nuanced, moreover, the prohibition of 'inhuman and degrading treatment' as laid down in Article 3 ECHR can be linked to the provision of basic means of subsistence needed for living a human life. Here, it is worth recalling the effectiveness thesis outlined in Chapter 2 of this book.[64] Combining the idea of effectuating ECHR rights with a search for what this essentially demands, some socio-economic guarantees appear to be crucial, because without those one cannot even start ensuring the further realization of the respective rights.[65]

Second, consensus or broad agreement can also provide a valuable point of departure for core socio-economic rights protection by the ECtHR. The essential socio-economic guarantees that have been agreed

---

[60] Ch. 6, S. 6.3.2.

[61] Rosalind Dixon, 'Creating Dialogue about Socio-Economic Rights: Strong Form Versus Weak-Form Judicial Review Revisited', *International Journal of Constitutional Law*, 5 (2007), pp. 391–418, 415–416 (see also Ch. 5, S. 5.2.2).

[62] *Kjeldsen, Busk Madsen and Pedersen v. Denmark*, ECtHR 7 December 1976, 5095/71, 5920/72 and 5926/72, para. 53.

[63] Cf. Ch. 2, S. 2.1.   [64] Ibid.   [65] Cf. Bilchitz 2007 (n. 14), 189.

upon at the national and international levels may be considered, and in particular the core obligations that have been recognized by the CESCR. After all, the ICESCR has been broadly ratified, including by states parties to the ECHR. It hence seems unproblematic for the ECtHR to at least give these core requirements some consideration in dealing with cases under the Convention. Such consensus interpretation fits the interpretative practice of the Strasbourg Court as well as its recognition of the indivisibility of civil and political and economic and social rights.[66] Yet what the idea of core rights protection adds is that rather than taking into account economic and social rights generally, the attention is directed towards the core aspects thereof. It suggests a take on indivisibility that entails a focus on minimum essential levels and other core requirements, linking these to the Convention in a more transparent manner.

7.3   Core Indicators and Proportionality Review

7.3.1   Socio-Economic Scope

The ECtHR reviews limitations of Convention rights through a proportionality test. It asks whether a limitation serves a legitimate aim, as well as whether it was 'necessary in a democratic society'.[67] In principle, though not always in a structured, multi-pronged way, this means that it investigates whether the impugned measure was suitable and necessary, and proportional *stricto sensu*. Alternatively, it is asked whether a fair balance has been struck, or if the limitation resulted in 'individual and excessive burden'.[68] The requirement of proportionality can be said to be inherent in the Convention. It is, moreover, in line with the global perception of proportionality review and balancing as the best approaches to fundamental rights review.[69] Another inherent aspect of the Court's review is its margin of appreciation, i.e., the doctrine through which the Court ensures deference towards decisions taken at the national level. Recently, the margin has become more prominent in the discussions on the role of the ECtHR and on its reasoning.[70] However, criticism is vented concerning the opaqueness of the implications of the margin for the Court's review, as well as the doctrine's relation to the

---

[66] Ch. 2, S. 2.2.2.   [67] Cf. Article 8-11 ECHR.   [68] Cf. the case law on Art. 1 P1 ECHR.
[69] Cf. Barak 2012 (n. 45), 243.
[70] Cf. the Brighton Declaration, 20 April 2012, which has resulted in an explicit reference to the margin in Art. 1 Protocol No. 15 ECHR.

different aspects of the proportionality test.[71] In any case, in explicating the role of core rights in the adjudication of socio-economic rights by the ECtHR, the doctrines of proportionality and the margin of appreciation cannot be overlooked.

Yet before expounding further on a core rights perspective for the Court's review of limitations of rights, we must embark in more detail on its determination of the protective scope of the ECHR. After all, in order to balance these rights against other interests, their content should be clarified. In Chapter 2, I argued that the economic and social dimension of the ECHR can be explained by the aim of effectuating the rights enumerated in the ECHR. Besides, the idea of the indivisibility of fundamental rights suggests that socio-economic rights are expressly taken into account when interpreting the Convention.[72] While justifying the Court's engagement in this field, however, the notions of effectiveness and indivisibility fail to sufficiently pinpoint the limits thereto.[73] Once an interest is recognized as falling within the protective scope of a right, this interpretation acquires a certain permanence.[74] In this connection, core socio-economic rights allow for the necessary focus, and prevent the Court from skipping the interpretation stage altogether. In addition, a clear and focussed interpretation may ensure that socio-economic interests are taken seriously at the review stage.[75]

Socio-economic issues falling within the scope of Article 6 (fair trial) or relating to negative aspects of the right to respect for the home (Article 8) are naturally covered by the Convention. Beyond this, at least minimum core socio-economic rights should be prima facie protected. I explained in the previous section that Convention rights can be interpreted to include minimum social protection. This is corroborated by the minimum cores that have been recognized in the context of socio-economic rights, according to which states are required to guarantee minimum levels of these rights. The Court need not get into details here: recognizing that a social minimum, or subsistence minimum, is prima facie protected provides a sufficient starting point for reviewing cases in which the state interfered with or failed to provide this minimum.[76] This

---

[71] See, for criticism of this doctrine, for example, Jan Kratochvíl, 'The Inflation of the Margin of Appreciation by the European Court of Human Rights', *Netherlands Quarterly of Human Rights*, 29 (2011), pp. 324–357.

[72] Ch. 2, S. 2.1 and 2.2.   [73] Ch. 2, S. 2.3.

[74] Stephen Gardbaum, 'Limiting Constitutional Rights', *UCLA Law Review*, 54 (2007), pp. 798–854, 803; Barak 2012 (n. 45), 23. See Ch. 3, S. 3.2.1.

[75] See further, S. 7.3.2. and Ch. 8.   [76] Cf. Ch. 5, S. 5.3; Ch. 6, S. 6.3.

would also address the criticism that the Court regularly tends to skip the interpretation stage.[77] Interpretation does not demand that the ECtHR explains in detail what is covered by the Convention and what is not. Yet it should make clear why an individual interest deserves prima facie protection, which can be done by referring to the importance of core socio-economic rights. The fulfilment of minimum essential levels of food, health care, housing, social security and education can be considered a prerequisite for the (further) enjoyment of the rights enshrined in the ECHR. In turn, when such minimum levels are absent, socio-economic rights are not taken seriously.[78] Being devoid of food or basic health care can amount to inhuman treatment (Article 3) or have a serious impact on someone's private life (Article 8). A revocation of social benefits (minimum means of subsistence) may be seen to involve proprietary interests protected under Article 1 P1.

A few more things must be noted regarding the prima facie protection of minimum essential levels of social rights under the Convention. First, this guarantees not only negative protection by allowing for review of deprivations of existing basic provisions, but also ensures positive protection of the right to be provided with minimum essential levels. The right to have the very core of one's socio-economic position protected is mirrored by the obligation of states to ensure a subsistence minimum by making the necessary budgetary choices and designing the required legislative and policy framework. Today, a clear distinction between the negative and positive aspects of rights seems no longer feasible.[79] Prima facie recognition in this regard authorizes the Court to review issues concerning minimum social rights, but does not imply that these are automatically rendered definitive. Second, especially since positive protection is included, we are indeed dealing with minimum requirements. States are of course encouraged to provide a higher level of socio-economic arrangements, yet this cannot be claimed under the Convention. Expansive protection may be considered desirable in practical terms, but given the genesis of the ECHR, the wording of the rights it contains and the competences of the ECtHR, the recognition of positive socio-economic guarantees is not self-evident and in any way limited.

---

[77] See the examples given in Ch. 8.

[78] Cf., on the idea of the indivisibility of different fundamental rights, Ch. 2, S. 2.2.

[79] See, for example, Laurens Lavrysen, *Human Rights in a Positive State: Rethinking the Relationship between Positive and Negative Obligations under the European Convention on Human Rights* (Antwerp/Oxford/New York: Intersentia, 2016).

Third, a reason for emphasizing the protection of minimum socio-economic rights, rather than, for example, human dignity, is that the former allows for clarifying the *socio-economic* scope of the Convention. Even though human dignity is one of the basic principles underlying the Convention, in terms of socio-economic protection it is not an entirely unequivocal requirement.[80] It is difficult to determine what it means to speak of a life in dignity, and equally complicated to establish to what extent subjective interpretations should thereby be taken into account. It could be considered that living off the state cannot lead to a dignified existence as this means a loss of independence, whereas dignity could also be understood as involving a relatively high standard in terms of food, housing and care, regardless of by whom this standard is provided. Even though the requirement of minimum essential levels is also not unambiguous, it points into one direction and acknowledges the importance of socio-economic, in addition to civil and political, rights protection. Finally, the wording of the rights norms of the Convention remains leading. Whereas this is different for Article 8 (the right to respect for private life), it is not logical to protect a positive right to a minimum level of subsistence on the basis of Article 1 of Protocol No. 1.[81] The right to protection of property protects possessions, and it is hard to convincingly argue that even if the state does not grant a certain minimum benefit, a property right entitlement to this benefit nevertheless exists. This is one of the examples I will discuss in more depth in the next chapter, where the Court's case law takes centre stage and it is illustrated what a core rights perspective has to add.

However, not only complaints about minimum levels of social rights deserve review under the Convention. There are socio-economic issues that might appear more peripheral at first glance, but nevertheless require protection. Additional core indicators allow for spotting these while not losing sight of the scope of the Convention. It was explained in Chapter 6 that core socio-economic rights not only concern substantive guarantees, but also entail additional requirements. In particular, in the various General Comments the CESCR has underlined that states should at all times ensure non-discrimination in the socio-economic domain as well as direct their efforts to disadvantaged and marginalized individuals and groups. In line with this, the fact that a complaint concerns this kind

---

[80] Cf. Jeff King, *Judging Social Rights* (Cambridge University Press, 2012), 22–23, 27.

[81] See, for my critical reflection on the case of *Bélané Nagy v. Hungary* (ECtHR (GC) 13 December 2016, 53080/13) in this regard, Ch. 8, S. 8.3.3.

of protection signals that there is a core issue at stake requiring the Strasbourg Court to step in. Let me explain why promoting non-discrimination in the socio-economic sphere and protecting the social rights of vulnerable groups and individuals fits particularly well with the aims of the Convention.

First, to be treated in a non-discriminatory fashion is an essential right, both in the context of civil rights as well as in relation to social rights. Discrimination, even when it occurs in the social field, cannot be seen as a strictly socio-economic, or a second-rank concern. Therefore, whereas broad socio-economic arrangements cannot generally be demanded under the Convention, what must always be guaranteed is that the entitlements a state creates comply with the principle of non-discrimination.

Besides holding that the Covenant's non-discrimination provision is an immediate requirement,[82] the CESCR has highlighted that the non-discriminatory provision of socio-economic rights belongs to the state's core obligations. States must, as a matter of priority, 'ensure the right of access to health facilities, goods and services on a non-discriminatory basis',[83] as well as 'the right of access to public educational institutions and programmes on a non-discriminatory basis'.[84] Accordingly, as soon as particular socio-economic schemes are available, at least discrimination-free access to such facilities needs to be provided. The core requirement of non-discrimination allows for some variation amongst states: given that not all states have the means for providing a similar (high) level of socio-economic arrangements, and cannot be required to provide for certain facilities right away, it adjusts to factual possibilities and political and other preferences.

Non-discrimination is not an easy requirement though. It is one of the hallmarks of social policies that distinctions are made between different categories of persons who may receive different levels of assistance due to specific criteria, such as need. Conditions related to someone's place of residence, immigration status or age can be reason for granting less, or even no assistance at all. Yet it cannot be said that such differentiation always amounts to discrimination: whether this is the case at least to

---

[82] Cf. the Limburg Principles on the Implementation of the International Covenant on Economic, Social and Cultural Rights, UN doc. E/CN.4/1987/17, Annex, reprinted in *Human Rights Quarterly*, 9 (1987), 123, paras. 22 and 35. See Ch. 5, S. 5.1.

[83] CESCR, General Comment No. 14, para. 43(a).

[84] CESCR, General Comment No. 13: The Right to Education (Art. 13 of the Covenant), 8 December 1999, E/C.12/1999/10, para. 57.

some extent depends on the ground for differentiation. Moreover, the non-discriminatory provision of social entitlements could require that they be extended to those who would otherwise be excluded. The requirement of non-discrimination may thus demand positive, but also very costly action. A danger in this regard is that the state lowers the level of entitlements altogether in order to prevent discrimination.

Notwithstanding these objections, protection against discrimination provides a fitting example of what core socio-economic protection under the Convention entails. It provides a reasonable answer to the need for the Court to respect diversity and subsidiarity, as it remains for the states to decide what kind and what exact level of socio-economic guarantees is provided. At the same time, it ensures review of those cases that relate to what lies at the heart of the ECHR, namely the effort to ban discrimination throughout the different areas of society. This at least can be inferred from the pivotal role of Article 14 ECHR as well as the adoption of a free-standing non-discrimination requirement in Protocol No. 12.[85] Thus, even when they do not concern minimum essential levels, socio-economic complaints that involve alleged discrimination deserve to be reviewed under the Convention.

Second, another indicator suggesting that a core socio-economic issue is concerned is the fact that a complaint concerns the interests of vulnerable individuals or groups. On top of the protection of minimum essential levels of socio-economic rights for all, the Court should have an extra eye for the needs of vulnerable persons. The Convention is there to protect especially the interests of those who cannot stand up for themselves. Vulnerable individuals and groups are most likely to lack access to basic goods and an adequate standard of the various socio-economic rights, as well as the possibility to improve their socio-economic situation on their own. Effectuating the Convention rights in conformity with the rationales of effectiveness and indivisibility thus requires that cases brought by these persons are assessed and given particular concern, even when they do not directly concern their minimum social needs.

Again, the CESCR's practice may serve as a source of inspiration. In many of its General Comments, it has recognized that to progressively realize the ICESCR rights, it is important to start by helping those whose situation is most in need of improvement and who lack the capacity to alter their circumstances singlehandedly. Already in the 1991 Comment

---

[85] Cf. Ch. 1, S. 1.2.2.

on the right to housing, the Committee held that 'States parties must give due priority to those social groups living in unfavourable conditions by giving them particular consideration'.[86] It has also held that especially for 'disadvantaged and marginalised individuals and groups', access to social security systems and schemes and health care facilities needs to be guaranteed.[87] When defining disadvantaged, marginalized and vulnerable individuals and groups, one could think of religious or ethnic minorities, i.e., groups or individuals whose interests do not correspond with the prevalent status quo and require protection against majority decisions. In the socio-economic context, vulnerable persons are particularly those whose well-being, including their enjoyment of fundamental rights, primarily depends on the state. Asylum seekers lacking any means to facilitate their self-support or severely disabled persons that have to rely on state arrangements can be counted amongst those that need extra attention, and the same goes for children and the elderly.[88] This rationale of Convention protection has recently been foregrounded in the literature, also as a means to direct the Court's efforts to where they are most needed.[89]

7.3.2   Proportionality and Procedural Protection

What was called an absolute-relative understanding of core rights forms the starting point for the core rights perspective that can help explain but also guide the reasoning of the ECtHR in socio-economic cases. This means that once the Court decides that the Convention applies to a socio-economic complaint, its review must have 'bite' although the protection offered remains of a relative kind. There can be justifications

---

[86] CESCR, General Comment No. 4: The Right to Adequate Housing (Art. 11(1) of the Covenant), 13 December 1991, E/1992/23, para. 10.

[87] CESCR, General Comment No. 18: The Right to Work (Art. 6 of the Covenant), 6 February 2006, E/C.12/GC/18, para 31(a); CESCR, General Comment No. 14, para. 43(a).

[88] See, however, *V.M. a. O. v. Belgium*, ECtHR (GC) 17 November 2016, 60125/11, dissenting opinion of Judge Ranzoni, joined by Judges López Guerra, Sicilianos and Lemmens, para. 4 (arguing that the Court should clarify the concept of vulnerability in its case law).

[89] See, for example, Lourdes Peroni and Alexandra Timmer, 'Vulnerable groups: The promise of an emerging concept in European Human Rights Convention law', *International Journal of Constitutional Law*, 11 (2013), pp. 1056–1058; Veronika Flegar, 'Vulnerability and the Principle of Non-Refoulement in the European Court of Human Rights: Towards an Increased Scope of Protection for Persons Fleeing from Extreme Poverty?', *Contemporary Readings in Law and Social Justice*, 8 (2016), pp. 148–169.

for interfering with or for failing to provide socio-economic guarantees. Nevertheless, once core socio-economic rights are concerned, weighty justifications must be provided. Thus, whereas the scope of the Convention in some instances may be limited to core social rights issues, a core rights perspective holds that at the review stage core social rights are taken seriously.

The promise of a core rights perspective is that besides clarifying what the ECtHR has been embarking on thus far, it can suggest a more structured analysis that does justice to the individual interests at stake as well as to the role of the Court. As will also be shown in Chapter 8, in socio-economic cases the Court might be inclined to take a very deferential stance and apply an overall balancing test. Especially when combined with a lack of interpretation, this results in insufficient as well as obscure protection. Just like the notions of effectiveness and indivisibility, thus, the doctrines of the margin of appreciation and proportionality alone seem insufficiently capable of providing a response to the challenge of supranational judicial protection of socio-economic rights on the basis of classical rights norms.

To sum up, complaints concerning socio-economic rights can be reviewed under the Convention when they naturally fall within the scope of the (procedural) rights listed therein,[90] as well as when they concern minimum essential levels of socio-economic rights, alleged discrimination or the protection of vulnerable individuals. In most instances, the Court will then continue with a proportionality or fair balance test. At least in theory, the former entails more than a mere balancing of interests: proportionality analysis typically requires an examination of whether the interference or omission served a legitimate aim, whether it was suitable and necessary and whether it was proportional *stricto sensu*.[91] Notwithstanding this, the emphasis generally lies on the last aspect, namely on the balance that has or has not been struck between the rights of the individual and the general interests concerned. This is particularly so when positive socio-economic protection is demanded.[92] Balancing takes place in an often blurry and confusing manner: it results in an ad hoc exercise in which it is often not clear how much 'weight' is

---

[90]   Such as under Artt. 6, 8 and 14 ECHR, or Art. 1 of the First Protocol to the ECHR.

[91]   See, on (the different subtests of) the proportionality test, Ch. 3, S. 3.3.2; Barak 2012 (n. 45).

[92]   Cf. Möller 2012 (n. 44), 179–180.

attached to the different aspects relevant to the case.[93] The predictive value of ad hoc balancing exercises can be close to nil.

Core socio-economic rights reasoning suggests two possible, more transparent approaches in this regard. The first ties in with a more structured approach to proportionality review as a multi-pronged and rational way of approaching conflicts involving rights. The second forms a procedural alternative to proportionality review as we know it, which is in line with current trends in the Court's case law. Here the idea of core socio-economic rights protection can ensure that fundamental rights – despite a procedural focus – are sufficiently protected. Indeed, the two suggested approaches start from the idea that there is at least some clarity on what in terms of substantive protection is prima facie protected. I will expound on both approaches, including their interconnectedness in a general fashion. More specific remarks will be made in relation to the Court's case law in Chapter 8.

First, the idea of core socio-economic rights suggests that a differentiation is made between core and non-core rights at the review stage.[94] This distinction can form a workable point of departure for reviewing a case in the sense that where a core right is concerned, this forms a normative justification to accord particular weight to the position of the individual. From an indivisible perspective and in the light of the aim of effectuating the rights enshrined in the Convention, this also holds true when core socio-economic cores are at stake. Although a state may still provide a sufficient justification, this is especially burdensome when the interference or omission concerned is a very serious one. For example, when instead of a temporary or limited reduction the provision of minimum means of subsistence is revoked completely, or when a case concerns minimum needs and unequal treatment or vulnerable individuals, the ECtHR's approach should be a strict one.

A presumption in favour of the individual and his core rights means that his interests are more difficult to be outbalanced, but also that the Court can opt for more thorough review of the legitimacy of the aim pursued and the suitability and necessity of the means chosen to realize it. The legitimate aim of socio-economic measures is generally for the government to determine, yet this does not mean that no legitimate aim

---

[93] This also has to do with the fact that it often takes place in a vacuum, in the sense that when the Court fails to identify prima facie rights and obligations, the interests of the individual easily move to the background. See also the examples given in Ch. 8.

[94] See, for a somewhat comparative point, Barak 2012 (n. 45), 531 ff.

needs to be identified.[95] When core socio-economic interests are neg-lected for democratically agreed-upon purposes, the Court should take a close look at the suitability and necessity of the infringement in the light thereof. It is up to the state to present the necessary information on why the choices made are fitting as well as needed to achieve the proclaimed aim(s). If the impugned measure passes the legitimate aim, necessity and suitability test, core socio-economic interests should be given appropriate weight in the balancing test. In case the Court determines the applicable margin of appreciation, moreover, the leeway granted should be adjusted accordingly.

Our present discussion focuses on the protection on the basis of limitable rights. This brings up the question of how the Court should deal with cases under the absolute prohibition of inhuman and degrading treatment of Article 3 ECHR. For an issue to amount to such treatment, it must likely concern the lack of a minimum level of socio-economic rights of a vulnerable individual who for his subsistence minimum is dependent on the state. The socio-economic threshold should be a high one, but once it has been reached, the Convention is violated and a proportionality test is not required.[96]

As a second possible approach, the examples of core socio-economic rights protection propose that core socio-economic rights may be trans-lated into more or less neutral, i.e., non-substantive requirements. It is inappropriate for the Court to identify specific social policy demands or quantitative obligations. In order to give hand and feet to the protection of minimum essential levels of socio-economic rights, though, it could rely on procedural demands that national authorities have to comply with in order for measures taken to be in compliance with the Convention. This could be an alternative to a structured proportionality test when such a test, for example in cases concerning positive obligations, is less feasible. The issue of whether a specific measure (or the lack thereof) was disproportionate may then dissolve into the question of whether the procedural safeguards available to the applicant were sufficient. Such safeguards may for example include duties of consultation or timely information. Remember in this regard the emphasis placed by the CESCR in the context of evictions on appropriate procedural protection and due process. This entails, amongst other things, 'an opportunity for genuine

---

[95] See, however, Möller 2012 (n. 44), 179, and Ch. 3, S. 3.3.2.

[96] Cf. *Paposhvili v. Belgium*, ECtHR 13 December 2016, 41738/10, discussed in Ch. 8, S. 8.1.1.

consultation with those affected', adequate and reasonable notice, information, provision of legal remedies and, where possible, of legal aid.[97] More generally, and in line with the notion of proportionality that is inherent in the Convention, it would be required that the core socio-economic interests of the individual are sufficiently taken into account when deciding upon the proportionality of the interfering measure at the national level. This requirement may apply to the legislature, as well as to the executive and the national courts. An example concerning the former are the procedural demands formulated by the German *Bundesverfassungsgericht* in order to determine whether the right to a subsistence minimum is complied with.[98] These demands require the decisions made in this regard to be the result of adequate methods for determining such a minimum that are transparent and consistently applied,[99] i.e., based on the actual needs and situations of those involved. Compared to defining detailed (legislative and administrative) requirements, an obligation to take the minimum socio-economic needs of those involved into account seems sufficiently harmless while adding a material component.[100] It allows the Court to respect the prerogatives of the member states while setting a transparent standard in regard to how a state can comply with the socio-economic rights included in the Convention.[101]

A trend of 'proceduralization' is clearly visible in the case law of the Court, not only with regard to socio-economic rights. The ECtHR increasingly identifies procedural obligations on the basis of substantive rights norms, as well as opting for procedural review.[102] This has led to a vibrant debate on whether procedural tests can replace substantive review.[103] Some have questioned whether decisive interferences – be it

---

[97] CESCR, General Comment No. 7: The right to adequate housing (Art.11(1)): forced evictions, 20 May 1997, E/1998/22 para. 15.

[98] See Ch. 5, S. 5.3.   [99] See *Hartz IV* (n. 9), para. 143.

[100] See, for risks attached to procedural review by the ECtHR, Angelika Nussberger, 'Procedural Review by the ECtHR: View from the Court', in Janneke Gerards and Eva Brems (eds.), *Procedural Review in European Fundamental Rights Cases* (Cambridge University Press, 2017), pp. 161–176.

[101] Gerards 2012 (n. 44).

[102] See, for example, Oddný Mjöll Arnardóttir, 'The "Procedural Turn" under the European Convention on Human Rights and Presumptions of Convention Compliance', *International Journal of Constitutional Law*, 15 (2017), pp. 9–35.

[103] See, for some contributions, Gerards 2012 (n. 44); Eva Brems, 'Procedural Protection: An Examination of Procedural Safeguards Read Into Substantive Convention Rights' in E. Brems and J.H. Gerards (eds.), *Shaping Rights in the ECHR: The Role of the European Court of Human Rights in Determining the Scope of Human Rights* (Cambridge University Press, 2014), pp. 137–161; Arnardóttir 2017 (n. 102); Patricia Popelier and Catherine

negative of positive – can be drawn from procedural requirements. Can the fact that the state met such requirements suffice in concluding that it complied with the Convention? Core rights protection suggests that procedural demands should not be substantively empty; the very fact that it is required that the socio-economic needs of the individual(s) concerned are sufficiently taken into account implies the impossibility of meeting these requirements without giving due weight to core interests. Here, a core rights perspective adds to a debate that is still insecure as to the implications of procedural review. Moreover, borrowing again from the example of the German right to a subsistence minimum, the Court should retain the final say in the sense that even if procedural requirements are met, it can still be concluded that the protection or provision of essential guarantees is evidently insufficient.[104] When taking a procedural route, this should, however, only be concluded in exceptional circumstances. It nevertheless ensures that the Court retains its judicial responsibility, even if only as a back-up option.[105] In this approach, the margin seems to be built-in: there is a structural margin included in the fact that the proportionality analysis is left to the national authorities. By requiring consideration of socio-economic needs and retaining the possibility to conclude that the balance struck at the national level in the light thereof was insufficient, the margin attached to social policy however does not overshadow the fundamental interests at stake therein.

Procedural protection fits the sensitive position of the Court – especially in the socio-economic field – as well as the idea of separation of powers more generally.[106] Similar to the proposed proportionality analysis, procedural review leaves it to the state to articulate core socio-economic guarantees. Although it is clarified at the interpretation stage that such guarantees are in principle required, it is up to the government to show that the impugned measure served a legitimate aim and was suitable and necessary, or that the core socio-economic needs of the individual were sufficiently taken into account. The conclusion that a measure was disproportional *stricto sensu* or evidently insufficient can only be reached if the prior (procedural) requirements have been met.

Van de Heyning, 'Subsidiarity Post-Brighton: Procedural Rationality as Answer', *Leiden Journal of International Law*, 30 (2017), pp. 5–23; Janneke Gerards and Eva Brems (eds.), *Procedural Review in European Fundamental Rights Cases* (Cambridge University Press, 2017).

[104] See Ch. 5, S. 5.3.   [105] Cf. Arnardóttir 2017 (n. 102), 35.
[106] Gerards 2012 (n. 44), 197.

Such sequence circumscribes the discretion of the Strasbourg Court, while ensuring robust core socio-economic rights protection. The main difference with a reasonableness approach to the protection of socio-economic rights in this regard is the following: instead of an overall inquiry into whether the impugned acts or omissions were reasonable – a test that may or may not be infused by elements of proportionality and core rights protection[107] – the core rights approach developed here is a two-stage approach that assesses proportionality in the light of core socio-economic rights. Whereas sophisticated reasonableness review is no doubt successful in different socio-economic rights contexts,[108] this approach is more in line with the extensive experience of fundamental rights protection on the basis of the Convention as well as the limits thereto.

Conclusion

Core rights protection is more promising than is often assumed. This chapter showed that there are different approaches that vary in strictness and that are in keeping with a two-stage approach to rights adjudication. Moreover, core rights protection is compatible with proportionality review:[109] it aligns with the idea that when socio-economic rights are at stake, there can be room for justifications. At the same time, stating what is prima facie required in terms of core socio-economic rights can make this test more insightful.

The core rights perspective that was developed on the basis of the different core rights experiences elsewhere is said to fit the practice of the Strasbourg Court. It connects the dots in the sense that – together with the ideas of effectiveness and indivisibility – it turns into a comprehensive explanation what is already visible in the Court's case law. Adjudicating socio-economic cases under the civil and political rights norms of

---

[107] Cf. Young 2017 (n. 27).

[108] Cf. the South African example (Young 2017 (n. 27); King 2012 (n. 80), 116–7).

[109] See also Landau 2015 (n. 1). Referring to the approach of Colombian Constitutional Court, he holds that 'proportionality review and the minimum core did not appear to be viewed by the Court as antagonistic concepts. Instead, they were seen as complementary and as playing distinct roles; the minimum core was critical in interpreting the socio-economic rights at issue, giving them clearer con- tent by requiring prioritisation of the interests of the poor. Proportionality was then used at a subsequent stage in order to compare the infringement on the socio-economic rights with the government's justifca-tion' (284).

the Convention requires a focus on non-discrimination, vulnerable individuals but also minimum essential social rights protection. The ECtHR is not equipped to specify this minimum, yet recognizing that it is required for complying with the Convention may ensure that core socio-economic rights are not easily outbalanced. Whether an interference or omission was proportional then depends on whether the different proportionality requirements were met. Alternatively, these requirements may be translated into procedural requirements with a substantive element. Core rights protection entails a targeted approach in which the margin cannot depend merely on the socio-economic nature of a complaint.

I will now turn to the case law of the Court to illustrate that it can be more fully understood from a core rights perspective. Where the Court's reasoning is still unclear, a core rights approach provides suggestions for improvement.

8

Core Socio-Economic Rights in the Case Law of the ECtHR

In the prior chapter I outlined a core rights perspective for the protection of socio-economic interests under the ECHR. This perspective connects the Court's developing socio-economic dimension to the role of the Strasbourg system of fundamental rights protection. It adds to the justifications given based on the ideas of effectiveness and indivisibility, and suggests a more transparent use of proportionality review and the margin of appreciation. The core rights perspective was derived from insights on core rights protection as it is theorized and used elsewhere. And although the idea of absolute-relative core rights reasoning has been linked to the position and task of the ECtHR, it is necessary to have a closer look at the Strasbourg case law. What exactly does a core rights perspective add to our comprehension of the Court's dealing with complaints on social rights? Throughout its case law, a kind of core socio-economic rights standard seemingly emerges – that is, if one is willing to look at the Court's reasoning through a core rights lens. Besides aiming for the effective realization of ECHR rights and showing signs of indivisibility, the Court's practice can be understood as granting, at least prima facie, minimum socio-economic rights protection. However, it mostly does so in an implicit manner. As I mentioned at the outset of this book, the ECtHR's socio-economic reasoning fails to convince in terms of the gap between what falls within the Convention's scope and what is eventually protected, as well as due to its opaque and ad hoc character. Here a core rights perspective not only helps to comprehend and justify the ECtHR's practice, but could guide its further development as well.

To illustrate this, this chapter delves deeper into the Court's reasoning in socio-economic cases and the (potential) role of core rights protection in this regard.[1] Three thematic illustrations will be presented that focus on housing rights, social security and health and health care. I do not

---

[1] Generally, judgments rendered after 2016 could not be taken into account. A few exceptions have been made for interesting cases dating from the first months of 2017.

intend to provide a comprehensive overview of the Court's social rights case law. Not only is this impossible due to the volume of case law, it would also miss the point of zooming in on where core rights may help to understand or improve the Court's reasoning. In Section 8.1, the protection under the ECHR of housing rights is discussed. Under Article 8 (the right to private and family life), but also under Article 3 ECHR (the prohibition of torture), the Court is moving towards the recognition of a minimum right to housing. This can be seen most clearly in its case law on Roma housing, which signals a procedural specification of what are still rather implicit prima facie core social rights. Cases concerning health and health care are discussed in Section 8.2. The most intriguing developments in this regard are visible in the context of expulsion cases dealt with under Article 3, yet also Articles 2 (the right to life) and 8 play an important role, for example, in cases involving health damage resulting from environmental pollution. The thresholds the Court has developed in this regard could be used more consistently in accordance with a core rights perspective. Finally, social rights protection is particularly visible in the ECtHR's social security case law. In Section 8.3, I discuss this important subset and show how core rights reasoning would allow for more transparent and consistent protection. I will argue that the scope of the right to protection of property (Article 1 P1), contrary to that of Articles 3 and 8, does not admit the protection of a positive right to social security benefits. The case law is going astray in this regard and I will demonstrate how a core rights perspective could get it back on track.

8.1   Housing

8.1.1   Minimum Housing Protection

On one hand, it is natural that the Convention covers issues related to housing. Especially in the context of state interferences with an individual's home or house, the link with the right to respect for the home (Article 8) or property protection (Article 1 of Protocol No. 1) is readily apparent. On the other hand, the role of the Convention is less obvious when positive claims to housing are made. When an individual requests adequate housing that meets his specific needs, or alternative housing if he is evicted, the social dimension of the Strasbourg housing case law becomes visible. Besides in relation to Article 8, social housing issues are dealt with under the inhuman and degrading treatment aspect of

Article 3. How they are construed as such will be discussed later in this section. First I will say something on Article 8 and the way in which its home as well as private life limb are interpreted to protect basic housing rights.

In the 2001 judgment in *Chapman v. the United Kingdom*, the Grand Chamber held:

> Article 8 does not in terms recognise a right to be provided with a home. Nor does any of the jurisprudence of the Court acknowledge such a right. While it is clearly desirable that every human being have a place where he or she can live in dignity and which he or she can call home, there are unfortunately in the Contracting States many persons who have no home. Whether the State provides funds to enable everyone a home is a matter for political not judicial decision.[2]

According to the wording of Article 8 ECHR, this provision provides the individual only with a right to respect for his home. To benefit from its protection, thus, it appears that one already needs to have a home. In that case, the Convention provides guarantees against unjustified interferences by the state. Notwithstanding this, the Court has interpreted 'respect for the home' in a broad manner. In *McCann v. the United Kingdom*, it defined the notion of 'home' in explicitly factual terms.[3] Mr McCann and his wife had been joint and secure tenants until they divorced, and the applicant's ex-wife eventually gave up the tenancy. Mr McCann had continued living in the house although he was no longer legally entitled to do so. The Court stressed that 'whether a property is to be classified as a "home" is a question of fact and does not depend on the lawfulness of the occupation under domestic law'.

Decisive is 'the existence of sufficient and continuous links with a specific place'.[4] This requirement may be met in the case of temporary stays or frequent absence,[5] or indeed in the case of unlawful occupation. This can also be seen in different cases involving Roma housing. In most of these cases the applicants had resided on a plot of land or site for a significant period of time and with the intention to stay

---

[2] *Chapman v. the UK*, ECtHR (GC) 18 January 2001, 27238/95, para. 99. Similar phrasing has been used in many more (recent) cases.

[3] *McCann v. the UK*, ECtHR 13 May 2008, 19009/04, para. 46.

[4] A recent example is *Lazarenko a. O. v. Ukraine*, ECtHR 11 December 2012 (dec.), 27427/02, para. 53.

[5] Ibid.

permanently, but without initially establishing their home in a legal manner. This does not prevent the conclusion that the right to respect for the home is engaged.[6]

The Court's indivisible interpretation, however, does not include situations in which an individual does not have a place to stay in the first place. In a case concerning the allocation of a replacement flat in lieu of one that had been destroyed during the war, it held that '[t]he interests protected by the notion of a "home" within the meaning of Article 8 include the peaceful enjoyment of one's *existing* residence'.[7] The complaint was declared inadmissible *ratione materiae*. Nevertheless, the Court's interpretation can be understood as granting, at least prima facie, core housing rights protection. After all, in the context of the right to housing, (negative) protection against evictions is considered of essential importance.[8] This protects mostly vulnerable individuals from becoming homeless, i.e., from being deprived of basic rights without which their enjoyment of other fundamental rights is put at risk as well.

Whether eventually a violation of the right to respect for the home is found depends on whether there was a 'pressing social need' and in particular on the proportionality of the interference.[9] The fact that this right is considered an important right relating to someone's personal security and well-being, does not mean that it easily prevails over conflicting interests. A recent example is the case of *Berger-Krall and Others v. Slovenia*.[10] This case concerned the privatization of social dwellings on the basis of the Slovenian Housing Act. Those whose dwellings had been expropriated after the Second World War could only buy the flats if the previous owners agreed within a year. The result was that several applicants eventually had to leave their homes involuntarily. The Court found that the new system 'was aimed at ensuring a fair balance between the protection of the rights of the tenants on the one hand and those of the "previous owners" on the other'.[11] Therefore no violation had occurred.

---

[6] S. 8.1.2. Only when a stay is interrupted *and* illegal, however, it is less likely that the Court nevertheless accepts that the sufficient and continuous link requirement is met. Cf. the discussion in *Yordanova a. O. v. Bulgaria*, ECtHR 24 April 2012, 25446/06.

[7] *Dukic v. Bosnia and Herzegovina*, ECtHR 19 June 2012, 4543/09, para. 40 [emphasis added].

[8] Ch. 6, S. 6.1.1.   [9] E.g., *Gillow v. the UK*, ECtHR 24 November 1986, 9063/80, para. 55.

[10] *Berger-Krall a. O. v. Slovenia*, ECtHR 12 June 2014, 14717/04.

[11] Ibid., para. 274. The applicants also complained under Art. 1 P1, which was also found not to be violated.

The Court's deferential review at first glance provides little guidance on what the Convention in the field of housing requires. A core rights perspective in this regard, however, could clarify two things. First, a closer look reveals that the Court gives hand and feet to the prima facie social protection under Article 8 by holding that the procedural safeguards provided must be adequate. This means that

> a person at risk of losing his or her home should in principle be able to have the proportionality and reasonableness of the measure determined by an independent tribunal in the light of the relevant principles under Article 8 of the Convention, notwithstanding that, under domestic law, his or her right of occupation had come to an end.[12]

This approach is in line with what was said on the possibility of securing socio-economic rights by translating them into procedural obligations. Second, from the facts of *Berger-Krall* it appears that the situation of the complainants did not evidently conflict with their basic housing rights.[13] Core socio-economic rights review would suggest that had there been such a conflict, the Court could have still found a violation – even if procedural safeguards had been provided.

In the case of *McCann*, the Court did not conclude that the measure McCann was confronted with was disproportional. Rather, it found a violation of the Convention because in reaching the decision to evict him, the national authorities had failed to consider his needs.[14] This kind of procedural review is also visible in the recent case of *Yevgeniy Zakharov v. Russia*.[15] After the death of his partner, Zakharov was evicted from the room in a communal flat he had shared with her for ten years. Although he was registered elsewhere, he had no other place to stay, and the eviction thus interfered with his right to respect for his home. The fact that the Regional Court, in reviewing the measure, had not taken the applicant's housing needs into account was 'sufficient to enable the Court to conclude that the interference complained of was not "necessary in a democratic society"'.[16] A procedural violation, but, like in *McCann*, one that emphasizes the applicant's substantive minimum needs. In this way, the Court ensures a core socio-economic standard without unduly interfering with the state's social policies.

---

[12] Ibid., para. 270.   [13] Ibid., paras. 208, 210.
[14] *McCann v. the UK*, ECtHR 13 May 2008, 19009/04, para. 50. See further S. 8.1.2.
[15] *Yevgeniy Zakharov v. Russia*, ECtHR 14 March 2017, 66610/10.   [16] Ibid., para. 37.

Besides the right to respect for the home, Article 8's private and family life limb has also proven increasingly relevant in the housing sphere. There lies great social potential in the Court's recognition of positive obligations in relation to this provision, even though taking core social rights seriously would require minimum social rights to be recognized in a more straightforward manner.

The case of *Marzari v. Italy* concerned a severely disabled person's request for adequate accommodation.[17] After the building in which he lived had been expropriated, he had moved to other accommodation that, in his view, was inadequate to meet his special needs. He stopped paying his rent, which led to an eviction order. Eventually Marzari refused to accept another apartment that was allocated to him. Marzari complained before the Court about the authorities' failure to provide him with adequate accommodation, notwithstanding a local law-based obligation to do so. The Court held that

> although Article 8 does not guarantee the right to have one's housing problem solved by the authorities, a refusal of the authorities to provide assistance in this respect to an individual suffering from a severe disease might in certain circumstances raise an issue under Article 8 of the Convention because of the impact of such refusal on the private life of the individual. The Court recalls in this respect that, while the essential object of Article 8 is to protect the individual against arbitrary interference by public authorities, this provision does not merely compel the State to abstain from such interference: in addition to this negative undertaking, there may be positive obligations inherent in effective respect for private life. A State has obligations of this type where there is a direct and immediate link between the measures sought by an applicant and the latter's private life.[18]

While the right to respect for the home demands that there is an existing home, respect for private life may require positive state action even if – or especially when – someone does not have a place to live. For this to be the case, it is required that there is a direct and immediate link between the latter provision and the housing measures an applicant demands. This threshold requirement fits the aim of providing effective Convention protection, but in social housing cases the case law would benefit

---

[17] *Marzari v. Italy*, ECtHR 4 May 1999 (dec.), 36448/97.

[18] Ibid. [emphasis added]. Cf. also *Botta v. Italy*, ECtHR 24 February 1998, 21439/93, paras. 33–34.

from a more explicit recognition of a prima facie positive obligation to provide minimum protection in this field.

In *O'Rourke v. the United Kingdom*, the Court repeated that an issue under Article 8 might arise when housing assistance to an individual suffering from a serious disease is refused because of the impact of such refusal on his private life.[19] Yet it considered that Article 8 does not lay down a right to be provided with a home, and that therefore 'the scope of any positive obligation to house the homeless must be limited'. Even though the Court suggests that states have a duty to do at least something if a seriously ill person is in need of a home,[20] its tentative and negative phrasing in this regard is not very helpful. Just like when concluding in *Marzari* that 'no positive obligation for the local authorities can be inferred from Article 8 to provide the applicant with a specific apartment', the Court here missed a chance to clarify that the obligation that nevertheless exists had been complied with. More generally, its reasoning would benefit from a more explicit two-stage approach. This would allow the Court to be more clear on why a case is reviewed, namely because minimum core housing protection for vulnerable individuals is something that falls within the scope of Article 8. Taking account of the state's efforts at the review stage, it could then nevertheless conclude that minimum protection had been provided. Rather than dealing with cases because there might be a positive obligation, this would provide more guidance. It would also allow the Court to abstain from reviewing cases that are not sufficiently linked to what is protected by the Convention.

In *O'Rourke*, the complainant also relied on Article 3 ECHR, but the Court stated that his situation had not attained the requisite level of severity to engage this article.[21] Although the absolute prohibition of inhuman and degrading treatment at first glance seems to have little to offer those lacking adequate housing, there is an interesting set of cases linking it to the right to housing. In fact, it appears that Article 3 can be understood as providing minimum protection in this field, although the Court seems hesitant to explicitly recognize this.

---

[19] *O'Rourke v. the UK*, ECtHR 26 June 2001 (dec.), 39022/97.
[20] Cf. Arno Frohwerk, *Soziale Not in der Rechtsprechung des EGMR* (Tübingen: Mohr Siebeck, 2012), 132.
[21] *O'Rourke v. the UK*, ECtHR 26 June 2001 (dec.), 39022/97.

Moldovan and Others v. Romania involved individuals whose houses and property had been burned.[22] As a result, for years they had no choice but

> to live in hen-houses, pigsties, windowless cellars, or in extremely cold and deplorable conditions: sixteen people in one room with no heating; seven people in one room with a mud floor; families sleeping on mud or concrete floors without adequate clothing, heat or blankets; fifteen people in a summer kitchen with a concrete floor ... etc.[23]

While the Court in *Moldovan* could not review the actual destruction of the homes,[24] because at the time this happened Romania had not yet ratified the Convention, the living conditions of the applicants formed the reason why Article 3 had been violated.[25] In other words, rather than the interference by the state (the destruction of the homes), the evidently insufficient housing conditions of the applicants triggered the application of the prohibition of inhuman and degrading treatment.

The conclusion that Article 3 provides minimum protection in relation to housing, at least when vulnerable individuals are concerned, can also be inferred from the Court's judgment in the case of *M.S.S. v. Belgium and Greece*.[26] In *M.S.S.*, the Court held that when someone is dependent on state support and faces 'serious deprivation or want incompatible with human dignity', a responsibility for the state could arise.[27] It concluded that although there is no general obligation to give refugees financial assistance, in this case the applicant refugee was confronted with such deplorable circumstances that Article 3 had nevertheless been breached. After having been sent back to Greece, he had spent months in extreme poverty, while being unable to cater for his most basic needs, like a place to stay.

A related example is the 2014 case of *Tarakhel v. Switzerland*, where the Court held that returning an Afghan family to Italy without individual guarantees concerning their accommodation would be in violation of

---

[22] *Moldovan a. O. v. Romania*, ECtHR 12 July 2005, 41138/98 and 64320/01.

[23] Ibid., para. 69.

[24] Cf. *Selçuk and Asker v. Turkey*, ECtHR 24 April 1998, 23184/94 and 23185/94.

[25] *Moldovan a. O. v. Romania*, ECtHR 12 July 2005, 41138/98 and 64320/01, para. 113.

[26] *M.S.S. v. Belgium and Greece*, ECtHR (GC) 21 January 2011, 30696/09. Cf. also *Budina v. Russia*, ECtHR 18 June 2009 (dec.), 45603/05; *Laroshina v. Russia*, ECtHR 23 April 2002 (dec.), 56869/00.

[27] *M.S.S. v. Belgium and Greece*, ECtHR (GC) 21 January 2011, 30696/09, para. 253. See Marc Bossuyt, 'The Court of Strasbourg Acting as an Asylum Court', *European Constitutional Law Review*, 8 (2012), pp. 2013–2245.

Article 3 of the Convention.[28] It repeated that there is no obligation to provide everyone within a state's jurisdiction with a home, and that Article 3 does not entail 'any general obligation to give refugees financial assistance to enable them to maintain a certain standard of living'.[29] At the same time, it placed particular weight on the fact that the applicant belonged to a 'particularly underprivileged and vulnerable population group in need of special protection'.[30] Moreover, the requirement of special protection for asylum seekers 'is particularly important when the persons concerned are children, in view of their specific needs and their extreme vulnerability'.[31] Sending the applicant family back to Italy would thus be in violation of Article 3. In *A.S. v. Switzerland* it was clarified that this is not a general requirement, but one that indeed only applies when the Court is convinced that the applicant's vulnerability so demands.[32]

Finally, in this regard, the case of *V.M. and Others v. Belgium* should be mentioned.[33] This case concerned the reception conditions of a Serbian family in Belgium that, following an order to leave the country, was left without basic means of subsistence. The family, with their disabled daughter, spent nine days on a public square before taking up residence in Brussels North railway station for three weeks until their return to Serbia was arranged. The Court held that no matter how overstretched the reception network was at the time, the authorities had not given due consideration to the applicants' vulnerability – because they were asylum-seekers, but also since (disabled) children were involved. With a majority of four to three judges, the Court held that the level of severity required under Article 3 had therefore been attained.

Unfortunately, after having been referred to the Grand Chamber, the case of *V.M.* was struck off the list as the applicants had not maintained contact with their lawyer.[34] Since the Chamber had been divided on the issue, this means that the ECtHR missed a chance to elucidate its position on the issue of a subsistence minimum for vulnerable individuals. In his dissenting opinion, Judge Ranzoni, joined by three other judges, pointed out the 'serious questions affecting the interpretation or application of the Convention' which required that the application continue to be

---

[28] *Tarakhel v. Switzerland*, ECtHR (GC) 4 November 2014, 29271/12. [29] Ibid., para. 95.
[30] Ibid., para. 97. [31] Ibid., para. 119.
[32] *A.S. v. Switzerland*, ECtHR 30 June 2015, 39350/13, para. 36.
[33] *V.M. a. O. v. Belgium*, ECtHR 7 July 2015, 60125/11.
[34] *V.M. a. O. v. Belgium*, ECtHR (GC) 17 November 2016, 60125/11.

examined.[35] According to the dissenters, the Court should have clarified its case law, especially in respect of the concept of 'vulnerability' and to what extent this makes a difference for meeting the threshold of severity of Article 3. Seen from a core rights perspective, they have a point: the Grand Chamber could have seized the opportunity to affirm that the lack of a subsistence minimum for vulnerable individuals triggers Article 3 of the Convention in the sense that when both minimum protection and the needs of disadvantaged or marginalized persons are concerned, this provision applies.[36]

8.1.2   Roma Housing and Procedural Protection

It is well known that the Roma form a vulnerable group in need of special protection. According to the Parliamentary Assembly of the Council of Europe '[t]he Roma people are still regularly victims of intolerance, discrimination and rejection based on deep-seated prejudices in many Council of Europe member states'.[37] For that reason,

> [t]he situation of Roma with regard to education, employment, housing, health care and political participation is far from satisfactory. The Assembly is convinced that effective and sustainable access to education and decent housing are the first decisive steps towards breaking the vicious circle of discrimination in which most of the Roma are locked.[38]

The precarious housing situation of great numbers of Roma, combined with the fact that their particular way of settling is integral to their identity, entails that this issue is intimately linked to their fundamental rights and dignity. The Strasbourg case law on this topic forms a good illustration of the Court's indivisible rights reasoning. It shows how the Court stops short of recognizing minimum core housing rights under the Convention, but also that it has come a long way since earlier Roma cases in which it seemed unwilling to move in this direction in the first place. Corroborating what was noted in the previous section, the Court in these cases opts for procedural review in order to ensure the effective

---

[35] Ibid., dissenting opinion of Judge Ranzoni, joined by Judges López Guerra, Sicilianos and Lemmens, para. 4.

[36] See, however, for an illustrative example of where the threshold of Art. 3 is not met, *Hunde v. the Netherlands*, ECtHR 5 July 2016 (dec.), 17931/16.

[37] Resolution 1740 (2010) of the Parliamentary Assembly of the Council of Europe on 'The situation of Roma in Europe and relevant activities of the Council of Europe', para. 7.

[38] Ibid.

protection of the positive rights that follow from Article 8. In the following, I will elaborate on these developments and indicate what a core rights perspective can offer here.

I already mentioned that complaints of Roma, even when they did not establish their 'homes' in accordance with national regulations, fall within the scope of Article 8 of the Convention. In *Buckley v. the United Kingdom* and *Chapman v. the United Kingdom*, for example, the applicants owned land but had not obtained planning permission to settle there.[39] In *Chapman*, the Court, for the first time, also discussed the right to respect for private and family life in this context. It stressed that measures affecting the stationing of her caravans 'also affect her ability to maintain her identity as a Gypsy and to lead her private and family life in accordance with that tradition'. Therefore, 'the applicant's right to respect for her private life, family life and home is in issue in the present case'.[40]

It appears that the interpretation of the Convention in Roma housing cases generally involves merely negative duties. In the different cases, the Court explicitly paid attention to 'whether there was an "interference" by a public authority'.[41] A negative focus may also explain why in the case of *Codona v. the United Kingdom*, the Court found it 'far from obvious that Article 8 is engaged'.[42] Now that these cases generally involve eviction orders, at first glance it seems unnecessary for the Court to take a stance on whether Article 8 involves a prima facie right to adequate (alternative) housing for this group as well. The review of Roma housing issues under Article 8 ECHR is done in a fairly ad hoc, case-specific fashion. That is, the Court pays attention to the specific facts of the case at hand to decide whether or not this provision has been violated. Still, the case law shows some relevant trends that can be comprehended in light of the idea of core rights protection.

---

[39] *Buckley v. the UK*, ECtHR 29 September 1996, 20348/92; *Chapman v. the UK*, ECtHR (GC) 18 January 2001, 27238/95. See also *Beard v. the UK*, ECtHR (GC) 18 January 2001, 24882/94; *Coster v. the UK*, ECtHR (GC) 18 January 2001, 24876/94; *Lee v. the UK*, ECtHR (GC) 18 January 2001, 25289/94 and *Jane Smith v. the UK*, ECtHR (GC) 21 January 2001, 25154/94.

[40] *Chapman v. the UK*, ECtHR (GC) 18 January 2001, 27238/95, paras. 73–74. Cf. also *Yordanova a. O. v. Bulgaria*, ECtHR 24 April 2012, 25446/06, para. 105.

[41] *Winterstein a. O. v. France*, ECtHR 17 October 2013, 27013/07, para. 143. Cf. also *Buckley v. the UK*, ECtHR 29 September 1996, 20348/92, paras. 56–60; *Chapman v. the UK*, ECtHR (GC)18 January 2001, 27238/95, paras. 75–78; *Yordanova a. O. v. Bulgaria*, ECtHR 24 April 2012, 25446/06, paras. 102–106.

[42] *Codona v. the UK*, 7 February 2006 (dec.), 485/05.

An important thread running throughout the Court's Roma housing judgments is the attention it pays to the procedural safeguards available to the applicant(s). In the earlier Roma housing cases, these procedural safeguards merely played a role in reviewing whether the negative interference at stake was proportional. In *Buckley v. the United Kingdom*, it was held that

> [w]henever discretion capable of interfering with the enjoyment of a Convention right such as the one in issue in the present case is conferred on national authorities, the procedural safeguards available to the individual will be especially material in determining whether the respondent State has, when fixing the regulatory framework, remained within its margin of appreciation. Indeed it is settled case-law that, whilst Article 8 contains no explicit procedural requirements, the decision-making process leading to measures of interference must be fair and such as to afford due respect to the interests safeguarded to the individual by Article 8.[43]

Since the procedural safeguards had been sufficient, the interference was justified. According to the Court 'Article 8 does not necessarily go so far as to allow individuals' preferences as to their place of residence to override the general interest'.[44] And '[a]lthough facts were adduced arguing in favour of another outcome at national level', the Court considered that the reasons given by the national authorities 'were relevant and sufficient ... to justify the resultant interference with the exercise by the applicant of her right to respect for the home'.[45] Also in *Chapman*, the Court partly relied on the fact that the regulatory framework contained adequate procedural safeguards, and ultimately showed a significant degree of deference.[46]

In *Connors v. the United Kingdom*, the Court did find a violation. Here, it held that the applicable procedural guarantees did not suffice because, for reasons of flexibility in the management of Roma sites, the eviction of the Connors family could be enforced without any proof of a breach of license. Noticing that 'this case is not concerned with matters of general planning or economic policy but with the much narrower issue of the policy of procedural protection for a particular category of persons', the Court did not have to move into the direction of recognizing more

---

[43] *Buckley v. the UK*, ECtHR 29 September 1996, 20348/92, para. 76. Cf. Resolution 1740 (2010) of the Parliamentary Assembly of the Council of Europe, para. 17.

[44] *Buckley v. the UK*, ECtHR 29 September 1996, 20348/92, para. 81.   [45] Ibid., para. 84.

[46] *Chapman v. the UK*, ECtHR (GC) 18 January 2001, 27238/95, para. 114.

positive, social housing obligations.[47] In the context of a classical interference with the applicant's lawful residence, the margin of appreciation
was narrowed and a violation could be found.

Core rights protection can be primarily negative, yet whether this
suffices cannot be seen in isolation from the basic needs of those involved.
Arguably, the interests of the applicants in the cases just mentioned were
quite similar,[48] and it could thus be argued that the distinction made
between negative and positive protection fails to do justice to the indivisibility of civil and social rights. Yet recently the Court's procedural test has
been given a 'positive twist'. Procedural requirements have been linked to
the issue of whether the state was required to provide for alternative,
suitable housing, as well as to the substantive individual interests involved.

Two cases in particular must be mentioned. In *Yordanova and Others
v. Bulgaria*, the Court for the first time fully appreciated the vulnerable
position of Roma and ensured effective protection in the field of housing.[49] Reviewing the proportionality of the measures, the Court repeated
that the margin of appreciation varies according to the nature of the
Convention right and its importance for the individual, as well as the
nature of the aim pursued by the restrictions. It held that in this respect
the following considerations are relevant: 1) in spheres involving the
application of social or economic policies, the margin is wide, as is the
case in the planning context; but 2) the margin might be narrower
whenever what is at stake for the applicant is of crucial importance for
ensuring his effective enjoyment of 'key rights'. Further, 3) procedural
safeguards are especially material, so that 4) any person at risk of losing
his home, which the Court considers the most extreme form of interference with one's right to respect for the home,

> should in principle be able to have the proportionality and reasonableness
> of the measure determined by an independent tribunal in the light of the
> relevant principles under Article 8, ... This means, among other things,
> that where relevant arguments concerning the proportionality of the
> interference have been raised by the applicant in domestic legal proceed-
> ings, the domestic courts should examine them in detail and provide
> adequate reasons.

---

[47] *Connors v. the UK*, ECtHR 27 May 2004, 66746/04, para. 86.
[48] Ida Elisabeth Koch, *Human Rights as Indivisible Rights: The Protection of Socio-Economic Demands under the European Convention on Human Rights* (Leiden: Martinus Nijhoff Publishers, 2009), 124.
[49] *Yordanova a. O. v. Bulgaria*, ECtHR 24 April 2012, 25446/06.

And finally, 5)

> [w]here the national authorities, in their decisions ordering and uphold-
> ing the applicant's eviction, have not given any explanation or put
> forward any arguments demonstrating that the applicant's eviction was
> necessary, the Court may draw the inference that the State's legitimate
> interest in being able to control its property should come second to the
> applicant's right to respect for his home.[50]

On the basis of these general principles, the Court concluded that the
prospective removal of the applicants was not justified under Article 8.
Relevant was that they had been tolerated for several decades and that no
alternative solutions had been sought for the risks associated with the
applicants' housing lacking basic sanitary and building requirements.
The authorities had not considered the risk of the applicants becoming
homeless, even though they had signed an agreement containing an
undertaking to secure alternative shelter.

Hence, the Court, in fact, did not conclude that the eviction was
disproportional. Decisive for finding a violation was instead that at the
national level, the proportionality of this measure had not been
reviewed.[51] At first glance this seems to corroborate the procedural
approach taken in the earlier Roma housing cases. Yet given its hints as
to what should be put on the scale, notably the interests of and risks for the
individuals involved, possible (tailor-made) alternatives, etc., the Court's
approach can be understood as procedural review taken to another level.
Emphasizing that too little, if any, attention had been given to the individual interests at stake, the requirement of proportionality review becomes a
requirement that is procedural in nature, yet also has a clearly substantive
dimension. Apparently, 'if forcibly removed persons do not have a self-
standing right to be re-housed, they nevertheless have the right to have the
state *consider* their risk of becoming homeless as well as their possibilities
to be re-housed, potentially with the state's support'.[52] Seen in this way,
the procedural breach found in *Yordanova* forms a concrete step towards
effective protection of the core housing interests of Roma.

The 2013 judgment in the eviction case of *Winterstein and Others v.
France* confirms this development.[53] Again in this case, the ECtHR found

---

[50]   Ibid., para. 118.   [51]   Ibid., para. 144.
[52]   Adélaide Remiche, 'Yordanova and Others v. Bulgaria: The Influence of the Social Right
       to Adequate Housing on the Interpretation of the Civil Right to Respect for One's Home',
       Human Rights Law Review, 12 (2012), pp. 787–800, 798.
[53]   *Winterstein a. O. v. France*, ECtHR 17 October 2013, 27013/07.

procedural shortcomings that led to a breach of the Convention. On top of this, it concluded that there had been another, separate violation of Article 8 in respect of the applicants who had not been provided with alternative accommodation. *Winterstein and Others* concerned the proceedings brought against a number of traveller families who had been living on the same spot for many years. In 2005, the domestic courts had issued orders for the families' eviction, on pain of penalty for noncompliance, because of the lack of the necessary permits and the resulting breach of the land-use plan. Instead of enforcing the order, a study was conducted by the municipal authorities in order to assess the situations of the individuals involved. For those who wished to be provided with alternative accommodation on family sites, no solution had been found and these families continued living in precarious conditions.

Like in *Yordanova and Others*, the Court summed up the considerations relevant for determining the margin of appreciation.[54] Referring to Council of Europe and other materials, the Court underlined that the vulnerable position of Roma needed to be taken into account also in regard to the offering of alternative housing.[55] After the situations of the families involved had been assessed, some of them – in line with their wishes – had obtained social housing. With regard to these individuals, the Court held that a sufficient solution had been found. However, those who had wanted to obtain alternative accommodation on family sites still found themselves in difficult circumstances since they either continuously faced the enforcement of the order under penalty, or had left without finding any adequate alternative. Here the Court concluded that the needs of the applicants had not been sufficiently taken into account.[56]

The *Winterstein and Others* judgment thus suggests that apart from whether the authorities reviewed the proportionality of an interference, the Court may conclude that their efforts in regard of the provision of alternative accommodation were deficient. In other words, an obligation to provide minimum housing protection to vulnerable Roma that is translated into procedural requirements still leaves room for the conclusion that what the authorities had done was evidently insufficient. Such an approach shows similarities to the FCC's protection of a right to a subsistence minimum and corroborates what was introduced as a core rights perspective for the protection of socio-economic interests under the Convention. What is lacking, though, in terms of an absolute-relative

---

[54] Ibid., para. 148.   [55] Ibid., para. 160.   [56] Ibid., para. 167.

core rights approach, is that the Court recognizes a prima facie positive obligation under the Convention to provide vulnerable Roma with (suitable) alternative accommodation – at least if they would otherwise become homeless or face very severe living conditions. This obligation can be met if the needs of the individuals concerned have been sufficiently taken into account in the decision-making process at the national level, although it is still possible for the Court to determine that the efforts made in regard to this prima facie requirement were evidently insufficient. This would also allow for clarifying the role of the margin of appreciation. It seems that the procedural requirements not merely determine the width of the margin, but that because key – or core social – rights[57] are at stake, procedural requirements must be strictly complied with and can be decisive for concluding that there had been a violation.[58]

8.1.3   Non-Discrimination

Protection against discrimination is of core importance for the realization of socio-economic rights. An approach that recognizes the connectedness of the ECHR norms and core socio-economic protection, thus, should pay sufficient attention to this issue. This seems unproblematic at first sight due to the broad ambit of Article 14 and the scope of Article 1 of Protocol No. 12.[59] However, safeguards against discrimination in the socio-economic field suffer from a bias a core rights perspective cannot entirely solve. This perspective does suggest that alleged discrimination in relation to socio-economic measures at least deserves to be reviewed under the Convention.

Article 14 in principle allows for recognizing that even when there is no obligation under Article 8 or Article 1 P1 to provide for certain housing arrangements, once such arrangements have been provided in a discriminatory fashion, they must be extended.[60] An example of how this works is the 1999 Grand Chamber judgment in *Larkos v. Greece*.[61] The issue at stake concerned a civil servant who was a tenant of the state.

---

[57] *Yordanova a. O. v. Bulgaria*, ECtHR 24 April 2012, 25446/06, para. 118; *Winterstein a. O. v. France*, ECtHR 17 October 2013, 27013/07, para. 148.

[58] Cf. also *Yevgeniy Zakharov v. Russia*, ECtHR 14 March 2017, 66610/10, para. 37.

[59] Ch. 1, S. 1.2.

[60] See, on the socialization of Art. 14, Pieter van Dijk, Fried van Hoof, Arjen van Rijn and Leo Zwaak (eds.), *Theory and Practice of the European Convention on Human Rights*, 4th ed. (Antwerp/Oxford/New York: Intersentia, 2006), 5, 1051.

[61] *Larkos v. Greece*, ECtHR (GC) 18 February 1999, 29515/95.

When he retired, Mr Larkos's tenancy agreement was terminated and his eviction was ordered. He complained that he had been confronted with unjustified discrimination in the enjoyment of his right to respect for his home as he did not obtain the protection of the Rent Control Law 1983 that private tenants received. Although the Convention does not require such protection, the Grand Chamber held that the issue fell within the ambit of Article 8 and that, therefore, Article 14 applied. It held that the applicant was in a similar situation to that of private tenants, and concluded that 'the Government have not provided any convincing explanation of how the general interest will be served by evicting the applicant'.[62] Regardless of the margin of appreciation in the area of the control of property, it found a violation of Article 14 in conjunction with Article 8. *Karner v. Austria* can be mentioned here as well.[63] Here the Court found that because the possibility of a life companion to succeed the tenancy after the death of his partner did not apply to same-sex couples, there had been a breach of the Convention. To comply with the Convention, thus, entitlements to succession had to be extended to this group.

As Koch has noted, *Larkos* and *Karner* have in common that they both concern situations in which the applicants were already living in the flats in question.[64] However, the requirement of non-discrimination extends also to positive measures.[65] *Bah v. the United Kingdom* concerned a woman who had been denied priority treatment under the housing legislation because of her son's conditional immigration status.[66] Here the Court held that 'there is no right under Article 8 of the Convention to be provided with housing', but if a state provides housing benefits, 'it must do so in a way that is compliant with Article 14'.[67] This approach can be explained as a means to provide effective or even indivisible protection. It can also be justified from a core rights perspective, which requires discrimination in the field of social housing to be given appropriate attention.

In *Bah*, the Court eventually held that the authorities' decision was not arbitrary. In case the applicant's risk of becoming homeless would have materialized, the applicable legislation would have required assistance from the local authorities. Now that she did not end up in such situation,

---

[62] Ibid., para. 31.   [63] *Karner v. Austria*, ECtHR 24 July 2003, 40016/98.
[64] Koch 2009 (n. 48), 127.
[65] Cf. *Petrovic v. Austria*, ECtHR 27 March 1998, no. 156/1996/775/976.
[66] *Bah v. the UK*, ECtHR 27 September 2011, 56329/07.   [67] Ibid., para. 40.

the Court's conclusion that Article 14 had not been violated seems reasonable. However, it also emphasized that 'any welfare system, to be workable, may have to use broad categorisations to distinguish between different groups in need',[68] and that states may justifiably 'limit the access of certain categories of aliens to "resource-hungry" sources', amongst which social housing can be counted.[69] In this regard, the Court considered important that the ground for the unequal treatment was considered 'immigration status' and not 'nationality', as the applicant had submitted. What this shows is that ensuring core socio-economic rights protection is not so much a matter of narrowing the margin in case of alleged discrimination in relation to minimum socio-economic needs. The strictness of the test in Article 14 cases is primarily dependent on the ground of discrimination.[70] When a distinction is made on a suspect ground, 'very weighty reasons' are required.[71] However, as *Bah* shows, grounds of distinction in the field of social policy are by no means always 'suspect' or need not be labelled as such.[72]

A final point is that in all of the Roma cases just presented, the applicants also explicitly relied on the prohibition of discrimination. Since this is one of the most precarious issues where Roma are concerned,[73] it might come as a surprise that in none of these cases a violation of Article 14 was found. The Court seems remarkably hesitant to address this matter. In *Buckley v. the United Kingdom*, for example, it held that

> [i]t does not appear that the applicant was at any time penalised or subjected to any detrimental treatment for attempting to follow a traditional Gypsy lifestyle. In fact, it appears that the relevant national policy was aimed at enabling Gypsies to cater for their own needs.[74]

In *Chapman v. the United Kingdom*, it was considered that because the interference under Article 8 was proportionate, there was no reason to

---

[68] Ibid., para. 49.   [69] Ibid., para. 49.

[70] See, on the intricate link between the margin of appreciation and the grounds of discrimination, Janneke Gerards, 'The Margin of Appreciation Doctrine, the Very Weighty Reasons Test and Grounds of Discrimination' in M. Balboni (ed.), *The Principle of Non-Discrimination and the European Convention of Human Rights* (forthcoming). Available at SSRN: https://ssrn.com/abstract=2875230.

[71] Cf. *Karner v. Austria*, ECtHR 24 July 2003, 40016/98.   [72] See, further, S. 8.3.2.

[73] Resolution by the Parliamentary Assembly of the Council of Europe (Resolution 1740 (2010)), para. 7 (mentioning 'the vicious circle of discrimination in which most of the Roma are locked').

[74] *Buckley v. the UK*, ECtHR 29 September 1996, 20348/92, para. 88.

conclude that there had been a violation of Article 14.[75] Similarly, where there was a violation of Article 8, the Court stated that 'no separate issue' arose with regard to non-discrimination.[76]

In regard to these considerations, it can be concluded that, if anything, the Court does not treat the requirement of non-discrimination as a core issue in relation to Roma housing that is worth attention for reasons of its own. Although it can be argued that sometimes the Court implicitly takes into account equal treatment concerns in discussing the complaint under Article 8, Article 14 hardly plays a role in these cases. Of course, it is difficult to review often implicit or indirect unequal treatment or discrimination. Yet stating that it is 'no separate issue' fails to explicitly address what the applicants probably consider to be an essential aspect of their complaints.

8.2   Health and Health Care

8.2.1   A Right to Health Care

It must be admitted from the outset that the core of the right to health is hard to determine. An obligation to ensure minimum protection related to health can mean many things. With technologies constantly improving, it can moreover be understood to proliferate over time.[77] What it means in the context of the Convention is thus also hard to define. At the same time, it was explained that judicial core socio-economic rights protection does not require a detailed interpretation of core aspects related to the right to health. The protection offered is to be determined by the member states, and it is then for the Court to see if this suffices for complying with the Convention.

A right to health is not contained in the Convention. Nevertheless, a vast number of health- and health care-related decisions and judgments can be found in the ECtHR's case law. This can be explained by the fact that there are close links between health issues and provisions such as Article 2 ECHR (the right to life) or Article 8 (the right to respect for private and family life). Think of matters like abortion and euthanasia,

---

[75] *Chapman v. the UK*, ECtHR (GC) 18 January 2001, 27238/95, para. 129.

[76] *Connors v. the UK*, ECtHR 27 May 2004, 66746/04, para. 97; *Yordanova a. O. v. Bulgaria*, ECtHR 24 April 2012, 25446/06, para. 149; *Winterstein a. O. v. France*, ECtHR 17 October 2013, 27013/07, para. 179.

[77] Katherine G. Young, *Constituting Socio-Economic Rights* (Oxford University Press, 2012), 77.

but also self-determination and the issue of informed consent.[78] More social health complaints, however, involve claims to treatment, (expensive) medication, etc. Applicants may complain about the lack of certain medical arrangements they consider themselves entitled to as a human being or because of their particular state of health. In this regard, next to Articles 2 and 8, the prohibition of inhuman and degrading treatment (Article 3) has also proven relevant.

One of the first health-related cases under Article 2 was *L.C.B. v. the United Kingdom*.[79] It concerned the applicant's father's exposure to radiation during nuclear tests. The question was whether there had been an obligation to inform the applicant's parents or monitor her health as her leukaemia was most likely caused by this event. Albeit answering this question in the negative, the Court held that 'the first sentence of Article 2 § 1 enjoins the state not only to refrain from the intentional and unlawful taking of life, but also to take appropriate steps to safeguard the lives of those within its jurisdiction'.[80] Not much later, in *Powell v. the United Kingdom*, a case that concerned a boy who had died allegedly because his disease had not been timely diagnosed, the Court emphasized that it 'cannot be excluded that the acts and omissions of the authorities in the field of health care policy may in certain circumstances engage their responsibility under the positive limb of Article 2'.[81] In *Calvelli and Ciglio v. Italy*, it was clarified that the duty to take appropriate steps to safeguard the lives of those within its jurisdiction

> require[s] States to make regulations compelling hospitals, whether public or private, to adopt appropriate measures for the protection of their patients' lives. They also require an effective independent judicial system to be set up so that the cause of death of patients in the care of the medical profession, whether in the public or the private sector, can be determined and those responsible be made accountable.[82]

Just like when dangerous activities are carried out, besides arranging for an effective judicial response, the state is hence required to ensure the regulation – via *inter alia* governing the licensing, operation or monitoring – of health care.

From the cases in which a violation was found, it can be inferred that the ECtHR's protection is targeted at a minimum level, as well as at

---

[78] See the Court's different factsheets on Health, to be found on the Court's homepage.
[79] *L.C.B. v. the UK*, ECtHR 9 June 1998, 14/1997/198/1001.   [80] Ibid., para. 36.
[81] *Powell v. the UK*, ECtHR 4 May 2000 (dec.), 45305/99.
[82] *Calvelli and Ciglio v. Italy*, ECtHR (GC) 17 January 2002, 32967/96., para. 49.

(other) core aspects of the right to health. In the 2013 case of *Mehmet Senturk and Bekir Senturk v. Turkey*, a double violation of Article 2 was found.[83] The case concerned a pregnant woman who died after a series of misjudgments and a refusal of the hospital authorities to provide her with appropriate emergency treatment because she was not able to pay for such treatment on the spot. The procedural breach followed from the statute of limitations that barred conviction, the fact that the doctor had not been prosecuted and the length of the proceedings. Besides, the state's failure to provide appropriate care resulted in a substantive violation. Maternal (prenatal as well as postnatal) health care is considered of 'comparative priority' by the CESCR.[84] A refusal to provide emergency medical treatment in this field, moreover, seems contrary to what in the CoE minimally can be expected in terms of the right to health care.

The violation found in *Nencheva a. O. v. Bulgaria*, again in 2013, can also be explained with the help of a core rights perspective. It shows that a minimum level of health care, especially for vulnerable individuals, is required.[85] *Nencheva* involved the death of fifteen children and young adults in a care home after the authorities had failed to provide them with the necessary care. Material in this regard was that the children had been entrusted to the care of the state and were under the exclusive supervision of the authorities. The authorities had been fully aware of the extremely worrisome circumstances in the care home that, in the harsh winter of 1997 and during a severe economic crisis, had to cope with a lack of heating, food, medical care and medication. There was no doctor available at the time, and the nearest hospital was 40 kilometres away. Besides the authorities' knowledge and responsibility, the vulnerability of the children added to the conclusion that the state had failed to provide the required care.[86]

The core requirement of non-discrimination is visible in the Court's case law on health care as well. *Cyprus v. Turkey* involved complex questions on the situation in Northern Cyprus after Turkey's military operations had started there in 1974.[87] One of these questions concerned the provision of health care that had been available at the time. The applicant state pointed out the restrictions on the ability of enclaved

---

[83] *Mehmet Senturk and Bekir Senturk v. Turkey*, ECtHR 9 April 2013, 23423/09.

[84] CESCR, General Comment No. 14: The Right to the Highest Attainable Standard of Health (Art. 12 of the Covenant), 11 August 2000, E/C.12/2000/4, para. 44.

[85] *Nencheva a. O. v. Bulgaria*, ECtHR 18 June 2013, 48609/06.   [86] Ibid., para. 124.

[87] *Cyprus v. Turkey*, ECtHR (GC) 10 March 2001, 25781/94.

Greek Cypriots and Maronites in Northern Cyprus to receive medical treatment, and argued that this amounted to a violation of their right to life. The Grand Chamber held that 'an issue may arise under Article 2 of the Convention where it is shown that the authorities of a Contracting State put an individual at risk *through the denial of health care which they have undertaken to make available to the population generally*'.[88] In the circumstances of the case, it had not become clear that health care was actively withheld, nor were the lives of the individuals concerned put in danger on account of any delay in obtaining medical services that might have occurred. Nevertheless, it can be inferred from the quoted remark that the care a state provides must be available to all. Can it then decide not to provide any health care at all? In *Cyprus v. Turkey* the Grand Chamber did not consider it necessary to examine '*the extent to which* Article 2 may impose an obligation on a Contracting State to make available *a certain* standard of health care'.[89] With Harris et al., it can be argued that '[i]t is reasonable to infer from the word "extent" that the Court accepts that such a general obligation exists to some undefined degree'.[90] It seems that at least some level of care must be provided, although it remains unclear what the required standard entails. This is understandable, because determining exact core obligations related to the right to health is too complex to be left to a supranational court. Should another case in which this issue is at stake come before the Court, however, it could in accordance with a core rights perspective clarify that at least a minimum level of health care is demanded under the Convention.

In line with this, it can be concluded from *Nitecki v. Poland* that it is in principle for the state to determine how it complies with the right not to be denied health care that has been made available generally.[91] Nitecki was diagnosed with amyotrophic lateral sclerosis (ALS), and his request for a refund covering the cost of the drug prescribed to him was denied. As a pensioner he was unable to pay for this drug himself. The government submitted that this right was '*ratione materiae* hardly applicable', but the Court referred to *Cyprus v. Turkey* and repeated that Article 2 entails positive obligations. Yet it concluded that

---

[88] Ibid., para. 219 [emphasis added].   [89] Ibid. [emphasis added].

[90] David J. Harris, Michael O'Boyle, Edward P. Bates, and Carla M. Buckley, *Harris, O'Boyle and Warbrick: Law of the European Convention on Human Rights*, 3rd ed. (Oxford University Press, 2014), 213.

[91] *Nitecki v. Poland*, ECtHR 21 March 2002 (dec.), 65653/01.

the complaint at hand was manifestly ill-founded. The applicant had access to a standard of health care, which also meant that the drug was refunded for 70% by the state. Therefore, 'the respondent State cannot be said, in the special circumstances of the present case, to have failed to discharge its obligations under Article 2'.[92] In regard to Article 14, the Court found a justification for the alleged discrimination 'in the present health care system which makes difficult choices as to the extent of public subsidy to ensure a fair distribution of scarce financial resources'.[93] Thus, the Court leaves room for making choices – in the light of the available resources – as regards what and to whom care is provided, as long as a standard of care is provided generally.[94] This makes sense both for the purpose of effective social rights protection and in the context of the ECtHR's indivisible reasoning.[95] Defining far-reaching (absolute) individual guarantees may benefit an individual complainant while being to the detriment of the provision of health care generally. Hence this is something a court, and *a fortiori* a supranational court reasoning on the basis of classic rights norms, should avoid in principle.

When a violation is found in relation to the provision of expensive medication, this stems not from the Court's definition of expansive health rights, but can be explained otherwise. In *Panaitescu v. Romania* a failure to provide specific anti-cancerous medication for free was considered in breach of Article 2 of the Convention.[96] The domestic courts had ordered the authorities to provide the applicant with the medication. The state could therefore not cite a lack of resources. By contrast, when an omission is not in conflict with national procedural rules or requirements, a complaint about expensive or unauthorized medication seems unlikely to be successful. In *Hristozov and Others v. Bulgaria*, the applicants did not argue that generally available health care was denied. Rather, what they claimed was that the applicable law should be framed in a way that would entitle them, exceptionally, to 'an experimental and yet untested product that would be provided free of charge by the company which developed it'.[97] According to the Court, 'Article 2

---

[92] Ibid., para. 1.   [93] Ibid., para. 3.

[94] Cf. the South African case on a request for free treatment Soobramoney v. Minister of Health, KwaZula-Natal, 1997 (12) BCLR 1696 (CC) (Ch. 5, S. 5.2.1).

[95] Cf. Octavio Ferraz, 'Harming the Poor through Social Rights Litigation: Lessons from Brazil', *Texas Law Review*, 89 (2010), pp. 1643–1668.

[96] *Panaitescu v. Romania*, ECtHR 10 April 2012, 30909/06.

[97] *Hristozov a. O. v. Bulgaria*, ECtHR 13 November 2012, 47039/11 and 358/12, para. 107.

cannot be interpreted as requiring that access to unauthorized medicinal products for the terminally ill be regulated in a particular way'.[98]

In *Hristosov*, the applicants had also invoked Article 3 due to the pain and suffering resulting from the fact that they had to await their death knowing that there was an experimental product that might improve their health. The Court held that in the case of naturally occurring illness, Article 3 comes with a high threshold, 'because the alleged harm emanates not from acts or omissions of the authorities but from the illness itself'.[99] It repeated that the applicants did not complain about a lack of adequate medical treatment, and concluded that the refusal of access to the medication had not led to inhuman and degrading treatment. That 'Article 3 does not place an obligation on the Contracting States to alleviate the disparities between the levels of health care available in various countries' can also be read in various expulsion cases.[100] Nevertheless, in these cases an obligation to provide the necessary care can be found as well. In *D. v. the United Kingdom*, the Court concluded that there would be violation of Article 3 if the United Kingdom were to remove the applicant to St Kitts. The government had argued that his 'hardship and reduced life expectancy would stem from his terminal and incurable illness coupled with the deficiencies in the health and the social-welfare system of a poor, developing country', and that he would therefore not be worse off than other AIDS victims in St Kitts.[101] The Court however held that it was

> not prevented from scrutinising an applicant's claim under Article 3 where the source of the risk of proscribed treatment in the receiving country stems from factors which cannot engage either directly or indirectly the responsibility of the public authorities of that country, or which, taken alone do not in themselves infringe the standards of that Article. To limit the application of Article 3 in this manner would be to undermine the absolute character of its protection.[102]

Important for finding a violation was that the applicant was in 'the advanced stages of a terminal and incurable illness'.[103] His removal would not only accelerate his death, but also subject him to 'acute mental and physical suffering'.[104] That these were 'exceptional circumstances'

---

[98] Ibid., para. 108. For this reason there had not been a violation of Art. 2.
[99] Ibid., para. 111 (referring to *N. v. the UK*, ECtHR (GC) 27 May 2008, 26565/05).
[100] Ibid., para. 113.   [101] *D. v. the UK*, ECtHR 2 May 1997, 30240/96, para. 42.
[102] Ibid.   [103] Ibid., para. 51.   [104] Ibid., para. 52.

was later confirmed in *N. v. the United Kingdom*.[105] Taking a more deferential stance, the Grand Chamber there held that 'Article 3 does not place an obligation on the Contracting State to alleviate such disparities through the provision of free and unlimited health care to all aliens without a right to stay within its jurisdiction. A finding to the contrary would place too great a burden on the Contracting States.'[106] N. was about to be removed to Uganda even though she was HIV-infected. This would mean a serious drop in the level of treatment she received. However, N. was not 'at the present time critically ill', and the rapidity of the health deterioration she would suffer from and the amount of treatment and help she would receive involved a certain degree of speculation. For that reason, the Court held that removal would not amount to a violation of Article 3.[107]

The dissenters in *N.* criticized the majority's remark that '[a]lthough many of the rights it contains have implications of a social or economic nature, the Convention is essentially directed at the protection of civil and political rights'.[108] They emphasized that the reference to *Airey v. the Ireland*[109] in this regard was incomplete as the Court had there in fact recognized the extension of the Convention into the socio-economic sphere.[110] Another point of criticism concerned the Grand Chamber's statement that 'inherent in the whole of the Convention is a search for a fair balance between the demands of the general interest of the community and the requirements of the protection of the individual's fundamental rights'.[111] How does this relate to the absolute – and thus to some extent indivisible – protection Article 3 prescribes?

This point was taken up in a recent case that seems to 'save' the Court's protection of minimum health rights under Article 3. It does so with the help of requirements that are of a procedural, rather than of a

---

[105] *N. v. the UK*, ECtHR (GC) 27 May 2008, 26565/05. [106] Ibid., para. 44.
[107] See for a critical analysis of this case Virginia Mantouvalou, 'N v UK: No Duty to Rescue the Nearby Needy?', *Modern Law Review*, 72 (2009), pp. 815–828; but see also Vanessa Bettinson and Alwyn Jones, 'The integration or exclusion of welfare rights in the European Convention on Human Rights: The removal of foreign national with HIV after N v UK (Application No. 26565/05; decision of the Grand Chamber of the European Court of Human Rights, 27 May 2008)', *Journal of Social Welfare & Family Law*, 31 (2009), pp. 83–94.
[108] *N. v. the UK*, ECtHR (GC) 27 May 2008, 26565/05, para. 44.
[109] *Airey v. Ireland*, ECtHR 9 October 1979, 6289/73, para. 26 (see Ch. 1, S. 1.2.1).
[110] *N. v. the UK*, ECtHR (GC) 27 May 2008, 26565/05, joint dissenting opinion of Judges Tulkens, Bonello and Spielmann, para. 6.
[111] Ibid., para. 44 (dissenting opinion, para. 7).

(purely) substantive kind. In *Paposhvili v. Belgium*, the Grand Chamber clarified that the 'other very exceptional circumstances' referred to in *N*.

> should be understood to refer to situations involving the removal of a seriously ill person in which substantial grounds have been shown for believing that he or she, although not at imminent risk of dying, would face a real risk, on account of the absence of appropriate treatment in the receiving country or the lack of access to such treatment, of being exposed to a serious, rapid and irreversible decline in his or her state of health resulting in intense suffering to or a significant reduction in life expectancy. The Court points out that these situations correspond to a high threshold for the application of Article 3 of the Convention in cases concerning the removal of aliens suffering from serious illness.[112]

It then set out in detail the authorities' obligation to protect the integrity of the persons concerned primarily through appropriate procedures. When someone adduces evidence that he would be exposed to a real risk of being subjected to treatment contrary to Article 3 in relation to his state of health, it is for the authorities of the returning state to assess this risk. More precisely, they 'must verify on a case-by-case basis whether the care generally available in the receiving State is sufficient and appropriate in practice for the treatment of the applicant's illness'.[113] *Paposhvili* concerned the order of removal to Georgia of a man suffering from chronic lymphocytic leukaemia. Since in the proceedings the opinions issued regarding his state of health had not been examined from the perspective of Article 3, the authorities could not conclude that the applicant, if returned, would not have run a real and concrete risk of treatment contrary to Article 3.

Thus, the Court made clear that the health situation of seriously ill persons who are to be removed must be taken seriously, even if the removal would not imply a more or less immediate death. Instead of defining what level of care is required to prevent a violation of Article 3, the Grand Chamber formulated procedural requirements to ensure that medical needs like that of the applicant are sufficiently taken into account. These requirements allow it to nevertheless protect a minimum level of health care. After all, should the state conclude that a removal would entail a risk of inhuman or degrading treatment due to the lack of (adequate) care, this removal would not be allowed.

---

[112] *Paposhvili v. Belgium*, ECtHR 13 December 2016, 41738/10, para. 183.
[113] Ibid., para. 189.

From the perspective of indivisible core rights protection it is however somewhat disappointing that the Court phrases the overall obligation of the state as a negative one that in fact has not much to do with social rights. It holds that what engages the state's responsibility is not the lack of medical infrastructure in the receiving state, while repeating that it is not for the returning state to alleviate disparities in health care 'through the provision of free and unlimited health care to all aliens without a right to stay within its jurisdiction'.[114] Instead, the responsibility of the state stems from its act – the expulsion – which would lead to a risk of treatment contrary to Article 3. It is understandable that the Court stresses this negative aspect in order to promote acceptance by the member states. However, from the obligation to take the health situation of a seriously ill person into account follows the requirement to provide that person with care, the lack of which would result in an inhuman and degrading situation. This has nothing to do with providing *free and unlimited* health care' for '*all* aliens without a right to stay'. More targeted wording could instead have been used to identify a positive obligation that acknowledges the indivisible yet minimum character of the obligation at stake: when a person is vulnerable due to a severe health condition and the fact that he is dependent on the state, then the state has the obligation to prevent inhuman and degrading situations – also when this means it should (continue to) provide the necessary and generally available care.

A final point worth mentioning is that the Grand Chamber in *Paposhvili* allowed the relatives of the applicant to pursue his application after he had died. The GC explained that its judgments serve 'to elucidate, safeguard and develop the rules instituted by the Convention, thereby contributing to the States' observance of the engagements undertaken by them'.[115] It observed that the case involves important issues concerning seriously ill aliens, and that the impact of the case thus extends beyond the individual application. That it continued the examination of Paposhivili's case can be contrasted with what the Grand Chamber did in the case of *V.M. and Others v. Belgium*, discussed earlier in this chapter.[116] This case was struck off the list after the applicant family had lost contact with their lawyer. I agree with the dissenters in *V.M. and Others* that for similar reasons as mentioned in *Paposhivili*, the GC should also have

---

[114] Ibid., para, 192.   [115] Ibid., para. 130.
[116] *V.M. a. O. v. Belgium*, ECtHR 7 July 2015, 60125/11. S. 8.1.1.

continued that application in order to provide more clarity on the core socio-economic standard set by the Convention.

Finally, let me briefly mention two Article 8 cases before I move to the issue of environmental health, which is also primarily linked to this provision. What these exemplify is that the Court's proportionality test appears biased against positive protection in the field of health, while a clearer focus on the rights and needs of the individual concerned may mitigate this. In *Sentges v. the Netherlands*, the issue at stake was the authorities' refusal to provide the applicant, who suffered from Duchenne muscular dystrophy, with a robotic arm.[117] The Court repeated that in case of a direct link between the measures sought and the applicant's private life, 'there may be positive obligations inherent in the effective respect for private or family life. These obligations may involve the adoption of measures designed to secure respect for private life even in the sphere of the relations of individuals between themselves'.[118] However,

> [e]ven assuming that such a special link indeed exists ... regard must be had to the fair balance that has to be struck between the competing interests of the individual and of the community as a whole and to the wide margin of appreciation enjoyed by the States in this respect in determining the steps to be taken to ensure compliance with the Convention.[119]

The Court's review was characterized, thus, by an inchoate determination of Article 8's scope combined with an overall balancing test. Focusing almost entirely on the interests of the state, including the difficult context of the allocation of limited state resources and the fact that the national authorities are better placed to assess how to deal with an issue like this, it held this to be reason for an even wider margin of appreciation. Unsurprisingly, as they did not exceed this margin, the complaint was manifestly ill-founded.

This is not to say that with the help of a core socio-economic rights approach, the Court would have found a violation. What the core rights perspective I outlined suggests, however, is a two-stage approach that clarifies, first, why a complaint concerning core socio-economic interests is covered by the Convention, in order to thereafter ensure that these interests are visible in the Court's review. In *Sentges* the Court supported

---

[117] *Sentges v. the Netherlands*, ECtHR 8 July 2003 (dec.), 27677/02.
[118] Ibid. Cf. also *Botta v. Italy*, ECtHR 24 February 1998, 21439/93, paras. 33–34.
[119] *Sentges v. the Netherlands*, ECtHR 8 July 2003 (dec.), 27677/02.

its conclusion by stating that it 'should also be mindful of the fact that . . . a decision issued in an individual case will nevertheless at least to some extent establish a precedent'.[120] Inversely, however, not applying any threshold for allowing Convention review can just as well be seen to invite a flood of new complaints. In this connection, it may be better to sometimes instead conclude that Article 8 is inapplicable *ratione materiae*, or in turn clarify why prima facie protection is deserved.

It is not the task of the Court to determine the exact right balance between the interests of the state and an applicant's request for medication or care. However, if a complaint is phrased as a negative one, the Court's test appears a more robust one. *McDonald v. the United Kingdom* concerned a woman's claim to night-time care because she has problems with her bladder and due to mobility problems is unable to safely access a toilet or commode unaided.[121] She had initially been provided with a night-time carer, so that the Court could deal with the issue 'without entering into the question whether or not Article 8 § 1 imposes a positive obligation on the Contracting States to put in place a level of entitlement to care equivalent to that claimed by the applicant'.[122] As the interference had, at first, not been in accordance with the law, this resulted in a violation. In regard to the remaining period – during which the law did not require the continuation of the care – the Court took account of the fact that the proportionality of the decision not to provide this care had been duly considered by the local authorities, as well as by the domestic courts. Thus, as the Court found that the interests of the applicant as prima facie protected under Article 8 were adequately balanced against 'the more general interest of the competent public authority in carrying out its social responsibility of provision of care to the community at large', it concluded that the authorities had not 'exceeded the margin of appreciation afforded to them, notably in relation to the allocation of scarce resources'.[123]

It appears from these cases that when positive measures are claimed, the individual interests at stake run a risk of being overshadowed by a general balancing of interests that is often informed by a very wide margin of appreciation. This is not only the case because positive obligations appear to bring about more costs, but also because the Court often leaves open the question whether a sufficient link exists for engaging Article 8 in the first place, and does not determine what is prima facie

---

[120] Ibid.   [121] *McDonald v. the UK*, ECtHR 20 May 2014, 4241/12.
[122] Ibid., para. 48.   [123] Ibid., para. 57.

required. This may hinder meaningful, effective and indivisible protection based on a clear indication of what interests are actually protected by Article 8. Additionally, it also fails to provide the necessary guidance for the member states – as well as for (potential) applicants – on both the interpretation of and review under the Convention.

8.2.2   Environmental Health

Even though the Court's case law on environmental pollution is vast,[124] it suffices to make only a few remarks on the relation between this case law and the core rights perspective developed in this book. This has to do with the fact that it is generally difficult to single out the health aspects in these cases.[125] Still, two things are worth noting that support the points made in the context of health care. What is to follow illustrates the fact that the Court sometimes does not engage with the scope of Article 8, while granting overall and deferential protection in fields not traditionally covered by the Convention. At the same time, in its environmental case law, the Court seems willing to set minimum standards for the application of the Convention while recognizing that there is sometimes reason to narrow the wide environmental margin and ensure strict (procedural) protection. This strategy shows similarities with a core rights perspective. I will first say something on the interpretation of the right to respect for private life, to then discuss the way in which the Court in environmental cases renders this right definitive.

In its environmental case law under Article 8, the Court has developed a threshold for this provision's application. Early judgments left open the question whether any effect on someone's private life could trigger prima facie protection. In *Powell and Rayner v. the United Kingdom*, in 1990, the Court held that 'the quality of the applicant's private life and the scope for enjoying the amenities of his home have been adversely affected by the noise generated by aircraft using Heathrow Airport ... Article 8 is therefore a material provision in relation to both Mr Powell and Mr Rayner'.[126] Moreover, in *López Ostra v. Spain*, it held that '[n]aturally, severe environmental pollution may affect individuals' well-being and

---

[124] Cf. the Court's factsheet on 'Environment and the European Convention on Human Rights', available on the Court's homepage.

[125] In fact, also housing issues may be involved if someone's place to live becomes uninhabitable.

[126] *Powell and Rayner v. the UK*, ECtHR 21 February 1990, 9310/81.Ibid., para. 40.

prevent them from enjoying their homes in such a way as to affect their private life adversely, without, however, seriously endangering their health'.[127] However, it was clarified in *Kyrtatos v. Greece* that disturbances must reach a 'sufficient degree of seriousness to be taken into account for the purposes of Article 8'.[128,129]

In the 2005 *Fadeyeva v. Russia* judgment the Court confirmed that these threshold requirements are indeed a matter of scope, i.e., they determine whether an environmental issue deserves review under the Convention in the first place.[130] Ms Fadeyeva was living in close proximity to a severely polluting plant that was operating in breach of domestic environmental standards and endangering her health. The Court made crystal clear that

> the adverse effects of environmental pollution must attain a certain minimum level if they are to fall within the scope of Article 8 ... The assessment of that minimum is relative and depends on all the circumstances of the case, such as the intensity and duration of the nuisance, and its physical or mental effects. The general context of the environment should also be taken into account. There would be no arguable claim under Article 8 if the detriment complained of was negligible in comparison to the environmental hazards inherent to life in every modern city.[131]

In concreto, this means that 'complaints relating to environmental nuisances have to show, firstly, that there was an actual interference with the applicant's private sphere, and secondly, that a level of severity was attained'.[132] In *Fadeyeva*, the Court referred to a 'very strong combination of indirect evidence and presumptions' that made it likely the applicant's health deteriorated as a result of the industrial emissions. 'Even assuming that the pollution did not cause any quantifiable harm to her health', it stressed that 'the actual detriment to the applicant's health and well-being reached a level sufficient to bring it within the scope of Article 8 of the Convention'.[133]

Thus, the environmental case law creates room for indivisible review of fundamental interests. In fact, the criterion of a 'minimum level of severity' explicitly demands taking into account the issue of health. Even

---

[127] *López Ostra v. Spain*, ECtHR 9 December 1994, 16798/90.Ibid., para. 51.
[128] *Kyrtatos v. Greece*, ECtHR 22 May 2003, 41666/98, para. 44.   [129] Ibid., para. 54.
[130] *Fadeyeva v. Russia*, ECtHR 9 June 2005, 55723/00.   [131] Ibid., para. 69.
[132] Ibid., para. 70.
[133] Ibid., para. 88. Cf. also *Ledyayeva, Dobrokhotova, Zolotareva and Romashina v. Russia*, ECtHR 26 October 2006, 53157/99; 53247/99; 56850/00; and 53695/00.

though – partly for evidentiary reasons – they do not seem to be an absolute prerequisite,[134] 'physical and mental effects' increase the likelihood that an interest is prima facie protected under the Convention. When health effects are clearly present, this makes it likely that review is granted,[135] whereas when there are no health issues involved at all this may be (part of the) reason for holding the case inadmissible.[136]

Yet the threshold set is not always applied in a consistent manner. In *Zammit Maempel v. Malta*, for example, a family complained about fireworks that are let off on the occasion of certain village feasts, twice a year for a few hours, at about 150 meters from their home. The Court here explicitly referred to the minimum level of severity nuisances must have attained for a case to be admissible, but as there was 'at least a temporary effect on both the physical and ... the psychological state of those exposed to [the fireworks]', and because 'the applicants' family may be exposed to some physical and personal risk',[137] the complaint was nevertheless reviewed. The lack of concrete, severe risks or any health effects further on in the judgment played an important role in concluding that there had not been a violation.[138] Another example is the 2012 case of *Di Sarno and Others v. Italy*.[139] The issue at hand concerned the waste crisis in Italy, where garbage had been piling up in the streets for months without the government being able to take any effective measures. In *Di Sarno* the Court placed particular emphasis on these general, rather than on individual circumstances. It mentioned a direct effect of the waste on the applicants *propre bien-être* (well-being),[140] and moreover held that it could foresee that the situation *could* lead to a 'deterioration of their life quality'.[141] However, also because of the lack of any health effects, it is questionable whether the criteria set in *Fadeyeva* were actually applied.

---

[134] Eva Brems, 'Indirect Protection of Social Rights by the European Court of Human Rights' in D. Barak-Erez and A.M. Gross (eds.), *Exploring Social Rights: Between Theory and Practice* (Oxford: Hart Publishing, 2007), pp. 135–167, 148.

[135] See, for example, *Bâcilă v. Romania*, ECtHR 30 March 2010, 19234/04, paras. 63–64. Cf. also *Brânduse v. Romania*, ECtHR 7 April 2009, 7586/03, paras. 66–67; *Marchis a. O. v. Romania*, ECtHR 28 June 2011 (dec.), 38197/03, para. 38; *Orlikowsci v. Poland*, ECtHR 4 October 2011, 7153/07, para. 98; *Darkowska and Darkowski v. Poland*, ECtHR 15 November 2011 (dec.), 31339/04, para. 69.

[136] Cf., for example, *Walkuska v. Poland*, ECtHR 29 April 2008 (dec.), 6817/04; *Fägerskiöld v. Sweden*, ECtHR 26 February 2008 (dec.), 37604/04; *Furlepa v. Poland*, ECtHR 18 March 2008 (dec.), 62101/00.

[137] *Zammit Maempel v. Malta*, ECtHR 22 November 2011, 24202/10, para. 38.

[138] Ibid., para. 67.   [139] *Di Sarno a. O. v. Italy*, ECtHR 10 January 2012, 30765/08.

[140] Ibid., para. 81.   [141] Ibid., para. 108.

Just as in cases concerning housing or health care, and even though it has developed interpretive standards, the prima facie scope of the Convention at times seems of little concern to the Court. Yet an overbroad interpretation tends to invite a wide margin especially in social and other issues that may appear to be only tacitly linked to the ECHR.[142] In *Hatton and Others* the Grand Chamber discussed the issue of whether the state's regulations on limitations for night flights had struck a fair balance between the individual and the general interests involved. It considered:

> [O]n the one hand, the Government claim a wide margin on the ground that the case concerns matters of general policy, and, on the other hand, the applicants' claim that where the ability to sleep is affected, the margin is narrow because of the "intimate" nature of the right protected. This conflict of views on the margin of appreciation can be resolved only by reference to the context of a particular case.[143]

It found that the issue of sleep deprivation was not intimate enough for concluding that the margin of appreciation had to be a narrow one, and instead opted for the wide environmental margin. This turned out to be one of the most important reasons why the Grand Chamber judgment in *Hatton* has been criticized.[144] Indeed, in *Hatton*, the fact that the severity of the individual interests at stake could also mitigate the margin – rather than only turn it into a very narrow one – is not even considered, which illustrates that it difficult to overcome the wide margin the Court generally grants in the field of environmental policy.

Notwithstanding this, even when it does not explicitly narrow the margin, the Court has in more recent cases turned its deferential fair balance test into stricter, often procedural review. In earlier cases, violations mostly resulted from national irregularities. In *López Ostra v. Spain*, a case about serious industrial pollution from a nearby waste-treatment

---

[142] See, for some examples of the wide margin in environmental cases, *Taskin a. O. v. Turkey*, ECtHR 10 November 2004, 46117/99, paras. 116–117; *Fadeyeva v. Russia*, ECtHR 9 June 2005, 55723/00, para. 104; *Giacomelli v. Italy*, ECtHR 2 November 2006, 59909/00, para. 80; *Dubetska a. O. v. Ukraine*, ECtHR 10 February 2011, 30499/03, para. 141; *Zammit Maempel v. Malta*, ECtHR 22 November 2011, 24202/10, para. 66; *Deés v. Hungary*, ECtHR 9 November 2010, 2345/06, para. 23; *Mileva a. O. v. Bulgaria*, ECtHR 25 November 2010, 43449/02 and 21475/04, para. 98. A 'considerable' margin was applied in *Grimkovskaya v. Ukraine*, ECtHR 28 June 2011, 38182/03, par. 65.

[143] *Hatton a. O. v. the UK*, ECtHR (GC) 8 July 2003, 36022/97, para. 103.

[144] See the dissenting opinion of Judges Costa, Ress, Türmen, Zupancic, and Steiner, under III. Cf. Koch 2009 (n. 48), 69 ff.

plant, the Court emphasized the fact that the factory was operating without the necessary municipal licence. Therefore, '[i]t has to be noted that the municipality not only failed to take steps ... but also resisted judicial decisions to that effect'.[145] A fair balance between the economic well-being of the town and the applicant's fundamental right had thus not been struck. *Guerra and Others v. Italy* dealt with the issue of access to information regarding the health risks related to environmental pollution.[146] The fact that in this case there had been a violation, however, was premised on the fact that there was a national law concerning the dissemination of information, with which the state had failed to comply. Finally, in *Fadeyeva v. Russia* the Court also confirmed the importance of 'national irregularities' for concluding whether or not there had been a violation. It mentioned that 'in all previous cases in which environmental questions gave rise to violations of the Convention, the violation was predicated on a failure by the national authorities to comply with some aspect of the domestic legal regime'.[147] However, different from in cases concerning negative obligations,[148] it considered that when positive claims are concerned, such irregularities do not necessarily suffice for concluding on a violation.[149] Moreover, even though 'in today's society the protection of the environment is an increasingly important consideration', because of the complexity of the issues involved, the Court's task remains a primarily subsidiary one.[150]

The Court in *Hatton and Others v. the United Kingdom* considered that the 'element of domestic irregularity is wholly absent in the present case', which added to the conclusion that there had not been a violation.[151] However, the Grand Chamber also held here that in cases 'involving State decisions affecting environmental issues', besides an assessment of the substantive merits of the case, 'it may scrutinise the decision-making process to ensure that due weight has been accorded to the interests of the individual'.[152] And although in *Hatton* the applicants were not much aided by this test, more recently it has been shown to form a workable starting point for investigating environmental health

---

[145] *López Ostra v. Spain*, ECtHR 9 December 1994, 16798/90, para. 56.
[146] *Guerra a. O. v. Italy*, ECtHR 19 February 1998, no. 116/1996/735/932.
[147] *Fadeyeva v. Russia*, ECtHR 9 June 2005, 55723/00, para. 97.
[148] 'The breach of domestic law in these cases would necessarily lead to a finding of a violation of the Convention'. See *Fadeyeva v. Russia*, ECtHR 9 June 2005, 55723/00, para. 95.
[149] Ibid., para. 98.   [150] Ibid., para. 103.
[151] *Hatton a. O. v. the UK*, ECtHR (GC) 8 July 2003, 36022/97, para. 120.
[152] Ibid., para. 99.

complaints in a meaningful manner. Focusing explicitly on the role of the health- and housing-related interests in the national procedure, a procedural focus allows the Court to guarantee indivisible protection even if the authorities did not act contrary to domestic legislation.

A few examples illustrate this. In *Taskin and Others v. Turkey*, which concerned a complaint about the issuing of a permit to use a cyanidation operation process that posed a risk for human health and safety, the Court recalled the possibility of procedural review.[153] It only briefly reflected on the substantive aspect and referred to the wide margin of appreciation granted in this regard. Concerning the procedure aspect, however, it held that in complex issues of environmental and economic policy,

> the decision-making process leading to measures of interference must be fair and such as to afford due respect for the interests of the individual as safeguarded by Article 8 ... It is therefore necessary to consider all the procedural aspects, including the type of policy or decision involved, the extent to which the views of individuals were taken into account throughout the decision-making process, and the procedural safeguards available.[154]

More concretely:

> [T]he decision-making process must firstly involve appropriate investigations and studies in order to allow them to predict and evaluate in advance the effects of those activities which might damage the environment and infringe individuals' rights and to enable them to strike a fair balance between the various conflicting interests at stake ... The importance of public access to the conclusions of such studies and to information which would enable members of the public to assess the danger to which they are exposed is beyond question ... [They must] be able to appeal to the courts against any decision, act or omission where they consider that their interests or their comments have not been given sufficient weight in the decision-making process.[155]

Because in *Taskin* the authorities had 'deprived the procedural guarantees available to the applicants of any useful effect', the Court concluded that Article 8 had been breached.

Giacomelli v. Italy concerned an applicant who lived thirty metres away from a plant for the storage and treatment of 'special waste'.[156] An environmental impact assessment had only been initiated years after

---

[153] *Taskin a. O. v. Turkey*, ECtHR 10 November 2004, 46117/99, para. 115.
[154] Ibid., para. 118.   [155] Ibid., para. 119.
[156] *Giacomelli v. Italy*, ECtHR 2 November 2006, 59909/00.

the detoxification of the hazardous waste had begun to take place. The Court in this regard

> considers that the procedural machinery provided for in domestic law for the protection of individual rights, in particular the obligation to conduct an environmental-impact assessment prior to any project with potentially harmful environmental consequences and the possibility for any citizens concerned to participate in the licensing procedure and to submit their own observations to the judicial authorities and, where appropriate, obtain an order for the suspension of a dangerous activity, were deprived of useful effect in the instant case for a very long period.[157]

There had hence been a violation of the Convention.

In a later case, the Court has found a violation on the basis of the fact that the state had failed to provide the information known in order for those involved to take the necessary steps, thereby referring to the importance of the precautionary principle.[158] Elsewhere, it held that the fact that it had taken ten years before an issue was settled before the domestic authorities made that the state had failed to show due diligence and give proper consideration to all competing interests.[159] In other instances, the Court has concluded that the procedural safeguards were sufficient, and combined with a deferential stance on the substantive issue, this then often led to the conclusion that Article 8 had not been breached.[160] In any case, it seems that by now, the Court has moved from a rather narrow focus on national irregularities, to a test that encompasses an explicit focus on the decision-making procedures concerned and whether these have shown due account of the health, housing and other needs of the individuals involved. Thereby, it seems to have found an approach that at least has the potential of providing effective and indivisible socio-economic protection while preventing the Court from overstepping the boundaries of its delicate task. In this regard, in line with a core rights perspective, it is advised to apply the thresholds for Article 8's application in a consistent manner. When this is done having regard to the essential importance of the health interests concerned, it can be said that the Court's approach comes close to what individual core rights protection in a complex field like environmental policy would entail.

---

[157] Ibid., para. 94.   [158] *Tâtar v. Romenia*, ECtHR 27 Januray 2009, 67021/01.

[159] *Udovicic v. Croatia*, ECtHR 24 April 2014, 27310/09.

[160] *Hardy and Maile v. the UK*, ECtHR 14 February 2012, 31965/07. See also *Luginbühl v. Switzerland*, ECtHR 17 January 2006 (dec.), 42756/02; *Gaida v. Germany*, ECtHR 3 July 2007 (dec.), 32015/02.

8.3 Social Security

8.3.1 Social Security as a Convention Issue

In terms of core social protection, the protection of social security under the right to protection of property may appear most promising and most tricky at the same time. What does a core rights perspective add to the Court's vast case law on social security issues? Briefly stated, it helps to explain why the Court from time to time concludes that a revocation or reduction of a social benefit was disproportional. Yet it also points out the weak points in the Court's reasoning. These relate to its sometimes opaque balancing test, as well as to the interpretation of social security benefits as 'possessions' protected under the Convention. Before having a look at the Court's complex case law, including the issue of non-discrimination in relation to social security, a few general things can first be said on the strained relationship between this domain and the Convention.

Not only do many individuals receive some kind of social assistance, a significant number of them today are dependent on the provision of state-organized support. When private social networks fail to provide the necessary safety nets and this task is largely left to fine-grained social security schemes, the relation between individuals and the 'social state' becomes a prominent one. Indeed, this relation is an asymmetrical one, characterized by the power of the state and the vulnerability of the individual concerned, thus creating a situation in which vital individual interests can be harmed.[161]

The inherent nexus between social security and fundamental individual interests explains why, besides in the context of economic and social rights, this topic is relevant under the Convention. Still, and this may be unsurprising given the lack of a textual reference in the Convention, the obvious effects of the revocation of social security measures for an individual's private and/or family life have not automatically led to the applicability of Article 8 and the prohibition of disproportional interferences or omissions. In a similar vein, the importance of pecuniary support has not compelled the straightforward recognition of all social security benefits as 'possessions' protected under Article 1 of Protocol No. 1 to the ECHR. The Convention does not unequivocally guarantee a subjective right to be provided with social security. Yet a close look at

---

[161] Cf. Jo Kenny, 'European Convention on Human Rights and Social Welfare', *European Human Rights Law Review*, 5 (2010), pp. 495–503, 502.

the case law prevents the conclusion that a social security benefit not awarded to an individual at the national level can never be successfully claimed with the help of it.

Article 3, in a few cases, has been linked to social security-related issues as well.[162] The absolute protection of this article can only be triggered when the circumstances 'attain a minimum level of severity'.[163] The assessment of this minimum is relative and allows for taking social needs into account. In *Larioshina v. Russia* the applicant complained about the insufficient amount of pension and other benefits she received for maintaining a proper standard of living. In deciding on the admissibility of her complaint, the Court considered:

> [A] complaint about a wholly insufficient amount of pension and the other social benefits may, in principle, raise an issue under Article 3 of the Convention which prohibits inhuman or degrading treatment. However, on the basis of the material in its possession, the Court finds no indication that the amount of the applicant's pension and the additional social benefits has caused such damage to her physical or mental health capable of attaining the minimum level of severity falling within the ambit of Article 3 of the Convention.[164]

In *Budina v. Russia* the Court confirmed that it is very difficult to satisfy the high threshold of 'a minimum level of severity', especially when someone is not left bereft of 'essential medical treatment'.[165] Yet as the case of *M.S.S. v. Greece and Belgium* shows, when a vulnerable individual[166] lacks practically any means of subsistence and is dependent on the state[167], it nevertheless can be met. Thus, whereas the Court makes clear that Article 3 does not entail 'any general obligation to give refugees financial assistance to enable them to maintain a certain standard of living',[168] a more targeted minimum obligation nevertheless exists. Seen through a core rights lens, this seems justified and in line with the aims of effective and indivisible protection. Yet as mentioned earlier, the Court could more clearly indicate that minimum social protection is required, while leaving it to the state to determine how exactly this is arranged for and what it in detail implies.

---

[162] See also S. 8.1.1.   [163] *Ireland v. the UK*, ECtHR 18 January 1978, 5310/71, para. 162.
[164] *Larioshina v. Russia*, ECtHR 23 April 2002 (dec.), 56869/00.
[165] *Budina v. Russia*, ECtHR 18 June 2009 (dec.), 45603/05. Cf. also Brems 2007 (n. 133). See also Koch 2009 (n. 40), 181–182.
[166] *M.S.S. v. Belgium and Greece*, ECtHR (GC) 21 January 2011, 30696/09, para. 251.
[167] Ibid., para. 253.   [168] Ibid., para. 249.

Via the prohibition of discrimination (Article 14), the rights under Article 8 and Article 1 P1 have increasingly become relevant to matters of social security.[169] The prohibition of discrimination is not a self-standing requirement. However, its scope of application is generous as it covers the broader ambit of the substantive right invoked together with Article 14.[170] In *Petrovic v. Austria*, the Court held that 'the refusal to grant Mr Petrovic a parental leave allowance cannot amount to a failure to respect family life, since Article 8 does not impose any positive obligation on states to provide the financial assistance in question'.[171] Nonetheless,

> this allowance paid by the State is intended to promote family life and necessarily affects the way in which the latter is organised as, in conjunction with parental leave, it enables one of the parents to stay at home to look after the children. The Court has said on many occasions that Article 14 comes in play whenever "the subject-matter of the disadvantage ... constitutes one of the modalities of the exercise of a right guaranteed" ... or the measures complained of are "linked to the exercise of a right guaranteed" ... By granting parental leave allowance States are able to demonstrate their respect for family life within the meaning of Article 8 of the Convention; the allowance therefore comes within the scope of that provision. It follows that Article 14 – taken together with Article 8 – is applicable.[172]

The Court's reasoning can be understood to imply that only because parental leave allowances directly relate to the organization of family life, the connection with Article 8 is a sufficient one. At the same time, given the broadness of the notion of private life, and the fact that the Court has often underlined that 'Article 14 comes into play whenever "the subject-matter of the disadvantage ... constitutes one of the modalities of the

---

[169] Cf. Marc Bossuyt, 'Should the Strasbourg Court Exercise More Self-Restraint? On the Extension of the Jurisdiction of the European Court of Human Rights to Social Security Regulations', *Human Rights Law Journal*, 28 (2007), pp. 321–332, 321.

[170] Cf. Robert Wintemute, '"Within the Ambit": How Big Is the "Gap" in Article 14 European Convention on Human Rights? Part 1', *European Human Rights Law Review* (2004), pp. 366–382 and Robert Wintemute, 'Filling the Article 14 "Gap": Government Ratification and Judicial Control of Protocol No. 12 ECHR: Part 2', *European Human Rights Law Review* (2004), pp. 484–499. See also Oddný Mjöll Arnardóttir, *Equality and Non-discrimination under the European Convention on Human Rights* (Leiden: Martinus Nijhoff Publishers, 2003), 35–37.

[171] *Petrovic v. Austria*, ECtHR 27 March 1998, 20458/92, para. 26.

[172] Ibid., paras. 27–29. Cf. Koch 2009 (n. 48), 188–188. Cf. also *Di Trizio v. Switzerland*, ECtHR 2 February 2016, 7186/09.

exercise of a right guaranteed"',[173] the variety of social security arrangements that can be reviewed under Article 8 and 14 does not seem very limited.[174] A generous interpretation aligns with the idea that non-discrimination is an essential guarantee inherent in the right to social security. Also in light of the rationale of Article 1 of Protocol 12, complaints of alleged discrimination in this field deserve to be reviewed under the Convention. What is more, when minimum essential levels of social security and/or the protection of vulnerable individuals is at stake, Article 8 taken alone could also be applied. In fact, as I will argue at the end of this chapter, the Article 8 route in some cases would be preferable to relying on the right to protection of property. Article 1 P1 has become the main avenue for seeking Convention rights protection in case benefits or pensions are revoked, reduced or not granted at all. The extensive case law under this provision can be seen as a corollary of the application of the principle of non-discrimination in relation to property rights in this field. I will first turn to this non-discrimination case law, and then address the protection of property taken alone.

8.3.2   Non-Discrimination and Property Rights

Taken together with Article 1 P1, Article 14 plays an important role in the Strasbourg social security case law. From a core rights perspective, this is understandable: even if there is no general positive obligation to create social benefits, the arrangements that have been put in place must be non-discriminatory.[175] Just as in the context of housing, besides emphasizing the need for review of cases concerning alleged discrimination, the core socio-economic rights approach that was outlined in Chapter 7 would require that sufficient attention is paid to the socio-economic needs involved. Especially if there is unequal treatment in the provision of minimum subsistence rights, or if this treatment negatively

---

[173] Ibid., para. 29; *Konstantin Markin v. Russia*, ECtHR (GC) 22 March 2012, 30078/06, para. 129.

[174] See, for example, *Karner v. Austria*, ECtHR 24 July 2003, 40016/98, discussed in S. 8.1.3; Oddný Mjöll Arnardóttir, 'Discrimination as a Magnifying Lens: Scope and Ambit under Art. 14 and Protocol No. 12' in E. Brems and J.H. Gerards (eds.), *Shaping Rights in the ECHR: The Role of the European Court of Human Rights in Determining the Scope of Human Rights* (Cambridge University Press, 2014), pp. 330–349.

[175] Ida Elisabeth Koch and Jens Vested-Hansen, 'International Human Rights and National Legislatures – Conflict or Balance', *Nordic Journal of International Law*, 75 (2006), pp. 3–28, 20.

affects vulnerable individuals, a sufficient justification is required. However, the question of what reasons the Court requires for unequal treatment is closely intertwined with the grounds on which this treatment is based.[176] Moreover, the element of whether situations are relevantly similar plays a pivotal role. For these reasons, the eventual protection granted by Article 14 remains complex.

The applicability of Article 1 P1 normally depends on the economic value of the individual interest central to the complaint.[177] Moreover, for a property right to be recognized as justiciable, it should generally be an existing right.[178] Alternatively, there should be a legitimate expectation of obtaining effective enjoyment of such right.[179] The fact that a right to acquire property is not recognized[180] has not withheld the Court from generally allowing review under Article 14.[181] When a benefit falls 'within the ambit' of the protection of property and is not awarded because of a failure to fulfil an allegedly discriminatory criterion, Article 14 applies. Whereas it first appeared that this could only be the case when a benefit was linked to prior paid contributions,[182] the Court has clarified that this is not material when applying Article 14. In *Stec and Others v. the United Kingdom*, the Court held that the variety of funding methods in the member states, among other things, made it 'appear increasingly artificial' to include only contributory benefits. Moreover,

> [i]n the modern, democratic State, many individuals are, for all or part of their lives, completely dependent for survival on social security and welfare benefits. Many domestic legal systems recognize that such individuals require a degree of certainty and security, and provide for benefits to be paid – subject to the fulfilment of the conditions of eligibility – as of right.[183]

---

[176] Cf. Gerards (n. 70).

[177] Pieter van Dijk, Fried van Hoof, Arjen van Rijn and Leo Zwaak (eds.), *Theory and Practice of the European Convention on Human Rights*, 4th ed. (Antwerp/Oxford/New York: Intersentia, 2006), 866.

[178] *Stran Greek Refinieries and Stratis Andeadis v. Greece*, ECtHR 9 December 1994, 13427/87, the Court noted that an existing right should be 'sufficiently established to be enforceable' (para. 59).

[179] Mere hope is not enough. See *Prince Hans-Adam II of Liechtenstein v. Germany*, ECtHR (GC) 12 July 2001, 42527/98.

[180] See, for example, *Van der Mussele v. Belgium*, ECtHR 23 November 1983, 8919/80, para. 48; *Pistorova v. the Czech Republic*, ECtHR 26 October 2004, 73578/01, para. 38.

[181] Cf. Mel Cousins, 'The European Convention on Human Rights, Non-Discrimination and Social Security: Great Scope, Little Depth?', *Journal of Social Security Law*, 16 (2009), pp. 118–136.

[182] *Gaygusuz v. Austria*, ECtHR 16 September 1996, 17371/90.

[183] *Stec a. O. v. the UK*, ECtHR (GC) 6 July 2005 (dec.), 65731/01 and 65900/01, para. 51.

Thus, if a state creates a benefits scheme, and regardless of whether this scheme is a contributory or a non-contributory one, 'it must do so in a manner which is compatible with Article 14'.[184]

Unsurprisingly, this rule has invited many new social security-related applications. This has led to the admissibility of complaints about highly complex social security issues.[185] It has become clear, moreover, that when *access* to a social security system and the future possibility to obtain a benefit, instead of a concrete benefit, is concerned, there is sufficient reason to apply Article 14 as well.[186] Thus, the unequal treatment an applicant complains about does not need to be directly related to the granting of a benefit as such.[187] Besides, whereas the Court has repeatedly held that Article 1 P1 does not guarantee a right to a pension of any particular amount, when a non-discrimination complaint concerns the level of a pension, this is no reason to hold the case inadmissible.[188]

Yet in some cases the Court appears more hesitant to apply Article 14 in conjunction with Article 1 P1. In *Valkov and Others v. Bulgaria*, the Court was asked to review the applications lodged by nine Bulgarian nationals who claimed that the statutory cap on their pensions breached their rights under the Convention.[189] The applicants considered that they had been discriminated against compared to those individuals who fell below the cap, as well as compared to those whose pensions were exempted from it.[190] The Court held here that it 'does not consider it necessary to determine whether the facts of the case fall within the ambit of that provision'. This because, '[e]ven assuming that they do, and that Article 14 is thus applicable, the Court finds that there has been no violation of that provision for the reasons that follow'.[191] Such an approach undermines the clarity of its case as well as the importance of the guarantee of non-discrimination. In *Ramaer and Van Willigen v. the Netherlands*, the Court's caution seems justified – yet its approach lacks

---

[184] Ibid., paras. 54–55.

[185] Cf. *Andrejeva v. Latvia*, ECtHR (GC) 18 February 2009, 55707/00, and *Andrle v. the Czech Republic*, ECtHR 17 February 2011, 6268/08.

[186] *Luczak v. Poland*, ECtHR 27 November 2007, 77782/01. See also *Stummer v. Austria*, ECtHR (GC) 7 July 2011, 37452/02.

[187] See, for example, *B. v. the UK*, ECtHR 14 February 2012, 36571/06.

[188] See, for example, *Carson a. O. v. the UK*, ECtHR 4 November 2008, 42184/05.

[189] *Valkov a. O. v. Bulgaria*, ECtHR 25 October 2011, 2033/04, 19125/04, 19475/04, 19490/04, 19495/04, 19497/04, 24729/04, 171/05 and 2041/05.

[190] Ibid., para. 102.   [191] Ibid., para. 113.

sufficient clarity as well.[192] This case dealt with the effects of the new Dutch health care system for pensioners living abroad. The applicants argued that the health care insurance they could obtain under the new system was not equivalent to that available to Dutch residents. The Court held that the protection of property, taken alone, did not apply because the expectations the applicants had were 'based on the hope to see their insurance contracts continued, or renewed, on terms no less favourable for them than those which they enjoyed previously'.[193] It then held that *because* Article 1 P1 taken alone did not apply, it could also not review the issue under Article 14.[194] This fails to recognize the broad(-er) ambit of the Convention rights when read in conjunction with Article 14, even though it can be argued that the interest of the applicants does not fall within this broader area of protection either. If a proprietary right is wholly absent, recourse must be had to Article 1 of Protocol No. 12.[195] Alternatively, where a sufficient link with this provision exists, Article 8 could provide solace.

When the Court reviews a non-discrimination complaint, it first asks whether the differential treatment was made on a ground covered by Article 14 and whether the applicant found himself in a 'relevantly similar situation'.[196] In the end, only when no 'objective and reasonable justification' has been given for the differentiation made, it will be held to violate Article 14.[197] This will be the case when the distinction does not pursue a legitimate aim, or lacks a 'reasonable relationship of proportionality between the means employed and the aim sought to be realised'.[198] In this connection, the Court generally grants a wide margin of appreciation. Pension schemes that distinguished between men and women

---

[192] *Ramaer and Van Willigen v. the Netherlands*, ECtHR 23 October 2012 (dec.), 34880/12. See on this case Ingrid Leijten, 'Social Security as a Fundamental Rights Issue in Europe: Ramaer and Van Willigen and the Development of Property Protection and Non-Discrimination under the ECHR', *Zeitschrift für ausländisches öffentliches Recht und Völkerrecht*, 73 (2013), pp. 177–208.

[193] *Ramaer and Van Willigen v. the Netherlands*, ECtHR 23 October 2012 (dec.), 34880/12, paras. 81–82.

[194] Ibid., para. 87.   [195] Ibid., para. 88ff.

[196] See, for example, *Fredin v. Sweden (No. 1)*, ECtHR 18 February 1991, 12033/86, para. 60.

[197] For a recent example of where this justification was lacking, see *Fábián v. Hungary*, ECtHR 15 December 2015, 78177/13 (concerning the revocation of old age pensions after pensioners had taken up work in the public sector; the case has been referred to the Grand Chamber).

[198] See, for example, *Chassagnou a. O. v. France*, ECtHR (GC) 29 April 1999, 25088/94, 28331/95 and 28443/95, para. 91; *Serife Yigit v. Turkey*, ECtHR 2 November 2010, 3967/05, para. 67.

have, for example, passed the Article 14 test.[199] The Court accepts that adjustments to such schemes must be carried out gradually and should not be forced on the state by a supranational Court.[200]

Frequently, also, the Court does not take a stance on whether or not differential treatment was objectively justified. Its conclusion with regard to complex social security-related discrimination issues may be that the applicants simply were not in a relevantly similar situation to those who received the treatment they too desired. The applicant in *B. v. the United Kingdom* had for some time received too high an amount of income support because she had failed to notify the relevant authorities of the fact that her children had been taken into care.[201] B. complained about a difference in treatment between persons who could not reasonably be expected to report a material fact to the social security authorities because they were unaware of the fact, and persons who, like herself, could not reasonably be expected to report a fact because they were not aware of its materiality. The ECtHR held that 'although neither could be said to be "to blame" for the failure to report, the Court considers the situation of persons who are not aware of a fact to be qualitatively of a different nature to that of persons who are aware of a fact but who are not aware of its materiality'.[202] In the landmark case of *Carson and Others v. the United Kingdom*, the Chamber had held that the pensioners who had emigrated to countries in which their pensions were not up-rated in line with inflation were not in a relevantly analogous situation to those residing inside the United Kingdom 'insofar as concerns the operation of pension or social security systems'.[203] Neither could they be compared to pensioners residing in other countries where up-rating was available.[204] The Grand Chamber confirmed this conclusion, albeit on the basis of somewhat different reasoning.[205] It explicated that the applicants had misconceived the relationship between National Insurance contributions and the state pension: according to the Grand Chamber, these were not exclusively linked. Further, it emphasized the 'essentially national character of the social security system',[206] and

---

[199] Cf. *Stec a. O. v. the UK*, ECtHR (GC) 12 April 2006, 65731/01 and 65900/01.
[200] *Andrle v. the Czech Republic*, ECtHR 17 February 2011, 6268/08.
[201] *B. v. the UK*, ECtHR 14 February 2012, 36571/06.   [202] Ibid., para. 57.
[203] *Carson a. O. v. the UK*, ECtHR 4 November 2008, 42184/05, para. 78; *Carson a. O. v. the UK*, ECtHR (GC) 16 March 2010, 42184/05.
[204] *Carson a. O. v. the UK*, ECtHR 4 November 2008, 42184/05, para. 79. Cf. Cousins 2009 (n. 181), 134.
[205] *Carson a. O. v. the UK*, ECtHR (GC) 16 March 2010, 42184/05.   [206] Ibid., para. 85.

expressed that it is generally hard to draw comparisons, because of the great variety of applicable social and economic variables.[207] It thereby underlined the complexity of social security issues, and the limited role of the Strasbourg Court therein.

However, regardless of the leeway the Court generally grants the state, not all social security complaints are dismissed on the merits. In *Luczak v. Poland* the applicant had been barred from joining the Polish Farmers' Social Security Fund solely on the basis of his nationality.[208] In this case the Court concluded that Article 14 in conjunction with Article 1 P1 had been violated. *Andrejeva v. Latvia* concerned the complaint of a former USSR citizen who had worked in Latvia since 1973.[209] After the Soviet Union ceased to exist, she became stateless and was eventually granted the status of permanently resident non-citizen. For her pension, this meant that only periods of work in Latvia could be taken into account; but because Andrejeva had been working for a Moscow-based employer, her working years in Latvia were treated as an extended business trip and therefore could not add to any pension.[210] The Court required very weighty reasons for justifying the distinction. Since it was not convinced of a 'reasonable relationship of proportionality', it concluded that the Convention had been violated.

The violations in *Luczak* and *Andrejeva* can be explained by the fact that the distinctions were made on the suspect ground of nationality.[211] Arguably, however, also the fact that a case concerns minimum essential levels of social security does not seem wholly irrelevant.[212] In *Luczak* the Court underlined that the exclusion of a person from a social security scheme 'must not leave him in a situation in which he is denied any social insurance cover, whether under a general or a specific scheme, thus posing a threat to his livelihood'. Moreover, 'to leave an employed or self-employed person bereft of any social security cover would be incompatible with current trends in social security legislation in Europe'.[213]

---

[207] Ibid., para. 86.   [208] *Luczak v. Poland*, ECtHR 27 November 2007, 77782/01.
[209] *Andrejeva v. Latvia*, ECtHR (GC) 18 February 2009, 55707/00.   [210] Ibid., para. 18.
[211] That the Court is less strict when no suspect ground is involved can be seen in, for example, *Stummer v. Austria*, ECtHR (GC) 7 July 2011, 37452/02.
[212] In a recent case that concerned the ground of nationality, but not minimum protection, the Court's test was more deferential, and no violation was found. See *British Gurkha Welfare Society a. O. v. the UK*, ECtHR 15 September 2016, 44818/11 (where the margin applicable to measures of economic and social policy prevented a 'very weighty reasons' test).
[213] *Luczak v. Poland*, ECtHR 27 November 2007, 77782/01, para. 52.

Andrejeva did not concern the applicant's subsistence minimum: rather than a basic, minimum pension, her complaint concerned additional entitlements. Yet this was exactly one of the reasons why the Court's conclusion was criticized.[214]

It seems appropriate to take account of the fact that minimum benefits are involved in the analysis under Article 14. If this is the case, the Court would be advised to also ensure that this is reflected in the margin of appreciation. Even if the answer to the question of whether there has been discrimination always depends on the comparability of situations and grounds of treatment, this would allow for a more coherent core rights-inspired approach.

8.3.3   Possessions, Benefits and Fair Balance

The core rights perspective for the ECtHR I defend in this book is premised on the idea that interpretation comes before application. What I will do in this final section, however, is start with the Court's review of social security claims under Article 1 P1, and then turn to its interpretation of the possessions that must be present for this provision to apply. I show how a core rights perspective helps to explain why a social security or pension cut is disproportional or not. Still, the Court's inchoate reasoning in this respect would benefit from further clarification. In connection to the Court's interpretation, however, core social rights have little to add. However, a core rights perspective's focus on interpretation does suggest that the Court should pay more attention to the issue of when a complaint about an essential social benefit does *not* fall within Article 1 P1's scope.

I have argued elsewhere that the application of Article 1 P1 to complaints about social security does not always lead to meaningful protection.[215] In this social rights context, the Court grants a wide margin due to the fact that 'general measures of economic and social strategy' are concerned. In consonance with this, it is often concluded that an interference

---

[214] According to the dissent of Judge Ziemele, 'Latvia decided to guarantee a minimum pension to everyone living in the country [including Andrejeva], citizens and non-citizens alike, and additionally to compensate for losses incurred as a result of the demise of the USSR on the basis of the criteria of citizenship and territory' (para. 6; see also para. 1 and para. 7).

[215] Ingrid Leijten, 'From Stec to Valkov: Possessions and Margins in the Social Security Case Law of the European Court of Human Rights, *Human Rights Law Review*, 13 (2013), pp. 309–349.

was proportional. Nevertheless, the Court has started to develop several criteria that could assist it to provide robust and especially more insightful protection, which are moreover in line with the idea of core rights protection.

It is generally not easy for the Court to judge upon the proportionality of interferences with individual social security rights. Frequently, on the other side of the scale there are considerations related to ideological preferences, budgetary considerations and/or austerity concerns. Balancing these against individual interests is a delicate task, especially for a supranational court. However, in some cases, the Court does not have to enter this slippery field, for example when it concludes that a measure or decision was unforeseeable and hence does not meet the lawfulness test. In *Damjanac v. Croatia* the Court explained why the applicant could be considered to meet the relevant requirements in order to continue to receive his military pension. This pension was discontinued after he had moved to Serbia. According to the Court's interpretation of the applicable law, the revocation was not provided for and the measure was therefore unlawful.[216] This meant that no balancing test was required, and the Court could immediately conclude that there had been a violation. The same conclusion was reached in *Grudic v. Serbia*.[217] In this case, Mr and Mrs Grudic complained about the suspension of their disability pensions, and the Court held that because this suspension was based on Opinions of the Ministry for Social Affairs and the Ministry for Labour, Employment and Social Policy, which do not amount to legislation, the lawfulness requirement had not been complied with. Like in *Damjanac*, this made it

> unnecessary for it to ascertain whether a fair balance has been struck between the demands of the general interest of the community on the one hand, and the requirements of the protection of the individual's fundamental rights on the other ..., the seriousness of the alleged financial implications for the respondent State notwithstanding.[218]

Such an approach, implying that the Court takes seriously the requirements preceding the eventual balancing test, is especially apt when core social security issues are at stake.

Yet most social security measures are considered to be based on national law, as well as accessible and foreseeable. The requirements of

[216] *Damjanac v. Croatia*, ECtHR 24 October 2013, 52943/10, para. 102.
[217] *Grudic v. Serbia*, ECtHR 17 April 2012, 31925/08.   [218] Ibid., para. 81.

a legitimate aim, suitability and necessity, moreover, hardly play a role in judgments on social security and property rights. Generally, the outcome instead turns on whether a fair balance has been found. A clear example that this invites abstruse reasoning is formed by the cases of *Maggio and Others v. Italy* and *Stefanetti and Others v. Italy*.[219] These cases concerned Italian citizens who for some time had been working in Switzerland, and due to a legislative change obtained a lower pension than expected. With regard to Maggio, the Court had regard 'to the particular context in which the issue arises in the present case, namely that of a social security scheme'.[220] It considered that '[s]uch schemes are an expression of a society's solidarity with its vulnerable members'.[221] Since the applicant lost 'considerably less than half' of his pension, he had to endure 'a reasonable and commensurate reduction, rather than the total deprivation of his entitlements'.[222] It was considered that the new method of calculating the pensions of those who had worked in Switzerland – where they had paid lower contributions – yet decided to retire in Italy, in fact equalized a state of affairs and avoided unjustified advantages. Accordingly, there had not been a violation of the Convention. *Stefanetti* concerned the same legislative change, but in this case the Court reached the opposite conclusion.[223] It noted that unlike in *Maggio*, the eight applicants in *Stefanetti* had lost more than half of what they would have received in pension had the calculation not been altered. At the same time, the Court stated that account must be had to more than just the amount or percentage of the reduction, as well as that it is material whether the benefit concerned was based on actual contributions rather than being 'gratuitous welfare aid solely funded by the taxpayer in general'.[224] Eventually, the Court held that the reductions had 'undoubtedly affected the applicants' way of life and hindered its enjoyment substantially'.[225] Given also their legitimate expectation of receiving higher pensions, the lack of a compelling general interest and the unforeseeability of the new law, the Court concluded that 'the applicants had

[219] *Maggio a. O. v. Italy*, ECtHR 31 May 2011, 46286/09, 52851/08, 53727/08, 54486/08 and 56001/08. *Stefanetti a. O. v. Italy*, ECtHR 15 April 2014, 21838/10, 21849/10, 21852/10, 21855/10, 21860/10, 21863/10, 21869/10 and 21870/10.

[220] *Maggio a. O. v. Italy*, ECtHR 31 May 2011, 46286/09, 52851/08, 53727/08, 54486/08 and 56001/08, para. 61.

[221] Ibid.   [222] Ibid., para. 62.

[223] *Stefanetti a. O. v. Italy*, ECtHR 15 April 2014, 21838/10, 21849/10, 21852/10, 21855/10, 21860/10, 21863/10, 21869/10 and 21870/10.

[224] Ibid., para. 60.   [225] Ibid., para. 64.

not suffered commensurate reductions but were in fact made to bear an excessive burden'.[226]

A few things may be noted in regard to *Maggio* and *Stefanetti*. First, from the perspective of individual protection, it is perfectly understandable that the Court considers a legislative change proportional in one case, while finding a violation in another. At the same time, the Court explicitly did not base its conclusion in *Stefanetti* solely on the percentage of the reduction. Since most of the other circumstances were similar to those in *Maggio*, it remains unclear when and why exactly the measure became disproportional.[227] The similarity of the facts of both cases makes painfully clear that it is difficult, if not impossible, to draw the line. Second, the dissenters in *Stefanetti* emphasized the wide margin, as well as the 'huge and unjustified disparity there would have been, to the advantage of the applicants, had the system not been amended'. They noted that none of the applicants fell into the lowest pension bracket, and that 'still less the old-age pensions actually received by the applicants ... are at such a level as to deprive the applicants of the basic means of subsistence'.[228] Thereby the dissenters suggest that (only) if minimum social security rights had been at stake, this would have been reason to hold that the reduction was disproportional.

Mention can also be made of *N.K.M. v. Hungary*.[229] The applicant in this case complained that the tax levy at a rate of 98% on part of her severance pay had amounted to a breach of Article 1 P1. Although the Court's approach to tax issues is normally a very hesitant one,[230] in *N.K.M.* the Court held that 'considered as a whole, the circumstances conferred on the applicant title to a substantive interest protected by Article 1 of Protocol No. 1'.[231] The same mixture of circumstances, moreover, was reason for concluding on a violation of this provision. In the applicant's case, the tax measure had led to an overall tax burden

---

[226] Ibid., para. 66.

[227] Moreover, the issue in *Stefanetti* concerned eight applicants, yet the Court does not distinguish amongst these, although it can be asked whether the reduction was as disproportional for all of them.

[228] *Stefanetti a. O. v. Italy*, ECtHR 15 April 2014, 21838/10, 21849/10, 21852/10, 21855/10, 21860/10, 21863/10, 21869/10 and 21870/10, partly dissenting opinion of Judge Raimondi joined by Judge Lorenzen.

[229] *N.K.M. v. Hungary*, ECtHR 14 May 2013, 66529/11.

[230] Which also has to do with what is stated in Art. 1 P1, namely that this right shall not 'impair the right of a State to ... secure the payment of taxes'.

[231] *N.K.M. v. Hungary*, ECtHR 14 May 2013, 66529/11, para. 33.

of about 52% on the entirety of her severance pay, yet 'given the margin of appreciation the applicable tax rate cannot be decisive in itself'.[232] The Court noted that the applicant 'had to suffer a substantial deprivation of income in a period of considerable personal difficulty, namely that of unemployment'.[233] Referring to Article 34 of the Charter of Fundamental Rights of the European Union and the importance of providing protection in the case of loss of employment, the Court considered it quite likely that the applicant had been exposed to 'substantial personal hardships'.[234] Since other civil servants had not been required to contribute to a comparable extent to the public burden, the relevant tax statute entered into force only weeks before the termination of the civil service relationship and no transitional period had been granted, the Court concluded that there had been a violation.[235] Unsurprisingly, in a similar case where the applicant was notified of her dismissal only six weeks after the law was enacted and was confronted with an overall tax burden of 60%, the Court concluded in a like manner.[236] However, this exceptional review of a tax issue has made the Court enter a discussion of proportionality *stricto sensu* in this field, and also here it will not always be easy to reach conclusions in a transparent manner. After all, even though the cases mentioned arguably were clearly disproportional, what if the Court were confronted with a case in which the overall tax burden was significantly lower? Would the fact that part of the severance pay was taxed at a rate of 98% then still amount to a violation?[237] While hardly paying attention to the lawfulness, suitability or necessity tests,[238] and balancing all the circumstances of the case in an unordered way, the judgment gives rise to more questions than it answers.

Notwithstanding the predominance of the fair balance test, the ECtHR has also developed criteria that arguably can improve its reasoning in social security cases. These criteria can be identified when looking at the case law through a core rights lens. That is, the importance of procedural safeguards, non-discrimination and minimum essential levels is often recognized. When these issues are at stake, it is more likely that a violation is found.

First, in *Moskal*, the Court relied on the principle of good governance for concluding that no fair balance had been struck between the demands

---

[232] Ibid., paras. 66–67.   [233] Ibid., para. 70.   [234] Ibid.   [235] Ibid., paras. 71–76.

[236] *Gáll v. Hungary*, ECtHR 25 June 2013, 49570/11.

[237] Cf. *R.Sz. v. Hungary*, ECtHR 2 July 2013, 41838/11, paras. 19–22, 54.

[238] But see *N.K.M. v. Hungary*, ECtHR 14 May 2013, 66529/11, para. 59.

of the general interest and the protection of the individual's fundamental rights.[239] This principle 'requires that where an issue in the general interest is at stake it is incumbent on the public authorities to act in good time, in an appropriate manner and with utmost consistency'.[240] The test it applied was a rather stringent one: even though the interference was provided for by law and pursued a legitimate aim,[241] the effects of the relatively late withdrawal of an erroneously granted benefit, and the fact that it took three years before she received a replacement, made the case turn out in Moskal's favour.[242] The judgment thereby can be seen as suggesting that a lawful revocation of means of subsistence requires the national authorities to scrutinize the individual hardship that might thereby be caused and act accordingly.[243] The dissenters in the case argued that in judging the proportionality of the interference, the majority had lost sight of the fact that the right to the benefit could not be relied on indefinitely.[244] Moreover, the revocation of the benefit had been subjected to careful examination at three levels of jurisdiction at the national level, and the applicant had never been required to pay back the sums that had mistakenly been paid to her. It had taken a while for her to obtain an alternative and less valuable pension, but the award of these benefits was backdated to the year she had lost her pension.[245] A response could, however, be that a focus on good governance in regard of minimum entitlements in fact formed an appropriate way for the Court to secure the basic benefits this case was about.[246]

The Court, in its review of social security issues, also has paid particular attention to the notion of equality. In reviewing whether the 98% tax the applicant was confronted with amounted to a violation, the Court in *N.K.M.* gave particular attention to the 'unequal treatment aspect', i.e., to the fact that compared to the applicant, other civil servants had not been confronted with a similar tax burden.[247] Even though these are normally dealt with under Article 14, the Court apparently seems willing to weigh in the unequal treatment issue in a pure property rights issue. In

---

[239] *Moskal v. Poland*, ECtHR 15 September 2009, 10373/05, paras. 68–76.
[240] Ibid., para. 51.   [241] Ibid., paras. 54–63.
[242] The government's error in granting the pension in the first place seems to have been important here, too. See ibid., para. 73.
[243] Cf. Kenny 2010 (n. 162), 500.
[244] *Moskal v. Poland*, ECtHR 15 September 2009, 10373/05, partly dissenting opinion of Judges Bratza, Hirvelä, and Bianku, para. 7.
[245] Ibid.   [246] See also, for example, *Czaja v. Poland*, ECtHR 2 October 2012, 5744/05.
[247] *N.K.M. v. Hungary*, ECtHR 14 May 2013, 66529/11, para. 71.

fact, in regard to the applicant's Article 14 complaint the Court held 'that the inequality of treatment of which the applicant claimed to be a victim has been sufficiently taken into account in the above assessment that has led to the finding of a violation of Article 1 of Protocol No. 1 taken separately'.[248] It can be a point of discussion whether this is a desirable approach. After all, if a case hinges on the aspect of non-discrimination, Article 14 seems to be the appropriate route. In any case, however, foregrounding the aspect of equality can make the Court's test more insightful. It fits the centrality of non-discrimination in relation to the provision core socio-economic rights protection, in the sense that unequal treatment makes it harder for the individual interest to be outbalanced.

Finally, the Court also regularly refers to the essence of the social security right concerned. It does not explicate what exactly this essence is and what role it plays in its review. Still, the question whether the essence of the applicant's right to social security is impaired is seen to form an increasingly relevant consideration in reviewing a case under Article 1 P1.[249] In *Lakicevic and Others v. Montenegro and Servia* the applicants complained about the suspension of their pensions because they had reopened their legal practices on a part-time basis. The Court considered that

> [w]hile it must not be overlooked that Article 1 of Protocol No. 1 does not restrict a State's freedom to choose the type or amount of benefits that it provides under a social security scheme ... it is also important to verify whether an applicant's right to derive benefits from the social security scheme in question has been infringed in a manner resulting in the impairment of the essence of his pension rights.[250]

The suspension of the applicants' pensions had not been due to any changes in their own circumstances, but solely resulted from changes in the law. No regard was thereby had to the amount of revenue generated by their part-time work, and the Court considered that the pension must still have constituted a considerable part of the applicants' gross monthly income.[251] The Court held that the applicants were made to bear an individual and excessive burden, and that this

---

[248] Ibid., para. 84; *Gáll v. Hungary*, ECtHR 25 June 2013, 49570/11, para. 79; *R.Sz. v. Hungary*, ECtHR 2 July 2013, 41838/11, para. 70.

[249] See, for example, *Kjartan Ásmundsson v. Iceland*, ECtHR 12 October 2004, 60669/00, para. 39; *Wieczorek v. Poland*, ECtHR 8 December 2009, 18176/05, para. 57.

[250] *Lakicevic a. O. v. Montenegro and Serbia*, ECtHR 13 December 2011, 27458/06, 33604/07, 37205/06 and 37207/06, para. 63.

[251] Ibid., para. 70.

could have been otherwise had the applicants been obliged to endure a reasonable and commensurate reduction rather than the total suspension of their entitlements ... or if the legislature had afforded them a transitional period within which to adjust themselves to the new scheme. Furthermore, they were required to pay back the pensions they had received as of 1 January 2004 onwards, which must also be considered a relevant factor to be weighed in the balance.[252]

Thus, it seems that when a pension or other benefit that forms a substantial part of someone's monthly income is suspended or discontinued entirely and cannot easily be substituted by another benefit, this is likely to be in breach of the Convention.[253] This focus on minimum social protection was recently confirmed in the case of *Baczúr v. Hungary*. Here, the Court explicitly stated that because the reduction of the applicant's benefit temporarily made him receive 'barely 60% of the minimum subsistence level' as determined by the state, he had to bear an excessive individual burden.[254] This case thereby shows that even if some benefit remains, the requirement of a subsistence minimum can lead to a violation of Article 1 P1.

In turn, the Court may also use the essence criterion for substantiating that an interference with social security rights is *not* in breach of the Convention. In *Maggio*, for example, it held that 'the applicant's right to derive benefits from the social insurance scheme in question has not been infringed in a manner resulting in the impairment of the essence of his pension rights'.[255] Another example is the case of *Da Conceição Mateus and Santos Januário v. Portugal*, which concerned austerity-related pension cuts in the form of (temporary) revocations of holiday

---

[252] Ibid., para. 72.

[253] Cf. also *Kjartan Ásmundsson v. Iceland*, ECtHR 12 October 2004, 60669/00. See also Brems 2007 (n. 133), 155. See *Valkov a. O. v. Bulgaria*, ECtHR 25 October 2011, 2033/04, 19125/04, 19475/04, 19490/04, 19495/04, 19497/04, 24729/04, 171/05 and 2041/05, para. 97; *Markovics a. O. v. Hungary*, ECtHR 24 April 2014 (dec.), 77575/11, 19828/13 and 19829/13, para. 42. In cases where there are alternative benefits, indeed, this can be reason for holding that a complaint is manifestly ill-founded, even if because of someone's savings or capital he is not eligible for these benefits (*Hoogendijk v. the Netherlands*, ECtHR 6 January 2005 (dec.), 58641/00).

[254] *Baczúr v. Hungary*, ECtHR 7 March 2017, 8263/15, paras. 30–32.

[255] *Maggio a. O. v. Italy*, ECtHR 31 May 2011, 46286/09, 52851/08, 53727/08, 54486/08 and 56001/08, para. 63. See also, for example, *Panfile v. Romania*, ECtHR 20 March 2012 (dec.), 13902/11, para. 24; *Khoniakina v. Georgia*, ECtHR 19 July 2012, 17767/08, para. 77; *Torri a. O. v. Italy*, ECtHR 24 January 2012 (dec.), 11838/07 and 12302/07, para. 45; *Arras a. O. v. Italy*, ECtHR 14 February 2012, 17972/07, para. 83; *Cichopek a. O. v. Poland*, ECtHR 14 May 2013 (dec.), 15189/10 (and 1,627 others), para. 153.

and Christmas allowances.[256] In this case, as well as in several other austerity cases,[257] the Court decided that the applicants' complaints were manifestly ill-founded. Amongst other things, it relied on the important consideration of whether the applicants' rights had been infringed in a manner resulting in the impairment of the essence thereof.[258]

It would likely benefit the clarity of the Court's reasoning if it developed the role of the essence criterion further, as well as the requirements of good governance and non-discrimination. However, it must be kept in mind that Article 1 P1 differs from Article 3 and Article 8 in an important respect: whereas minimum core (positive) social protection can be seen as inherently tied to private life and the prohibition of inhuman and degrading treatment, this link is a different one where the protection of property is concerned. Although entitlements to social benefits are of crucial importance in the welfare state, this does not mean that Article 1 P1 entails a prima facie right to obtain minimum social benefits under the Convention.

My final remarks on the ECtHR's case law concern its interpretation of the possessions protected by this provision. Even though the Court's generosity in this regard creates room for effective individual protection, it does not serve the aims of providing guidance as well as sufficient deference to decisions made at the national level. In this regard, a core rights perspective suggests a different course.

Elsewhere, I have extensively discussed the broad interpretation that has been given to the protection of property in social security cases.[259] I will not repeat this discussion here. Instead, I will focus on some recent cases that have increased rather than resolved the confusion about when property protection applies. A successful property claim should be 'sufficiently established' as well as 'adequately definable', and a right to acquire property is not recognized.[260] I explained that through its admissibility decision in *Stec*, the Court has clarified that in the context of discrimination cases it should not be material whether a benefit is or is not based on prior contributions.[261] This interpretation has travelled to 'pure'

---

[256] *Da Conceição Mateus and Santos Januário v. Portugal*, ECtHR 8 October 2013 (dec.), 62235/12 and 57725/12.

[257] See, for example, *Koufaki and Adedy v. Greece*, ECtHR 7 May 2013 (dec.), 57665/12 and 57657/12; *Savickas a. O. v. Lithuania*, ECtHR 15 October 2013 (dec.), 66365/09, 12845/10, 28367/11, 29809/10, 29813/10 and 30623/10.

[258] *Da Conceição Mateus and Santos Januário v. Portugal*, ECtHR 8 October 2013 (dec.), 62235/12 and 57725/12, para. 24.

[259] Leijten 2013 (n. 215).   [260] See S. 8.3.2.   [261] Ibid.

property cases. Moreover, the Court has allowed for review under Article 1 P1 when benefits were erroneously granted or when a complaint concerned access to a benefit or the height thereof. But does this simply mean that in principle all social security issues fall within this norm's scope? It is apparent from the Court's case law that this is not the case. An important exception seems to be that except for in cases concerning alleged discrimination,[262] the non-fulfilment of one or more of the criteria set for obtaining a benefit or pension means that there is no possession.[263] Besides, in a recent judgment, the Court more explicitly undermines the idea that in virtually all social security issues, Article 1 P1 applies. In *Damjanac v. Croatia* the applicant complained about the stopping of his military pension for thirteen months after he had changed his place of residence to Serbia.[264] The Court repeated that pension legislation can in principle be considered as creating proprietary interests, and that 'where the amount of a benefit or pension is reduced or eliminated, this may constitute an interference with possessions which requires to be justified in the general interest'.[265] However, it did not stop there, but continued by stating the following:

> Where, however, the person concerned does not satisfy, or ceases to satisfy, the legal conditions laid down in domestic law for the grant of any particular form of benefits or pension, there is no interference with the rights under Article 1 of Protocol No. 1 . . . Finally, the Court observes that the fact that a person has entered into and forms part of a State social security system does not necessarily mean that that system cannot be changed either as to the conditions of eligibility of payment or as to the *quantum* of the benefit or pension.[266]

Read together, these considerations seem to imply that Article 1 P1 is not concerned when someone no longer satisfies the legal conditions for being granted any particular benefit or pension due to changes in the system, i.e., because of alterations regarding the relevant conditions or the *quantum* of the benefit at stake. Yet although this may seem a sensible interpretation, normally the Court opts for a less strict understanding of the right to protection of property. The Court's interpretation

---

[262] After all, this could then be the result of a discriminatory condition.
[263] Sometimes, moreover, the Court leaves open the question of whether there was a possession. Cf. *Sali v. Sweden*, ECtHR 10 january 2006 (dec.), 67070/10; *Maggio a. O. v. Italy*, ECtHR 31 May 2011, 46286/09, 52851/08, 53727/08, 54486/08 and 56001/08, para 59.
[264] *Damjanac v. Croatia*, ECtHR 24 October 2013, 52943/10.   [265] Ibid., para. 85.
[266] Ibid., para. 86.

of Article 1 P1 has become known for its inclusiveness, at least when *at some point* the relevant conditions were met.[267] From the remarks in *Damjanac*, however, it may be inferred that one cannot complain under Article 1 P1 if the reason for a reduction or elimination of a benefit or pension lies in the fact that the applicable conditions are no longer met, or when it relates to a more general change in the system – which is indeed often the reason for no longer obtaining a benefit or a benefit of a certain amount. The reasoning in *Damjanac*, in other words, would enable the Court to exclude a large category of cases from review under the Convention.

The Court's cautious approach in *Damjanac*, however, can hardly be squared with its interpretation of the Convention in the recent case of *Bélané Nagy v. Hungary*.[268] This case concerned a woman who was granted a disability pension in 2001. Pursuant to a modification of the method of determining the level of disability, but apparently without any substantial change in her health, her entitlement to this pension was withdrawn in 2010. In 2012 a new law on disability allowances entered into force, introducing additional applicability criteria. Ms Béláné Nagy submitted a request for an allowance, and her condition was assessed as meeting the requisite level for entitlement. However, as she had not been in receipt of a disability pension on 31 December 2011 and had not accumulated the requisite number of days covered by social security required by the new law, she was not granted anything.

The Chamber, not having temporal jurisdiction to review the 2010 withdrawal, concluded that the refusal of the new request in 2012 amounted to an excessive and disproportionate individual burden. According to the Chamber, as of 2001, the applicant had a 'legitimate expectation to receive a disability pension/allowance as and when her medical condition would so necessitate', and this was reason for her interest to be covered by the 'possessions' protected by Article 1 P1. The dissenters argued that

> Article 1 of Protocol No. 1 to the Convention has never, before today, been interpreted by this Court as obliging member States to provide persons with the right to social security benefits, in the form of disability pensions, independently of their having an assertable right to such a pension under domestic law. The majority have thus expanded the scope

---

[267] Cf. *Moskal v. Poland*, ECtHR 15 September 2009, 10373/05
[268] *Bélané Nagy v. Hungary*, ECtHR 10 February 2015, 53080/13; ECtHR (GC) 13 December 2016.

of the right to property under the Convention in a manner that is flatly inconsistent with this Court's case-law and the object and purpose of Article 1 of Protocol No. 1. As the right to property under the European Convention on Human Rights is not an autonomous repository for economic and social rights not granted by the member States, we respectfully dissent.[269]

Notwithstanding this critical point, in December 2016 the Grand Chamber reached the same conclusion as had the Chamber.[270] Yet the majority's lengthy elaboration on the reasons why in this case a legitimate expectation was at stake, again appeared unconvincing to the dissenters as well concurring Judge Wojtyczek.[271] Lacking a concrete asset that was tied to this expectation, the Court's extensive interpretation of this concept may have far-reaching consequences. As the eight dissenters noted, 'hard cases do not make good law'.[272] It is obvious form the Court's reasoning that its focus here concerned effective, indivisible rights protection. Béláné Nagy was left without any social benefit, and the way in which her pension was revoked was dubious to say the least. The judgment can be read, however, as recognizing a positive right to obtain minimum social benefits under the right to protection of property even if the requirements set by national law have not been complied with. The question whether the fulfillment of the contribution criterion was crucial in this regard, is still left to be answered.

It is true that the protection of basic socio-economic guarantees is of crucial importance in the light of the aims of the Convention. What I have argued in this book, however, is that this should not come at the cost of insightful reasoning that besides ensuring effective protection, also is aimed at providing guidance while granting deference to choices made at the national level. In *Béláné Nagy*, the Court seemingly failed to strike the right balance in its approach under Article 1 P1. After all, for protection to be granted in socio-economic cases under this provision, it must convincingly be argued that the protection of *property* applies.

Does this mean that those in social need are left bereft of Convention review when they do not meet the requirements for obtaining any social

---

[269] *Béláné Nagy v. Hungary*, ECtHR 10 February 2015, 53080/13, dissenting opinion of Judges Keller, Spano and Kjølbro, para. 1.

[270] *Béláné Nagy v. Hungary*, ECtHR (GC) 13 December 2016, 53080/13.

[271] See ibid., concurring opinion of Judge Wojtyczek, in which he is very critical of the quality of the reasoning of the Court.

[272] Ibid., dissenting opinion of Judges Nussberger, Hirvelä, Bianku, Yudkivska, Møse, Lemmens and O'Leary.

benefit? By no means. Rather than under Article 1 P1, however, such cases may be dealt with under Articles 8, 14 or even 3 ECHR. This because the refusal of a minimum benefit seriously affects an individual's private life and may result from discrimination or even amount to inhuman and degrading treatment. The fact that this complaint was brought and dealt with solely as a property rights complaint supports my claim that the Court should be more explicit about the prima facie core socio-economic rights protection offered by Article 1 P1 as well as by the other rights enshrined in the Convention.

Conclusion

With the help of a core rights perspective, we can make sense of the protection offered by the ECtHR in the fields of housing, health and health care and social security. Although the Court does not say so explicitly, the state has obligations to ensure minimum social protection under the different provisions, particularly when complainants are vulnerable and dependent on the state. In the context of Article 3, a failure to provide such protection can lead to inhuman and degrading treatment. Sometimes it results in a violation of the right to life. Under Article 8, especially, the Court has applied the Convention to a broad range of socio-economic complaints, ensuring substantive minimum protection with the help of procedural requirements. In the social security case law dealing with property rights, we see that when core social guarantees are concerned, this can help explain why a measure was disproportional.

Looking at the case law through a core rights lens also has shown some lacunas in the Court's approach. It regularly does not determine whether a complaint falls within the scope of a Convention right, let alone that it explicates that the Convention prima facie protects core socio-economic rights. The result is that positive social claims in particular will easily be overshadowed by a wide margin and overall balancing test in which the interests of the state take centre stage. A core rights perspective in this regard shows a more targeted approach. Yet it cannot work miracles: for example, when alleged discrimination is concerned, a core rights perspective may provide a helpful analytical tool without being able to explain why a socio-economic interest is eventually protected or not.

~

Conclusion

Fit and Future

The idea of core socio-economic rights protection fits the ECtHR's emerging socio-economic case law and provides suggestions for the further development thereof. In this book, I showed how core rights protection can fill a gap in the justificatory explanation that has been given for the ECtHR's protection of socio-economic rights. The ECtHR protects these rights on the basis of the civil and political rights norms enumerated in the Convention. The ideas of effectiveness and indivisibility provide important clarifications in this regard. First, it is clear that effectuation of the ECHR norms requires a broad interpretation. This interpretation can be teleological or autonomous, and is most likely an evolutive one. The Convention is said to be a living tree, the branches of which grow in different directions. One of these is the socio-economic sphere. Second, indivisibility means that civil and political rights and economic and social rights are indivisible, interdependent and inter-related. They must be treated as such, and hence the ECtHR refers to socio-economic rights and interprets the Convention norms accordingly. Especially now that socio-economic rights have become more widely accepted, indivisibility holds great promise. If these rights are considered to form another living tree, it should not come as a surprise that the branches of the different 'rights trees' grow more and more intertwined.[1]

Effectiveness and indivisibility justify the Court's engagement in the socio-economic sphere. They fail, however, to provide a comprehensive explanation. Both notions focus primarily on the creation of interpretive room in order to allow individual protection. Yet whereas holding a Convention right applicable is one thing, reviewing cases involving socio-economic interests is quite another. Moreover, besides effective individual protection, the ECtHR as a supranational Court should show deference to decisions made at the national level, as well as provide

---

[1] This is what came to my mind when encountering *Two Trees* by Jacoba van Heemskerck (1908–1910), the painting that ended up on the cover of this book.

sufficient guidance in order for member states to be able to comply with the Convention. Effectiveness and indivisibility do not provide an answer to the criticism that has been levelled at the Court's socio-economic case law, namely that it is too incremental, at times inconsistent and shows a significant gap between prima facie and definitive protection. Also the question of whether there are limits to the Court's socio-economic rights protection remains unresolved. What follows from the different strains of criticism is that the doctrines of proportionality and the margin of appreciation cannot complete the puzzle: a close look at these doctrines in fact draws attention to the opaque use of the proportionality test and unclear application of the margin. In this book, I proposed the idea of core rights protection as an additional explanation and justification. Together with effectiveness and indivisibility, a core rights perspective provides for a more complete understanding of the ECHR's socio-economic dimension. It moreover suggests ways for dealing with the interpretive room offered by the Convention and the potential thereof.

The idea of core rights deserves particular care. It can easily be misunderstood, and its technical finesses are not always appreciated. What is more, the idea of core rights protection may be perceived as going against what a belief in fundamental rights today seems to be primarily about, namely a broad coverage of rights combined with a balancing of case-specific interests. In this study an effort was made to shed a fresh light on core rights protection. Core rights theory and practice is diverse and has more to offer than is often assumed. On the basis of various examples, a core rights perspective was developed to fit the particular legal context of the ECtHR and its socio-economic rights protection. I will use these final pages to make some last remarks as to this perspective's added value. In addition, I will say something on the implications of this study in relation to the current trends and developments in fundamental rights protection.

In Part III I offered some insights on the nexus between the idea of core rights and the Strasbourg practice. There, the inspiration that could be drawn from the different core rights doctrines was combined and confronted with what was said on the position and task of the ECtHR. This Court is expected to effectively secure fundamental individual interests. The mechanism set up by the Convention serves as a last resort for those within the Council of Europe who feel their rights have not been duly respected or actively protected. As a judicial organ, and this is exacerbated by the fact that it does not form part of a national balance of powers, the ECtHR is slow, however, to interfere with democratic

decisions taken at the national level. The Court cannot assume lawmaking capacities, particularly in a field like socio-economic policy. This field
is characterized by sensitive budgetary and political choices, and moreover not traditionally covered by the Convention. Somewhat paradoxically, though, the ECtHR is also required to elucidate guidelines for the
member states to comply with the Convention. A web of both negative
and positive obligations has been inferred from the different rights in
the Convention and the protocols thereto. Yet a clear view of what is
demanded for compliance is often lacking. That there is a desire for
objective information in this regard is obvious from encounters with
national judges, lawmakers and the executive. This is where ECHR
scholars can make a difference in practice, namely by attempting to point
out red threads to the extent that these are discernible.

When it comes to the protection of socio-economic rights under the
Convention, the morning mist is slowly lifting. Since it first explicitly
recognized that the socio-economic sphere cannot be disconnected from
that of the Convention altogether, a rich socio-economic case law has
emerged. This case law covers issues related to pension payments, the
provision of medication, access to housing, etc. Yet the Court often does
not explicitly address why it considers a socio-economic interest to be
covered by the Convention, or what obligations follow from this. A core
rights perspective can elucidate things: it adds to the explanations given
to the socio-economic case law by clarifying the emphasis the ECtHR
places on certain issues and the conclusions it reaches. The core rights
perspective that I argued fits the practice of the Strasbourg Court, starts
from the idea of absolute-relative core rights protection. It was seen in
the various core rights examples that core rights are perceived as
absolute or relative with regard to either or both their content and
protection. This ties in with a two-stage approach to render rights definitive that starts from the interpretation of these rights, followed by
reviewing whether the right or the interest with which it conflicts,
prevails. Absolute-relative core rights protection means that socio-
economic cores are general rather than case-specific. Although interpretation always proceeds from the facts of individual cases, a general notion
of what core socio-economic interests deserve prima facie protection
can guide a decision on whether or not a particular issue falls within
the ECHR's scope. At the same time, the eventual protection offered is
relative. This means that under the Convention there can be justifications
for not complying with socio-economic cores, although the review by the
Court must have sufficient bite. Absolute-relative core rights protection

suits the Strasbourg fundamental rights context because it recognizes the need for a clear enough demarcation of the scope of the Convention rights. In turn, it emphasizes that the rights – even if they are not civil and political – that deserve prima facie protection must be taken seriously, even when in the light of the position and task of the Court, absolute protection cannot be demanded. At least, that is, when the limitable rights of the Convention are concerned. In that case, core socio-economic rights can intensify (the different aspects of) the proportionality test or be translated into procedural requirements that need to be met to comply with the Convention. This allows to take into account state concerns while providing robust protection. Inversely, under the absolute Article 3 ECHR, a state that fails to guarantee core socio-economic protection, i.e., minimum essential socio-economic protection for vulnerable and dependent individuals, does not comply with the Convention.

Core socio-economic rights protection, as a matter of rights reasoning, suggests the following: the Court should be more clear about what is and what is not prima facie covered by the ECHR rights. Rather than opting for an overbroad interpretation or skipping the interpretation stage altogether, for purposes of clarity and demarcating the Court's task, it needs to explain why a complaint falls within the Convention's scope before it proceeds to reviewing the issue. For socio-economic issues concerning fair trial or the respect for one's home, for example, this is uncomplicated. Beyond this, however, complaints about interferences with or the lack of minimum essential levels of socio-economic rights (a subsistence minimum) can be sufficiently linked to the scope and aims of the Convention to be included. The same goes for socio-economic complaints that involve alleged discrimination and the protection of vulnerable individuals, even if no minimum levels are at stake (although, in the latter case, this will often be the case). Determining negative and positive prima facie obligations in regard to core socio-economic rights protection need not be avoided. The standard this sets provides the necessary guidance while leaving (some) room for justifiable limitations. This means that the state must demonstrate that individual core socio-economic needs have adequately been taken into account. At the review stage, the Court should clarify what the fact that a core socio-economic issue is at stake means for its review: whether by means of a strict(-er) proportionality sequence or by relying on procedural-type review and reviewing whether the provision of minimum protection was evidently insufficient, socio-economic cores deserve serious consideration. Rather than inviting a wide margin and being easily outbalanced by state interests, this allows for effective indivisible protection without losing sight of the scope of the Convention. This is not to say that a core rights perspective is a solution to all the complexities of the Court's socio-economic practice. In cases concerning alleged discrimination, for example, core socio-economic rights cannot be straightforwardly protected. In this context, also the ground of discrimination and the question whether there was a relevantly similar position play an important role. Even if a core rights perspective cannot work miracles, however, it provides an analytical tool as well as an argument for a more targeted approach. Future research may further support the case for core socio-economic protection under the ECHR by looking more closely into issues of discrimination, vulnerability and existing (European) consensus on minimum social rights.

It was mentioned in the Introduction that the scope of this book is limited. It deals solely with the ECtHR's protection of socio-economic rights. The different findings are relevant, in other words, for the supranational protection of socio-economic interests under civil and political rights norms, particularly in Europe. Regardless of these limitations, however, in the Introduction I linked the practice, and especially the reasoning, of the ECtHR to broader developments in the field of fundamental rights adjudication. It was considered that in dealing with conflicts between individual and general interests, courts around the world frequently make use of proportionality review and balancing. An important trend, moreover, is the recognition of positive obligations – also when the norms concerned are phrased in negative terms. Finally, I mentioned the more constructive approach to economic and social fundamental rights protection that is visible today. The case law of the ECtHR can be seen as exemplary of these different trends. The Court has contributed to the consolidation of proportionality analysis as *the* approach to fundamental rights adjudication, as well as to the acceptance of positive obligations. Moreover, as I have amply shown, the ECtHR's case law also signals the possibility of (supranational) judicial socio-economic rights protection. It thereby confirms the emerging perception that next to civil and political rights, economic and social guarantees should also be taken seriously as legal constructs on the basis of which individual claims can be protected. Having introduced the practice of the ECtHR in connection with these trends, it may be asked what are the broader implications of the argument I presented.

Although the ECtHR was labelled a forerunner and its practice avant-garde, this Court in particular should remain cautious in its approach to fundamental rights protection. Its position is a sensitive one, as the acceptance and implementation of its judgments is dependent on the willingness of the member states. The Court is far removed not only from the actual effects of its decisions and judgments, but also from what occurred and was decided at the national level. Its human rights mandate may provide the ECtHR with some leeway in applying the Convention in an evolutive way in order to ensure effective protection. At the same time its role can neither be described as particularly transformative, nor is it expected that the Court supports certain social or political goals. In the light of this, as well as in the context of the criticism that is voiced, it was asked in the Introduction whether a combination of the various trends just mentioned could in fact also hamper the success of the Court. Its reliance on proportionality analysis or ad hoc balancing, in combination with the room for positive and, moreover, economic and social rights protection, may have the effect (or at least give the impression) that the Court is doing more than its competences allow for. Even when the ECtHR relies on a wide margin and does not often find a violation of the Convention in the socio-economic sphere, it may sometimes be considered that it is not for the Strasbourg Court to determine whether a fair balance has been struck in a particular field in the first place. In turn, little attention for the Convention's scope combined with a wide margin the moment socio-economic cases are concerned, may fail to give sufficient 'weight' to the important individual interests involved.

Besides providing a fuller explanation of the Convention's emerging socio-economic dimension, the core rights perspective provided sugges-tions for the Court's reasoning in socio-economic cases. It was not argued that proportionality review needs to be avoided, or that positive obligations or socio-economic rights cannot have a place in the Court's case law. Rather, for a combination of these to work in a way that leaves enough room for national decisions and that renders guidance for the domestic authorities, it was suggested that the interpretation stage should not be overlooked. Where Möller speaks of the 'global model of consti-tutional rights',[2] he rejects the traditional dominant narrative and pre-sents a modern account of judicial fundamental rights protection at both the constitutional and the ECHR level. This account is characterized by positive and socio-economic rights, horizontal protection, proportion-ality analysis and by rights inflation, i.e., by a very broad understanding

---

[2] Kai Möller, *The Global Model of Constitutional Rights* (Oxford University Press, 2012).

of the scope of rights that allows practically all (autonomy related) individual interests to automatically pass the interpretation stage. A similar conception is visible in many important academic works on fundamental rights adjudication. It is suggested that clear statements on the interpretation and scope of rights are no longer needed, because balancing – especially in the context of positive obligations – is in fact all that matters.

My point that interpretation and review must be dealt with in an integrated fashion is not to say that the two should be part of a single, overall test. Rather, the two stages cannot be analyzed in isolation. Ad hoc balancing combined with an opaque or even nonexistent interpretation of what the Convention prima facie protects is vulnerable to the criticism that the Court's reasoning is unstructured and unclear. In the supranational context of the ECtHR, it fails to recognize that the mandate of this Court is tied to specific norms the interpretation of which provides a benchmark for their application. For the protection by the ECtHR of (positive) socio-economic rights under civil and political rights norms – but perhaps also in other complex (supranational) judicial contexts, or in other cases where specific norms are concerned – a threshold applies. The Court should not balance the various interests at stake in a given case 'from scratch', regardless of their importance and character. It is often simply for the national legislator, aided by executive and national judiciary, to conduct this important task.

Moreover, and this was corroborated by the examples given from the Court's case law, neglecting the scope of rights can have the effect that the focus lies almost entirely on the general, rather than on the individual interests at stake. In the context of socio-economic rights this creates a bias against protection of (positive) socio-economic rights, even when such protection is demanded by their importance. The reasonableness test that is often applied in the adjudication of socio-economic rights may factor in this importance by clarifying the requirements a reasonable policy must meet, such as providing for marginalized groups and ensuring non-discrimination. If proportionality is the prescribed test, however, a court mostly does not explain in abstract terms what a proportional measure or decision looks like. In this connection, it is helpful to state prima facie rights and obligations (concerning minimum protection, non-discrimination and protection of vulnerable individuals) to give the test sufficient substantive bite while recognizing that the indivisible scope of fundamental rights – at least at the supranational level – is not unlimited.

Thus, the gist of the argument presented here is that the global model may fare better, at least in some judicial contexts, when inflation is viewed with some suspicion. A core rights perspective reveals a clear image of the socio-economic dimension of the Convention by allowing for more attention to be given to the initial stage of interpretation. The inclusion of core socio-economic rights in turn may lead to more insightful review as well as providing targeted protection.

In the end, thus, this book has some implications for contemplating judicial rights reasoning. Different to what current trends prescribe, it supports the argument that the demarcation of the scope of rights is not of inferior importance, at least not in every legal context. Even when the recognition of positive obligations, indivisible protection and proportionality review are applauded, this is no reason to stop discussing what is justiciable on the basis of a particular rights norm in the first place. As the example of the protection of minimum essential levels of socio-economic rights under the European Convention on Human Rights has shown, this does not require a detailed interpretation of rights norms detached from the facts of the cases that come before the Court. Engaging with the content of justiciable rights, however, allows for deliberation on the role of (supranational) judicial review amidst other avenues for decision-making. It also serves as a reminder of the importance of fundamental rights. And that is what core rights protection is fundamentally about.

BIBLIOGRAPHY

Aleinikoff, T. Alexander, 'Constitutional Law in the Age of Balancing', *Yale Law Journal*, 96 (1987), pp. 943–1005.

Alexy, Robert, *Theorie der Grundrechte* (Baden-Baden: Nomos, 1985).

Alexy, Robert, *A Theory of Constitutional Rights*, transl. Julian Rivers (Oxford University Press, 2002).

Alkema, Evert, 'The European Convention as a Constitution and Its Court as a Constitutional Court' in P. Mahoney et al. (eds.), *Protecting Human Rights: The European Perspective* (Studies in memory of Rolf Ryssdal) (Cologne: Carl Heymanns Verlag, 2000), pp. 41–63.

Alston, Philip, 'Out of the Abyss: The Challenges Confronting the New UN Committee on Economic, Social and Cultural Rights', *Human Rights Quarterly*, 9 (1987), pp. 332–381.

Alston, Philip, 'The Committee on Economic, Social and Cultural Rights' in Philip Alston (ed.), *The United Nations and Human Rights: A Critical Appraisal* (Oxford: Clarendon Press, 1992), pp. 473–508.

Alston, Philip and Quinn, Gerard, 'The Nature and Scope of States Parties' Obligations under the International Covenant on Economic, Social and Cultural Rights', *Human Rights Quarterly*, 9 (1987), pp. 156–229.

Arai-Takahashi, Yukata, *The Margin of Appreciation Doctrine and the Principle of Proportionality in the Jurisprudence of the ECHR* (Antwerp/Oxford/New York: Intersentia, 2002).

Arnardóttir, Oddný Mjöll, *Equality and Non-Discrimination under the European Convention on Human Rights* (Leiden: Martinus Nijhoff Publishers, 2003).

Arnardóttir, Oddný Mjöll, 'Discrimination as a Magnifying Lens: Scope and Ambit under Art. 14 and Protocol No. 12' in E. Brems and J.H. Gerards (eds.), *Shaping Rights in the ECHR: The Role of the European Court of Human Rights in Determining the Scope of Human Rights* (Cambridge University Press, 2014), pp. 330–349.

Arnardóttir, Oddný Mjöll, 'The "Procedural Turn" under the European Convention on Human Rights and Presumptions of Convention Compliance', *International Journal of Constitutional Law*, 15 (2017), pp. 9–35.

Barak, Aharon, *Proportionality: Constitutional Rights and Their Limitations* (Cambridge University Press, 2012).

Bates, Ed, *The Evolution of the European Convention on Human Rights: From Its Inception to the Creation of a Permanent Court of Human Rights* (Oxford University Press, 2010).

Bates, Ed, 'The Birth of the European Convention on Human Rights – and the European Court of Human Rights' in J. Christoffersen and M.R. Madsen (eds.), *The European Court of Human Rights between Law and Politics* (Oxford University Press, 2011).

Bates, Ed, 'Analysing the Prisoner Voting Saga and the British Challenge to Strasbourg', *Human Rights Law Review*, 14 (2014), pp. 503–540.

Bendor, Ariel L. and Sela, Tal, 'How Proportional Is Proportionality', *International Journal of Constitutional Law*, 13 (2015), pp. 530–544.

Bennett, Robert W. and Solum, Lawrence, *Constitutional Originalism: A Debate* (Ithaca: Cornell University Press, 2011).

Berchtold, Klaus, 'Council of Europe Activities in the Field of Economic, Social and Cultural Rights' in F. Matscher (ed.), *The Implementation of Economic and Social Rights, National, International and Comparative Aspects* (Kehl: N.P. Engel Verlag, 1991), pp. 355–370.

Bettinson, Vanessa and Jones, Alwyn, 'The Integration or Exclusion of Welfare Rights in the European Convention on Human Rights: The Removal of Foreign National with HIV after N v UK (Application No. 26565/05; decision of the Grand Chamber of the European Court of Human Rights, 27 May 2008)', *Journal of Social Welfare & Family Law*, 31 (2009), pp. 83–94.

Bickel, Alexander, *The Least Dangerous Branch: The Supreme Court at the Bar of Politics* (Yale University Press, 1986).

Bilchitz, David, 'Towards a Reasonable Approach to the Minimum Core: Laying the Foundations for Future Socio-Economic Rights Jurisprudence', *South African Journal on Human Rights*, 19 (2003), pp. 1–26.

Bilchitz, David, *Poverty and Fundamental Rights: The Justification and Enforcement of Socio-Economic Rights* (Oxford University Press, 2007).

Bilchitz, David, 'Does Sandra Liebenberg's New Book Provide a Viable Approach to Adjudication Socio-Economic Rights?', *South African Journal on Human Rights*, 27 (2011), pp. 546–557.

Bilchitz, David, 'Necessity and Proportionality: Towards a Balanced Approach' in L. Lazarus, Ch. McCrudden, and N. Bowles (eds.), *Reasoning Rights: Comparative Judicial Engagement* (Oxford: Hart Publishing, 2014), pp. 41–62.

Bilchitz, David, 'Socio-Economic Rights, Economic Crisis, and Legal Doctrine', *International Journal of Constitutional Law*, 12 (2014), pp. 710–739.

Bittner, Claudia, 'Casenote – Human Dignity as a Matter of Legislative Consistency in an Ideal World: The Fundamental Right to Guarantee a Subsistence

Minimum in the German Federal Constitutional Court's Judgment of 9 February 2010', *German Law Journal*, 12 (2011), pp. 1941–1960.

Bomhoff, Jacco, *Balancing Constitutional Rights: The Origins and Meanings of Postwar Legal Discourse* (Cambridge University Press, 2014).

Borowski, Martin, *Grundrechte als Prinzipien*, 2nd ed., (Baden-Baden: Nomos, 2007).

Bossuyt, Marc, 'Should the Strasbourg Court Exercise More Self-Restraint? On the Extension of the Jurisdiction of the European Court of Human Rights to Social Security Regulations', *Human Rights Law Journal*, 28 (2007), pp. 321–332.

Bossuyt, Marc, 'The Court of Strasbourg Acting as an Asylum Court', *European Constitutional Law Review*, 8 (2012), pp. 2013–2245.

Brand, Danie, 'The Minimum Core Content of the Right to Food in Context: A Response to Rolf Künneman' in D. Brand and S. Russell (eds.), *Exploring the Core Content of Economic and Social Rights: South African and International Perspectives* (Pretoria: Protea Book House, 2002), pp. 99–108.

Brand, Danie, 'Socio-Economic Rights and the Courts in South Africa: Justiciability on a Sliding Scale' in F. Coomans (ed.) *Justiciability of Economic and Social Rights: Experiences from Domestic Systems* (Antwerp/Oxford/New York: Intersentia, 2006), pp. 207–236.

Brand, Danie and Russell, Sage (eds.), *Exploring the Core Content of Economic and Social Rights: South African and International Perspectives* (Pretoria: Protea Book House, 2002).

Brems, Eva, 'Indirect Protection of Social Rights by the European Court of Human Rights' in D. Barak-Erez and A.M. Gross (eds.), *Exploring Social Rights: Between Theory and Practice* (Oxford: Hart Publishing, 2007), pp. 135–167.

Brüning, Christoph, 'Art. 19' in Klaus Stern and Florian Becker (eds.), *Grundrechte-Kommentar: Die Grundrechte des Grundgesetzes mit ihren europäischen Bezügen* (Cologne: Carl Heymanns Verlag, 2010).

Budlender, Geoff, 'The Role of the Courts in Achieving the Transformative Potential of Socio-Economic Rights', *ESR Review*, 8 (2007), pp. 9–11.

Byrne, Iain, 'Sandra Liebenberg, *Socio-Economic Rights: Adjudication under a Transformative Constitution*', (Book review), *Human Rights Law Review*, 12 (2012), pp. 183–186.

Callewaert, Johan, 'The Judgments of the Court, Background and Content' in R.S.J. Macdonald, F. Matscher and H. Petzold (eds.), *The European System for the Protection of Human Rights* (Leiden: Martinus Nijhoff Publishers, 1993), pp. 713–731.

Cassese, Antonio, 'Are Human Rights Truly Universal' in O. Savić (ed.), *The Politics of Human Rights* (London and Brooklyn: Verso Books, 1999), pp. 149–165.

Chapman, Audrey R., 'A "Violations Approach" for Monitoring the International Covenant on Economic, Social and Cultural Rights', *Human Rights Quarterly*, 18 (1996), pp. 23–66.

Chapman, Audrey R., 'Core Obligations Related to the Right to Health' in Audrey Chapman and Sage Russell (eds.), *Core Obligations: Building a Framework for Economic, Social and Cultural Rights* (Antwerp: Intersentia, 2002), pp. 185–215.

Chapman, Audrey R. and Russell, Sage (eds.), *Core Obligations: Building a Framework for Economic, Social and Cultural Rights* (Antwerp/Oxford/New York: Intersentia, 2002).

Chapman, Audrey R. and Russell, Sage, 'Introduction' in A.R. Chapman and S. Russell (eds.), *Core Obligations: Building a Framework for Economic, Social and Cultural Rights* (Antwerp/Oxford/New York: Intersentia, 2002), pp. 1–19.

Chlosta, Joachim, *Der Wesensgehalt der Eigentumsgewährleistung. Unter besonderer Berücksichtigung der Mitbestimmungsproblematik* (Berlin: Duncker & Humblot, 1975).

Christoffersen, Jonas, *Fair Balance: Proportionality, Subsidiarity and Primarity in the European Convention on Human Rights* (Leiden/Boston: Martinus Nijhoff Publishers, 2009).

Cleveland, Sarah H., Helfer, Laurence R., Neuman, Gerald L. and Orentlicher, Diane F., *Human Rights*, 2nd ed., (Eagan: Thomson Reuters Foundation Press, 2009).

Cohen-Eliya, Moshe and Porat, Iddo, 'American Balancing and German Proportionality: The Historical Origins', *International Constitutional Law Journal*, 2 (2010), pp. 263–286.

Cohen-Eliya, Moshe and Porat, Iddo, 'Proportionality and the Culture of Justification', *American Journal of Comparative Law*, 59 (2011), pp. 463–490.

Cohen-Eliya, Moshe and Porat, Iddo, 'Proportionality and Justification' (Article Review: Aharon Barak, *Proportionality: Constitutional Rights and Their Limitations*, Cambridge University Press 2012), *University of Toronto Law Journal*, 63 (2013), pp. 458–477.

Coomans, Fons, 'In Search of the Core Content of the Right to Education' in A.R. Chapman and S. Russell (eds.), *Core Obligations: Building a Framework for Economic, Social and Cultural Rights* (Antwerp/Oxford/New York: Intersentia, 2002), pp. 217–246.

Coomans, Fons, 'In Search of the Core Content of the Right to Education' in D. Brand and S. Russell (eds.), *Exploring the Core Content of Economic and Social Rights: South African and International Perspectives* (Pretoria: Protea Book House, 2002), pp. 159–182.

Cousins, Mel, *The European Convention on Human Rights and Social Security Law*, Social Europe Series (Antwerp/Oxford/New York: Intersentia, 2008), vol. XV.

Cousins, Mel, 'The European Convention on Human Rights, Non-Discrimination and Social Security: Great Scope, Little Depth?', *Journal of Social Security Law*, 16 (2009), pp. 118–136.

Craven, Matthew C.R., *The International Covenant on Economic, Social and Cultural Rights* (Oxford University Press, 1995).

Crocquet, Nicolas A.J., 'The European Court of Human Rights Norm-Creation and Norm-Limiting Processes: Resolving a Normative Tension', *Columbia Journal of European Law*, 17 (2011), pp. 307–373.

Davis, Dennis, 'The Case against the Inclusion of Socio-Economic Demands in a Bill of Rights Except as Directive Principles', *South African Journal on Human Rights*, 8 (1992), pp. 475–490.

Debeljak, Julie, 'Balancing Rights in a Democracy: The Problems with Limitations and Overrides of Rights under the Victorian Charter of Human Rights and Responsibilities Act 2006', *Melbourne University Law Review*, 32 (2008), pp. 422–469.

Dembour, Marie-Benedicte, '"Finishing Off" Cases: The Radical Solution to the Problem of the Expanding ECtHR Caseload', *European Human Rights Law Review*, (2002), pp. 604–623.

De Schutter, Olivier and Tulkens, Françoise, 'Rights in Conflict: The European Court of Human Rights as a Pragmatic Institution' in E. Brems (ed.), *Conflicts between Fundamental Rights* (Antwerp/Oxford/New York: Intersentia, 2008), pp. 169–216.

De Vos, Pierre, 'Pious Wishes or Directly Enforceable Human Rights? Social and Economic Rights in South Africa's 1996 Constitution', *South African Journal on Human Rights*, 13 (1997), pp. 67–101.

De Vos, Pierre, '*Grootboom*, The Right of Access to Housing and Substantive Equality as Contextual Fairness', *South African Journal on Human Rights*, 17 (2001), pp. 258–276.

Dixon, Rosalind, 'Creating Dialogue about Socio-Economic Rights: Strong Form versus Weak-Form Judicial Review Revisited', *International Journal of Constitutional Law*, 5 (2007), pp. 391–418.

Dreier, Horst, 'Art. 19 II' in H. Dreier (ed.), *Grundgesetz Kommentar*, Band I, 3rd ed. (Tübingen: Mohr Siebeck Verlag, 2013).

Drews, Claudia, *Die Wesensgehaltgarantie des Art. 19 II GG*, Diss. (Baden-Baden: Nomos, 2005).

Dürig, Günter, 'Der Grundrechtssatz von der Menschenwürde. Entwurf eines praktikablen Wertsystems der Grundrecte aus Art. 1 Abs. I in Verbindung mit Art. 19 Abs. II des Grundgesetzes', *Archiv des öffentlichen Rechts*, 81 (1956), pp. 117–157.

Dworkin, Ronald, *Taking Rights Seriously* (Cambridge, MA: Harvard University Press, 1977).

Dworkin, Ronald, 'Rights as Trumps' in J. Waldron (ed.), *Theories of Rights* (Oxford University Press, 1984), pp. 153–167.

Dworkin, Ronald, *A Matter of Principle* (Cambridge, MA: Harvard University Press, 1985).

Dyzenhaus, David, 'Law as Justification: Etienne Mureinik's Conception of Legal Culture', *South African Journal on Human Rights*, 14 (1998), pp. 11–37.

Edmundson, William, 'Rethinking Exclusionary Reasons: A Second Edition of Joseph Raz's Practical Reason and Norms', *Law and Philosophy*, 12 (1993), pp. 329–343.

Egidy, Stefanie, 'Casenote – The Fundamental Right to the Guarantee of a Subsistence Minimum in the Hartz IV Decision of the German Federal Constitutional Court', *German Law Journal*, 12 (2011), pp. 1961–1982.

Eide, Asbjørn, 'Realization of Social and Economic Rights and the Minimum Threshold Approach', *Human Rights Law Journal*, 10 (1989), pp. 35–50.

Eide, Asbjørn, 'Economic, Social and Cultural Rights as Human Rights' in A. Eide, C. Krause and A. Rosas (eds.), *Economic, Social and Cultural Rights: A Textbook*, 2nd ed. (Leiden: Martinus Nijhoff Publishers, 2001), pp. 9–28.

Ely, John Hart, *Democracy and Distrust: A Theory of Judicial Review* (Harvard University Press, 1980).

Enders, Christoph, 'Art. 19' in Volker Epping and Christian Hillgruber (eds.), *Beck'scher Online-Kommentar GG*, 16th ed. (Munich: Verlag C.H. Beck, 2012).

Faigman, David L., 'Reconciling Individual Rights and Government Interests: Madisonian Principles versus Supreme Court Practice', *Virginia Law Review*, 78 (1992), pp. 1521–1580.

Fallon Jr., Richard H., 'Individual Rights and the Powers of Government', *Georgia Law Review*, 27 (1993), pp. 343–390.

Feldman, David, 'The Developing Scope of Article 8 of the European Convention on Human Rights', *European Human Rights Law Review* (1997), pp. 25–247.

Ferraz, Octavio 'Harming the Poor Through Social Rights Litigation: Lessons from Brazil', *Texas Law Review*, 89 (2010), pp. 1643–1668.

Flegar, Veronika, 'Vulnerability and the Principle of Non-Refoulement in the European Court of Human Rights: Towards an Increased Scope of Protection for Persons Fleeing from Extreme Poverty?', *Contemporary Readings in Law and Social Justice*, 8 (2016), pp. 148–169.

Foster, Steve, 'Reluctancy Restoring Rights: Responding to the Prisoner's Right to Vote', *Human Rights Law Review*, 9 (2009), pp. 489–507.

Fredman, Sandra, *Human Rights Transformed: Positive Rights and Positive Duties* (Oxford University Press, 2008).

Fried, Charles, *Right and Wrong* (Cambridge, MA: Harvard University Press, 1978).

Frohwerk, Arno, *Soziale Not in der Rechtsprechung des EGMR* (Tübingen: Mohr Siebeck, 2012).

Fuller, Lon L., 'The Forms and Limits of Adjudication', *Harvard Law Review*, 92 (1978), pp. 353–394.

Gadamer, Hans-Georg, *Truth and Method*, 2nd ed. (London and New York: Continuum International Publishing Group, 1989).

Gardbaum, Stephen, 'Limiting Constitutional Rights', *UCLA Law Review*, 54 (2007), pp. 798–854.

Gearty, Conor and Mantouvalou, Virginia, *Debating Social Rights* (Oxford: Hart Publishing, 2011).

Gerards, Janneke, 'Intensity of Judicial Review in Equal Treatment Cases', *Netherlands International Law Review*, 51 (2004), pp. 135–183.

Gerards, Janneke, *Judicial Review in Equal Treatment Cases* (Leiden: Martinus Nijhoff Publishers, 2005).

Gerards, Janneke, 'Fundamental Rights and Other Interests: Should It Really Make a Difference?' in E. Brems (ed.), *Conflicts between Fundamental Rights* (Antwerp/Oxford/New York: Intersentia, 2008), pp. 655–690.

Gerards, Janneke, 'Judicial Deliberations in the European Court of Human Rights' in N. Huls, M. Adams and J. Bomhoff (eds.), *The Legitimacy of Highest Courts' Rulings. Judicial Deliberations and Beyond* (The Hague: T.M.C. Asser Press, 2009), pp. 407–436.

Gerards, Janneke, 'Pluralism, Deference, and the Margin of Appreciation Doctrine', *European Law Journal*, 17 (2011), pp. 80–120.

Gerards, Janneke, 'The Prism of Fundamental Rights', *European Constitutional Law Review*, 8 (2012), pp. 173–202.

Gerards, Janneke, 'How to Improve the Necessity Test of the European Court of Human Rights', *International Journal of Constitutional Law*, 11 (2013), pp. 466–490.

Gerards, Janneke, 'The Scope of ECHR Rights and Institutional Concerns: The Relationship between Proliferation of Rights and the Case Load of the ECtHR' in E. Brems and J.H. Gerards (eds.), *Shaping Rights in the ECHR: The Role of the European Court of Human Rights in Determining the Scope of Human Rights* (Cambridge University Press, 2014), pp. 84–105.

Gerards, Janneke, 'The European Court of Human Rights and the National Courts: Giving Shape to the Notion of "Shared Responsibility"' in J.H. Gerards and J. Fleuren (eds.), *Implementation of the European Convention on Human Rights and of the Case Law of the ECtHR in National Case Law* (Antwerp/Oxford/New York: Intersentia, 2014), pp. 13–93.

Gerards, Janneke, 'The Margin of Appreciation Doctrine, the Very Weighty Reasons Test and Grounds of Discrimination' in M. Balboni (ed.), *The Principle of Non-Discrimination and the European Convention of Human Rights* (forthcoming). Available at SSRN: https://ssrn.com/abstract=2875230

Gerards, Janneke and Brems, Eva (eds.), *Procedural Review in European Fundamental Rights Cases* (Cambridge University Press, 2017).

Gerards, Janneke and Fleuren, Joseph (eds.), *Implementation of the European Convention on Human Rights and of the Case Law of the ECtHR in National Case Law* (Antwerp/Oxford/New York: Intersentia, 2014).

Gerards, Janneke and Fleuren, Joseph, 'The Netherlands' in J.H. Gerards and J. Fleuren (eds.), *Implementation of the European Convention on Human Rights and of the Case Law of the ECtHR in National Case Law* (Antwerp/Oxford/New York: Intersentia, 2014), pp. 217–260.

Gerards, Janneke and Senden, Hanneke, 'The Structure of Fundamental Rights and the European Court of Human Rights', *International Journal of Constitutional Law*, 7 (2009), pp. 619–653.

Greer, Steven, *The European Convention on Human Rights: Achievements, Problems and Prospects* (Cambridge University Press, 2006).

Greer, Steven and Wildhaber, Luzius, 'Revisiting the Debate about "Constitutionalising" the European Court of Human Rights', *Human Rights Law Review*, 12 (2013), pp. 655–687.

Gunther, Gerald, 'The Supreme Court, 1971 Term – Foreword: In Search of Evolving Doctrine on a Changing Court: A Model for a Newer Equal Protection', *Harvard Law Review*, 86 (1972), pp. 1–48.

Häberle, Peter, *Die Wesensgehaltgarantie des Art. 19 II GG – zugleich ein Beitrag zum institutionellen Verständnis der Grundrecht und zur Lehre vom Gesetzesvorbehalt*, 3rd ed. (Heidelberg: C.F. Müller, 1983).

Habermas, Jürgen, *Between Facts and Norms. Contributions to a Discourse Theory of Law and Democracy* (Cambridge, MA: MIT Press, 1996).

Hamel, Walter, *Die Bedeutung der Grundrechte im sozialen Rechtsstaat. Eine Kritik an Gesetzgebung und Rechtsprechung* (Berlin: Duncker & Humblot, 1957).

Harris, David J., O'Boyle, Michael, Bates, Edward P. and Buckley, Carla M., *Harris, O'Boyle and Warbrick: Law of the European Convention on Human Rights*, 2nd ed. (Oxford University Press, 2009).

Harris, David J., O'Boyle, Michael, Bates, Edward P. and Buckley, Carla M., *Harris, O'Boyle and Warbrick: Law of the European Convention on Human Rights*, 3rd ed. (Oxford University Press, 2014).

Hart, H.L.A., *The Concept of Law* (Oxford: Clarendon Press, 1994).

Haysom, Nicholas, 'Constitutionalism, Majoritarian Democracy and Socio-Economic Rights', *South African Journal on Human Rights*, 8 (1992), pp. 451–463.

Helfer, Laurence R. and Slaughter, Anne-Marie, 'Toward a Theory of Effective Supranational Adjudication', *Yale Law Journal*, 107 (1997), pp. 273–392.

Hennette-Vauchez, Stéphanie, 'Constitutional v. International? When Unified Reformatory Rationales Mismatch the Plural Paths of Legitimacy of ECHR Law' in J. Christoffersen and M. Rask Madsen (eds.), *The European Court of Human Rights between Law and Politics* (Oxford University Press, 2011), pp. 144–164.

Herbert, Georg, 'Der Wesensgehalt der Grundrechte', *Europäische Grundrechte-Zeitschrift*, 12 (1985), pp. 321–335.

Hörmann, Jens-Hendrik, *Rechtsprobleme des Grundrechts auf Gewährleistung eines menschenwürdigen Existenzminimums: Zu den Auswirkungen des 'Regelleistungsurteils' auf die 'Hartz IV'-Gesetzgebung und andere Sozialgesetze* (Hamburg: Verlag Dr. Kovač, 2012).

Ignatieff, Michael, 'Human Rights as Ideology' in M. Ignatieff (A. Gutmann (ed.)), *Human Rights as Politics and Idolatry* (Princeton University Press, 2001).

Jäckel, Hartmut, *Grundrechtsgeltung und Grundrechtssicherung – eine rechtsdogmatische Studie zu Artikel 19 Abs. 2 GG* (Berlin: Duncker & Humblot, 1967).

Jakab, András, 'Re-Defining Principles as "Important Rules" a Critique of Robert Alexy' in M. Borowski (ed.), *On the Nature of Legal Principles* (Proceedings of the Special Workshop 'The Principles Theory' held at the 23rd World Congress of the International Association for Philosophy of Law and Social Science (IVR), Kraków, 2007) (Stuttgart: Franz Steiner Verlag/Baden-Baden: Nomos, 2010), pp. 145–160.

Jarass, Hans D., 'Art. 19' in Hans D. Jarass and Bodo Pieroth (eds.), *GG. Grundgesetz für die Bundesrepublik Deutschland. Kommentar*, 14th ed. (Munich: Verlag C.H. Beck, 2012).

Kaufmann, Arthur, 'Über den "Wesensgehalt" der Grund- und Menschenrechte', *Archiv für Rechts- und Sozialphilosophie*, 70 (1984), pp. 384–399.

Kavanagh, Aileen, *Constitutional Review under the UK Human Rights Act*, (Cambridge University Press, 2009).

Kende, Mark S., 'The South African Constitutional Court's Embrace of Socio-Economic Rights: A Comparative Perspective', *Chapman Law Review*, 6 (2003), pp. 137–160.

Kende, Mark S., 'The South African Constitutional Court's Construction of Socio-Economic Rights: A Response to the Critics', *Connecticut Journal of International Law*, 19 (2004), pp. 617–629.

Kenny, Jo, 'European Convention on Human Rights and Social Welfare', *European Human Rights Law Review*, (2010), pp. 495–503.

King, Jeff, *Judging Social Rights* (Cambridge University Press, 2012).

Kingreen, Thorsten, 'Schätzungen "ins Blaue hinein": Zu den Auswirkungen des Hartz IV-Urteils des Bundesverfassungsgerichts auf das Asylbewerberleistungsgesetz', *Neue Zeitschrift für Verwaltungsrecht* (2010), pp. 558–562.

Klatt, Matthias and Meister, Moritz, *The Constitutional Structure of Proportionality* (Oxford University Press, 2012).

Klug, Heinz *Constituting Democracy: Law, Globalism and South Africa's Political Reconstruction* (Cambridge University Press, 2000).

Knüllig, Werner, *Bedeutung und Auslegung des Artikels 19 Abs. I und II des Grundgesetzes*, doctoral thesis (Kiel, 1954).

Koch, Ida Elisabeth, 'Social Rights as Components in the Civil Right to Personal Liberty – Another Possible Step Forward in the Integrated Human Rights Approach?', *Netherlands Quarterly of Human Rights*, 20 (2002), pp. 29–51.

Koch, Ida Elisabeth, 'The Justiciability of Indivisible Rights', *Nordic Law Journal*, 72 (2003), pp. 3–39.

Koch, Ida Elisabeth, 'Dichotomies, Trichotomies or Waves of Duties', *Human Rights Law Review*, 5 (2005), pp. 81–103.

Koch, Ida Elisabeth, 'Economic, Social and Cultural Rights as Components in Civil and Political Rights: A Hermeneutic Perspective', *The International Journal of Human Rights*, 10 (2006), pp. 405–430.

Koch, Ida Elisabeth, *Human Rights as Indivisible Rights: The Protection of Socio-Economic Demands under the European Convention on Human Rights* (Leiden: Martinus Nijhoff Publishers, 2009).

Koch, Ida Elisabeth and Vested-Hansen, Jens, 'International Human Rights and National Legislatures – Conflict or Balance', *Nordic Journal of International Law*, 75 (2006), pp. 3–28.

Kratochvíl, Jan, 'The Inflation of the Margin of Appreciation by the European Court of Human Rights', *Netherlands Quarterly of Human Rights*, 29 (2011), pp. 324–357.

Krieger, Heike, 'Positive Verpflichtungen unter der EMRK: Unentbehrliches Element einer gemeineuropäischen Grundrechtsdogmatik, leeres Versprechen oder Grenze der Justitiabilität?', *Zeitschrift für ausländisches öffentliches Recht und Völkerrecht*, 74 (2014), pp. 187–213.

Krüger, Herbert, 'Der Wesensgehalt der Grundrechte i.S. des Art. 19 GG', *Die Öffentliche Verwaltung*, 8 (1955), pp. 597–602.

Kumm, Mattias, 'Constitutional Rights as Principles: On the Structure and Domain of Constitutional Justice', *International Journal of Constitutional Law*, 2 (2004), pp. 574–596.

Kumm, Mattias, 'Who Is Afraid of the Total Constitution? Constitutional Rights as Principles and the Constitutionalization of Private Law', *German Law Journal*, 7 (2006), pp. 341–369.

Künnemann, Rolf, 'The Right to Adequate Food: Violations to Its Minimum core Content' in A.R. Chapman and S. Russell (eds.), *Core Obligations: Building a Framework for Economic, Social and Cultural Rights* (Antwerp/Oxford/New York: Intersentia, 2002), pp. 163–183.

Landau, David, 'The Promise of a Minimum Core Approach: The Colombian Model for Judicial Review of Austerity Measures' in A. Nolan (ed), *Economic and Social Rights after the Global Crisis* (Cambridge University Press, 2015), pp. 276–298.

Langa, Pius, 'The Vision of the Constitution', *South African Law Journal*, 120 (2003), pp. 670–679.

Langford, Malcolm, 'The Justiciability of Social Rights: From Practice to Theory' in M. Langford (ed.), *Social Rights Jurisprudence: Emerging Trends in International and Comparative Law* (Cambridge University Press, 2008), pp. 3–45.

Lasser, Mitchel de S.-O.-l'E, *Judicial Deliberations: A Comparative Analysis of Judicial Transparency and Legitimacy* (Oxford University Press, 2004).

Laurens Lavrysen, *Human Rights in a Positive State: Rethinking the Relationship between Positive and Negative Obligations under the European Convention on Human Rights* (Antwerp/Oxford/New York: Intersentia, 2016).

Leckie, Scott, 'The Human Right to Adequate Housing' in A. Eide, C. Krause and A. Rosas (eds.), *Economic, Social and Cultural Rights: A Textbook*, 2nd ed. (Leiden: Martinus Nijhoff Publishers, 2001), pp. 149–168.

Lehmann, Karin, 'In Defense of the Constitutional Court: Litigating Socio-Economic Rights and the Myth of the Minimum Core', *American University International Law Review*, 22 (2006), pp. 163–197.

Leijten, Ingrid, 'From *Stec* to *Valkov*: Possessions and Margins in the Social Security Case Law of the European Court of Human Rights', *Human Rights Law Review*, 13 (2013), pp. 309–349.

Leijten, Ingrid, 'Social Security as a Fundamental Rights Issue in Europe: *Ramaer and Van Willigen* and the Development of Property Protection and Non-Discrimination under the ECHR', *Zeitschrift für ausländisches öffentliches Recht und Völkerrecht*, 73 (2013), pp. 177–208.

Leijten, Ingrid, 'Defining the Scope of Economic and Social Guarantees in the Case Law of the ECtHR' in E. Brems and J.H. Gerards (eds.), *Shaping Rights in the ECHR: The Role of the European Court of Human Rights in Determining the Scope of Human Rights* (Cambridge University Press, 2014), pp. 109–136.

Leijten, Ingrid, 'The German Right to an *Existenzminimum*, Human Dignity, and the Possibility of Minimum Core Socioeconomic Rights Protection', *German Law Journal*, 16 (2015), pp. 23–48.

Leijten, Ingrid, 'Separation of Powers and the Limits to the "Constitutionalization" of Fundamental Rights Adjudication by the ECtHR and the CJEU' in H.M.Th.D. Ten Napel and W.J.M. Voermans (eds.), *The Powers that Be: Rethinking the Separation of Powers: A Leiden Response to Christoph Möllers* (Leiden University Press, 2015) pp. 275–293.

Letsas, George, 'The Truth in Autonomous Concepts: How to Interpret the ECHR', *European Journal of International Law*, 15 (2004), pp. 279–305.

Letsas, George, 'Two Concepts of the Margin of Appreciation', *Oxford Journal of Legal Studies*, 26 (2006), pp. 705–732.

Letsas, George, *A Theory of Interpretation of the European Convention on Human Rights* (Oxford University Press, 2007).

Letsas, George, 'The ECHR as a Living Instrument: Its Meaning and Legitimacy' in Geir Ulfstein, Andreas Follesdal and Birgit Peters (eds), *Constituting Europe:*

The European Court of Human Rights in a National, European and Global Context (Cambridge University Press, 2013), pp. 106–141.

Letsas, George, 'The Scope and Balancing of Rights: Diagnostic or Constitutive?' in E. Brems and J.H. Gerards (eds.), *Shaping Rights in the ECHR: The Role of the European Court of Human Rights in Determining the Scope of Human Rights* (Cambridge University Press, 2014), pp. 38–64.

Leuprecht, Peter, 'Innovations in the European System of Human Rights Protection: Is Enlargement Compatible with Reinforcement?', *Transnational Law and Contemporary Problems*, 8 (1998), pp. 313–336.

Liebenberg, Sandra, 'The Right to Social Assistance: The Implications of *Grootboom* for Policy Reform in South Africa', *South African Journal on Human Rights*, 17 (2001), pp. 232–357.

Liebenberg, Sandra, 'South Africa: Adjudicating Social Rights Under a Transformative Constitution' in M. Longford (ed.), *Social Rights Jurisprudence: Emerging Trends in International and Comparative Law* (Cambridge University Press, 2008), pp. 75–101.

Liebenberg, Sandra, *Socio-Economic Rights: Adjudication under a Transformative Constitution* (Cape Town: Juta and Company, 2010).

Lord, Hoffmann, 'The Universality of Human Rights', *Judicial Studies Board Annual Lecture* (2009).

Lord Lester of Herne Hill, 'Universality versus Subsidiarity: A Reply', *European Human Rights Law Review* (1998), pp. 73–81.

Mahoney, Paul, 'Judicial Activism and Self-Restraint in the European Court of Human Rights', *Human Rights Law Review*, 11 (1990), pp. 57–88.

Mantouvalou, Virginia, 'Work and Private Life: Sidabras and Dziautas v. Lithuania', *European Law Review*, 30 (2005), pp. 573–585.

Mantouvalou, Virginia, 'N v UK: No Duty to Rescue the Nearby Needy?', *Modern Law Review*, 72 (2009), pp. 815–828.

Mantouvalou, Virginia, 'Labour Rights in the European Convention on Human Rights: An Intellectual Justification for an Integrated Approach to Interpretation', *Human Rights Law Review*, 13 (2013), pp. 529–555.

Masterman, Roger, 'The United Kingdom' in J. Gerards and J. Fleuren (eds.), *Implementation of the European Convention on Human Rights and of the Case Law of the ECtHR in National Case Law* (Antwerp/Oxford/New York: Intersentia, 2014), pp. 297–332.

Matscher, Franz, 'Methods of Interpretation of the Convention' in R.S.J. Macdonald, F. Matscher and H. Petzold (eds.), *The European System for the Protection of Human Rights* (Leiden: Martinus Nijhoff Publishers, 1993), pp. 63–81.

Merrills, J.G., *The Development of International Law by the European Court of Human Rights*, 3rd ed. (Manchester University Press, 1993).

Miller, Bradley W., 'Justification and Rights Limitations' in G. Huscroft (ed.), *Expounding the Constitution: Essays in Constitutional Theory* (Cambridge University Press, 2008).

Moellendorf, Darrel, 'Reasoning about Resources: *Soobramoney* and the Future of Socio-Economic Rights Claims', *South African Journal on Human Rights*, 14 (1998), pp. 327–333.

Möller, Kai, *The Global Model of Constitutional Rights* (Oxford University Press, 2012).

Möller, Kai, 'From Constitutional to Human Rights: On the Moral Structure of International Human Rights', *Global Constitutionalism*, 3 (2014), pp. 373–403.

Möllers, Christoph, *The Three Branches: A Comparative Model of Separation of Powers* (Oxford University Press, 2013).

Moseneke, Dikgang, 'Transformative Adjudication', *South African Journal on Human Rights*, 18 (2002), pp. 309–319.

Mowbray, Alastair, *The Development of Positive Obligations under the European Convention on Human Rights by the European Court of Human Rights* (Oxford: Hart Publishing, 2004).

Mowbray, Alastair, 'The Creativity of the European Court of Human Rights', *Human Rights Law Review*, 5 (2005), pp. 57–79.

Mowbray, Alistair, *Cases, Materials and Commentary on the European Convention on Human Rights*, 3rd ed. (Oxford University Press, 2012).

Mureinik, Etienne, 'Beyond a Charter of Luxuries: Economic Rights in the Constitution', *South African Journal on Human Rights*, 8 (1992), pp. 464–474.

Mureinik, Etienne, 'A Bridge to Where? Introducing the Interim Bill of Rights', *South African Journal on Human Rights*, 10 (1994), pp. 31–48.

Neumann, Volker, 'Menschenwürde und Existenzminimum', *Neue Zeitschrift für Verwaltungsrecht* (1995), pp. 426–432.

Nolette, Paul, 'Lessons learned from the South African Constitutional Court: Toward a Third Way of Judicial Enforcement of Socio-Economic Rights', *Michigan State Journal of International Law*, 12 (2003), pp. 91–119.

Nussbaum, Martha, *Women and Human Development: The Capabilities Approach* (Cambridge University Press, 2000).

Nussbaum, Martha, *Creating Capabilities: The Human Development Approach* (Oxford University Press, 2011).

Nussberger, Angelika, 'Procedural Review by the ECtHR: View from the Court', in Janneke Gerards and Eva Brems (eds.), *Procedural Review in European Fundamental Rights Cases* (Cambridge University Press, 2017), pp. 161–176.

O'Cinneide, Colm, 'A Modest Proposal: Destitution, State Responsibility and the European Convention on Human Rights', *European Human Rights Law Review* (2008), pp. 583–605.

O'Cinneide, Colm, 'The Problematic of Social Rights – Uniformity and Diversity in the Development of Social Rights Review' in L. Lazarus, Ch. McCrudden and N. Bowles (eds.), *Reasoning Rights: Comparative Judicial Engagement* (Oxford: Hart Publishing, 2014), pp. 299–317.

O'Connell, Paul, *Vindicating Socio-Economic Rights: International Standards and Comparative Experiences* (London: Routledge, 2012).

O'Neill, Onora, *Towards Justice and Virtue* (Cambridge University Press, 1996).

Örücü, Esin, 'The Core of Rights and Freedoms: The Limits of Limits' in Tom Campbell et al. (eds.), *Human Rights: From Rhetoric to Reality* (Oxford: Basil Blackwell, (1986), pp. 37–59.

Ost, François, 'The Original Canons of Interpretation of the European Court of Human Rights' in M. Delmas-Marty and Ch. Chodkiewicz (eds.), *The European Convention for the Protection of Human Rights* (Leiden: Martinus Nijhoff Publishers, 1992), pp. 283–318.

Palmer, Ellie, 'Protecting Socio-Economic Rights through the European Convention on Human Rights: Trends and Developments in the European Court of Human Rights', *Erasmus Law Review*, 2 (2009), pp. 397–425.

Palmer, Ellie, 'Beyond Arbitrary Interference: The Right to a Home? Developing Socio-Economic Duties in the European Convention on Human Rights', *Northern Ireland Legal Quarterly*, 61 (2010), pp. 225–243.

Peroni, Lourdes and Timmer, Alexandra, 'Vulnerable Groups: The Promise of an Emerging Concept in European Human Rights Convention Law', *International Journal of Constitutional Law*, 11 (2013), pp. 1056–1058.

Petersen, Niels, 'How to Compare the Length of Lines to the Weight of Stones', *German Law Journal*, 14 (2013), pp. 1387–1408.

Pieterse, Marius, 'Coming to Terms with Judicial Enforcement of Socio-Economic Rights', *South African Journal on Human Rights*, 20 (2004), pp. 383–417.

Pieterse, Marius, 'Resuscitating Socio-Economic Rights: Constitutional Entitlements to Health Care Services', *South African Journal on Human Rights*, 22 (2006), pp. 473–502.

Pildes, Richard H., 'Avoiding Balancing: The Role of Exclusionary Reasons in Constitutional Law', *Hastings Law Journal*, 45 (1994), pp. 711–751.

Popelier, Patricia and Van de Heyning, Catherine, 'Subsidiarity Post-Brighton: Procedural Rationality as Answer', *Leiden Journal of International Law*, 30 (2017), pp. 5–23.

Popelier, Patricia, Lambrechts, Sarah and Lemmens, Koen (eds.), *Criticism of the European Court of Human Rights: Shifting the Convention System: Counter-Dynamics at the National and EU Level* (Cambridge/Antwerp/Portland: Intersentia, 2016).

Porter, Bruce, 'The Crisis of Economic, Social and Cultural Rights and Strategies for Addressing it' in J. Squires, M. Langford and B. Thiele (eds.), *The Road to a Remedy: Current Issues in the Litigation of Economic, Social and Cultural*

Rights (Australian Human Rights Centre in collaboration with the Centre for Housing Rights and Evictions, 2005), pp. 43–69.

Prebensen, S.C., 'Evolutive Interpretation of the European Convention on Human Rights' in P Mahoney (ed.), *Protecting Human Rights: The European Perspective. Studies in Memory of Rolv Ryssdal* (Cologne: Carl Heymanns Verlag, 2000), pp. 1123–1137.

Rainey, Bernadette, Wicks, Elizabeth and Ovey, Clare, *Jacobs, White and Ovey: The European Convention on Human Rights*, 6th ed. (Oxford University Press, 2014).

Rawls, John, *A Theory of Justice* (Cambridge, MA: Harvard University Press, 1971) (1999).

Rawls, John, *Political Liberalism* (New York: Columbia University Press, 1993).

Raz, Joseph, 'On the Nature of Rights', *Mind*, 93 (1984), pp. 194–214.

Raz, Joseph, *Practical Reasons and Norms*, 2nd ed. (Oxford University Press, 1990).

Raz, Joseph, 'On the Authority and Interpretation of Constitutions' in L. Alexander (ed.), *Constitutionalism: Philosophical Foundations* (Cambridge University Press, 1998), pp. 152–193.

Remiche, Adélaide, 'Yordanova and Others v. Bulgaria: The Influence of the Social Right to Adequate Housing on the Interpretation of the Civil Right to Respect for One's Home', *Human Rights Law Review*, 12 (2012), pp. 787–800.

Remmert, Barbara, 'Art. 19' in Theodor Maunz and Günther Dürig (eds.), *Grundgesetz* (Munich: Verlag C.H. Beck, 2012).

Ress, George, 'The Effects of Decisions and Judgments of the European Court of Human Rights in the Domestic Legal Order', *Texas International Law Journal*, 40 (2005), pp. 359–382.

Rietiker, Daniel, 'The Principle of "Effectiveness" in the Recent Jurisprudence of the European Court of Human Rights: Its Different Dimensions and Its Consistency with Public International Law – No Need for the Concept of Treaty *Sui Generis*', *Nordic Journal of International Law*, 79 (2010), pp. 245–277.

Rivers, Julian, 'Proportionality and Variable Intensity of Review', *Cambridge Law Journal*, 65 (2006), pp. 174–207.

Roux, Theunis, 'Understanding *Grootboom* – A Response to Cass R. Sunstein', *Constitutional Forum*, 12 (2002), pp. 41–51.

Ryssdal, Rolv, 'The Coming of Age of the European Convention of Human Rights', *European Human Rights Law Review* (1996), pp. 18–29.

Sachs, Albie, 'The Judicial Eenforcement of Socio-Economic Rights', *Current Legal Problems*, 56 (2003), pp. 579–601.

Sachs, Michael, 'Art. 19' in Michael Sachs (ed.), *GG. Grundgesetz Kommentar*, 7th ed. (Munich: Verlag C.H. Beck, 2011).

Sadurski, Wojciech, 'Partnering with Strasbourg: Constitutionalisation of the European Court of Human Rights, the Accession of Central and East

European States to the Council of Europe, and the Idea of Pilot Judgments', *Human Rights Law Review*, 9 (2009), pp. 397–453.

Sadurski, Wojciech, *Constitutionalism and the Enlargement of Europe* (Oxford University Press, 2012).

Saul, Ben, Kinley, David and Mowbray, Jacqueline, *The International Covenant on Economic, Social and Cultural Rights: Commentary, Cases, and Materials* (Oxford University Press, 2014).

Schauer, Frederick, 'Categories and the First Amendment: A Play in Three Acts', *Vanderbilt Law Review*, 34 (1981), pp. 265–307.

Schauer, Frederick, 'A Comment on the Structure of Rights', *Georgia Law Review*, 27 (1993), pp. 415–434.

Schauer, Frederick, 'Do Cases Make Bad Law?', *The University of Chicago Law Review*, 73 (2006) pp. 883–918.

Scheinin, Martin, 'Economic and Social Rights as Legal Rights' in A. Eide et al. (eds.), *Economic, Social and Cultural Rights: A Textbook*, 2nd ed. (Leiden: Martinus Nijhoff Publishers, 2001), pp. 29–54.

Schlag, Pierre, 'Rules and Standards', *UCLA Law Review*, 33 (1985), pp. 379–429.

Schlink, Bernhard, *Abwägung im Verfassungsrecht* (Berlin: Duncker & Humblot, 1976).

Schnath, Matthias, 'Auswirkungen des neuen Grundrechts auf Gewährleistung des Existenzminimums auf die besonderen Hilfen nach dem Zwölften Sozialgesetzbuches (SGB XII)', *Sozialrecht aktuell* (2010), pp. 173–176.

Schneider, Ludwig, *Der Schutz des Wesensgehalts von Grundrechten nach Art. 19 Abs. 2 GG* (Berlin: Duncker & Humblot, 1983).

Scott, Craig, 'The Interdependence and Permeability of Human Rights Norms: Towards a Partial Fusion of the International Covenants on Human Rights', *Osgoode Hall Law Journal*, 27 (1989), pp. 769–877.

Scott, Craig, 'Reaching Beyond (Without Abandoning) the Category of Economic, Social and Cultural Rights', *Human Rights Quarterly*, 21 (1999), pp. 633–660.

Scott, Craig, 'Towards a Principled, Pragmatic Judicial Role', *ESR Review*, 1 (1999), pp. 4–7.

Scott, Craig and Alston, Philip, 'Adjudicating Constitutional Priorities in a Transnational Context: A Comment on *Soobramoney*'s Legacy and *Grootboom*'s promise', *South African Journal on Human Rights*, 16 (2000), pp. 206–268.

Seiler, Christian, 'Das Grundrecht auf ein menschenwürdiges Existenzminimum: Zum Urteil des Bundesverfassungsgerichts vom 9.2.2010', *JuristenZeitung*, 65 (2010), pp. 500–505.

Sen, Amartya, 'The Standard of Living: Lives and Capabilities' in G. Hawthorn (ed.), *The Standard of Living* (Cambridge University Press, 1987), pp. 20–38.

Sen, Amartya, 'Freedom and Needs', *New Republic* (10 January and 17 January 1994), pp. 31–38.

Sen, Amartya, *The Idea of Justice* (Oxford University Press, 2009).

Senden, Hanneke, *Interpretation of Fundamental Rights in a Multilevel Legal System: An Analysis of the European Court of Human Rights and the Court of Justice of the European Union*, doctoral thesis (Cambridge/Antwerp/Portland: Intersentia, 2011).

Shue, Henry, *Basic Rights: Subsistence, Affluence and U.S. Foreign Policy*, 2nd ed. (Princeton University Press, 1996).

Smet, Stijn, 'The "Absolute" Prohibition of Torture and Inhuman or Degrading Treatment in Article 3 ECHR: Truly a Question of Scope Only?' in E. Brems and J.H. Gerards (eds.), *Shaping Rights in the ECHR: The Role of the European Court of Human Rights in Determining the Scope of Human Rights* (Cambridge University Press, 2014), pp. 273–293.

Spielmann, Dean, 'Wither the Margin of Appreciation', *Current Legal Problems*, 67 (2014), pp. 49–65.

Steiner, Henry J., 'Securing Human Rights: The First Half-Century of the Universal Declaration, and Beyond', *Harvard Magazine* (September–October 1998), pp. 45–46.

Steiner, Henry J., Alston, Philip and Goodman, Ryan, *International Human Rights in Context: Law, Politics, Morals*, 3rd ed. (Oxford University Press, 2007).

Steinberg, Carol, 'Can Reasonableness Protect the Poor? A Review of South Africa's Socio-Economic Rights Jurisprudence', *South African Law Journal*, 123 (2006), pp. 264–284.

Stern, Klaus, *Das Staatsrecht der Bundesrepublik Deutschland. Band III/2. Allgemeine Lehren der Grundrechte* (Munich, Verlag C.H. Beck, 1994).

Stone-Sweet, Alec and Keller, Helen, 'The Reception of the ECHR in National Legal Orders' in A. Stone-Sweet and H. Keller (eds.), *A Europe of Rights: The Impact of the ECHR on National Legal Systems* (Oxford University Press, 2008), pp. 11–36.

Stone-Sweet, Alec and Mathews, Jud, 'All Things in Proportion? American Rights Doctrine and the Problem of Balancing', *Emory Law Journal*, 60 (2011), pp. 711–751.

Sullivan, Kathleen M., 'Post-Liberal Judging: The Roles of Categorization and Balancing', *University of Colorado Law Review*, 63 (1992), pp. 293–317.

Sunstein, Cass R., 'Incompletely Theorized Agreements', *Harvard Law Review*, 108 (1995), pp. 1733–1772.

Sunstein, Cass R., *Legal Reasoning and Political Conflict* (Oxford University Press, 1996).

Sunstein, Cass R., *Designing Democracy: What Constitutions Do* (Oxford University Press, 2001).

Sunstein, Cass R., 'Social and Economic Rights? Lessons from South Africa', *Constitutional Forum*, 11 (2000–2001), pp. 123–132.

Sunstein, Cass R., 'Incompletely Theorized Agreements in Constitutional Law', *Social Research*, 74 (2007), pp. 1–24.

Taskyrakis, Stavros, 'Proportionality: An Assault on Human Rights?, *International Journal of Constitutional Law*, 7 (2009), pp. 468–493.

Teitgen, Pierre-Henri, 'Introduction to the European Convention on Human Rights' in R.S.J. Macdonald, F. Matscher and H. Petzold (eds.), *The European System for the Protection of Human Rights* (Leiden: Martinus Nijhoff Publishers, 1993), pp. 3–14.

Toebes, Brigit, *The Right to Health as a Human Right in International Law* (Antwerp/Oxford/New York: Intersentia/Oxford: Hart Publishing, 1999).

Tomuschat, Christian, *Human Rights: Between Idealism and Realism*, 2nd ed. (Oxford University Press, 2008).

Tulkens, Françoise, *How Can We Ensure Greater Involvement of National Courts in the Convention System?* Dialogue between Judges (European Court of Human Rights, Council of Europe, 2012), pp. 6–10.

Urbina, Francisco J., 'A Critique of Proportionality', *American Journal of Jurisprudence*, 57 (2012), pp. 49–80.

Van der Schyff, Gerhard, *Limitation of Rights: A Study of the European Convention and the South African Bill of Right* (Nijmegen: Wolf Legal Publishers, 2005).

Van der Schyff, Gerhard, 'Interpreting the Protection Guaranteed by Two-Stage Rights in the European Convention on Human Rights: The Case for Wide Interpretation' in E. Brems and J.H. Gerards (eds.), *Shaping Rights in the ECHR: The Role of the European Court of Human Rights in Determining the Scope of Human Rights* (Cambridge University Press, 2014), pp. 65–83.

Van Dijk, Pieter, Van Hoof, Fried, Van Rijn, Arjen and Zwaak, Leo (eds.), *Theory and Practice of the European Convention on Human Rights*, 4th ed. (Antwerp/Oxford/New York: Intersentia, 2006).

Von Bernstorff, Jochen, 'Kerngehaltsschutz durch den UN-Menschenrechtsausschuss und den EGMR: vom Wert Kategorialer Argumentationsformen', *Der Staat*, 50 (2011), pp. 165–190.

Von Bernstorff, Jochen, 'Proportionality Without Balancing: Why Judicial Ad Hoc Balancing in Unnecessary and Potentially Detrimental to the Realisation of Individual and Collective Self-Determination' in L. Lazarus, Ch. McCrudden and N. Bowles (eds.), *Reasoning Rights: Comparative Judicial Engagement* (Oxford: Hart Publishing, 2014), pp. 63–86.

Von Hippel, Eike, *Grenzen und Wesensgehalt der Grundrechte* (Berlin: Duncker & Humblot, 1965).

Waldron, Jeremy, 'Liberal Rights: Two Sides of the Coin' in Jeremy Waldron, *Liberal Rights: Collected Papers 1981–1991* (Cambridge University Press, 1993), pp. 1–34.

Waldron, Jeremy, 'The Core of the Case against Judicial Review', *Yale Law Journal*, 155 (2006), pp. 1346–1406.

Warbrick, Colin, 'The Structure of Article 8', *European Human Rights Law Review* (1998), pp. 32–44.

Warbrick, Colin, 'Economic and Social Interests and the European Convention on Human Rights' in M.A. Baderin and R. McCorquodale, *Economic, Social and Cultural Rights in Action* (Oxford University Press, 2007), pp. 241–256.

Webber, Grégoire, *The Negotiable Constitution: On the Limitation of Rights* (Cambridge University Press, 2009).

Weinrib, Jacob, *Dimensions of Dignity. The Theory and Practice of Modern Constitutional Law* (Cambridge University Press, 2016).

Wesson, Murray, '*Grootboom* and Beyond': Reassessing the Socio-Economic Jurisprudence of the South African Constitutional Court', *South African Journal on Human Rights*, 20 (2004), pp. 284–308.

Wesson, Murray, 'The Emergence and Enforcement of Socio-Economic Rights' in L. Lazarus, Ch. McCrudden and N. Bowles (eds.), *Reasoning Rights: Comparative Judicial Engagement* (Oxford: Hart Publishing, 2014), pp. 281–297.

Wildhaber, Luzius, 'A Constitutional Future for the European Court of Human Rights?', *Human Rights Law Journal*, 23 (2002), pp. 161–166.

Wildhaber, Luzius, 'The European Court of Human Rights: The Past, The Present, The Future', *American University International Law Review*, 22 (2007), pp. 521–538.

Wintemute, Robert, '"Within the Ambit": How Big Is the "Gap" in Article 14 European Convention on Human Rights? Part 1', *European Human Rights Law Review* (2004), pp. 366–382.

Wintemute, Robert, 'Filling the Article 14 "Gap": Government Ratification and Judicial Control of Protocol No. 12 ECHR: Part 2', *European Human Rights Law Review* (2004), pp. 484–499.

Xenos, Dimitris, *The Positive Obligations of the State under the European Convention of Human Rights* (London/Oxford/Edinburgh: Routledge, 2012).

Young, Katherine G., 'The Minimum Core of Economic and Social Rights: A Concept in Search of Content', *Yale Journal of International Law*, 33 (2008), pp. 113–175.

Young, Katherine G., *Constituting Socio-Economic Rights* (Oxford University Press, 2012).

Young, Katherine G., 'Proportionality, Reasonableness, and Socio-Economic Rights' (20 January 2017) in V.C. Jackson and M. Tushnet (eds.) *Proportionality: New Frontiers, New Challenges* (Cambridge University Press, forthcoming 2017); Boston College Law School Legal Studies Research Paper No. 430. Available at SSRN: https://ssrn.com/abstract=2892707

Zivier, Ernst, *Der Wesensgehalt der Grundrechte* (Berlin: Ernst Reuter Gesellschaft der Förderer und Freunde der Freien Universität e.v.,1962).

INDEX

absolute core rights, 92, 130–40
  Existenzminimum and, 203–4
  in FCC case law, 134
  theories on, 133–6
  Wesensgehaltsgarantie and, 133–6, 203
absolute theories, 133–6
absolute-absolute core rights, 200–4
  ECtHR and, 216
absolute-relative core rights, 204–6,
  225–6
adjudication, of fundamental rights, 12,
  32–9, 118
  in ECtHR cases, 95
  intensity of review in, 113–17
  limitations of, 95
  scope of, 95
  under South African Constitution, of
    socio-economic rights, 150–6,
    167–8
  stages of, 88–117, 160
  supranational, 113–14
Article 1, ECHR, 55–7
Article 2, ECHR, 47–9
Article 3, ECHR, 49–52
Article 6, ECHR, 43–4
Article 8, ECHR, 52–4
Article 14, ECHR, 42, 44–6
Asylum Seekers Benefits Act (1993),
  Germany, 172–3
autonomous interpretation
  defined, 66
  ECHR and, 66–7
  by ECtHR, 97
autonomy, personal, 65

balancing, 109–11
  Bundesverfassungsgericht and, 110

criticism of, 110
formal structure of, 110–11
Law of Competing Principles and,
  109–10
positive socio-economic rights and,
  226–7
right to social security and,
  278–90
Bundesverfassungsgericht (German
  Federal Constitutional Court
  (FCC))
  absolute core rights and, 134
  Asylum Seekers Benefits Act 1993
    and, 172–3
  balancing by, 110
  Existenzminimum and, 171–6
  proportionality test and, 4
  subsistence minimum, procedural
    determination of, 229

capabilities theory, 74–5
categorical review, 111–13
  levels of intensity in, 115–16
  limitations of, 112
  proportionality and, 112–13
CESCR. *See* Committee on Economic,
  Social and Cultural Rights
Charter of Fundamental Rights of the
  European Union (CFR), 11
  core rights under, 125
  indivisibility thesis and, 71
  social security rights under, 282
children's rights, under South African
  Constitution, 153
civil and political interests, 60–1
civil rights obligations, 43
CoE. *See* Council of Europe

9 781316 648216